BRITISH POLICY TOWARDS THE SOVIET UNION
DURING THE SECOND WORLD WAR

BRITISH POLICY TOWARDS THE SOVIET UNION DURING THE SECOND WORLD WAR

Martin Kitchen

St. Martin's Press   New York

First published in the United States of America in 1986

Printed in Hong Kong

ISBN 0–312–10422–7

Library of Congress Cataloging-in-Publication Data
Kitchen, Martin.
British policy towards the Soviet Union during the
Second World War.
Includes bibliographical references and index.
1. World War, 1939–1945—Diplomatic history.
2. Great Britain—Foreign relations—Soviet Union.
3. Soviet Union—Foreign relations—Great Britain.
4. World War, 1939–1945—Peace. I. Title.
D750.K57 1986   940.53′22′41   85–24993
ISBN 0–312–10422–7

To James Duncan Ward

Contents

Acknowledgements

For their generous and continued support I am deeply grateful to the Social Sciences and Humanities Research Council of Canada. Simon Fraser University granted me one year free from undergraduate teaching duties which enabled me to complete the manuscript. At a time of severe financial stringency this assistance was especially appreciated. For their help and encouragement I am particularly grateful to Edward Ingram and Hugh Johnston.

I would also like to thank the archivists and librarians of the British Library, Department of Manuscripts; the British Library of Political and Economic Science; the Winston S. Churchill Library, Churchill College, Cambridge; the House of Lords Record Office; the Labour Party Archives; the Liddell Hart Centre for Military Archives; and the Public Record Office. Without their help and expertise this book could not have been written.

For granting me helpful interviews I would especially like to thank Sir Eric Berthoud, Lord Brimelow, Gwynne Elias, Lieutenant-General Sir Ian Jacob, Sir Fitzroy Maclean, Sir Frank Roberts, Sir John Russell and Sir Geoffrey Wilson.

Many months of research at the Public Record Office in Kew were made particularly enjoyable and profitable thanks to my friends Elizabeth Boross, Lynn Gasteen, Gabriel Gorodetsky, Bradley Smith and Yuen-Nui Thomas. Patricia Howlin and Roger Marchbanks were unfailing in their hospitality and listened to my anecdotes about Anglo–Soviet relations with what appeared to me to be genuine amusement.

Barbara Barnett typed the final manuscript under particularly trying circumstances, and I am most appreciative of her assistance.

MARTIN KITCHEN

1 The Russian Enigma

When the Red Army invaded Eastern Poland on 17 September 1939 it came as no great surprise to the British Government. Although nothing was known of the terms of the secret protocol to the Ribbentrop–Molotov Pact which had been signed just over one month before, and which made the Soviet Union a partner of Nazi Germany fully entitled to her share of the spoils of aggressive war, there were clear indications that the Red Army was about to pounce on a hapless Poland. The British Embassy in Moscow reported that the conclusion of the Soviet armistice with Japan and the concentration of troops in the west were indication that an attack on Poland was likely.[1] The Government was not particularly concerned about this report. The Foreign Secretary, Lord Halifax, told the Cabinet that Soviet mobilisation was a precautionary move, and added that the Soviets might desire to secure a portion of Polish territory to improve their defensive position against a possible threat from Germany. This point of view was not challenged by his Cabinet colleagues.[2] Five days after this Cabinet meeting Soviet troops crossed the borders of Poland. Speaking on behalf of the Foreign Office, Sir Lancelot Oliphant told the Cabinet that the Soviet invasion of Poland was not an eventuality covered by the Anglo–Polish Agreement of August 1939, which referred to a 'European power' which was understood by both parties to the agreement to mean Germany.[3] Halifax strongly supported the Foreign Office view and told the Cabinet that there was no obligation whatsoever to become involved in a war with the Soviet Union over Poland. The Prime Minister took a rather sterner view of the situation and suggested that the Government should issue a strongly-worded note condemning Soviet aggression; but Chamberlain was overruled by his colleagues who did not want a formal protest unless the French Government insisted on taking such a step.

The Government's official statement which resulted from these discussions was therefore extremely cautious. It underlined Britain's determination to fulfil her obligations to Poland and rejected the Soviet Government's arguments justifying its attack on Poland, but

1

it said little else. By stressing that 'The full implication of these events is not yet apparent' the Government was leaving the door open for further discussions with the Soviets. The Soviet Government did not fail to note the implications of Halifax's statement that 'Russia has only advanced the Russian boundary to what was substantially the line recommended by Lord Curzon.'[4] Winston Churchill wrote a memorandum for his War Cabinet colleagues in which he argued that the Soviet invasion of Poland was in many ways an advantage to the Allies in that the Germans would be obliged to keep up to 25 Divisions in the east to watch an untrustworthy ally, and also that it created the possibility of a 'Balkan bloc' being formed to counter a German threat to the Black Sea. He argued strongly in favour of a renewal of relations with Russia.[5] On 1 October Churchill made his first wartime broadcast on the BBC in which he spoke of the Soviet Union's 'cold policy of self-interest', and in a famous phrase referred to Russia as 'a riddle wrapped in a mystery inside an enigma', but he also spoke of the 'community of interests' between Britain, France and the Soviet Union which could be clearly seen through the 'fog of confusion and uncertainty'. Churchill told the Soviet Ambassador, Maisky, that their two countries had common interests against Hitler and that they would soon be fighting together.[6] No prominent figure in the Labour Party was prepared to make such a startling prediction, although Harold Lasky and Stafford Cripps agreed that the Soviet Union had invaded Poland to improve her defensive position against Germany.[7]

The British military authorities were not particularly perturbed that the Red Army had marched into eastern Poland. Although there was clear evidence of collusion between Russia and Germany to dismember Poland, it was argued that a valuable buffer state had been removed and that the two countries now stood face-to-face and that friction was bound to develop between them.[8] The Dominion Governments were less sanguine. They felt that the joint operation against Poland could well be the beginning of a Russo–German military alliance, and the Chiefs of Staff were requested by the Cabinet to examine the likely consequences of such a development.[9] The Chiefs of Staff saw little cause for concern. They had a singularly low opinion of Soviet military capability. Pre-war manoeuvres which had been attended by foreign observers had been a shambles, and Stalin's brutal purge of the Soviet High Command had decimated the leadership of the armed forces. On the other hand, the second agreement between Molotov and Ribbentrop, which was signed on

29 September, was taken as an indication that the Soviets might be tempted to stir up trouble elsewhere and give indirect help to the Germans. The Chiefs of Staff suggested that the most likely areas for such activity were the Baltic, Finland, the Balkans, the Caucasus or Afghanistan.[10] There was some concern that the Soviets might be tempted to attack Afghanistan and thus threaten India in a fresh round of the 'Great Game', but it was agreed that this was not an immediate danger.[11] Halifax was rather more concerned about a Soviet threat to Romania, for he knew that without the cooperation of Turkey and Italy a British guarantee was worthless. He also asked the Chiefs of Staff to examine the implications of a Soviet move into the Balkans, either with or without the support of their German allies.[12] In subsequent discussions in Cabinet it was agreed that any increased threat from the Soviet Union would increase the likelihood of Italy remaining neutral and thus would not be wholly disadvantageous to the Allied cause.[13] By that time the Soviet Union was bogged down in her campaign in Finland and was in no position to do much harm elsewhere.

Few statesmen shared Churchill's extraordinary conviction that sooner or later Germany would go for Russia's throat. No one at the Foreign Office had bothered to study *Mein Kampf* or to wade through the writings of lesser Nazi ideologues. Nor did they pay any attention to Soviet ideology in an attempt to understand something of the dynamics of Stalinist Russia. Few would listen to the broad hints dropped by Maisky that the Soviet attitude to Germany was totally lacking in mutual trust and understanding. The former Czech President, Dr Beneš, was the most outspoken in his conviction that Germany would attack Russia, and that with Russia as an ally the war would be won. Statements from Maisky and other senior Soviet officials that Chamberlain should be replaced by Churchill as soon as possible were some indication that this view was shared by certain members of the Soviet Government.[14] However, with the strident denunciations of British and French imperialism and the flattering references to the Nazis which poured forth from Moscow, it took a considerable effort of imagination to come to the conclusion that the Soviet Union was anything other than a loyal and enthusiastic ally of the Germans. Hugh Dalton, who was in regular contact with Maisky, felt that Russia was waiting until Germany became exhausted before delivering the *coup de grâce* to Germany and thus dominating Central Europe.[15] Those who felt that they knew more about the effectiveness of the Red Army would have dismissed the idea as absurd. However far-fetched this idea might have seemed it was the very first suggestion that the Soviet Union might emerge from the war as the dominant power in Europe. For the British Government, the Soviet Union in the early weeks of the war was a potential nuisance, but certainly not a serious threat.

Those who insisted that everything possible should be done to keep open the lines of communication between London and Moscow had a powerful argument in their favour. Britain badly needed Soviet timber for war production, particularly for aircraft, and it was agreed that the deficiency could not be made up by extra shipments from Canada. At the beginning of the war, export licences for a wide assortment of goods destined for the Soviet Union had been refused. The Admiralty was particularly emphatic in insisting that machine tools and machinery should no longer be sent to the Soviet Union as they were vital for the British war effort. The Cabinet, however, felt that such was the need for Soviet timber, that everything possible should be done to meet the terms of the Anglo–Soviet Trade Agreement of July 1936, and that export licences should only be refused for machinery which was deemed to be absolutely essential for wartime industry.[16] The Soviet Union urgently required rubber, tin, copper and machine tools, and so great was the need for timber that every effort was made to secure supplies of these valuable commodities.[17] The Soviets however took a characteristically intransigent attitude towards these negotiations, holding up all shipments to Britain and loudly denouncing the British Government for unilaterally breaking the trade agreement.[18] Churchill, who was determined that the Trade Agreement should be honoured and that the best possible relations should exist between Britain and the Soviet Union, warned the Cabinet that if the trade deal did not go through the Soviets would almost certainly seize all British ships in Archangel and Murmansk.[19]

Such alarmist talk was hardly necessary, for the Soviets were fundamentally as anxious as the British to conclude a satisfactory trade agreement. In his first interview with Halifax after the invasion of Poland, Maisky treated the Foreign Secretary to a long diatribe about the invasion being 'a great act of liberation' and gave profuse assurances that the Soviet Union had every intention of remaining neutral, not only in Western Europe but also in Romania and Estonia. Having expended this obligatory amount of official hot air the Ambassador turned to the more important issue of trade relations, complaining that the British authorities were refusing to grant export licences for goods which were badly needed by the Soviet Union.[20] Since both the British and the Soviet Governments were anxious to keep the trade treaty alive, a fresh agreement was quickly signed on 11 October.[21] The British got their timber and the Russians their rubber and tin. Thus although relations between London and Moscow were badly strained they were not severed, and some politicians argued that these trade negotiations might be used as the basis of a more comprehensive political agreement. Prominent among these were Eden, who was at that time Dominions Secretary, and R. A. Butler, Parliamentary Under-Secretary of State for Foreign Affairs, both of whom hoped that the Turks might act as intermediaries between the two Governments.[22] It was also hoped that the French Government might have some influence in Moscow. Halifax supported the idea of sending Stafford Cripps on a special mission to the Soviet Union even though the Ambassador, Sir Williams Seeds, was still in Moscow and was not recalled until the end of the year. Cripps' aunt, Beatrice Webb, somewhat maliciously reported this suggestion to Maisky, and confided in her diary that 'it was a frivolous and futile plan on the part of our clever and misguided nephew and Halifax must have had his tongue in his cheek when he sanctioned it'.[23]

The Trade Agreement of mid-October was *ad hoc* and strictly limited, and was not enough in itself to secure adequate supplies of timber. The need for timber continued to dominate Anglo–Soviet relations, and forced the British Government to be very circumspect in its reactions to Soviet policy in the Baltic and Finland. The Russians were, as ever, hard and relentless bargainers. Gladwyn Jebb told Dalton, in a mixture of despair and admiration, that 'It's wonderful how these peasant diplomats get the better of everyone.' Dalton concurred and added that come what may it was vitally important that 'Russia should not be publicly slanged too much at present.'[24] The Cabinet realised that it would be foolish to appear over-eager to conclude the trade agreement, but it was difficult for them to conceal their anxiety, and the Soviets were quick to exploit this situation to the full.[25] Another worry was that the Soviets would fail to honour their side of the bargain. As Soviet timber was sent CIF the Government feared that they might tip off the Germans who would then sink the ships and the Soviets could still demand their rubber and tin.[26] The Soviet Government was equally suspicious of British duplicity and suggested that the goods should be exchanged at sea, both fleets sailing under naval escort. This highly impractical proposal was supported by Churchill on behalf of the Admiralty.[27] Attlee and Greenwood speaking for the Labour Party, continually pressed for the prompt conclusion of a comprehensive trade agreement. Halifax agreed that the October arrangement did not go far enough, but feared that the growing Soviet threat to Finland might make any such agreement impossible.[28] Meanwhile Stafford Cripps continued to press for a trade mission to be sent to Moscow, provided that the Soviets did not invade Finland, and suggested that the mission should be headed by a Cabinet Minister. The Cabinet agreed in principle to this proposal, but the Chancellor of the Exchequer, Sir John Simon was strongly opposed to such a high-level mission.[29] The Soviet attack on Finland effectively put a stop to this suggestion.

Another matter of considerable concern was that goods sent to the Soviet Union would be passed on to the Germans. At the Foreign Office Fitzroy Maclean, who was bored with his desk job and eager to see some action in the British Army, was the most outspoken critic of Soviet policy. He argued that the Soviet Union was Germany's ally and suggested that 'Our aim is to damage Soviet interests by every means at our disposal short of actually going to war.' His minute was warmly endorsed by his head of department.[30] Yet at the same time the Foreign Office acknowledged the need to secure supplies of Soviet timber and sponsored a Consultative Committee on Anglo–Russian Trade, with A. G. Marshall in the chair, composed of representatives of the London Chamber of Commerce, the Federation of British Industry and the London Corn Exchange. The Committee was told that there should be no suggestion of 'running after the Russians' and that it was up to them to make the next move. They did concede, however, that it was unwise to 'annoy the Russians unnecessarily' with trade embargos and the heavy-handed enforcement of contraband regulations.[31] The Soviets thundered on about these measures, condemning them as 'unjustified and arbitrary' and 'in violation of the principles of international law', repeating the dubious argument that as all Soviet ships were owned by the state they were exempt from any such controls. The Foreign Office was probably quite correct in assuming that these outbursts were designed for German ears in an attempt to disguise what was to amount to a very considerable degree of economic cooperation with Britain. Amidst all this acrimony and confusion the British took a sensibly fatalistic attitude. If the Soviets wished to break off trade relations they would do so, and there was little to be done to prevent them. Everything depended on how badly the Soviets needed British supplies, how anxious they were to maintain some contacts with Britain and on their relations with Germany. The British Ambassador in Moscow was therefore instructed to take a low key approach in his discussions with Soviet officials.

These frustrating trade negotiations were conducted against the background of a growing Soviet threat to Finland. By the end of September Mr Snow, the Minister to Finland, was convinced that the Soviets had territorial ambitions. He felt that the Finns would be unlikely to attempt the seemingly hopeless task of offering armed resistance to the Soviets, and would buy time by negotiating away a few of their offshore islands. The Foreign Office had no great sympathy for the Finns in their unpleasant predicament, feeling that they had 'missed the boat' by failing to support the Estonians who, when faced with a similar situation, had been forced to lease naval bases on Oesel, Agoe and at Baltic Port to the USSR in what was to prove to be the first step towards the absorption of the Baltic States into the Soviet Union. Thus the day after the Soviet Government made the ominous announcement to the Finns that they wished to discuss 'certain political questions' Snow told the Finnish Minister of Foreign Affairs that it was only a matter of time before Germany and Russia quarrelled and made no suggestion that Britain might assist Finland. Indeed Lascelles wrote from Helsinki to the Foreign Office that 'we are under no obligation to defend Scandinavia against any power'.[32] Back in London the Finnish Minister complained bitterly to R. A. Butler at the British Government's lack of concern about developments in Finland, insisting that the Russians were a greater menace than the Germans. The Foreign Office dismissed such talk as pure rubbish, pointing out that the Soviet Union was greatly inferior to Germany as a military power.[33]

The major reason for this apparent indifference to the fate of Finland was the belief that the more the Soviets became involved in the Baltic the greater was the likelihood of a conflict between Germany and the Soviet Union. Seen from this perspective anything which might lead to the disruption of the Nazi–Soviet Pact was welcome. Lieutenant General Sir Ronald Adam, the Deputy CIGS, reported to Cabinet that the Germans would probably have to keep 30 divisions in the east to hold the Soviets in check, and the Prime Minister frequently stressed Germany's profound distrust of the Russians.[34]

These ideas were regularly aired at Cabinet meetings in October. The British Government had no desire to appear to be supporting

the Finns for fear that the Russians might break off the trade
negotiations, and it was also hoped that Russian ambitions in Finland
would poison their relations with Germany. The most outspoken
advocate of this view was Winston Churchill. On 16 October this
stalwart anti-Bolshevik crusader told his astonished Cabinet colleagues,

> No doubt it appeared reasonable to the Soviet Union to take
> advantage of the present situation to regain some of the territory
> which Russia had lost as a result of the last war, at the beginning
> of which she had been the ally of France and Great Britain. This
> applied not only to the Baltic territories but also to Finland. It was
> to our interests that the U.S.S.R. should increase their strength in
> the Baltic, thereby limiting the risk of German domination in that
> area. For this reason it would be a mistake for us to stiffen the
> Finns against making concessions to the U.S.S.R.

This was altogether too much for Halifax who had to remind the
First Lord of the Admiralty that Finland had a perfect right to
national independence.[35]

From Helsinki Lascelles sent reports which argued a similar case.
He suggested that a Soviet attack on Finland would relieve the threat
to British interests in Central Asia and would reduce the ability of
the Russians to send war materials to Germany.[36] Fitzroy Maclean
could not accept this line of reasoning and insisted that Russia's
ambitions were 'Asiatic' rather than European, and that India was
the ultimate prize.[37] This nagging suspicion of Soviet ambitions
towards Afghanistan would not disappear. As late as April 1940
Cabinet discussed what should be done if the Soviets did attack
Afghanistan. Halifax and the Chiefs of Staff wanted to send land
forces from India. The Government of India suggested air strikes
against Soviet oilfields. It was finally agreed that the Afghan Government should be offered every possible support against the Soviet
Union and should be given the 'stiffening' which the Government
had failed to give to Finland.[38]

As the threat of a Soviet attack on Finland became more serious
there was less inclination to indulge in speculation about the possible
benefits to the Allied cause from such a move, and a mounting
realisation that it would place the British Government in an exceedingly difficult situation in which the future of the whole of Scandinavia
might well be at stake. The British Minister in Helsinki changed his

tune completely. In a passionate message to the Foreign Office he wrote:

> I assume condonation of so cold blooded a crime to be out of the question on the part of protagonists in the idealist war against aggression and that, in view of earlier Soviet treachery, a complete breach with the Soviet government would command nation-wide support, while condonation would not only involve our profession in complete discredit in Scandinavia and elsewhere but also at home, and in our hearts as well.

Faced with the immediate prospect of a Soviet attack, Snow now endorsed the Finnish Government's view that Stalin was a greater menace than Hitler, and even went as far as to suggest that Britain should immediately begin negotiations with Japan for an anti-Soviet coalition.[39] At the Foreign Office, where feelings about an idealist war did not run quite so high, Maclean wisely minuted that a breach with the Soviet Union would not command nation-wide support, and in any case the Cabinet would not consider breaking off relations with the Soviet Union. His head of department, Collier, gloomily added that the Soviets were unlikely to do anything worse in Finland than they had done in Poland. The Cabinet reacted to these developments by ordering the Chiefs of Staff to prepare a paper on the advantages and disadvantages of declaring war on the Soviet Union should they attack Finland. The reply was quick and unequivocal.

> In our view we and France are at present in no position to undertake additional burdens and we cannot therefore, from a military point of view, recommend that we should declare war on Russia.[40]

The British Government thus had no real desire to go to the assistance of Finland and had no possible means of taking on the Soviet Union at a time when they were awaiting Hitler's attack on the West. Halifax told the Cabinet that he found Molotov's speech to the Supreme Soviet, in which he outlined Soviet demands on Finland, to be 'satisfactory', emphasising that although Molotov offered moral support to Germany he had made no promises of concrete assistance, and he repeated Soviet avowals to remain neutral in the event of a war in the west.[41] Thus the crisis over Finland placed a further strain on Anglo–Soviet relations, but did not lead to a breach. Some were prepared to accept what seemed to them to be inevitable, others hoped that there might be some strategic gain from Soviet aggression. No one supported Mr Snow's call for a moral crusade side-by-side with the Japanese who were in no position to complain about expansionist powers. When the Cabinet discussed the problem, Halifax urged the Prime Minister not to be too harsh about the Russians when answering questions in the House. He insisted that since the Government was not in a position to do anything effective Chamberlain should stress the Soviet Union's desire to secure a strong defensive position against possible aggression from Germany, and that the Finns should be urged to negotiate. Churchill interposed that it did not matter what the Prime Minister said as the Russians were 'impervious to words'. Chamberlain offered the helpful observation that the situation was difficult. At the end of the discussion it was agreed that the Prime Minister should express his 'strong disapproval' of Soviet actions.[42] This was hardly a satisfactory solution. It would give the indefatigable Soviet Ambassador, Maisky, further ammunition to hurl at the British Government and would do nothing either to help or to placate the Finns. But in the circumstances it is difficult to see what else could have been done.

Those who hoped that the Turkish Government might be persuaded to act as an intermediary with the Russians were quickly disillusioned. The Turkish Foreign Minister, Sarajoglu, was requested by Stalin and Molotov to revise the Anglo–Turkish Treaty so that the Turks would no longer be obliged to give active support to the Anglo–French guarantee to Romania and Greece, and asked that the Treaty should be suspended if the USSR became involved in a war with Britain and France. Although the British Government was relieved that the Turks did not give way to considerable Soviet pressure and that the Anglo–Turkish Treaty remained intact, they were disappointed that the Turks had not been able to use these discussions to build some kind of bridge between Britain and the Soviet Union. But of even greater concern was the feeling that these discussions were further evidence that the Soviets had made a deal with the Germans over the Balkans, and that they were aiming at Romania. It was agreed that nothing could be done to help Romania, but it was hoped that it might be possible to help defend Greece. Halifax still hoped to persuade Italy to support British efforts to form a neutral Balkan bloc.[43]

In November the Soviets unleashed a heavy-handed propaganda

campaign in preparation for the attack on Finland. The Comintern denounced the British and French 'slave empires' and called for a crusade against the imperialist bourgeoisie and their Social Democratic lackeys. The Communist press complained about the 'Scandinavian lackeys of British and American capital'.[44] On 27 November Maisky had a conversation with the Foreign Secretary, which Halifax, to use a favourite word, no doubt found extremely 'boring'.[45] The Soviet Ambassador bitterly complained about the unfriendly attitude of Britain 'in every part of the world', but when challenged by Halifax was unable to cite one single instance to support this allegation. Maisky outlined Soviet demands on Finland, but Halifax refused to discuss the relative merits of either side in the dispute and merely said that a Soviet attack on Finland would make it difficult for the British Government to improve relations with the Soviet Union by means of a trade agreement. Thus Halifax let Maisky know that the British Government had no intention of helping Finland, and were still anxious to secure a comprehensive trade agreement. Indeed the Cabinet was still very worried that the contraband regulations should not be enforced to the point where they might jeopardise friendly relations with the Russians.[46] It was agreed that the authorities should go through the motions of checking for contraband, but should not actually seize any goods. The Chiefs of Staff were also extremely concerned not to become involved in any military operations in Scandinavia, for they felt that this would merely give the Germans an excellent pretext to invade.[47]

On 30 November 1939 the Soviet Union attacked Finland. In Britain there was widespread and vociferous support for the Finns in their struggle against such a great and apparently brutal power. The intensity of public sentiment was something of an embarrassment to the Government. The Prime Minister, although no one could question the sincerity of his loathing of the Soviet Union and everything it stood for, still wished to tread softly in relations with Moscow, but he warned his Cabinet colleagues that 'It might be difficult politically to avoid a more open condemnation of her action in Finland in view of its similarity to German aggression in Poland.'[48] Chamberlain still believed that Soviet expansion in the Baltic would not adversely affect the Allies, and might well be the cause of dissension between the Soviets and their German partners, and he repeated the Chiefs of Staff's warning that it would be disastrous for Britain to become involved in a war with Russia. His real concern was not with Finland, but with the possibility of Russian expansion into south-eastern

Europe. He still hoped that the Soviet invasion of Finland might convince Mussolini of the need for cooperation in the face of a Soviet threat. The Cabinet agreed that representations should be made to Italy and Japan in an attempt to persuade the Russians to desist from any further aggression. At the same time Halifax was worried that the press might indulge in an anti-Soviet campaign which would make negotiations with the Russians over the trade agreement even more difficult.[49]

Within the Cabinet there was growing unease about this passive attitude towards the Russo–Finnish war. Although the Scandinavian states merely called for discussions between the two sides in the war, and for the registration of Soviet aggression by the League of Nations, the British Government became increasingly concerned that the problem of denying Swedish iron ore to the Germans would be even more difficult to solve and that the Soviets might well be aiming to grab these ore deposits themselves. The Secretary for War, Hore-Belisha, emphasised the menace of the global ambitions of Soviet Communism, which was a particular obsession of the War Office. Although Kingsley Wood, the Secretary for Air, insisted that his department had no spare aircraft, the Cabinet agreed to send material support to Finland.[50] It was suggested that 20 Gladiators should be sent to Finland as a private sale by the manufacturers to the Finnish Government.[51] In the following days Cabinet sanctioned the export of further arms for Finland, including 12 Blenheim bombers and anti-tank rifles.[52]

The astonishing success of the Finns in fending off the Russians, and the miserable performance of the Red Army in the early stages of the war, meant that the question of support for Finland was not particularly pressing. Indeed Sir Samuel Hoare told the Cabinet that in his opinion the war had reached a decisive point in Finland's favour.[53] Oliver Harvey went so far as to speculate that the failures of the Red Army in Finland might provoke a revolution in the Soviet Union which would result in the overthrow of Stalin.[54] There were even fears expressed in Cabinet that the Soviet Union might be defeated, for although no one wanted a Soviet victory it was generally felt that it was highly desirable that Scandinavia should be 'kept in anxiety' by continued Soviet pressure. At the same time it was agreed that all means of supporting Finland, short of direct military intervention, should be discussed. Hoare suggested sending volunteers to Finland in the manner of the International Brigades in Spain.[55]

Although Halifax hoped that effective support could be sent to Finland he was strongly opposed to severing diplomatic relations with the Soviet Union.[56] He favoured a condemnation of Soviet aggression but was opposed to sanctions or to the expulsion of the Soviet Union from the League.[57] Under strong pressure from the French the British Government agreed, if necessary, to support a resolution calling for the expulsion of the Soviet Union from the League, but refused to go along with French demands for sanctions.[58] R. A. Butler was sent to Geneva to argue the British case. He had a wonderful time. Accompanied by the Duke of Devonshire and that epicene socialite 'Chips' Channon he attended some splendid parties, the most enjoyable of which was given on the lakeside by Lady Diana Cooper at which he recited Lamartine's 'Le Lac' from the balcony.[59] He supported the resolution to expel the Soviet Union from the League, but was careful not to mention the question of sanctions, at the same time stressing the British Government's determination to assist the Finns in their struggle against aggression.

Throughout the crisis over Finland the British Government was thus unable to formulate a clear and consistent policy towards the Soviet Union. On the one hand they were pushed by public opinion to support Finland, on the other they were anxious not to break off trade negotiations. The fact that Halifax constantly told the Cabinet that British policy towards the Soviet Union should be made clear is ample indication that it was not.

Although Finland was uppermost in the minds of the British Government Romania continued to be of considerable concern. The Romanian Government was worried about the possibility of a Soviet attack and asked whether the British Guarantee would apply to Soviet as well as to German aggression. They warned that if the British reply was negative they might be tempted to do a deal with the Germans. Churchill told the Cabinet that he was convinced that the USSR and Germany would never act in unison and that a joint attack on the Balkans was therefore most unlikely. Furthermore, if these two powers ever became true allies this would force Japan and Italy, along with a number of smaller countries, to change their attitude.[60] Halifax argued that the British Government was in no position to give a guarantee to Romania without the active support of Italy and Turkey, and that pressure from the Soviet Union on Romania would increase the possibility of such an agreement.[61]

As long as the Red Army was heavily engaged in Finland concern about Romania was bound to remain secondary. In January the

Cabinet agreed to publish a Blue Book on the failure of the Anglo–Soviet talks in the summer of 1939, but it was emphasised that the introduction should not be too 'spirited'.[62] This idea was abandoned when the French Government pointed out that the record might create the embarrassing impression that the British and the French had been prepared to consider abandoning the interests of the Baltic States in order to placate the Soviet Union, and that the Blue Book could very well backfire.[63] Meanwhile aid to Finland was increased. The Chancellor of the Exchequer announced that the somewhat parsimonious Governor of the Bank of England was prepared to advance up to £500 000 to the Finnish Government.[64] In the middle of January the British observer, Brigadier Ling, returned to London after a visit to Finland and told the Cabinet that the present advantage enjoyed by the Finns was due to their mastery of winter warfare, particularly their use of ski troops, and also to the very poor quality of Russian staff work. He was convinced that when the snows melted in May the Russians would have a tremendous advantage which could only be offset by sending at least 30 000 volunteers and large numbers of aircraft and anti-aircraft guns. Brigadier Ling also passed on a message from Mannerheim that if the British would bomb the oilfields at Baku the Russians would be finished.[65] In a further report to the Cabinet Brigadier Ling was even more pessimistic, pointing out that the volunteers would be unlikely to do much good owing to the climate and their lack of experience in winter warfare. Cabinet therefore reached the gloomy conclusion that if nothing were done to help Finland she was almost certain to collapse in May. The General Staff was ordered to draw up a plan for 'effective intervention' in Finland, even if this meant risking general hostilities with Russia. Meanwhile it was agreed that some sort of recruitment bureau should be set up in London in order to vet applications for the volunteer force.[66] The Government was anxious that men should not be sent to Finland who might be a discredit to the country. It was further decided that Amery, who was champing at the bit to set up a committee to organise volunteers for Finland, would have to be dissuaded by being appraised of all the problems involved.[67] Thus although the Cabinet approved of sending volunteers, and the Military Co-ordination Committee supported this action, there were some important restraints. It was agreed that the volunteers should be militarily effective, and the problem of Norwegian and Swedish reactions to volunteers passing through neutral territory had to be settled.[68] After some tricky negotiations both Governments agreed to allow volunteers to pass provided that they came either as individuals or in small groups, and as long as they had valid Norwegian or Swedish visas.[69]

Some encouragement to those who hoped that Italy could be drawn closer to the Allied side by the threat of Soviet expansionism came from a report from the British Ambassador in Rome who had been told by Ciano that he favoured sending war material to Finland to stop the Russians.[70] Nothing came of this idea as Ciano lacked his father-in-law's backing, and the minor disagreement between Mussolini and his Foreign Minister could not be exploited to Britain's advantage. More hope was placed in the proposal, which was strongly supported by Churchill, that the United States should be asked to send credits and fighter planes to Finland. The British Ambassador in Washington was ordered to examine this possibility.[71] Meanwhile the British Government stepped up its efforts to send war material to Finland. It was decided to send 12 Hurricanes but without their RAF pilots for fear that Russia might use their presence as a pretext to declare war on Britain. Skilled mechanics were sent with the aircraft and Finnish pilots were trained to fly the aircraft in combat.[72] Permission was also granted to the Finns to open a recruiting office in London, although it was obliged to work in close consultation with the Ministry of Labour and National Service to make sure that the volunteers were not required in the armed forces or for essential war work.[73] Churchill told the Cabinet that the Admiralty was prepared to release 20 Skira dive-bombers and 13 Rocs to be sent to Finland.[74] In the following days the Cabinet agreed to send a number of other aeroplanes to Finland as well and, in a clear violation of the spirit of the agreement with Norway and Sweden, they were to be accompanied by RAF personnel, although they were to be demobbed for the purpose of this mission.[75]

The Prime Minister was by now becoming increasingly concerned that the Allies were embarking on a course of action which might very well lead to open hostilities with the Soviet Union.[76] An understandable enthusiasm for gallant little Finland in its heroic struggle against a nasty bully-boy seemed to be leading Britain to undertake serious commitments to a country which would probably be defeated in May. There was however general agreement that the British Government had a moral obligation to help Finland, even if it meant pouring money down a drain, and there were few critics of the Government outside the ranks of the Communist Party. Among the more influential opponents of the policy of aid to Finland were

Hugh Dalton and Stafford Cripps. Dalton felt that it was 'sheer political lunacy' to send aid to Finland, a country which was bound to be defeated and at a time when the first priority had to be to build up defences against the German threat to western Europe.[77] Dalton saw the Russians as old-fashioned imperialists and nationalists with Stalin as a Tsar rather than a Communist leader and, given the choice, decided that it was better to have eastern Europe overrun by the Russians than by the Germans. Such a point of view was by no means unusual at the time, although as the Russians became the arch-villains and the Germans victims and allies it became expedient to forget that one had ever held such wicked opinions. Dalton flatly refused Attlee's request that he should go to Finland on a fact-finding mission, but Stafford Cripps was even more outspoken. In an article in *Tribune* he offered a spirited defence of the Soviet Union's actions in Finland.[78]

The Foreign Office was becoming increasingly belligerent in its attitude towards the Soviet Union and less tolerant of the Ministry of Supply's concerns about the need for Soviet timber. The head of the Northern Department told the chairman of the Anglo–Soviet Trade Committee that the Finnish war had put an end to all chances of further trade with Russia, and that alternative sources of timber would have to be found.[79] The Foreign Office decided that nothing should be sent to the Soviet Union which might be of use against Finland, and this even included a shipment of Australian wheat. Fitzroy Maclean took the opportunity afforded by a request to permit the export of some herrings to the Soviet Union to object that they might be sent on by the Russians to Germany and that in any case there was nothing to choose between the Russians and the Germans. The Board of Trade took a more conciliatory attitude, pointing out to the Foreign Office that apart from the timber agreements of October and November 1939 there were no provisions for direct trade between Britain and the Soviet Union, so that private trade, such as Maclean's herrings, was governed by the same controls as were imposed on all neutrals. The Ministry of Supply was determined not to close off the timber market with Russia, and urged greater restraint in requisitioning machinery intended for the Soviet Union. The Foreign Office was unmoved by these appeals and stuck to the view that although the Soviet Union was still formally a neutral country it was Britain's prime aim to hurt Germany as much as possible, and that this could also be achieved by hurting Germany's Russian ally.[80] This line of argument failed to convince those who felt that Britain needed Russian supplies every bit as much as the Russians needed British machinery and raw materials. Some even went as far as to suggest that Britain's need was greater than theirs.

Although Brigadier Ling's report from Finland was accurate and perceptive the British Government was very short of detailed information of what was going on in Finland. Since there were only four British officers there the main source of information was the daily press. The Labour Party tried to rectify this situation by sending Walter Citrine and Noel-Baker, two of their staunchest anti-Soviet members, to Finland. They sent a glowing report of Finnish military prowess back to the Cabinet. They made the staggering claim that the Finns were killing the Russians at a ratio of 50:1 and that therefore they only needed a few specialists to help them out. They also pointed out that Soviet morale was terribly low, whereas the Finns were in fine fighting spirit.[81] At home their colleagues Attlee and Greenwood were determined that Britain should not become involved in a war with the Soviet Union over Finland.[82] They went to see Anthony Eden to present their case for not sending troops to Finland. Eden, who was in one of his anti-appeasement moods, replied disdainfully that 'We were disposed to think that the fear of Russia declaring war on us ought not to deter us from any course of action that would certainly seem wise.'[83]

In the middle of February 1940 Lord Davies and Harold Macmillan were sent to Finland on an official fact-finding mission. Their impressions were far less optimistic than those of the Labour team. They quickly realised that without massive support the Finns would soon be defeated. They returned to London in a depressed mood, particularly the unfortunate Lord Davies who had somehow managed to lose both his passport and his false teeth while travelling through Sweden.[84]

The Cabinet agreed in large part with Macmillan that more aircraft, artillery and ammunition should be sent to Finland. They were also under considerable pressure from the French, who seemed increasingly keen to wage an anti-bolshevik war in Finland rather than worry about the defence of France, to send bombers to Finland. The Chief of Air Staff resisted this proposal, stressing that the lack of ground staff in Finland would mean that the bombers would be ineffective. Lord Chatfield, the Minister for the Co-ordination of Defence, suggested that one or two squadrons of heavy bombers should be sent to Finland for a limited period to see what they could do.[85] Meanwhile due to the enthusiastic efforts of Teddy Roosevelt's son Kermit, volunteers were beginning to come forward at the rate of about 50 per week, although they were not a particularly impressive lot and certainly not up to the standard of the International Brigades.[86] The military authorities felt that it might be quite useful to send a few specialists to Finland to gain some practical experience of modern warfare, but very little was done. Convinced that the Finns would be defeated within a few weeks, the British Government was unable to produce any coherent policy towards Finland. Halifax even went so far as to ask the Cabinet what Britain was supposed to be doing in Finland. Should she allow the Finns to fight her battle for her, or should she give them everything she could spare to help them fight a common enemy? Unable to come up with any political answer to this question, Halifax suggested that the whole matter should be handed over to the Chiefs of Staff for their decision. The strongest opposition to this point of view came from Churchill who gained general assent for the argument that Finland was a highly political question and in no sense a purely military and technical matter. On one issue, however, there was some agreement. As long as the Soviet Union was embroiled in Finland the less use she was to Germany. Therefore, the longer the war lasted the better.

Churchill's interest in Finland was that it provided a useful cover for his schemes for an attack on Norway to cut off supplies of iron ore from Sweden to Germany. Two days after the Russo–Finnish war ended Churchill wrote: 'Our real objective was, of course, to secure possession of the Galivare ore fields, which would certainly shorten the war and save great bloodshed later on.'[87] The main proponents of this idea were the French. The French Commander-in-Chief, General Gamelin, accounced that the Germans would not dare to attack France in 1940 and therefore Scandinavia was an ideal theatre of war. The French favoured a landing at Petsamo, but the British quite understandably preferred Narvik.[88] Churchill was enthusiastic about this idea and pushed it for all it was worth. He proposed sending troops as if headed for the Middle East, and then regrouping them on board in order, as he put it with curious spelling, 'to fool the Bosch'. The Chiefs of Staff were far less sanguine than the French, refusing to entertain the idea of an attack on Petsamo which would require at least $4\frac{1}{2}$ divisions and would mean that no reinforcements could be sent to France until well into the summer. The Cabinet still argued that the longer the Russians went on fighting in Finland the better, and even managed to convince themselves that a serious threat of British intervention might have the disadvantage of forcing them to end the war.[89]

Although the Cabinet saw certain benefits in prolonging the Russo–Finnish war, and although the Chiefs of Staff did not want to become directly involved in the war, the Foreign Office was becoming increasingly belligerent. Cadogan, the Permanent Under-Secretary, wrote in his diary, 'I have been coming to wonder more and more lately, whether we need be deterred from any action that we may think advantageous, simply for fear of finding ourselves in a state of war with Russia.'[90] The Joint Planning Sub-Committee was more circumspect. At a meeting on 19 February it was minuted that:

The Directors of Plans held the view that on balance, from the purely military point of view, war with Russia will make it more difficult to achieve our primary object in this war, the defeat of Germany. Unless, therefore, there is some substantial compensating factor such as the opportunity to obtain control of the Galivare orefields or comparative certainty of the active support of the United States of America, they were not prepared to recommend to the Chiefs of Staff that we should accept the additional commitments involved in war with Russia.[91]

The Foreign Office did not accept this cautious view. Fitzroy Maclean told the committee that

It was questionable whether the Russian army forces exercised any restraint upon German military action. In the view of the Foreign Office, this was not so and it appeared to be to our advantage to bring about the complete downfall of Russian military power ... The collapse of Russia was likely to contribute materially to the early defeat of Germany. While it was true that the economic assistance which Germany was receiving from Russia was limited, this position was capable of considerable improvement and if Russia were knocked out of the war the economic effect upon Germany would be far-reaching. More important still, however, would be the psychological effect upon the German people.

The Foreign Office suggested an all-out bombardment of the Caucasus oilfields which, they were convinced, would quickly force the Soviet Union to her knees. The Red Army and OGPU would lose their grip over the Soviet people, and internal unrest would bring about the downfall of Stalin's empire.

As long as the fighting continued in Finland these wild ideas were not given any serious consideration. The British continued to send supplies to Finland, and a few hundred volunteers arrived just before the war ended, but as the tide turned in the winter war there was a growing feeling that this was merely a waste of valuable resources. On 8 March Chamberlain told Macmillan that there was no point in sending any more aid to the Finns as they were about to capitulate, and that further help could only be considered if the Scandinavian countries could be 'brought to reason to co-operate'.[92] The Prime Minister knew full well that this was most unlikely to happen, and there were those who feared that Finland might turn out to be a repeat performance of the Dardanelles campaign as Churchill continued to push for a raid on Norway.[93]

As had long been predicted the Finns were unable to continue their unequal struggle and in the middle of March were obliged to come to terms with the Soviets. This left the British in an even worse situation and without a coherent policy towards the Soviet Union. At the Foreign Office Orme Sargent, the Deputy Under-Secretary, plaintively inquired what was Britain's agreed policy. Did she hope to drive a wedge between Germany and Russia? Did she wish to have a *rapprochement* with Russia? Or was she going to bomb Baku?[94] The answers he got were widely different. R. A. Butler still hoped that a *rapprochement* with the Soviet Union was possible. He pointed out that the British working man was sympathetic to Stalin's Russia, saying, 'In war the home front is very important and I feel that a reckless alienation of the Soviet Union would do more harm than good both internally and in the realm of European diplomacy.' At the same time Butler was pushing for an improvement of relations with Japan.[95] Vansittart, the arch-opponent of appeasement, announced that the Russian and German systems were identical and that 'Teutoslavia' had to be destroyed. He wrote:

I am personally convinced that we have got to aim at the destruction of both Nazism and Communism in this war, and that we shall not have won it or peace if we don't succeed ... The Soviets have been a bloody fraud from the start, and have now nakedly and unashamedly reverted to the policy of conquest and imperialism of the Czarist predecessors.

He suggested that the Soviet Union was in exactly the same position as Germany in the 1930s, appeasement would be fatal, and Baku should be bombed as soon as possible.[96]

At first it seemed that the hardliners would win the argument. A few days after the end of the Russo–Finnish war the Inter-Service Project Board was requested to consider 'a certain method of attacking Russian oil supplies in the Caucasus'.[97] The War Office was by now in a very bellicose mood. They dismissed the ideas of those, like Stafford Cripps and R. A. Butler, who believed that a *rapprochement* with the Soviet Union was possible and desirable, as the illusions of men who failed to see that Russia wanted to keep out of the war simply because she was afraid of Britain. In early March a number of staff officers argued in favour of war with the Soviet Union as the only effective way of stopping Soviet supplies from reaching Germany. The fact that Military Intelligence estimated the size of the Red Army as $3\frac{1}{2}$ million men did nothing to cool the ardour of these desk-bound heroes.[98] With all this wild talk going on in high places it is hardly surprising that it reached the ears of the Soviet Ambassador, who let it be known that he was well aware of plans to bomb Baku.[99]

In spite of, or as some argued, because of these threats to Baku the Soviet Government was still anxious to keep the lines open to the British. Fitzroy Maclean had no doubt that 'The temporary improvement in the Soviet attitude towards Great Britain, which occurred in March, was entirely due to the fear of the Soviet Government that we were preparing to bomb the oilfields.'[100] It is impossible to know the true motives of Soviet policy in the Spring of 1940, but Maclean's argument sounded plausible and was useful to those who favoured an attack on the Caucasus.[101] The situation was not improved by the fact that the British Ambassador had been recalled from Moscow at the end of 1939, leaving the Embassy in the hands of a chargé d'affaires, de Rougetal, who was well known for his extreme dislike of socialists, even of the most moderate hue. As the Ambassador was hardly one of the Foreign Office's stars, this was little more than a mild rebuke to the Soviets, but it did mean that there was no influential British official in Moscow with whom they could communicate. In February Stafford Cripps was in China on a private tour, and at Chungking he met the Soviet Ambassador who urged him to go to Moscow in an attempt to improve relations between Britain and the Soviet Union. Cripps, who had always believed that a *rapprochement* with Moscow was possible, was delighted to accept the invitation. Without even waiting for Government approval for this action he boarded a Soviet aeroplane at Urumtschi on the Mongolian border and flew to Moscow. By the time the Cabinet was informed of Cripps' whereabouts it was too late to stop him, so they could do nothing but wait for his report.[102]

Cripps arrived in Moscow on 15 February and had a number of interviews with senior Soviet officials, including Molotov. He told the Cabinet that he was convinced that the Soviet Union was genuinely concerned to improve relations with Britain and that her alliance with Germany was based on convenience rather than conviction. He believed that once the war in Finland was over it would be possible to detach them from the alliance with Germany.[103] Halifax and Churchill supported Cripps' initiative, suggesting that he should be sent on an official mission to Moscow in the hope of concluding an economic and political agreement. The rest of the Cabinet was not particularly enthusiastic and felt that there was no great urgency in the matter.[104] Cripps was anxious to come back to London and discuss his trip in detail, but the Foreign Office was not at all impressed by this effort in private diplomacy. Maclean thought Cripps was nothing more than the willing tool of the Russians and the Germans who were using him to make sure that British support for Finland remained modest. He saw no point whatsoever in opening negotiations with the Russians. R. A. Butler was almost alone in supporting Cripps and minuted sadly: 'We are a proud people and seem to enjoy the world in arms against us.'[105] But Cripps could not be easily discounted. He was fiercely independent and commanded wide support at home. He had been convinced by the Russians and was determined to keep talking to them. At home the argument was essentially between those who felt that the Russians were Germany's faithful ally and therefore should be hurt as much as possible, and those who insisted that Soviet supplies, particularly timber, were essential and that concessions would have to be made in order to secure a trade agreement.

The Cripps mission did nothing to deter the Cabinet from further discussion of the possibilities of war with the Soviet Union. At the beginning of February the Chiefs of Staff had pointed out that there was nowhere in Russia where the British forces could strike that would bring about the early defeat of Germany. India and Iraq were both weak positions, and the Anglo–Iranian oilfields were not adequately defended. Anti-aircraft guns would have to be sent to improve defence in the Middle East, and these were needed at home.

Sending three long-range Blenheim squadrons to the Middle East to strike at the Caucasus would seriously weaken British ability to strike at Germany and would further impair home air defence. Maclean dismissed this report as a gross exaggeration of the difficulties and argued that 80 per cent of Soviet oil production could be destroyed with 'comparatively little effort'. At the same time Maclean was calling for increased supplies for Finland to stop the Germans from gaining full control over Swedish iron ore.[106] In a further report to the Cabinet a few weeks later the Chiefs of Staff repeated their reservations about an attack on the Soviet Union, but admitted that the most promising way to deal them a severe blow would be to attack the Caucasus oilfields. They felt that three bomber squadrons could do the job in six to twelve weeks, but they hastily added that there was a shortage of bombers and that the cooperation of Iran and Turkey would be necessary. In the subsequent discussion Halifax argued that neither Iran nor Turkey would agree to allow British bombers to attack the Soviet Union unless they were directly threatened by the Soviets. He further insisted that the Soviet Union had no desire to fight Britain and did not wish to see Germany become too powerful. The Secretary of State for India was very concerned about a possible Soviet threat to Afghanistan, and said that if that country were to be abandoned as Czechoslovakia had been the effect on the Muslim world would be disastrous. Churchill welcomed the idea of a few Soviet bombs on India as they might serve to show the Indians that they were unable to defend themselves. The Prime Minister, impatient at the direction the discussion was taking, said that war with the Soviet Union was most unlikely and that the only sensible course was to await the outcome of events, particularly in Finland.[107]

The idea of bombing the Soviet oilfields had first been suggested by the Minister of Supply in October 1939.[108] Once the Russo–Finnish war was over the Government became increasingly concerned about stopping Soviet supplies to Germany, and it was hoped that a raid on Norway to disrupt the iron ore traffic could be combined with action against the Caucasus oilfields.[109] An encouraging report came from the Washington Embassy saying that three American engineers who had recently been in the Caucasus claimed that the Baku–Batum pipeline was very poorly defended and could be easily destroyed in a determined attack. Professor Hall from the Ministry of Economic Warfare tried to dampen the enthusiasm caused by this despatch by pointing out that it was no easy matter to destroy oil installations from the air.[110] Churchill felt that Halifax should prepare the ground by visiting Turkey to get their consent for British submarines entering the Black Sea as part of a combined operation against the Caucasus oilfields. Halifax objected that the Soviets might well retaliate by bombing the oilfields in Iraq and Persia which were still very lightly defended. Chamberlain wisely called for further consideration of the full implications of bombing Baku.[111]

Within the Foreign Office there was a growing feeling in favour of a lightning attack on the Soviet Union. There was much talk of the Caucasus as an Achilles heel and complaints about the lack of offensive spirit by the Chiefs of Staff. Cadogan argued that if there was a reasonable chance of success it should be done, although he doubted whether three squadrons of Blenheims would be enough to do the job. Halifax was still very dubious and even felt that the Chiefs of Staff were 'rather more in favour of action against Russia than I at present feel'. Orme Sargent was concerned about the attitude of the Turkish Government and wanted the ground prepared carefully before even considering an attack. He also asked the pertinent question of how badly the Germans needed Soviet oil.[112] Meanwhile plans for the raid went ahead. The RAF undertook aerial reconnaissance of the oilfields and prepared detailed target maps. The Planning Staff of the Air Ministry drew up plans for the raid and felt that there would be no serious difficulties. A draft message was prepared for the Dominion Governments preparing them for the possibility of war with the Soviet Union. The New Zealand Government had already voiced their objections to the scheme, but these views were rejected by Maclean and by Victor Cavendish-Bentinck as those of a government frightened by its own left-wing.[113]

While the British Government discussed the pros and cons of a raid on the Caucasus, Maisky continued his efforts to secure a trade agreement. On 27 March he had a long conversation with Halifax in which he was exceptionally tactful, agreeing that Britain had a perfectly legitimate concern about essential goods reaching Germany from the Soviet Union, at the same time repeating his usual complaints about the interception of Soviet ships. The Cabinet agreed that Halifax should follow up this discussion in an attempt to begin serious negotiations for a trade agreement, and Churchill suggested that the threat to bomb Baku, which was no secret to Maisky, could be used as a bargaining counter.[114] The Foreign Office suggested that it might be possible to stop Soviet oil going to Germany by buying it themselves. Cadogan and Halifax both thought that this was as good an idea as bombing the Caucasus, but the Minister of Economic Warfare pointed out that the cost would be prohibitive and the idea was dropped. Cadogan then suggested that the trade discussions could be used to pre-empt exports to Germany, and if this tactic failed then force would have to be used.[115] Thus enthusiasm for a lightning attack on the Caucasus was beginning to wane and the plan was put on hold, awaiting the outcome of trade negotiations.

Indication that many Russians were far from enthusiastic about the alliance with Germany came from a well-placed source. The Soviet Ambassador in Stockholm, Madame Kollontai, was an independent and courageous woman who was prepared to let it be known that she felt singularly uncomfortable about the Nazi–Soviet pact. She became the unofficial spokeswoman of the opposition to Stalin's wartime policy and a champion of *rapprochement* with Britain. In February 1940 she told the British Ambassador that Stalin was convinced that Hitler could not win the war, and was therefore interested in establishing good relations with Britain.[116] There can be little doubt that Madame Kollontai genuinely wished to improve Soviet relations with the west, but it is impossible to tell how far these remarks reflected the thoughts of Stalin's inner-circle. The Foreign Office discounted the whole incident as an attempt to confuse the issue. Cadogan, encouraged by all the sabre-rattling that was going on in Whitehall, even suggested that an attack on the Soviet Union might encourage the Japanese to join in an anti-Bolshevik crusade. He then began to speculate about Soviet policy:

> Being fairly self-sufficient I should have thought she [Russia] might be content to sit within her own frontiers and watch the belligerents exhaust themselves, giving a push here and a push there occasionally to keep the war going, hoping to be the one in the end to profit from the war.

Halifax commented on this view, which was soon to prevail in the Foreign Office, 'It is a very uncertain world.' Orme Sargent doubted whether the Soviets would be able to play this waiting game with any degree of success. He believed that it was impossible for the Soviets and the Germans to be true allies, and that the Soviet Union might well look to Britain, just as Britain had looked to France rather than Germany after the Boer War. But he still agreed with Cadogan that it would be greatly to Russia's advantage if the war lasted as long as possible so as to wear down both sides.

Maisky gave some indication that this was indeed the basis of Soviet policy when he told Sir Bernard Pares, 'After a long war neither side would have anything left; *both* would start again from scratch and the Germans would be more efficient.'[117] Pares, who acted as a special adviser to the Foreign Office where he was regarded as a frightful *bête noire*, consistently argued that the Soviet Union was genuinely neutral and was improving its defences against Germany in the Baltic and the Carpathians. Although he had a tremendous affection and respect for the Russian people he was certainly not a fellow-traveller. His greatest opponent at the Foreign Office was Fitzroy Maclean who minuted: 'Sir Bernard Pares ought to be subsidized by M. Maisky rather than by H.M.G. . . . Could not Sir Bernard Pares be got rid of?' The wheels were promptly set in motion to remove this man whose views no one wished to hear.

Although the Foreign Office was still deeply suspicious of Soviet intentions, particularly about a possible deal between the Russians and the Germans over Scandinavia, which would give Narvik to the Soviet Union, it was agreed that trade talks should continue and that, in the Foreign Secretary's words, 'war with the USSR would not be forced'.[118] Halifax also supported trade negotiations 'as a lubricant, to ensure a better reception in certain parliamentary quarters for our recent trade agreement with Spain and for the trade agreement which we hoped to negotiate with Italy'.[119] Fitzroy Maclean remained unconvinced. He argued that the Soviet Union had never been particularly keen on trade agreements in the past, and that her foreign trade was very small. He felt that the Soviets wanted to use these talks to prevent the Allies from taking any drastic action against them, and in order to weaken the blockade so as to be in a better position to supply Germany.[120] He felt that the British had nothing to fear from the Soviet Union as she was far more useful to the Germans as a neutral power. Maclean wanted to ditch the entire barter agreement, saying that if it went ahead

> our action would also be bound to produce a disastrous effect both
> on Allied and neutral opinion by displaying weakness and giving
> the impression that in return for a little timber we were prepared
> to overlook Soviet aggression against Poland, the Baltic States and
> Finland not just to mention Soviet cooperation with Germany.

He felt that Maisky had been exceptionally skilful in creating the impression that the Soviet Union and Germany were far apart and that Moscow could be won away from Germany. This myth was being disseminated by the *Daily Worker*, the *News Chronicle* and the Beaverbrook press. It was time that something was done to prepare public opinion to be more anti-Soviet, 'especially as we are on the verge of war'. But the general feeling in the Foreign Office was that the trade talks were important and should not be jeopardised by excessive anti-Soviet propaganda.

Part of the reason for this shift in opinion away from an aggressively anti-Soviet stance was that Cripps' mission to Moscow encouraged those who favoured negotiation over confrontation. In May Andrew Rothstein, the Russian-born Communist journalist who was soon to become the leading spokesman of the Soviet Union in Britain, almost to the point of becoming something of an unofficial ambassador, had a long and friendly talk with Ridsdale of the Foreign Office News Department. Rothstein suggested that instead of an endless exchange of memoranda, a method which he described as 'Byzantine', there should be an exchange of delegations. Then serious discussion of the trade agreement could begin.[121] The unmistakable impression is that Maisky, knowing the belligerent mood of the Foreign Office and the antipathy of its officers to him, preferred to intrigue elsewhere, and that he was using Rothstein as his spokesman. Meanwhile, returning to London via Washington, Cripps had won over the British Ambassador, Lord Lothian, who told the Foreign Office that the Soviet Union and Germany were fundamentally antagonistic, that the Soviets wished to remain neutral and were providing the Germans with very little besides foodstuffs, and that Britain should not blockade Vladivostok as some Foreign Office officials were urging.[122] One of the wilder schemes being entertained at the time was that a blockade of Vladivostok would help bring the Japanese into a British-sponsored anti-Comintern pact which hopefully might include Italy.

There was thus considerable uncertainty whether there was indeed a fundamental antagonism between the Soviet Union and Germany, or whether they were kindred spirits. The Foreign Office made no attempt to analyse the dynamics of Soviet and Nazi society. The works of Stalin and Hitler were left unread. Ideology was totally discounted, and all analogies were taken from nineteenth-century history, with Hitler as a Kaiser and Stalin as a Tsar, playing the same game according to the same rules. Any specialised knowledge of contemporary Russia or Germany was thus deemed to be an unnecessary diversion from the eternal truths of the diplomatist's art. There were distinct advantages to this approach with its insistence on Britain's national interest and a refusal to be bamboozled by ideological claptrap, but for all its supposed realism it made it almost impossible to assess the motives, intentions and thrust of Soviet and German policy.

Although the Foreign Office was in a distinctly anti-Soviet mood and felt that the Soviet Union was merely taking a breathing space before embarking on fresh adventures, it was obliged to hold its fire for the time-being by a Cabinet decision to send Sir Stafford Cripps to Moscow in the hopes of negotiating a satisfactory trade agreement and of reaching a workable political arrangement between the two countries.

2 Sir Stafford Cripps Goes to Moscow

As the German army poured into France the need for a more satisfactory arrangement with the Soviet Union became a matter of some urgency. Something more than an endless and frustrating exchange of notes was badly needed. Halifax felt that if a mission were to be sent to Moscow Cripps was the man best suited for the task. Cripps was eager to go, confident that he could build on the foundations he had laid in his brief visit, and readily accepted the Foreign Secretary's invitation. The British Government was willing to send him, and the Soviets, in spite of the fact that he was a social democrat and a teetotaller, were anxious to have him, and Maisky was delighted. But there remained the thorny, if somewhat arcane problem of his official status. Halifax wanted him to go to Moscow simply to test the water. The Soviet Government wanted the British to have an Ambassador in Moscow. There was no great enthusiasm on either side for the suggestion that Seeds might return to his post, and it was agreed that it would confuse the situation if Seeds and Cripps were to travel to Moscow together. Halifax therefore suggested that Cripps should go as an 'ambassador on a special mission'.[1]

Cripps was already on his way to Moscow, little concerned about the precise nature of his appointment, when Tass released a communiqué that the Soviet Government refused to discuss trade relations with anyone other than the regular ambassador in Moscow.[2] Although Halifax had already told Maisky that Cripps would not be appointed to replace Seeds, the British Government had no alternative but to give way and make Cripps Ambassador to the Soviet Union.[3] But the Foreign Office was at a loss to know how this could be done. Ambassadors had to be given their credentials by the King, but Cripps had left the country and could hardly be recalled in midair. Those who wanted to scotch the entire mission were delighted at this unexpected turn of events, but the ever-ingenious Maisky stepped in with a solution to the problem. Much to the horror of the traditionalists he suggested that the King could telegraph his consent to the appointment to Moscow.[4] With much reluctance it was agreed that this unusual method should be used, and the Soviet Government got its way. Cadogan was disgusted with the whole affair, saying that Cripps 'is an excellent lawyer and a very nimble debater in parliament, but he has not yet won his spurs in diplomacy', and adding, 'I personally attach no great importance to Russia. Russia is in no event going to do us any good and I am not optimistic enough to think she could do something later.'[5]

If the Soviet Government had been banking on a prolonged stalemate between Germany and the Allies from which they might eventually benefit, they certainly had to rethink their position after the fall of France. Any apparent balance had been brutally destroyed, the Soviets had to consider the possibility that Hitler's insatiable appetite for conquest might lead him to strike eastwards. They did not want to strengthen Germany, but they could not afford to do anything that might provoke their dangerous ally. They needed to strengthen their ties with Britain, but at the same time leave all their options open. As a consequence of their arrangement with Nazi Germany they were now placed in a very awkward position from which they were unable to extricate themselves. The uncertainty of Soviet policy made it almost impossible for the British Government to make an accurate assessment of their aims and intentions. In the summer of 1940 both governments were hanging on by the skin of their teeth and hoping for the best. This was hardly a promising background for top level discussions.

One thing was clear: the Soviets, with their chronic shortage of foreign exchange, wanted a barter agreement. Furthermore, a barter arrangement would make it easier to avoid entanglements over the British contraband regulations and obviate the need for a discussion of the sensitive issue of Soviet trade relations with Germany.[6] They were also anxious that political questions should be excluded from the trade talks, and firmly stated that, 'The Soviet Government cannot accept the viewpoint of the British Government to the effect that the trade policy of the Union of Soviet Socialist Republics should be subordinated to the war aims of one or another foreign state.'[7]

Although the Foreign Office was fed up with the endless exchange of increasingly vituperative notes on Anglo–Soviet trade, they did not feel that Cripps was likely to do any better. Cripps was a very independent man who wanted to be much more than a mere executant of Government policy, and he had no time at all for the anti-Soviet faction within the Foreign Office. He agreed that Russia under Stalin was repressive, backward, and inefficient, but he was convinced that without the cooperation of the Soviet Union Germany could not be defeated. The national interest rather than his left-wing philosophy was the guiding principle behind his determination to secure an agreement with the Soviets, and he firmly believed that it was in their national interest to agree to his proposals. This somewhat high-minded independence was the cause of considerable concern to the Foreign Office. Collier minuted: 'Mr. Lascelles, I hope, will see to it that Sir S. Cripps does not commit us politically to anything too outrageous; but he will have his work cut out for him, I fear.'[8] Dalton, the Minister of Economic Warfare, also had some reservations about Cripps, thinking that he might run too much of a one-man show. He was an equally strong advocate of better relations with the Soviet Union, and had no patience with those whom he was pleased to call 'The palsied pansies of the F.O.'. He therefore decided to send the eminent Russian-born economic historian, Professor Postan, 'as policeman with Cripps'.[9] Unfortunately for Dalton the Soviet authorities refused to allow Postan to enter the country, and the Foreign Office was delighted to report that the unfortunate Professor had disappeared somewhere in equatorial Africa in his desperate attempt to find a way home. One official remarked gleefully, 'Fortunately his movements are no longer any concern of ours.'[10]

Professor Postan made his circuitous way home and Orme Sargent was furious that he had suffered such a humiliation from the Soviet Government. Above all Sargent blamed Dalton for sending his right-hand man even though he knew full well that he was unlikely to be welcomed by his erstwhile countrymen. Sargent was however in a minority position at the Foreign Office, for most of his colleagues had no interest in reaching any sort of agreement with the Soviet Union and were rather pleased with the Postan affair. Cripps' strongest supporter at the Foreign Office was R. A. Butler who felt that he might get some results which would significantly improve Britain's position. Butler was also greatly encouraged by the attitude of the new Government under Churchill and pointed out that there was 'a fairly strong urge in this new Government both on the right and the left for a *rapprochement*'.[11]

The imminent defeat of France and the change in government in Britain thus spurred on those who were hoping for better relations with the Soviet Union. They agreed that Cripps was the best man for the job, even though there was some concern that he might be a tricky man to handle. Their main difficulty was that they wanted an agreement which would hurt the Germans, whereas the Soviets wanted to avoid this at all costs.

Cripps arrived in Moscow on 12 June and two days later was granted an interview with Molotov. They readily agreed that the problems of Anglo–Soviet trade should be settled as soon as possible, but when Cripps turned the conversation towards political questions he got no encouragement. He told Molotov that once the Germans had finished with France they would round on the Soviet Union, and suggested that the two countries had a common interest in stopping aggression in the Balkans and the Far East. Molotov muttered that he found these ideas interesting, but that he had no time to discuss them any further, owing to other pressing engagements. He mentioned Soviet interests in Romania and his fear that the United States was unlikely to agree on a common policy in the Far East.[12]

In his report of the meeting, Cripps suggested that American pressure could be applied to convince the Soviets to enter the war. Ambassador Kennedy quickly put an end to any such hopes by saying that the only thing his country could offer the Soviets were machine tools, a remark which infuriated Halifax because they were badly needed in Britain to increase industrial production. Cripps further argued that the Soviets were unlikely to 'acquiese in a German hegemony of Europe', but hastily added that they were unlikely to do anything very much about it.[13] This report from Moscow further strengthened Halifax's conviction that the reported Soviet military build-up in the Baltic States was an entirely defensive move. He told the Cabinet that 'there could be little doubt that the intention behind Russia's moves was to strengthen her position against Germany, whose military successes were not to her liking.'[14] Halifax did not believe that there was any question of the Soviet Union attacking East Prussia from these positions, but he urged Churchill to talk to Maisky, for Cripps was about to meet Stalin and there was some indication that circumstances were favourable for a political initiative.

During the night of 24/25 June the text of the Prime Minister's message to Stalin was sent to Moscow along with instructions to Cripps on how he should approach the interview with the Soviet leader. Churchill's letter stressed the terrible danger of German hegemony over the continent of Europe and expressed the hope that, in spite of the wide differences between Britain and the Soviet Union and the mutual suspicions which had hampered relations between the two countries in the past, it might be possible to work together in the face of a common danger. The note was skilfully worded so as to avoid the impression that the British Government was chasing after the Russians in a desperate search for an ally and was a blunt statement of Churchill's conviction that Germany would sooner or later turn on a country that had become her 'friend, almost at the same moment as she became our enemy'.[15] In an accompanying note, Orme Sargent suggested that Cripps should tell Stalin that he thought his recent actions in the Baltic had been dictated by the 'imminence and magnitude of the German danger'.[16]

The general feeling in the Foreign Office was that Cripps was hopelessly optimistic in believing that he could reach an agreement with the Soviets, and that his mission offered further proof that amateurs should not dabble in diplomacy. They were not particularly impressed with the argument that Stalin was improving his strategic frontier, taking it as further evidence that the Germans had a very low opinion of the Red Army and were therefore indifferent to such developments. In spite of Andrew Rothstein's efforts to convince the Foreign Office that the Soviets had no interest in allowing Hitler to overrun the whole of Europe and that they knew perfectly well that they were next on Hitler's list, most officials in Whitehall believed that the Russians still hoped to remain on close and friendly terms with the Germans. But some diplomats were beginning to have doubts about this analysis. Orme Sargent carefully deleted the following passage from a letter he wrote to Dalton.

> There is reason to believe that he [Stalin] still favours co-operation with Germany, and intends that any trade agreement with us shall help Germany by weakening our blockade rather than be the first step towards an Anglo–Soviet political *rapprochement*.[17]

Sargent believed that Stalin was playing games with Cripps, using him as a pawn against the Germans, and remarked sourly that he would have to stick to it. He agreed with the majority of his colleagues that this was hardly a matter of great concern and that it served Cripps right. R. A. Butler, who was a staunch supporter of Cripps, was horrified at this attitude. Commenting on a minute by Sargent he wrote, 'We must be very careful about comment on such envoys who with complete disregard for their own private convenience undertake duties such as this which must at times be odious.'[18] Maclean was still convinced that the barter agreement had probably been approved by the Germans as a means of getting hold of those raw materials they badly needed. He hoped that the Government would be prepared to use the threat of an attack on the Caucasus oilfields in order to bring the Soviets round. Collier did not go quite as far, arguing that a trade agreement should be made conditional on the Soviets giving a solemn undertaking not to send any further supplies to Germany. If they would do this he was prepared to suggest that the Government should recognise the new Russo–Polish border. No mention was made of Lithuania, which had been occupied by Soviet troops on 15 June, nor of Latvia and Estonia which had suffered a similar fate two days later. No thought was given to the reactions of the Polish Government to such a suggestion, even though Britain had ostensibly gone to war to preserve the territorial integrity of Poland; nor was it asked whether Britain was in any position to offer such a recognition.[19]

Cripps eventually met Stalin on 1 July, and was granted an interview which lasted three hours.[20] Stalin argued that since Germany did not have control of the seas it would be impossible for them to dominate Europe, and that Churchill's basic premise was therefore entirely false. He hoped that it would be possible to reach a tripartite agreement with Turkey over the Dardanelles. Cripps managed to get Stalin to confess that some of the non-ferrous metals imported from Britain would indeed go to Germany in order to fulfil Soviet contracts. The Ambassador was encouraged by the length of the conversation and by the 'friendly and severely frank' tone of the interview and was hopeful that a trade agreement would soon be forthcoming. Predictably the Foreign Office did not share this optimism. Maclean felt that Stalin's enthusiasm for an accord on the Dardanelles was simply an attempt to use Britain's good offices to secure the Soviet Union's long-standing imperialist aims. Orme Sargent immediately sent a telegram to Knatchbull-Hugessen, the British Ambassador in Turkey, telling him that Britain was not going to do Stalin's work for him.[21] Many felt that Stalin's open admission that he would re-export British raw materials to Germany was clear proof of his pro-German stance and the worthlessness of the trade agreement, but Sargent told Cripps that this was no serious obstacle to further negotiations.[22]

Although Cripps found his talk with Stalin encouraging nothing further happened for weeks. Molotov declined to speak with him, in spite of frequent requests, and he was left hanging about in Moscow with precious little to do – a highly frustrating situation for such an active and ambitious man. The Foreign Office debated whether

Cripps should be recalled, but decided against such a step. It was argued that the Soviets would then claim that Cripps had been foisted on them, and had not been given proper instructions by his Government. They would probably think that the Cripps mission had been nothing more than a ploy to keep them in play. Another important consideration was the effect of a growing public sentiment that closer ties with the Soviet Union were highly desirable. On 17 June Michael Foot had written an article in Beaverbrook's *Evening Standard* in which he had made a strong plea for an alliance with the Soviet Union, arguing that it was a country which 'holds the power at any moment of her choice to shift the whole balance'. This article met with a tremendous response, and was duly noted by the Foreign Office. But probably the strongest argument of all was that the failure of the Cripps mission would give comfort to Hitler. Hermann Rauschning, the author of the influential book *Germany's Revolution of Destruction*, suggested to the Foreign Office that the Soviets should be told that there had been peace feelers from Germany which were designed to set the stage for an attack on Russia. This idea was seriously considered, but finally rejected as unlikely to be successful. It was therefore decided that Cripps should remain in Moscow and be left, as some officials felt, to stew in his own juice. Butler was still virtually alone in giving his full support to Cripps. He wrote, 'I feel that Sir S. Cripps will still survive to lead the conservative or "Traditional Party" in England.'[23] This is possibly the first hint that Cripps was to be seriously considered as a suitable Prime Minister to replace Winston Churchill, although for the moment this was far from men's minds.

The Soviet occupation of the Baltic States was also a major problem affecting Anglo–Soviet relations in the summer of 1940. Halifax and the Foreign Office believed that the States had been incorporated into the Soviet Union as a result of naked aggression and fraudulent elections, and that, all Soviet protestations to the contrary, it was carried out against the will of the people. British assets in the Baltic States were seized and there was no likelihood of any compensation. The United States' Government made it abundantly plain that they would not tolerate any suggestion that recognition should be given to the Soviet occupation of the Baltic States. Although the British Government sympathised with the American position, and was in no doubt about the legitimacy of any Soviet claims for recognition, they were also anxious that nothing should stand in the way of a *rapprochement* with the USSR. It was therefore argued that Stalin had invaded the Baltic States to protect himself against German aggression and that this should be seen as an extenuating circumstance. In reply to the Cabinet's request for his views on the Soviet position in the Baltic States and the effects of this move on his negotiations in Moscow, Cripps emphatically stated that he saw no objection to a *de facto* recognition of the Soviet presence in the area, and pointed out that they had gone to great lengths to give an air of legality to their activities. Cripps was also strongly opposed to the suggestion that the Bank of England should seize the gold reserves of the Baltic States in lieu of compensation for the loss of British assets. At a Cabinet meeting on 13 August these arguments were discussed. The Chancellor of the Exchequer suggested that the gold holdings of the Baltic States should be kept until all British losses were recouped. After some discussion it was agreed that the United States should be consulted about the question of the Baltic gold, but that Cripps should be told that there was no serious objection to a *de facto* recognition of the Soviet presence in the Baltic States.[24] The United States' Government made it very clear that they were strongly opposed to releasing the gold deposits and did not wish to grant any recognition whatever to Soviet aggression.[25] The British Government therefore happily kept the gold, but argued that *de facto* recognition was nothing more than an acknowledgement that something, however reprehensible, had indeed taken place.

Meanwhile Cripps was becoming increasingly impatient and was on the point of threatening to pack up his bags and leave, when Molotov agreed to talk to him on 7 August.[26] Molotov made some acid remarks about the Baltic gold and the conversation was far from satisfactory. Cripps took cold comfort in the fact that Molotov had at least agreed to talk to him and had consented to the suggestion that he should discuss the trade agreement with Mikoyan. The interview left Cripps with the conviction that little could be done for the moment to improve relations between the two countries, but he still felt that things might change for the better and he was prepared to remain at his post to await further developments.

On 22 August Cripps eventually met Mikoyan who immediately launched into a violent diatribe against the British for seizing the assets of the Baltic States and for holding Estonian and Latvian ships in British ports.[27] Always an exceptionally tough negotiator, Mikoyan was on this occasion at his most rude. He announced that the behaviour of the British authorities was intolerable and there could be no talk of a comprehensive trade agreement. However, he did suggest that Soviet flax could be exchanged for British rubber. Cripps, who was also a very able negotiator, stood up very well against this onslaught and scored a number of telling points against his opposite number. He took some comfort in the thought that this was a beginning, even if an unpromising one, and that the door had not been completely closed and bolted. He was not to see Mikoyan again until 16 October.

The Foreign Office was uncertain what to make of all this. Maclean felt that it was further indication that the Soviets were not at all interested in coming to an agreement. Butler asked for some information on the leading Soviet figures and was told by Laurence Collier,

> Mikoyan is, of course, an Armenian, with all the well-known characteristics of his race; but these characteristics have probably been caused by environment, and the same sort of semi-oriental and semi-commercial environment, producing in each case a certain inferiority complex together with a suspicious and indirect approach to any question, doubtless accounts for the similar methods of M. Maisky, a Siberian Jew.

Butler found this memorandum, worthy of some minor Nazi functionary, to be most helpful. But the major cause of concern was that Cripps had requested the release of the Baltic gold and of all ships held in British ports and appeared to be likely to be sucked into a discussion of the future position of the Baltic States, an issue which the Foreign Office felt had nothing to do with trade and which was certain to infuriate the United States. The exchange of flax for rubber was the only suggestion which seemed encouraging. Although Britain had no need for the flax, it was agreed that it could be used to make linen which could then be exported to the dollar countries. It was estimated that the British stood to make a profit of £3 million on the deal.[28]

Cripps' difficulties in Moscow reinforced the Foreign Office's belief that the Soviet Union was not in the least bit interested in coming to any arrangement with Britain, and that there was no point whatever in making major concessions in the Baltic or elsewhere if nothing could be gained in return. The Soviets appeared to be staunchly pro-German and in no mood to change their alliances. Cadogan wrote to the Northern Department:

The Soviet Government will make no anti-German move at present, as they are frightened of Germany. If, however, Germany were to decline, and we looked like winning, the Soviet Government would become even more disturbed as they would almost sooner see us beaten rather than Germany.[29]

In his diary, Cadogan wrote that it was foolish of Cripps to even think of giving anything to the Russians because they would never change their minds until they were ready to do so.[30] Cripps in fact agreed with Cadogan that there was very little chance of winning the Russians away from the Germans for the time being. Russia was frightened of Germany, and for this reason had strengthened her defences by seizing the Baltic States, Bessarabia and the northern Bukovina, and had absorbed parts of Poland and Finland. But since he also believed that when things began to go badly for Germany, Russia would be prepared to risk getting closer to Britain, Cripps felt that the Soviet Union was an unwilling ally of Nazi Germany, forced by circumstances into a distasteful cooperation with an essentially hostile power. Under these circumstances Cripps felt that he could do little but help prepare the way for the Soviet Union to change alliances, and to undo the harm that had been done by the British Government's failure to reach an agreement with the Soviets in the summer of 1939. For the moment the only hope was that it might be possible to reach an agreement with the Soviet Union over Turkey.[31] Halifax was of the opinion that it would be most unwise to place any hope in acting as a go-between to reach a settlement of the highly sensitive issue of the Straits. Britain's position in the Middle East and the Mediterranean was such that she could not possibly afford to alienate the Turkish Government, who might well feel that they were being sold out to the Russians, and might therefore move closer to the Germans. On the other hand, the Turks were anxious to be on better terms with the Russians and might favour a British initiative on their behalf. Cripps therefore felt that Turkey was the only card he had to play, but it would need a great deal of luck and much skill to use it effectively.

The Foreign Office took this to mean that Cripps was becoming disillusioned and the implication was that it served him right. Orme Sargent felt that Cripps would have to learn the virtues of patience, forebearance, and long-suffering, which were needed in abundant measure by any ambassador in Moscow. Cripps was merely learning the necessary lesson that diplomacy needs more than high-mindedness and political flair. R. A. Butler continued to defend Cripps, insisting that what one saw was not disillusionment but patience.[32] On the Soviet side only Madame Kollontai in Stockholm dared to voice her fulsome admiration for Cripps, and used the opportunity to express once again her conviction that Germany would eventually be defeated and that the Soviet Union was looking forward to that day.[33] The Soviet Union had ample reason to be concerned by the signing of the Tripartite Pact between Germany, Italy, and Japan on 27 September 1940, and Cadogan suggested that this might be the right psychological moment to call off the trade talks and threaten to bomb Baku in a final attempt to make the Soviets switch sides.[34]

Orme Sargent, on thinking about Cripps' experiences in Moscow, came to the conclusion that Stalin had hoped that war between Britain and Germany would weaken both sides to such an extent that Communism would inherit the earth. Now Stalin found himself in a most uncomfortable situation. Germany was immensely powerful having defeated France, and the Russian armed forces now faced 'an unexhausted and megalomaniac Germany'. Stalin had therefore begun a 'flirtation' with Britain simply to put some pressure on the Germans, but he was not serious about this because he saw the British Empire as his greatest rival, and a far greater threat to his ambitions than Nazi Germany. Therefore Russia and Germany were likely to do a deal. Germany would gain control over the Middle East and Turkey; Russia would be given *carte blanche* in Iran and Afghanistan. The only bone of contention between these two robber states would be the Straits. It was therefore essential for the British Government to be on good terms with Turkey, otherwise they were likely to lose the Middle East and their oil supplies as Russia triumphed in a fresh round of traditional nineteenth-century imperialism in its threadbare Communist disguise. The Ministry of Economic Warfare was less pessimistic. They pointed out that Soviet supplies to Germany had in fact gone down, and asked whether this was due to deliberate policy or to inefficiency. Sargent argued that on the contrary oil supplies from Russia had increased, and this strengthened his conviction that Turkey, as the key to the Middle East, should be the centre of British diplomatic attention. Fitzroy Maclean had no stomach for such speculation and historical erudition. For him the solution was simple: 'We are solely concerned with the mental processes of a middle-aged Georgian brigand.'[35]

Such frustration was a reflection of the fact that the British Government was in no position to make the Soviets an offer which would tempt them to consider moving away from their alliance with Germany. Given the parlous state of the British armed forces and the clear threats to Romania, the Balkans, and the Mediterranean posed by Germany and Italy, the Government could not threaten the Russians with anything at all convincing. Given the notorious suspiciousness of the Soviets it was hardly possible to begin discussions of the post-war settlement, and it might have been difficult to persuade the Russians that the British were likely to have anything very much to say about the organisation of the post-war world. There was some evidence that the Russians were mildly impressed by the courage and the determination of the British resistance to German bombing raids, but this was certainly not taken as a reliable indication that the tide was turning in Britain's favour. In the summer of 1940 odds on a German defeat were still very long. The only real hope for an improvement of relations with the Soviet Union thus lay in trade relations, as the Soviets with their often brutal realism had made abundantly clear. Modest progress was made in these talks. On 16 October Cripps had a further meeting with Mikoyan who announced that the Soviet Union was prepared to export lubricating oil and chrome.[36] At the end of the month the Soviets offered a more comprehensive barter arrangement.

The successful conclusion of these barter agreements opened up the difficult question of trade routes. It was felt that the safest route would be through Iran, but there were two major problems: the railway was in very poor condition and would need extensive repairs before large quantities of goods could be sent along it; even more difficult was the fear that using this route would open up the question of a partition of Iran between Britain and the Soviet Union. The Ministry of Economic Warfare did not think that this latter concern was justified. They saw no reason why the Soviet Union should not have control over the route in Northern Iran, but the Foreign Office was horrified at the suggestion. Professor Postan at the MEW suggested that Northern Iran should be given to the Russians as a bribe to win them away from the Axis powers. Those Foreign Office officials who had managed to convince themselves that the Soviet Union was out to take over the world felt that Postan was giving them positive encouragement in this endeavour. There were some sighs of relief at the Foreign Office when Dalton, the Minister of Economic Warfare, suggested to Halifax that as the Iranian route raised all manner of political and strategic questions there should be a top-level discussion of all the difficulties.[37]

Sir Stafford Cripps' mission was made all the more difficult by the fact that it was widely discussed in the British press. Articles by Kingsley Martin, D. N. Pritt, and Vernon Bartlett in the *New Statesman* blamed all his difficulties on the intransigent attitude of the British Government. The Foreign Office was bombarded with letters from Trades Unions, local Labour Party groups, and concerned individuals all demanding closer ties with the Soviet Union. Hardliners on the right denounced Cripps as a dupe of the Russians. Meanwhile, Maisky busily leaked information about the negotiations in Moscow to the *Daily Worker* and the *News Chronicle*. The *Daily Worker* wrote:

Behind this new campaign is no desire for friendship with the Soviet Union. There is the desire to extend the war and to recreate the anti-Soviet front which Chamberlain so miserably failed to build.[38]

Cripps complained bitterly to the Foreign Office that his negotiating position was being undermined by this public discussion of his mission and by the frequent leaks to the press. But given the existing censorship regulations, little could be done to improve the situation.[39]

With this constant criticism from the left-wing press, little support from the Foreign Office and with Soviets dragging their feet, Cripps was getting increasingly frustrated. On 11 November he asked the Foreign Office for permission to withdraw the trade proposals when he saw fit. The Foreign Office was strongly opposed to this suggestion, saying that the Russians would then blame the British for destroying everything at the last minute and for having negotiated in bad faith.[40]

Cripps had already reached the conclusion that it would be grossly unfair to place all the blame for this unfortunate situation on the Soviet Government. In a long letter to Halifax he argued that the Russians had every right to be suspicious of British intentions. The British Government had long been openly hostile to the Soviet Union. There were still too many prominent representatives of the traditional anti-Soviet line in the Government. The Soviets were convinced that the British were simply out to get something for themselves, and they were not seriously interested in improving relations between the two countries. Nor could they really be blamed for taking this attitude, for the British Government still refused to talk seriously about outstanding problems in Turkey, the Baltic or the Far East. The Soviet Union was still in no position to stand up to Germany, and thus could not afford to edge away from the Axis. Cripps continued,

> If you want to win over this country it has got to be on the basis of recognising a continuing friendship and partnership in post-war reconstruction and not merely upon the basis of getting them to help us out of our awkward hole after which we might desert them and even join the enemies who now surround them.

One Foreign Office official summed up the Northern Department's feelings about this message by writing, 'The trouble with Russian foreign policy is that it is much too good.'[41]

On 22 October Cripps gave Vyshinskii a copy of the British proposals for improving relations between the two countries. It called on the Soviet Government to extend towards Britain the same degree of benevolent neutrality as they gave to Germany. The Soviets were further asked to assist in the defence of Turkey and Iran should they be attacked by an Axis power. They were also asked to continue to help China in her struggle against Japan. If the trade or barter agreement did not provoke a hostile reaction from Japan, the Soviet Government was asked to conclude a non-aggression pact similar to that which they had signed with Germany. In return the British Government agreed to consult the Soviet Union about the post-war settlement and undertook not to form or enter any anti-Soviet coalition. They agreed to extend *de facto* recognition of Soviet sovereignty in the Baltic States, Bessarabia and the Northern Bukovina, and Cripps, on his own initiative and somewhat to the dismay of the Foreign Office, extended this to include those parts of Poland which were now under Soviet control. The British Government also agreed to offer the Soviets every possible expert assistance and material needed for the defence of the country against any future attack.[42]

These proposals were not particularly attractive to the Soviet Union for they were asking for concrete assurances in return for vague promises. Furthermore, they were made at a time when Molotov was going to Berlin, in the words of the official communiqué 'to extend and deepen, by the renewal of personal contact, current exchanges of views within the framework of friendly relations existing between the two countries'. Cripps got no reply from Vyshinskii, and Maisky complained to Butler that the proposals were without substance. The proposals were not officially rejected until the beginning of February, by which time they had been published in the *News Chronicle* having been given by Maisky to Mr Kuh of the United Press in an attempt to put pressure on the British Government to make further concessions. Kuh was soon to develop a considerable appetite for political intrigue and became a willing accomplice of the Ambassador. Cripps was furious at this leak, but was uncertain whether to blame Maisky or those in the Foreign Office who wanted to sabotage his efforts to reach an understanding with the Soviet Union. In fact the publication of the proposals had little effect on the outcome of the negotiations. There was nothing in them that seriously tempted the Soviets and they were met with a deafening silence.

After months of frustrating inactivity during which he saw his hopes of becoming the architect of an Anglo–Soviet *rapprochement* dashed, Cripps came to the conclusion that the only way to deal with the Soviets was to be tough. When the Soviet Government suggested that the British Military Attaché should visit units of the Red Army he replied that the offer should be refused. He felt that it was merely a sop, and would involve a reciprocal arrangement which might not be advantageous. He was furious when he learnt that owing to an administrative blunder the Soviet Attaché had already been allowed to visit units of the British Army.[43] The Foreign Office was amused and delighted that Cripps was beginning to take a firmer stand against the Soviets, and felt that he was at last coming down to earth and learning something about diplomacy.

On 23 December Anthony Eden was appointed Foreign Secretary. He had long been an advocate of closer ties with the Soviet Union, and made the improvement of relations with Moscow one of his first priorities. Much to his dismay he found the Ambassador in Moscow utterly fed up and ready to break off negotiations. He therefore went to great lengths to convince Cripps to change his mind, telling him that he was particularly anxious to improve relations with the Soviet Union and pointing out that it would be a disastrous beginning to his tenure of office if Cripps were to break off the talks, for this would convince the Soviets that the new Foreign Secretary was not interested in coming to terms with the Soviets.[44] As almost every minister, including Dalton, had lost patience with the Soviets, Eden had little support, but he was determined to do what he could to improve the situation. He suggested to Cripps that his appointment as Foreign Secretary offered a useful opportunity to send a message to Stalin expressing his sincere desire to have the best possible relations with the Soviet Union. Cripps replied somewhat reluctantly that he was prepared to continue the trade talks and asked Eden where he should draw the line in any forthcoming negotiations.

When Eden asked Oliver Harvey to become his private secretary in January 1941 he told him that he was horrified at the 'deadness' and 'woolliness' of the Foreign Office. Harvey was equally appalled by the anti-liberal attitude of the Foreign Office and hoped that Eden would be able to do something to change the atmosphere. Both men were somewhat to the left of the Conservative Party at the time, and Eden, greatly impressed by his Labour colleagues in the Cabinet, was even toying with the idea of joining the left after the war. Both men agreed that improvement of relations with the Soviet Union and a comprehensive programme of social reform should be top priorities.[45] Eden was much more sensitive to the feelings of the Soviet Union than was the Foreign Office, and immediately set out to restrain some of its more outspoken anti-Soviet officials. But for the time being there was little he could do but wait and hope that Cripps would be successful.

British policy towards the Soviet Union was seriously hampered by lack of intelligence information. Almost all intelligence efforts were directed against the Axis powers, and the Soviet Union was largely ignored. The Soviet meteorological cypher had been broken, and some naval, army and police messages had been decoded, but this yielded little of strategic importance.[46] No serious attempt was made to assess Soviet war potential, and information on the political situation was equally jejune. Estimations of Russo–German relations were thus based on guesswork, and although the results were sometimes perceptive they were never based on solid intelligence. The Head of MI3(b), the German section of military intelligence, claimed in late 1939 that Russo–German friendship was superficial and that a conflict between the two countries was inevitable.[47] In the summer of 1940 it was generally agreed that Germany would not attack the Soviet Union until Britain had been defeated; but at the end of October Churchill told his military advisers that he believed Germany would attack the Soviet Union in 1941 in order to grab the oilfields.[48] This piece of inspired guesswork was discounted by military intelligence who insisted that the German build-up in the east was not the prelude to an attack, but a defensive move designed to restrain the Soviet Union.[49] By the end of January 1941 military intelligence argued that Germany would only attack the Soviet Union if the invasion of Britain failed and they found themselves in need of either a success or a bargaining counter. Another reason for an invasion of Russia would be if the Soviets failed to meet the terms of their trade agreement with Germany.[50] Eden did not agree and argued that 'There is every indication that the German threat to Russia – indirect if not direct – will increase in the next few months.'[51] Fitzroy Maclean was not convinced by Eden's assessment and felt that military intelligence provided a more accurate reflection of the situation. He wrote,

> The War Office have reached, on military grounds, the same conclusion as we have reached on political grounds, namely that there is at present no reason to anticipate an early German attack on the Soviet Union.

At most he was prepared to concede that there was a certain degree of mutual suspicion between the two countries.[52] Military intelligence believed that Stalin's policy was to allow Britain and Germany to exhaust themselves, and they were even prepared to predict that if Germany did eventually attack the Soviet Union, the Russians would not even bother to fight.[53]

Amid all these rumours, speculations and guesses Cripps remained steadfast in his conviction that the Germans would attack the Soviet Union regardless of the outcome of their plans to invade Britain. During a meeting with Eden and the CIGS in Ankara, at the end of February 1941, Cripps announced that Germany would attack the Soviet Union 'not later than the end of June'. Whether this was a piece of brilliant intuition, or whether it was based on solid military intelligence passed to him by the American Embassy in Moscow, remains uncertain.[54] The British military authorities estimated that the Germans would defeat the Russians in four to six weeks and, given this low opinion of Soviet military capabilities, there was no question of the British hoping that Germany would move east. They feared that Hitler would have no difficulty in overrunning the Caucasus and taking the oilfields, and that he would then be in an excellent position to launch a full-scale attack on British positions in the Middle East. Given these grave implications of a German attack on the Soviet Union it is truly extraordinary that British military intelligence made no serious effort to estimate Soviet war potential, and that no contingency plans were made of the strategic significance of the rapid collapse of the Soviet Union in the face of a German attack.

On 1 February Cripps had another meeting with Molotov. Six

months had passed since they had last met and the talks were, in the Ambassador's words, 'quite unproductive'.[55] The sole reason for the meeting was that Eden had complained to Maisky that Molotov had not seen Cripps for several months. As neither side had anything to offer, Cripps concluded that the meeting was arranged simply to show that Molotov was not totally inaccessible. Apart from some sour remarks about the attitude of the British Government to the Soviet position in the Baltic States, Molotov was grimly silent and frequently showed his obvious boredom with the proceedings. The Foreign Office was concerned that Cripps might be tempted to give way on the Baltic States and therefore sent him strict instructions to stand firm, reminding him that the Prime Minister's declaration of 5 September, that the British Government would not accept any territorial changes that were not brought about by the free consent of the people involved, must be the basis of all such discussions. The Foreign Office also did not wish to prejudice relations with the United States by giving way to the Russians over the Baltic States. Indeed, the Foreign Office took a firmer line on this issue than the Cabinet, and would not accept the argument that there was any significant difference between a *de facto* and a *de jure* recognition of the Soviet take-over in the Baltic States.[56]

Knowing that Eden had a genuine desire to improve relations with the Soviet Union, and hoping that it might be possible to begin some serious discussions with the Soviets, Cripps suggested that the Secretary of State might visit Stalin on his way back from the Middle East.[57] Cripps had been hanging around Moscow for months and had nothing to show for his efforts and hoped that Eden might be able to convince the Russians that the British Government was seriously interested in negotiations. Churchill was strongly opposed to this suggestion, particularly as the British position in Greece was so terribly weak and she was in no position to offer the Soviets anything remotely tempting. The Prime Minister told Eden that 'it is no good running after these people ... Events alone will convince them.' Indeed he was so strongly opposed to the suggested visit that he wrote to Eden that he 'would hardly trust them for your personal safety or liberty'.[58] It is difficult to believe that Churchill seriously thought the Soviets might arrest the Secretary of State, but it is an indication of how little he liked the whole idea. Eden agreed, saying that it was bad policy to 'run after the Soviet Government'.[59] He was prepared to talk to the Soviets at any time, but only when there seemed to be some chance of success. Thus, instead of Eden going to Moscow, Cripps travelled to Ankara. The two men agreed on the broad outlines of policy towards the Soviet Union, and Cripps managed to get a promise from Eden that he would reconsider the problem of the Baltic States on his return to London.

The Foreign Office was implacable in its opposition to the idea of making any concessions to the Russians, and Eden, in spite of his belief that something should be done, was not the man to put up much of a fight in the face of such strong opposition. 'I agree' tended all too often to be his favourite marginal note, even when it must often have been against his better judgement. At the end of April 1941 Orme Sargent summed up Foreign Office thinking: 'The truth of the matter is, of course, that until and unless the Soviet Government change their policy of appeasing Hitler there is no possibility of our reaching an understanding with them on any basis and at the price of any concession.'[60] Cadogan also agreed that making concessions to the Soviets over the Baltic would do no good at all, and for this reason alone he was against them.[61] Had the Foreign Office thought that concessions over the Baltic States would have significantly changed relations with the Soviet Union they would have quickly forgotten their legal and moral objections, and would certainly have discounted the effect such a move would have had on relations with the United States. The Foreign Office was very angry with Cripps for ignoring much of their advice and for indulging in bouts of wishful thinking when he imagined that the Soviets might change their minds. Just when Cripps had begun to show something of the cool realism of the professional diplomat he had begun once again to chase the phantom of Anglo–Soviet *rapprochement*. Eden was almost alone in thinking that Cripps had some grounds for his guarded optimism, and pointed out that on some issues the Soviet Government appeared to be a trifle more helpful. He therefore attempted to reach a reconciliation between the Foreign Office and Cripps. Eden wrote, 'While I do not want to indulge in useless gestures, I do want to disabuse the Soviet Government of some of the suspicions which, however unjustifiably they do entertain of us.' At the same time he admitted that this was 'a difficult hand to play'.[62] Eden suggested that the British Government should be prepared to discuss the future of the Baltic States with the Soviet Union once they were convinced that the Russians were no longer helping the Germans. Churchill was convinced that it was only possible to start serious talks with the Soviets from a position of strength, and this was palpably not the case. He therefore counselled 'sombre restraint on our part, and let them do the worrying'.[63] There was thus general agreement in London that the Soviet Government was well aware of the British position and that it was up to them to make the next move.

The Prime Minister's call for 'sombre restraint' was made against the background of mounting speculation that Germany might soon attack the Soviet Union. At the end of March the Foreign Office received word from Belgrade that Hitler had told Prince Paul of Yugoslavia (Churchill's 'Prince Palsy') that he would attack the Soviet Union on 30 June. The Foreign Office agreed that it might be unwise to pass this information on to the Soviet Government, feeling that it might encourage them to make further concessions to the Germans.[64] The British military attaché in Berne also forwarded information that he had received from the Romanian military attaché in Berlin to the effect that the Germans had decided to attack the Soviet Union rather than continue planning for the full-scale invasion of England. The report also included a number of significant details of German preparations for an invasion of the Soviet Union.[65] Military intelligence discounted these reports and pointed out that the Germans could get more out of the Soviet Union with their present agreements than they could by war. The German army would not move east at a time when they still hoped to defeat Britain and were on the point of mounting a major campaign in the Balkans. R. A. Butler found this 'a very sane point of view' and most of the Foreign Office agreed with this assessment. At the time British intelligence agreed with Hitler's belief that in the face of a German attack the Soviet Union would fall apart. Every village would seek autonomy, and there would be complete administrative chaos.[66]

The Foreign Office therefore continued to discount the flood of rumours of an impending attack, suggesting that they were deliberately put out by the Germans to blackmail the Russians and to convince the rest of the world that they were indeed a great anti-Communist power. Frank Roberts was almost alone in thinking that 'there must be fire behind the increasing clouds of smoke'.[67] Churchill, who had long been convinced that Germany would eventually attack the Soviet Union, was also inclined to believe that there was fire behind the smoke. Enigma decrypts had shown that three of the five Panzer divisions in Romania had been ordered to move towards the German–Soviet border, but that following the Yugoslav coup on 27 March these orders were cancelled. He told Eden that he believed that 'Bear will be kept waiting a bit,' but that these troop movements clearly revealed the 'magnitude of design' of Germany's ambitions in the Balkans and against the Soviet Union.[68] After some careful thought, Churchill decided to inform Stalin. On 3 April he drafted the message in which he concealed the fact that his information came from Enigma:

> I have sure information from a trusted agent that when the Germans thought they had got Yugoslavia in the net, that is to say after March 20, they began to move three out of the five Panzer Divisions from Romania to Southern Poland. The moment they heard of the Serbian revolution this movement was countermanded. Your Excellency will readily appreciate the significance of these facts.[69]

Churchill was furious when he heard that Cripps had refused point-blank to deliver this message to Stalin, saying that he had already said much the same thing, though in more forceful language, to Vyshinskii. Eden supported Cripps's position, but Churchill was adamant. On 16 April Churchill wrote to Eden complaining that 'The Ambassador is not alive to the military significance of the facts' and adding that this was 'an extremely pregnant piece of information'. The Prime Minister's orders were sent to Cripps on 19 April, Eden apologising to Churchill for the delay, saying that he had been visiting the King at Sandringham. The following day Cripps handed the message to Vyshinskii, but pointedly avoided making any comment.[70]

Churchill never forgave Cripps for his 'effrontery' in first refusing to send the message to Stalin, then waiting for sixteen days and finally for handing it to Vyshinsky rather than to Stalin in person. Writing in October 1941 to Beaverbrook and Eden he said,

> It was the only message before the attack that I sent Stalin direct ... Its brevity, the exceptional character of the communication, the fact that it came from the Head of Government and was to be delivered personally to the Head of the Russian Government by the Ambassador were all intended to give it special significance and arrest Stalin's attention.

Churchill blamed his later difficulties with Stalin on Cripps' 'obstinate, obstructive handling of the matter'.[71] The Foreign Office was not impressed by this flap, and thought that the Prime Minister was getting carried away by spurious rumours. The Yugoslavian revolution had completely altered the situation and this intelligence could be discounted. Cavendish-Bentinck of the Joint Intelligence Committee also felt that Churchill's concerns were based on nothing more than rumour. The JIC was not privy to the Enigma material and reached the conclusion that German preparations in the east were designed to frighten the Russians into making further concessions. Those who were in possession of Enigma decrypts, principally the Government Code and Cypher School and Air Intelligence, were convinced that Germany was about to attack the Soviet Union, and part of Churchill's anger must be attributed to the fact that he was unwilling to reveal the source of his information beyond the small circle of those who knew about Enigma.

Further reports reached the Foreign Office from Stockholm where the Ambassador, Mallet, had managed to gather a considerable amount of information on discussions in Berlin. He wrote, 'All military circles in Berlin are convinced of conflict with Russia this Spring and consider success certain.' In a further report he gave added details of discussions in Germany and in the Soviet Union of the possibility of an early conflict.[72] Supporting evidence was also given to those who chose to discount these reports when Mallet wrote that Madame Kollontai, although fervently anti-German, believed that the Soviet Union would do everything to avoid a war as the armed forces would not be ready to fight the Germans until 1944.[73] From Moscow Cripps reported that the military were expecting a war, but that they were 'separated from the Party' who firmly discounted all such talk.[74] Tass reported that these rumours were part of a campaign in the west designed to encourage Hitler to attack the Soviet Union, at which time peace would be made with Nazi Germany and Churchill would be replaced by the old appeasers. Reports from the Polish Embassy in London also indicated that the Red Army, unlike the Party, was expecting an attack, but that Stalin showed no signs of concern. Jack Scott of the *News Chronicle* told the Foreign Office that Stalin had been exceptionally friendly to the German Military Attaché, Krebs, and also to the Japanese Minister of Foreign Affairs, Matsuoka, who had appeared in front of the press hideously drunk after a vodka-session with Stalin.[75]

Cripps had for some sime thought that it was a good idea to threaten the Soviets with the suggestion that the British were contemplating a separate peace with Germany. He had tried this out on Vyshinskii in October and November 1940 and on Molotov in February. He sent an *aide-mémoire* to Molotov suggesting that Britain 'might be tempted to make peace with Germany at Russian expense'. Churchill and Eden were furious with Cripps for bringing up such a sensitive issue without instructions from Whitehall and for giving the Russians further grist for their propaganda mill. Cadogan and Sargent agreed that Cripps should be recalled and given a good dressing-down, but R. A. Butler suggested that 'If Sir S. Cripps were to revert to politics it would be important that he should not give up his post under a cloud and therefore a hurried evacuation of his piggery seems fairly difficult to arrange.'[76] Cripps pressed on regardless, and when Hess landed in Scotland in May he suggested that this bizarre event could be used to drop a hint to the Russians that peace negotiations had begun. In fact no such suggestion was needed, for the Russians were obsessed that this was the sole purpose of the Hess mission. The Foreign Office sensibly rejected this proposal. Orme Sargent wrote, 'The idea of our hinting at the possibility of a compromise peace with Germany is, I am certain, far too dangerous to be even considered.' Cadogan was fully in agreement with these sentiments.[77]

Hess turned out to be a nuisance and an embarrassment. The Soviets were convinced that there was some sinister purpose behind his mission. The British could find no useful purpose for him at all, particularly as he showed every sign of being deranged. In a richly comic scene Hess was interviewed by Sir John Simon, masquerading as the psychiatrist 'Dr Guthrie', Ivone Kirkpatrick as 'Dr Mackenzie' and, to really fool the prisoner, Beaverbrook as 'Dr Livingstone'. They listened to endless waffle from their patient, 'Jonathan', who in execrable English complained of being drugged and tortured. The three distinguished Scottish experts were quite unable to decide whether Hess was mad, or whether he was merely pretending. It is doubtful whether men with higher qualifications in psychiatry could have done any better. Clearly nothing could be gained politically from this episode.[78]

In May Brigadier Skaife of the Political Intelligence Department prepared a lengthy memorandum in which he argued that Germany was most unlikely to go to war with the Soviet Union. There was no reason why Germany, whose economic relations with the Soviet Union were, so favourable, should risk everything in a major campaign. Skaife, who was a great admirer of traditional Russia and an expert on Russian military affairs, disagreed with the prevailing assessments of Soviet military and political strength. He was convinced that Stalin would be able to unite the country by appeals to national sentiment and the glories and horrors of past wars. He would be prepared to burn Moscow and to retreat to Sverdlovsk. The regime would not only survive the war, it would be strengthened by it, and would fight with total dedication because it would not be able to survive a peace dictated by Germany.[79] The Foreign Office thought highly of this memorandum and felt that Hitler would be most unlikely to embark on such a hazardous adventure for such little economic or political gain. Skaife's paper was immediately forwarded to Cripps. Meanwhile Cavendish-Bentinck of the Joint Intelligence Committee was beginning to have second thoughts, and did not feel that it was wise to assume that Hitler was motivated by such rational considerations. He wrote, 'Hitler has a tendency sooner or later to revert to the tenets enunciated in *Mein Kampf* and: *on revient toujours à ses premiers amours!*'[80] The Foreign Office had little sympathy for such views. No one had bothered to study *Mein Kampf* and there was a general belief that Hitler's anti-Bolshevism was every bit as fraudulent as Stalin's communism. Even at this late stage Cavendish-Bentinck was almost alone in the Foreign Office in believing that Hitler really intended to use the forces which he was building up on such a massive scale in the east for an attack on the Soviet Union. He did get some support from Professor Postan at the Ministry of Economic Warfare, who thought that Germany might go to war for purely economic reasons because the Soviet Union was unlikely to make the sacrifices needed to increase supplies to Germany, although he did not entirely rule out such a possibility.

By the beginning of June the evidence of an imminent German attack was so overwhelming that the Foreign Office could no longer ignore it. The most perplexing aspect of the situation was the attitude of the Soviet Government. Tass scoffed at the 'Evident absurdity of these rumours' which they felt was 'a clumsy propaganda concoction of Powers which are hostile to the Union of Soviet Socialist Republics and Germany and interested in further spreading and unleashing a war'.[81] Christopher Warner was struck by the contrast between the reports of the concern of the people of Moscow and the attitude of the Soviet Government. Given the fact that there appeared to be little military activity in the Soviet Union he asked whether this was indication that Government was privy to certain information about German intentions.[82] On 2 June Eden told Maisky of the heavy concentration of German troops on the Soviet border and his belief that they would soon attack. Maisky shrugged this off with the remark that the Germans would not dare to attack as 'we won't have to fight with sticks as we did last time!' Eden replied that he was giving him this information in good faith. Maisky simply demanded concessions from the British Government on the question of the Baltic States.

Eden asked what the Soviets had to offer in return, adding that he did not believe in appeasement to Germany, to the Soviet Union, or to anybody. He suggested that the Soviets should undertake not to interfere in the Middle East, particularly in Iran and Iraq, as a first step towards an understanding. The Ambassador promised to pass on these comments to his Government.[83]

On 10 June Cadogan repeated these warnings of an impending German attack to Maisky but made no impression on him either. Two days later Macdonald of *The Times* had a long talk with Maisky who was extremely angry at the 'cock and bull story' of Germany preparing to attack the Soviet Union. Andrew Rothstein telegraphed to Moscow complaining about the 'cataracts of rumour' in the British press on impending war.[84] Eden saw Maisky again on 13 June and was told that all the talk about German troop concentrations was greatly exaggerated. Eden replied that if the Soviet Union were attacked the British Government would give every possible support.[85] By now the Joint Intelligence Committee felt that war was a distinct possibility, but unlike Brigadier Skaife they thought that the Germans would be in Moscow in six weeks.[86] Orme Sargent told Knatchbull-Hugessen in Ankara that there was now 'overwhelming evidence of imminent German attack'.[87]

The Foreign Office finally began to think about what should be done if the Germans launched their attack. One particular concern was that Hitler would be likely to win considerable support for an anti-Communist crusade. As there was general agreement that the Soviet Union would collapse within a few weeks, there was also the question of how to counter the shattering effect on Allied morale if Germany were to have yet another spectacular victory. At a high-level meeting in the Foreign Office it was agreed that the ideological motives behind Hitler's attack on the Soviet Union should be totally discounted and that it should be presented as yet another example of the worthlessness of his pledges. This new campaign would mean that the British would be fighting alongside the Soviet Union and that there would be tremendous sympathy for the Russians. This would create a most unpleasant situation, and as the report of the meeting suggested, 'There would probably be strong pressure in some circles to treat Russia as an ally. This should be resisted.' Another fear was that the United States with its aversion to the Soviet Union might leave Germany and Russia to fight it out and destroy one-another, in which case they might cut back their supplies to Britain.[88]

Curiously enough, just at the time when British military intelligence was convinced that the Germans would attack the Soviet Union in late June, and when the Foreign Office had been won over to this view, Cripps began to waver. Having been the strongest advocate of the view that Hitler would inevitably turn east, by mid-June he began to feel that Germany and the Soviet Union were beginning to negotiate.[89] No doubt the reason for this change of mind was the apparent lack of concern shown by Stalin and his immediate subordinates in the face of such clear indications that the Germans were about to attack. This is indeed one of the most curious aspects of the whole affair. Was Stalin totally fooled by the Germans, blindly refusing to accept the evidence presented to him from all quarters? Was he really caught totally by surprise? All the evidence suggests that he was living in a dream-world, refusing to listen to the terrible reports which came from all quarters. We have no possible means of knowing what really went on in the Kremlin during those days and Cripps, who knew Stalin as a brutal realist, can be excused for thinking that there must have been secret negotiations between Moscow and Berlin, and that German troop concentrations were designed to put additional pressure on the Soviet Government to make further economic concessions.

Cripps paid a brief visit to London in the middle of June where he attended Cabinet meetings, but his second thoughts on the likelihood of a German attack had no effect. Almost everyone was now convinced that the Germans were about to move. On 18 June a special meeting was held at the Foreign Office to discuss what could be done when the Germans attacked. Fears were expressed that Wall Street might become fervently anti-communist and pro-Nazi, and this could well have disastrous consequences for American aid to Britain. It was agreed that every possible support should be given to the Soviet Union to resist the Germans, but it did not look as if this would amount to very much.[90] On the following day Cabinet addressed the same issue. Churchill had no doubt about the political line to be taken: 'Germany should be represented as an insatiable tyrant' who had attacked Russia in order to obtain the materials needed to continue the war.[91] There was considerable doubt expressed about the desirability of having the Soviet Union as an ally, and a general feeling that the Germans would be victorious within a few weeks. It was agreed that every possible support should be given to the Soviets, but it seemed very doubtful that this would do anything to avert yet another crushing defeat.

Thus on the eve of the German attack on the Soviet Union the

British Government expected the worst. They felt that Germany would have little difficulty in grabbing the resources of the Soviet Union. They saw little chance of giving the Soviets any real assistance, and did not want to find themselves allied to the Soviet Union. They were also very much afraid that the United States might cut back the support which was essential if Britain was to continue the war. With the Soviet Union defeated there seemed to be nothing to stop the Germans from sweeping on into the Middle East and India. No contingency plans were drawn up to meet this eventuality. It seemed that nothing could be done but to wait and hope for the best.

3 Reluctant Allies

On Sunday, 22 June, Hugh Dalton was told by his wife at breakfast that she had heard on the seven o'clock news that Germany had attacked Russia, but she decided not to wake her husband. Later in the day Dalton wrote in his diary, 'I am mentally prepared for headlong collapse of the Red Army and Air Force. On the other hand, it is possible that they may do much better than we think.'[1]

The Prime Minister was staying at Chequers where the news of the invasion was relayed shortly after four in the morning. Churchill was not told until eight o'clock, for strict instructions had been given that he was not to be aroused before that hour unless England had been invaded. His immediate reaction was to tell his private secretary that he would broadcast to the nation at nine o'clock that evening. He then sent Eden a large cigar to celebrate this welcome news. Eden could not face a cigar at such an early hour, but shared Churchill's sense of relief. Churchill spent the rest of the day at Chequers with Beaverbrook, Stafford Cripps, and Lord Cranborne, working on the text of his speech. Beaverbrook felt that the Soviet Union would be able to stand up to the invader, but Cripps was very sceptical. There was no doubt in Churchill's mind that the Soviet Union should be given every assistance.[2] The previous evening he had told his private secretary that 'I have only one purpose, the destruction of Hitler. If Hitler invaded Hell I would make at least one favourable reference to the Devil in the House of Commons.' Colville argued that this was 'bowing down in the House of Rimmon'; a reference to II Kings 5: '. . . when my master goeth into the house of Rimmon to worship there, and he leaneth on my hand, and I bow myself in the house of Rimmon: when I bow down in the house of Rimmon, the Lord pardon thy servant in this thing.'

Churchill spoke on the BBC that evening without consulting the War Cabinet. The text was not completed until shortly before the broadcast, causing Eden no little concern as he was unable to vet the text of a speech which was bound to be of enormous political significance. The broadcast was one of the finest performances of a

56

great orator. It was also an exceptional act of statesmanship. Churchill began by emphasising his unwavering opposition to Communism and all that it stood for, and said that the Nazi regime 'is indistinguishable from the worst features of Communism', but that in this new situation all this was of little consequence. 'The past, with all its crimes, its follies, and its tragedies, flashes away.' In an unfortunate phrase, which was to cause no end of difficulties later on in the war, he spoke of 'Russian soldiers standing on the threshold of their native land, guarding the fields which their fathers have tilled from time immemorial.' The fact that Russian soldiers were standing in Eastern Poland and the Baltic States seems to have been forgotten as Churchill was swept away by his own rhetoric, and the Soviets were quick to point out that the speech gave at least tacit recognition to their annexations since 1939. Referring to fears that some might not support a war in which the Soviet Union was a partner, he was careful to say, 'This is no class war, but a war in which the whole British Empire and Commonwealth of Nations is engaged, without distinction of race, creed or party.' He argued that Hitler's invasion of Russia was a prelude to the invasion of Britain and that

> The Russian danger is, therefore, our danger, and the danger of the United States, just as the cause of any Russian fighting for his hearth and home is the cause of free men and free peoples in every quarter of the globe. Let us learn the lessons already taught by such cruel experience. Let us redouble our exertions, and strike with united strength while life and power remain.

A post-mortem on the speech was held at Chequers later that evening along with a discussion of whether there should be a debate on Russia in the House of Commons. Eden and Cranborne insisted that politically Russia was every bit as bad as Germany and half the country would object vigorously to being an ally of such a power. Churchill disagreed. He felt that the whole issue of Communism should be forgotten and that it was simply a matter of innocent people being slaughtered by a brutal invader.[3] Cabinet met the following day, and the Prime Minister expressed his hope that there was general approval of his speech. No adverse comment was made.[4] In Moscow, Mr Baggallay, who was holding the fort while Cripps was in London, saw Vyshinskii on the day of the invasion. He said that since Germany had attacked the Soviet Union their two countries now had a common interest in cooperation. Vyshinskii 'gave a very cautious assent'.[5]

Churchill was eager to see some immediate military reaction to the invasion of the Soviet Union and suggested to the Chiefs of Staff that there should be a large-scale raid across the Channel 'now the enemy is busy in Russia', and inspired by a suggestion from H. G. Wells thought of burning down the Black Forest with incendiary bombs. Nothing came of these schemes, but Churchill was more successful in pressing for aid for Russia, even though the Generals thought this was a terrible waste of valuable material which would all go down the spout as it had done in France in 1940. After several weeks of fighting the odds for Hitler being in Moscow by Christmas were Dill 5–4 on, Churchill even money, and Ismay 10–1 against. Few of the Generals shared Churchill's initial enthusiasm for the Russians. Ismay thought that 'the prospect of being allies with the Bolsheviks was repugnant'.[6] The Foreign Office was also not particularly enthralled, and D. N. Pritt wrote to Eden that the Foreign Office treated the Soviet Union like a mistress who suddenly arrives in the middle of a wife's garden party.[7]

As a first step towards an improved and closer relationship with the Russians, and in answer to the promptings of Maisky, a military mission was sent to Moscow, headed by Lieutenant-General F. N. Mason-Macfarlane, a soldier of whom the Chiefs of Staff wrote, 'He has great drive and personality, and goes down extremely well with foreigners.'[8] In fact 'Mason-Mac' detested the Russians and laboured under the frustrating delusion that the only way to tackle their tiresome authorities was to be tough with them. As the military mission had so little to offer, this policy was bound to fail. In spite of the Chiefs' enthusiasm, his attitude was no secret in London. Dalton wrote, 'Mason-Macfarlane went out very pessimistic and didn't want to go. He doesn't like the Russians anyhow. One should not believe too much in his reports.'[9] His news conferences in Moscow soon became legendary. He would open the proceedings by saying, with the utmost seriousness, 'I haven't much information, and please remember anything I say is off the rocker.'[10] His obvious hostility towards the Soviet Union soon provoked a number of demands for his dismissal. Beaverbrook, having seen him in action in Moscow, drafted a memorandum for Churchill calling for the removal of the military attaché and all other British officials in Moscow who were obviously anti-Soviet.[11] Eden referred to him as that 'ridiculous general' and felt that his approach would make matters far worse than they were already.[12] After a year at the job, Eden remarked that 'The good general has worked very hard, but he has been unable to learn this lesson' that it is pointless to bargain with the Soviets, particularly from a position of weakness. But the problem was compounded by the fact that CIGS still believed him to be right and would 'endorse his error and we must watch to correct it'.[13] Although Mason-Macfarlane was not at all suitable for the job it must be admitted that he faced considerable difficulties. As he pointed out in one of his reports, the Russians were unlikely to cooperate 'as long as the British Army is doing nothing on land to help us in our struggle'.[14] It was also well known in London that the military mission received many requests for help from the Russians but was given virtually nothing in return.[15]

An SOE officer, Colonel Hill, was also sent along with the military mission to establish a permanent liaison with the NKVD in Moscow. Hill was a colourful figure, whose father had been a merchant in Russia, and who, unlike anyone else involved in Soviet affairs, spoke fluent Russian. He was fat, bald, garrulous, and given to embroidering some remarkably tall stories. He had been a British secret agent in Russia after the Bolshevik revolution, along with Bruce Lockhart, and was a friend of Sidney Reilly who had laid ingenious but unsuccessful schemes to assassinate Lenin and Trotsky. Hill had initially thought that the Bolsheviks were resolutely anti-German and would fight for the Allied cause, but after the Treaty of Brest–Litovsk he found himself fighting both the Germans and the Bolsheviks. He claimed to have been a friend of Trotsky, when he had advised on the formation of the Red Air Force. After a spell running guns to the Ukrainian patriots he lived underground in Moscow. Eventually he left Russia by joining up with Bruce Lockhart's mission. With such a background he was a very strange choice for the job, and his deputy was equally unsuitable. Major Turkouski was a Pole who combined a deep loathing for the Russians with a passionate anti-Communism. Hill's mission was given the codename 'Sam' and arrived in Moscow in September 1941. An SOE/NKVD agreement was signed at the end of the month.[16]

The gist of the agreement was that they would not mount subversive operations in each other's territory, and the British promised to help the Soviets drop their agents into western Europe. Hill's opposite number, Colonel A. P. Ossipov studiously avoided any reference to his past, and professed to admire his professionalism. The NKVD however took their normal precautions of following every move made by the SOE mission and of having their offices bugged. No doubt that British did much the same to the Russians, and the claim that British intelligence ceased to decrypt the Soviet codes after 22 June 1941 is singularly hard to believe.[17] Soviet army and police codes had been broken as well as the meteorological cypher, and the official history of British intelligence rather coyly admits that the meteorological cypher was 'read again for a period beginning October 1942'. The fact that the British were relatively well-informed about Soviet troop deployments, without the Soviets volunteering the information, does suggest that the Government Code and Cypher School were listening to more than the weather reports.

During 1941 neither SOE nor NKVD were in any position to undertake serious subversive actions. There was rather more serious fighting to be done. The British provided the Russians with some low-grade intelligence and seem to have got very little in return. Early in 1942 Colonel Hill was taken behind the German lines and given the opportunity to observe Soviet partisans in action. With characteristic *chutzpah* Hill claims to have helped Ossipov write the official Soviet handbook on partisan warfare, making use of the information gained on this trip.[18] Hill then travelled to the Middle East to examine the possibility of joint SOE/NKVD operations, causing no little alarm at headquarters in Cairo. He then went to London and won the approval of Sir Stewart Menzies ('C') for a plan to bring NKVD agents to England by sea and to drop them into western Europe.

The proposal to drop Soviet agents into Italy and France was viewed with considerable misgivings at 64 Baker Street, SOE's London headquarters, but the Foreign Office had no serious objections. Eventually SOE came round to the Foreign Office's point of view, in spite of the fact that the French authorities had vetoed the proposal.[19] It is impossible to tell how many Soviet agents were dropped in western Europe, for the British files have been carefully weeded to remove this politically sensitive material, but it is doubtful if there were very many. An SOE paper of January 1945 refers to a small number of agents, most of whom were dropped in 1943.[20] SOE also arranged to drop Soviet agents into Germany and the Balkans. NKVD was not at all happy about their SOE partners and constantly complained, not without some justification, that they were not being given sufficient information. Nor were many of SOE's 'toys' (various gadgets for assassination and sabotage) passed on to the Soviets. Although the Russians were gratified that Hill was an enthusiastic

supporter of a second front, they complained that he was snooping –
a curious complaint from the NKVD. They were in a very good
position to know what he was doing because he was engaged in an
intense affair with an NKVD girl. Under the impression that he could
learn more from her than *vice versa* he even managed to persuade
the Foreign Office to send him a large supply of diamonds to loosen
her tongue.[21] Eden became increasingly annoyed with these antics
and complained that Colonel Hill 'does not know his onions', was
wasting the taxpayers' money, and sent reports which were sloppy
and inaccurate.[22] It is not clear from the files whether Eden was
referring to the £20 000 which the Foreign Office is said to have spent
at Hatton Garden for gems for his *mozhno* girl.

In March 1945 the Foreign Office produced a paper on 'Principal
Heads of SOE Contact with NKVD and Results Thereof' which gives
a valuable summary of their joint activities.[23] In March 1944 SOE
agreed to send Major K. K. Krassowski to Tito's headquarters.
Krassowski was a member of the NKVD mission in London which
was headed until May 1945 by Colonel Ivan Chichaev, who was then
sent to Prague as 'Minister-Counsellor'. The visit was not a success,
and Krassowski was recalled to Moscow, Ossipov telling Hill that
'perhaps Krassowski was the wrong type to send'. In April 1943 a
proposal to send five Soviet agents into Italy was cancelled by the
NKVD. The NKVD also told Brigadier Hill that they had decided
not to appoint a representative in Istanbul, although a proposal to
this effect had been made in May 1944. SOE/NKVD cooperation
had been broken off in Turkey for security reasons late in 1941. SOE
did not invite the Russians to participate in their joint mission to
Romania with the American OSS. Hill claimed that the NKVD had
been invited but had declined, but there was a massive broadside
from Molotov aimed at Churchill, accusing the British of attempting
to hatch a sinister Balkan plot. SOE also got themselves into trouble
with the NKVD by attempting to suborn Russian prisoners of war
who had been impressed by the Germans into service with the
Wehrmacht. Colonel Smith and Major Manderstam of SOE suggested
that it might be possible to get the Gestapo interested in Vlasov's
officers, thus hopefully undermining the efforts of the 'Liberation
Army' and also taking the heat off the French resistance. Hill
reported from Moscow that the NKVD thought this was a good idea,
but there are no details of what happened. Presumably NKVD
changed their minds and decided to keep the Russian prisoners of
war exclusively within their own field of operations.[24]

SOE were understandably interested in obtaining information on NKVD activities in Germany, but predictably the Soviets would say nothing. Brigadier Hill was merely told by Ossipov that it was desirable to work closely together in Germany. Ossipov was equally uncommunicative about NKVD operations in Poland and Czechoslovakia. He flatly refused to send any arms to the Polish Underground Army or to the Czechs.

It was obvious that the original agreement between SOE and NKVD was hopelessly out of date, and that it had achieved very little. It was therefore suggested that a new agreement should be considered. The main field of operations would now be Germany, and SOE proposed that a common plan should be made to subvert foreign workers in Germany, encourage dissident elements within the state, party, army and SS, sabotage the communications system and the manufacture, maintenance, and operation of U-boats, and make a concerted action against any long-term plans laid by the Germans for underground activity. It was also hoped that it would be possible to cooperate in assisting the resistance in Czechoslovakia. SOE were already engaged in varying degrees in these tasks and suggested that SOE and NKVD liaison officers should be appointed to field HQs where British and Russian forces were operating on a common front. These proposals came to nothing, for SOE were merely trying to hang on to their few remaining contacts in eastern and central Europe. Relations with the Soviet Union steadily deteriorated in the final weeks of the war, and hopes that it might be possible to continue the SOE/NKVD connection in the post-war period were shown to be hopelessly unrealistic. Their last cooperative venture was when SOE dropped NKVD agents into the open city of Prague in May 1945.[25]

Within very strict limits SOE were able to cooperate with NKVD and the Russians allowed Brigadier Hill to stay in Moscow until the end of the war. The situation with the military mission, however, was quite different and was the cause of almost constant friction. A number of officers attached to the mission were outspokenly anti-Soviet and by October 1941 the Russians were demanding that three naval officers should be removed from the Military Mission because of their hostile attitude. In part this demand was a cover for Soviet refusals to give any information to the Mission. Cripps believed that this was due to the fact that the Soviet system was plagued by a combination of over-work and inefficiency, but he was furious at this insistence that the three naval officers should be sent home, and suggested that the entire Military Mission should be dissolved if the Russians persisted. The Foreign Office thought that the Ambassador was making far too much fuss about a minor incident, and felt that it was not worth fighting the Russians over three naval officers. Churchill drafted a letter to Cripps which read, 'This is not a matter to make heavy weather about. It should be handled in a very cool fashion.' He added the very curious proposition that 'They are far more dependent upon us than we are upon them.'[26]

Along with the Military Mission and a representative of SOE it was also decided to send a press attaché to the Moscow Embassy who would be responsible for British propaganda in the Soviet Union. The Foreign Office began to look for a suitable candidate and were soon given the name of someone whom a referee described as an '*ideal* man' – Guy Burgess. One referee wrote, 'Burgess is unquestionably the most brilliant man I know of my own generation, and has a special understanding of Russian political matters.'[27] With the enthusiastic support of G. M. Trevelyan and E. H. Carr, Burgess was deemed to be too good a man to waste on such a minor posting, and thus the Soviets were unable to place their own man in the British Embassy in Moscow. The Soviets had every reason to be pleased that Burgess' friend Kim Philby was reading the messages from the War Office to the Military Mission in Moscow which were sent over SIS channels.[28] Thus the Soviets knew exactly what was going on in the Military Mission, and were given a golden opportunity to break the SIS codes.

Burgess did not get the job he wanted, and in October Walter Monckton was sent to Moscow to sign a propaganda agreement. On his return he suggested that Michael Foot or another left-winger, Konni Zilliacus, would make an admirable press attaché. The Foreign Office were appalled at this suggestion and appointed an old-Etonian, John Lawrence, to the post. Lawrence had no qualifications whatsoever for the job, but proved nevertheless to be an excellent press attaché. He was assisted by Vernon Bartlett of the *News Chronicle* who worked in Moscow on behalf of the Ministry of Information.

Although the administrative structure was now in place, there was still considerable uncertainty about how the Soviet Union should be approached. Just before the invasion of the Soviet Union the historian G. M. Young had been asked by the Foreign Office to prepare a pamphlet on the Comintern. He found this task singularly perplexing and wrote to the Foreign Office for guidance. 'Personally I don't know whether Moscow is to us the seat of a quaint foreign superstition, like Salt Lake City and Mormonism or an active force with a substantial following.'[29] The Foreign Office had no answer to this query. The fact that the Russians were now fighting on the same side as the British was greeted in some quarters with a singular lack of enthusiasm. Churchill's concerns about talk of a 'class war' were not wholly unfounded. There was much grumbling in Clubland about the awfulness of fighting alongside these atheistic Communists.[30] Such people felt a deep revulsion for the Soviet regime and an intense contempt for the Soviet fighting forces. Harold Nicholson, who was working at the Ministry of Information, was very concerned at the effect of cooperation with the Soviet Union on Catholic and Conservative opinion, but comforted himself with the thought that this would only be a temporary problem. 'They [the Soviets] are so incompetent and selfish that they will be bowled over at a touch.'[31] Such an attitude made the whole question of allied propaganda extremely difficult. The Minister of Information, Duff Cooper, felt that it was all well and good to boost modern Russian culture, but as he said to Eden, this was difficult to do without in some way 'implying some approval of the experiment that has been going on there these last 24 years'.[32]

Official thinking about the Soviet Union is clearly reflected in the instructions given to the censors:

> For the time being Russia is to be regarded as an associate, not as an ally. Censors are not therefore under an obligation to regard Russia as an 'allied country' for the purpose of censorship. There is no objection to reasonable criticisms and expressions of dislike for the behaviour of the Soviet up to yesterday, e.g. the attack on Finland, their occupation of Estonia, Latvia, Poland, Bessarabia, etc. Nor is there any objection to reasonable criticism and expressions of dislike for Communism. Messages, however, which are very insulting for Russia and which indicate that the behaviour from now on may be treacherous, etc. should be referred to D.A.D.[33]

These instructions were printed in full in *Tribune*, but the Foreign Office did not find this in the least bit embarrassing. On the basis of this directive the BBC refused to allow Andrew Rothstein to give a talk on the Soviet Union for schools broadcasting, on the grounds that it was pure propaganda.[34] The ban on the *Daily Worker* continued, pending the arrival of more acceptable orders to the editorial board from Moscow.[35]

In spite of this unpromising atmosphere, the Soviet Ambassador went immediately into action, demanding to know what military, economic and political collaboration his country could expect from Britain. Eden coolly replied that militarily and economically the British had more than enough on their plate trying to defeat Germany, but that a political settlement in the Middle and Far East might be possible.[36] Maisky continued to press for the opening of a sea route to Murmansk, daytime raids on Germany, and hit-and-run attacks on France to destroy the Atlantic bases. Eden continued to promise to do everything possible, but was clearly avoiding the issue. The Soviets were calling for the closest possible cooperation, but for the first few weeks of the campaign the British refused, not wishing to waste their valuable resources on a country which seemed to be on the brink of defeat and for which they had little sympathy.[37] The CIGS referred to the members of the Soviet Military Mission to Britain as 'pig-stickers', and his deputy, Lieutenant-General Henry Pownall, wrote in his diary on 29 June:

> I avoid the expression 'Allies' for the Russians are a dirty lot of murdering thieves themselves, *and* double crossers of the deepest dye. It is good to see the two biggest cut-throats in Europe, Hitler and Stalin going for each other.[38]

With such an attitude it is hardly surprising that the British resisted Maisky's requests for aid and Churchill's calls for offensive action across the Channel. They were even able to support their prejudices with sound military arguments. The British had suffered serious defeats in Greece and Crete, were losing shipping far faster than it could be replaced and were heavily engaged in an unpromising campaign in the desert. The invasion of the Soviet Union eased the pressure on Britain, but since there was general agreement that the Red Army would soon be defeated and that the Germans would then mount an invasion, this was seen merely as a temporary breathing space. Very few people thought that Russia had a chance of survival, and the terrible losses which the Red Army suffered in the early days of the campaign confirmed the view of those who thought that the Germans would triumph within a few weeks. Dalton found some comfort in Bruce Lockhart's remark that the Chiefs of Staff had been wrong over Norway, Belgium, France, Libya, Greece and Crete, and they were just as likely to be wrong over Russia.[39] Among the military however there was much talk of a hot knife through butter, and the Joint Intelligence Committee saw no reason to revise its estimate that the Soviet Union would be unable to continue its resistance for more than a few days.[40]

Maisky in London and Molotov in Moscow both continued to press for some action which might divert some of Germany's military might away from the eastern front, and hinted that the outbreak of the war between Russia and Germany might tempt the British to relax their efforts.[41] Cripps strongly urged a landing on the French coast and naval action on the Petsamo and Murmansk coast as had been suggested by Beaverbrook to Maisky. The Army insisted that they could not spare the men and equipment for a large-scale landing in France, and the First Sea Lord strongly opposed action in the Arctic on the grounds that the Russians would be unable to give adequate air cover to ships which would be terribly vulnerable in the endless Arctic daylight. The British Government promised to study these proposals and sent two officers to Murmansk and Archangel. The Soviet demands for something more concrete had some limited success on 7 July when Eden told Maisky that he 'was authorised to say that His Majesty's Government had agreed in principle to certain naval action in the Arctic'. Two submarines were sent to support the Soviet Northern Fleet and two aircraft carriers went to attack German positions in Norway.

Meanwhile Molotov continued to urge Cripps for a detailed agreement between the two countries, but the Ambassador stalled these demands by saying that it would take time for the two countries to build up that degree of mutual trust necessary to make such an agreement effective. Neither Cripps nor Mason-Macfarlane was told what was going on at the front, and this made it almost impossible for them to begin serious talks about military support. In addition Stalin remained aloof in the Kremlin, prompting Cripps to believe that there was a power struggle between the Party and the military which made the situation even more difficult. Cripps believed that the British had to be far more open with the Soviets, but he also told the Foreign Office that unless he got more help from the Soviet authorities he was wasting his time in Moscow.[42] In order to break the deadlock Cripps suggested that he should visit Stalin to find out his views on military cooperation. He suggested that the Prime Minister should write to Stalin and thus give him the opportunity to meet the Soviet leader. On 7 July Churchill sent a telegram to Stalin promising every possible help, giving a brief account of bombing raids on Germany, promising a 'serious operation' in the Arctic, and ending with the words, 'We have only to go on fighting to beat the life out of these villains.'[43]

Cripps delivered the Prime Minister's message on 8 July and was impressed by Stalin's frank and open response. Stalin suggested that there should be an agreement on mutual assistance, and a declaration that neither country would make a separate peace with Germany. He told Cripps that it had not been possible to make an agreement with Britain in 1940 because that would have been tantamount to a declaration of war on Germany, a step which the Soviet Union had been in no position to take. In a curious aside, he warmly praised Churchill for his profound understanding of the working class which enabled him to form a government of genuine national unity.[44] Clementine Churchill, who complained that her husband knew nothing of the common man, would no doubt have been amused by this compliment from the self-styled leader of the world's proletariat.

Cripps urged that Stalin's 'advance should be met with an immediate and generous response'. The Cabinet was uncertain. They wanted to avoid a treaty which might have 'a somewhat unfavourable reaction on public opinion in certain countries'. Above all they objected to Churchill's suggestion that the treaty should make some mention of post-war frontiers. Eden also objected to this idea, and the US Ambassador, Winant, was strongly opposed to such a statement being written into a formal treaty. It was therefore agreed that a joint declaration was the best solution, and the treaty idea was quickly dropped. Churchill played for time by replying to Stalin that he would first have to consult the Dominions, while Cripps informed him that public opinion in Britain would be opposed to any binding agreement. Cripps then told Molotov that 'the political basis was the common enmity against Hitler but while this was a sound basis for military and economic cooperation it was not a satisfactory basis for a political agreement'. These sentiments were echoed in Churchill's draft reply to Stalin which added a reference to the post-war settlement.

> You will of course understand that at the victorious Peace Conference in which the United States will certainly be a leading party, our line would be that the territorial frontiers will have to be settled in accordance with the wishes of the people who live there and on general ethnographical lines, and secondly, that these units, when

established, must be free to choose their own form of government and systems of life, so long as they do not interfere with the similar rights of neighbouring peoples.[45]

This passage was not included in the Prime Minister's message to Stalin which merely spoke of the need for cooperation and an undertaking never to negotiate a separate peace or armistice. It was agreed that any discussion of post-war frontiers was liable to antagonise the Polish Government and was best ignored for the time being. There was thus full agreement between the Prime Minister and the Ambassador that political questions should be avoided and that the absolute priority was to fight Germans as effectively as possible. The Anglo–French declaration of March 1940 was taken as a suitable model for a joint declaration.

Cripps delivered Churchill's message to Stalin on 10 July. Stalin agreed wholeheartedly with the text and urged that it should be signed as soon as possible. Two days later Cripps and Molotov signed the declaration which stated in language which was oddly Russian in wording and grammar that both powers would 'render to each other assistance of all kinds in present war against Hitlerite Germany'.

In spite of the dire predictions of the military experts and the frightful losses they had sustained, the Russians were still fighting. In July Rex Leeper of the Foreign Office wrote a memorandum which raised the possibility of the Russians actually defeating the Germans and the consequences of such an eventuality. He wrote, 'Since a fortnight ago there has been something of a revolution in men's minds.' Stalin, by talking of liberation and not of Communism, was making a bid for European leadership, and it was possible that Communism might save Europe from German domination. 'It might break the hold of Nazism in Germany, capture the imagination of the Czechs, Yugoslavs, and Bulgarians, sweep through France.' If Britain was not careful she might be accused of standing idly by while Soviet Communism got on with the job. Eden found these ideas 'interesting'.[46] Cadogan wrote, 'Certainly Russian resistance would appear to have given us an unlooked for opportunity. And comparative inaction on our part will have a very bad effect.' Thus, whereas the British military authorities continued to be deeply suspicious and often contemptuous of the Russians, the Foreign Office began to push for maximum cooperation, agreeing with Cripps' statement that 'we must not try to play too safe on information if we want the Russians to fight our battle all out'.[47] For the Prime Minister the question was simply a matter of 'killing Huns', and all political questions should be left until the fighting was over. To the First Lord he wrote, 'As long as they [the Russians] go on, it does not matter so much where the front lies.'[48] He was soon to find out that this was a completely unrealistic attitude to take towards the Soviet Government.

To the Soviet Union it mattered very much where the front lay. They desperately needed something to happen that would relieve the relentless pressure of the *Wehrmacht* on their crumbling forces. On 15 July Molotov suggested to Cripps that Spitzbergen and Bear Island should be occupied, and the Germans driven out of northern Norway. The following day Maisky asked Eden for a large-scale raid on France to create an important diversion. Eden replied that the matter was being 'carefully and sympathetically considered', but cautioned the Ambassador that such an operation presented enormous difficulties.[49] On 19 July Maisky handed Churchill a message from Stalin. It was the first message from the Soviet leader since the beginning of the war in Russia, since he had left Churchill's two previous notes unanswered. In it he made an open admission of Soviet weakness and requested the establishment of a second front in France and in the Arctic. This appeal from Stalin was a desperate call for help and was strongly endorsed by Sir Stafford Cripps. In a personal note for the Prime Minister Cripps stressed the need to overcome twenty years of mutual distrust and suspicion. 'What is required now above all things is some *action* by us to demonstrate our desire to help even at some risk to ourselves if necessary.' Even a 'demonstration' at Murmansk or Northern France would help, but above all something had to be done as soon as possible.[50]

Churchill replied to Stalin's note on the following day.[51] He pointed out that since there were forty German divisions in France protected by heavy coastal fortifications, an attack on northern France on a large scale would be a disaster, and 'petty raids would only lead to fiascoes doing far more harm than good to both of us'. He also ruled out the possibility of an attack on Norway, stressing the bitter experience the British had gained at Namsos and Crete. He told Stalin that the most effective form of aid would be naval operations to protect the Russian Arctic flank, and suggested joint operations around Spitzbergen. He also suggested that the RAF should establish an air base at Murmansk.

On 21 July the War Cabinet discussed this exchange of notes between the Prime Minister and Stalin.[52] Eden told his colleagues that Maisky was likely to be very disappointed by the reply to Stalin's request for substantial support, and would probably ask for considerable material aid, particularly aircraft. The Secretary of State for Air felt that it might be possible to give the Soviets some of the American planes which were on order. After further discussion it was agreed that the best course of action would be to begin joint discussions with the United States' Government about supplies for the Soviet Union, and that this issue should be taken up with Hopkins and Harriman who were in London to attend meetings of the War Cabinet's Technical Assistance from the United States of America Committee.

Eden's fears about Maisky's reaction were fully justified. Later that day the Soviet Ambassador told Eden that he was very disappointed with the Prime Minister's reply to Stalin, and he suggested that if the British were unable to launch operations against German positions in France then at least they should try to assist Russia with supplies, particularly aeroplanes and Bofors guns.[53] This request came as no surprise to Eden. At the end of June the Soviets had requested enormous quantities of military and civilian supplies which included 3000 fighters, 3000 bombers, 20 000 light anti-aircraft guns, all manner of raw materials, food, and military equipment, as well as three million pairs of boots and ten million metres of woollen cloth.[54] The service departments were appalled at these requests partly because they had nothing to spare and partly because they expected the Soviet Union to collapse at any moment. The Foreign Office agreed with these views and saw no reason to rush supplies to the Soviet Union. At first they suggested that a joint Soviet–American–British committee on supplies might be good psychologically, but then decided that such a committee would not work. Eden complained that the Russians would say nothing about their productive capacity, and that it was essential to know this before sending any military aid. The Chiefs of Staff also insisted that 'the Russians may only be given information or equipment which, if it fell into German hands, would not give the enemy any appreciable advantage.'[55] Rather grudgingly the Soviets were offered one Hurricane and some 1000lb bombs.

As the Soviets suffered a series of defeats and with the British unable to mount an offensive in the desert or anywhere else, the need to do something to help the Soviets became increasingly apparent. The Soviets did not press their initial demands, and Stalin was exceptionally gracious when he received Churchill's reply, telling

Cripps that he fully understood the Prime Minister's arguments about the difficulties involved in any of the suggested operations and that he had 'no questions and no reproaches'.[56] After much heart-searching the Air Ministry decided that it might be possible to send 200 Tomahawks, a fighter aircraft that was not used at home and was scheduled to be phased out of the Middle East theatre. The War Cabinet endorsed this proposal, and on 25 July Churchill wrote to Stalin promising to send these aircraft along with large quantities of raw materials and between two and three million pairs of boots. The Prime Minister also told Stalin that Harry Hopkins was hoping to go to Moscow and stressed how important such a mission could be.

> I must tell you that there is a flame in this man for democracy and to beat Hitler. He is the nearest personal representative of the President ... You can trust him absolutely. He is your friend and our friend. He will help you to plan for the future victory and for the long-term supply of Russia.[57]

On the same day Churchill also fired off a memorandum urging the service departments to consider aid for the Soviet Union as an urgent priority.

The military were far from pleased about these commitments to the Soviet Union. Intelligence reports indicated that the Germans would be in the Caucasus by mid-August and would then be in a position to launch a major attack on British positions in the Persian Gulf. Furthermore the Americans agreed that the Tomahawks could be sent to Russia but insisted that the British should supply the ammunition, spare parts and ground supplies. This would place a considerable strain on the RAF's very limited resources, but there was little that could be done since the Prime Minister had already given his word to Stalin. The situation was somewhat improved when Roosevelt managed to convince the War Department to send more spares and thus to counteract some of their considerable reluctance to support the Soviet war effort.[58] Harry Hopkins went to Moscow at the end of July and was given a most cordial reception. He pointed out to Stalin that it was necessary to know details of Soviet weapons, resources and industrial capacity, as well as to be given a full account of the situation at the front, before it would be possible to judge how best to meet his requests for assistance. Stalin readily agreed, and Hopkins returned from Moscow convinced of Soviet goodwill and determination to continue the struggle.[59]

Hopkins travelled back to the United States on the *Prince of Wales* with Churchill who was to meet Roosevelt at Placentia Bay in Newfoundland. During their discussions Churchill told the President that supplies had to be sent to the Soviet Union if the front was to be maintained. He warned that if Russia fell and if Britain were uncertain of extensive American support the situation would be desperate. He added that he intended to send Beaverbrook to Moscow to work out an agreement on supplies and that Eden would hammer out the political issues. In spite of the objection of his senior military staff, who were very concerned to build up American strength in the Philippines, Roosevelt endorsed Churchill's plea for aid to Russia, and Churchill could telegraph back to Attlee the announcement of the 'Arrival of Russia as a welcome guest at hungry table.' The Americans agreed that a supply conference should be held in Moscow, but wanted to postpone it until their own supply priorities had been set in the 'Victory Programme' which was still under discussion. They disguised their lack of preparation by arguing that it was necessary to wait until the Russian front was stabilised before the onset of winter, and this gave rise to serious misunderstandings with the British in the following weeks. Churchill and Roosevelt sent a joint message to Stalin on 12 August promising to send the very maximum of supplies, and suggesting that preparations be made for a supply conference to be held in Moscow. To underline the importance of supplies to Russia Churchill instructed Beaverbrook to remain in Washington to urge the Americans to make every effort to increase their production. The 'Riviera' meeting thus resulted in a joint agreement to assist the Soviet Union, but there were still a large number of difficulties to be overcome before any significant results could be expected.[60]

As a preliminary to the Moscow meeting a low-level mission was sent to Moscow in August under Mr Cadbury, a member of the chocolate family, who was working for the Treasury. Cadbury was considered by the Foreign Office to be charming but ineffective and, getting little response from the Soviets, he was sent home. On 16 August, while Churchill was sailing back across the Atlantic, Cripps and Molotov signed an Anglo–Soviet agreement on the exchange of goods, credit and clearing. Britain gave the Soviet Union £10 million over five years at 3 per cent, but this was obviously insufficient and was merely regarded as an interim agreement before the Anglo–American mission went to Moscow.[61] Trade relations with the Soviet Union were clearly still most unsatisfactory, and there was some unsavoury profiteering. One Foreign Office official noted that boots were being sold to Russia for 23/– a pair, when identical boots could be bought at the Army and Navy Store in Victoria for 21/4, including purchase tax.[62] Nor were the Russians particularly helpful. In spite of Stalin's assurances to Hopkins, virtually no information of Soviet war production, weapons or troop deployments was forthcoming. The Soviet Ambassador in Washington, Oumansky, was singularly tight-lipped and in Moscow Mason-Macfarlane was still given no useful information, although he was treated to a brief visit to the front.

The British were also becoming increasingly annoyed with the Americans for dragging their feet over the Moscow conference. In spite of the Foreign Office's promptings and constant prodding from the Russians the Americans said that they would be unable to send a delegation to Moscow before the middle of October. Cripps was insistent that there should be no delay and wrote, 'I feel that we are still underestimating the enormous and absolutely vital importance of this front to us as our one insurance against the future.'[63] Churchill was also determined that the conference should take place as soon as possible. He urged the Americans to go to Moscow not later than the end of September, and told the War Cabinet that Beaverbrook's mission was prepared to go whenever the Americans were ready.[64]

On 26 August Maisky told Eden that his Government, when reviewing events of the campaign and asking themselves what in the meantime the British had done for the general cause, could only reply 'very little'.[65] German troops were now within one hundred miles of Leningrad and were threatening the Caucasus. On 29 August Churchill again telegraphed to Stalin promising 200 further fighter aircraft and two RAF squadrons of Hurricanes for Murmansk.

Maisky delivered Stalin's note in reply to this stop-gap offer to 10 Downing Street on 4 September. The Soviet leader requested a second front in either the Balkans or France which would be capable of drawing 30 to 40 German Divisions away from the Eastern Front and thus relieving the 'mortal menace' to Leningrad and the Ukraine. Stalin claimed that without the second front the Soviet Union would be defeated or so weakened as to be unable to give any assistance to the Allied cause for a long period of time. Churchill was furious when Maisky began to drive Stalin's message home with a singularly heavy hand. He told the Soviet Ambassador,

Remember that only four months ago we in this Island did not know whether you were not coming in against us on the German side. Indeed, we thought it quite likely that you would, even when we felt we should win in the end. We never thought our survival was dependent on your action either way. Whatever happens, and whatever you do, you of all people have no right to make reproaches to us.[66]

The Prime Minister had every right to resent these Soviet insinuations that they had been fighting all on their own against the Nazis while the British stood idly by. But he was keenly aware of the terrible losses which the Soviets had suffered and was frustrated that there was so little he could do to help. Since the War Cabinet agreed with the Chiefs of Staff that Britain was in no position to mount a Continental operation that would have the effect of drawing substantial German forces away from the Eastern Front, the only alternative was to attempt to increase the flow of military supplies to the Soviet Union in the hope that they would help the Russians to hang on through the winter and make some offensive action possible in the spring of 1942. In his reply to Stalin Churchill promised 200 aircraft and 250 tanks per month from British production, and expressed the hope that this amount could be doubled to meet Stalin's initial request by the Americans extending Lend-Lease to the Soviet Union. He undertook to increase the number of trains on the Persian railway from two to twelve per day. He made no promise about a Second Front and merely said that the ability of the British armies to invade the Continent would depend on 'unforeseeable events'. In a covering letter to Cripps he pointed out that 'Neither sympathy nor emotion will overcome the kind of facts we have to face.' He ruled out any possibility of a landing in France or the Balkans, and expressed his wonder 'that the losses sustained by our shipping and the Fleet in the evacuation of Greece and Crete have been forgotten'. Cripps accepted this criticism of his impassioned call for 'a superhuman effort to help Russia' which Churchill said implied 'an effort rising superior to space, time and geography'. 'Unfortunately,' he added, 'these attributes are denied us.'[67]

The United States War Department was not at all enthusiastic when they learnt of Churchill's promises of tanks and aeroplanes to the Soviets. When Harriman and Beaverbrook began their discussions in London on 15 September it soon became apparent that Churchill had made a very rash promise to Stalin and that there were a number of reasons why the United States was not an unlimited 'arsenal of democracy'. Beaverbrook insisted that the Americans should guarantee that their supplies to Britain would be as promised. Harriman wanted an agreement on how the total of American arms export should be apportioned. After much wrangling it became clear, in Beaverbrook's words, that 'The promise of 400 aircraft and 500 tanks a month ... can be fulfilled by a sacrifice. This sacrifice will fall almost entirely on us.'[68]

The promise of aid to the Soviet Union was thus not enough to satisfy the Russians and was a very serious drain on British resources which left the service departments bitter and resentful. The situation was made even worse when Stafford Cripps reported from Moscow that Stalin was utterly unmoved by the British offer. He reported that he found the Soviet leader 'very depressed and tired', that Stalin talked of withdrawing behind the Volga and complained that the lack of supplies was a major problem.[69] General Macfarlane had to listen to insinuations that the British were not doing enough for the common cause, a criticism which he generously attributed to the frayed nerves of the Soviet liaison officer, General Panfilov.

Stalin's reply to Churchill's message arrived on 15 September. He complained that the absence of a 'second front simply favours the designs of our common enemy' and made the preposterous suggestion that 'Great Britain could without any risk land 25–30 Divisions or transport them across Iran to the southern regions of the USSR'.[70] Since the suggested number of divisions was roughly equal to the total number of troops stationed in Britain, and since the Iranian railway was incapable of handling such numbers of men, Churchill concluded that Stalin was living in a world of fantasy. In his response Churchill repeated that all possible theatres in which effective military cooperation might be possible had been examined by the Staffs, although he made no mention of the suggestion that British troops should be sent to the South of Russia. He also pointed out that a survey of monthly deliveries to the Soviet Union was being made prior to the departure of the Beaverbrook–Harriman Mission to Moscow.[71] Cripps delivered this message to Stalin who told him that he doubted whether the British tanks would ever arrive. Cripps reported back to London that the Russians 'are still doubtful of the degree of help that we are going to give them, and ... are inclined to underestimate the help that we have already given'.

With the Soviets suspicious that the British would not live up to their promises and the British resentful at the sacrifices they were being called upon to make to such an ungrateful ally, it was clear that the Beaverbrook–Harriman Mission would have a very difficult political task in overcoming these mutual recriminations and accusations. Churchill was determined that the Mission should be successful and did everything humanly possible to convince the War Cabinet and the service departments that aid to Russia was of the utmost importance. As Beaverbrook and Harriman left for Moscow Churchill telegraphed: 'All good wishes to you both and colleagues for your memorable journey on which you carry with you the hope of the world.'[72]

The Mission arrived in Moscow not without incident. General Ismay, who travelled with the Mission to discuss joint military planning, came under Soviet anti-aircraft fire as his plane approached Moscow, no doubt strengthening his misgivings about fighting alongside the 'Godless despotism' of Bolshevism and prompting Beaverbrook to tell Churchill not to send any more anti-aircraft guns to Russia.[73] Beaverbrook was still annoyed that American supplies to the Soviet Union would have to come from allocations already made to Britain. Ismay echoed the feeling of the British military departments when he wrote that sending supplies to Russia was 'like having all one's eye-teeth drawn out at the same time, but there was nothing to do but grin and bear it'.[74] The situation was further complicated by Beaverbrook's profound dislike of Sir Stafford Cripps, based on deep personal and political differences and because each man saw himself as the champion of Anglo–Soviet cooperation and was tempted to use the Soviet card to further his own political career. Harriman also had a very low opinion of the American Ambassador, Steinhardt, and therefore agreed with Beaverbrook that the Ambassadors should be excluded from the talks. Cripps found this situation intolerable, and the crowning insult came when Beaverbrook commandeered the British Embassy for an official banquet to which Cripps was not even invited. Whereas Cripps believed that the conference offered the British a golden opportunity to win some concessions from the Soviets, Beaverbrook strongly disagreed. He felt that this was a 'Christmas-tree party' with himself playing the improbable role of Santa Claus. Cripps, although he did not share Ismay's conviction that the only way to get anything out of the Russians was to be utterly tough and ruthless, felt that some skilful bargaining might make the Soviets more forthcoming and that generosity with no strings attached would not meet with any gratitude.

The Beaverbrook–Harriman Mission was greeted in Moscow with extraordinary pomp and ceremony and with quite exceptional hospitality. To emphasise the importance of the event, Stalin met the two men on three occasions. At their first meeting he was friendly, but at the second they were given the full Stalin treatment. He complained bitterly that the list of supplies was totally inadequate, and suggested that the British and Americans were willing to allow the Soviet Union to be defeated. When Beaverbrook handed him a letter from Churchill he refused to read it. At their third and final private meeting Stalin was more genial, but at the concluding banquet which was felt by some to have been the most lavish affair since the Revolution, Stalin turned to Beaverbrook and said, 'What is the good of having any army if it does not fight?' Ismay attempted to explain why an invasion of France was not possible, but Stalin refused to listen. Beaverbrook had already told Stalin that Ismay had come to Moscow to have strategic discussions, but Stalin, who wanted to say nothing about the deployment of Soviet forces, saw to it that Ismay was left out in the cold. On a strictly personal level Beaverbrook got on quite well with Stalin. When Stalin brought up the question of Hess and suggested that he had gone to Scotland with Hitler's knowledge but not at his request, Beaverbrook replied that Hess hoped to oust Churchill and establish an autocratic government that would join with Hitler against the Soviet Union, and was able to amuse Stalin with some details of his bizarre interview with Hess.[75] Beaverbrook asked Stalin if he really thought that Britain was in a position to invade France, and Stalin drily replied that he had confidence in Churchill's judgement. Beaverbrook was somewhat put out when Stalin reminded him of the precise horse-power of a Spitfire.[76] Beaverbrook generously conceded that there was nothing wrong with Cripps except that he was a bore, adding 'like Mrs Maisky'. Stalin is reported to have been much amused by this quip. While Beaverbrook spoke Stalin chain-smoked and drew pictures of ravening wolves.[77]

The conference lasted four days and was an undoubted success. The Russians got less than half the number of tanks they requested, and got neither the types nor quantity of aeroplanes they desired, but raw materials and non-military supplies were increased in an attempt to sugar the pill. The concluding protocol named 24 items, including 400 aircraft per month and 500 tanks in addition to all manner of things such as diamonds, army boots and cocoa beans.[78]

Churchill was delighted with Beaverbrook's performance in Moscow. When the conference ended Beaverbrook received a telegram from the Prime Minister which read, 'No one could have done it but you. Now come home and make the one group undecypherable stuff.'[79] There were complaints that Beaverbrook had not been able to discuss strategy more fully with the Soviets, but he argued that this had not been the purpose of the Mission as envisaged by the War Cabinet. Churchill disagreed, pointing out that Ismay had been sent with the Mission and that he had given Beaverbrook a memorandum on the over-all military situation.[80] Ismay and Mason-Macfarlane were angry that Beaverbrook had not been tougher with the Soviets, and argued that they should have been given nothing until they divulged all the information the British required. Beaverbrook complained to Churchill that he had had a number of altercations with Stafford Cripps in Moscow, and that the Ambassador had wanted to be present whenever he met Stalin. Cripps was still extremely annoyed that he had been excluded from these talks, particularly as they had touched on such political issues as the possibility of a long-term treaty between the two countries. In a letter to Eden he threatened to resign over this issue. Eden prepared a long reply in order to smooth the Ambassador's ruffled feathers.[81]

Although there can be no doubt that Cripps had every reason to be annoyed with Beaverbrook, the extent to which he engaged in political discussions is uncertain. Averell Harriman, who could write shorthand, took notes of their discussions with Stalin which give some indication of what was said.[82] When asked about peace objectives Beaverbrook had referred to the Atlantic Charter. He told Stalin that he favoured a treaty which would extend into the post-war period. He raised no objections when Stalin insisted that Britain should recognise the 1941 frontiers of the Soviet Union, and by showing no particular interest in the Polish question he must have given Stalin the impression that this was an issue of no great concern to the British Government. Eden took no exception to any of these remarks, and suggested that they were an indication that Stalin was anxious to improve Anglo–Soviet relations.[83]

Beaverbrook returned to London in triumph, and for the moment it seemed that he had overtaken Cripps as the leader of those who called for all-out cooperation with the Soviet Union. He began to imagine himself as a possible leader of the radical left, and in his wilder moments, even as Prime Minister.[84] These fantasies were encouraged by the odious band of sycophants who surrounded him, but they soon proved baseless. British workers could be swayed by his oratory, but would never accept him as their leader and no responsible figure ever saw him as a serious contender for supreme office. But for the moment Beaverbrook was the hero of the hour, and there was only one incident that clouded his glorious return.

Philip Jordan, a British journalist in Moscow, reported that he had bought a vast quantity of caviare for Churchill. At a time of stringent austerity it was feared that such high-living might have a damaging effect on public opinion.[85] But there must have been few people in Britain in 1941 who begrudged the Prime Minister's well-known liking for the good things of life. Churchill was no doubt delighted. When Harry Hopkins brought him an offering of caviare after his trip to Moscow in July he remarked that 'It was very good to have such caviare, even though it meant fighting with the Russians to get it.'[86] Beaverbrook was furious that the story had been leaked to the press and threatened to get John Russell of the Moscow Embassy sacked if he did not reveal the source. Russell, to his great credit, flatly refused to give way to such threats and Beaverbrook was unable to touch him.

The Moscow protocol seemed to be a hopeful new beginning in Anglo–Soviet relations. It was warmly greeted in the Soviet press, and British public opinion was enthusiastic. But it soon became clear that it was easier to make promises than to deliver the goods. Furthermore the service departments were bitterly resentful that so much was being given to a country they did not trust, like or admire. Soviet enthusiasm for the protocol soon began to wane, and they reverted to their habitually surly insinuations that the British were not seriously concerned to help Russia; but the British also failed to see that the supplies they sent were only a drop in the bucket, and the Latin tag which Churchill sent to Stalin, '*Bis dat qui cito dat*' (he gives twice who gives quickly), did nothing to disguise this fact. The frightful ferocity of the fighting in the Soviet Union can be seen by the fact that among the early shipments were 800 000 forceps, 20 000 amputation knives, 15 000 amputation saws and 10 000 000 surgical needles.[87]

On the Russian front there was no respite. Kharkov fell at the end of October and the Germans pushed on towards the Crimea. Cripps was seething with anger. It was not only the slights he had suffered from Beaverbrook which rankled, it was also his feeling that the British Government's policy towards the Soviet Union was seriously misguided. He believed that London was deliberately ignoring Moscow, thus making his job as Ambassador almost impossible. At the end of the month he wrote to Churchill,

You will recall that it was thought worthwhile to send the Foreign Secretary and the Chief of Imperial Staff for some weeks to the

Middle East in order to try and organise the defence of the Balkans when conditions there became serious and yet so far as this country is concerned, where conditions are no less important from our point of view, not only is His Majesty's Government unwilling to enter into consultations with the Soviet Government as to the best method of employing our combined forces against the common enemy but they are apparently not prepared to give the Soviet Government a reasoned statement through the mouth of someone fully qualified by status and knowledge to explain matters to Stalin . . . We seem to be trying to carry on two relatively unrelated wars to the great benefit of Hitler instead of a single war upon the basis of a common plan.

As far as Cripps was concerned the British Government had paid more attention to the Greeks and Turks than to the Soviet Union, and it was thus hardly surprising that the Russians were so resentful and suspicious.[88]

Churchill told Cripps that he sympathised with him in his difficult position and with Russia in her agony, but he told him to remain at his post and attributed Soviet resentments to 'the guilt and self-reproach in their own hearts' for what they had done in the first two years of the war when Britain had stood alone against Nazi Germany. Cripps did manage to secure an offer by the Prime Minister, sent directly to Stalin, to send General Wavell and General Paget to Moscow, or anywhere else in the Soviet Union, to explain the British position, but this was not enough for the Ambassador. He complained bitterly at the Government's refusal to discuss peace objectives, and at the futility of a mere promise of post-war collaboration with the Soviet Union 'for the purposes of working out terms of a new settlement of Europe'. He asked the Foreign Office how he was supposed to prepare the ground for this 'in a hard frost without any implements'. Once again he threatened to resign, announcing that 'Owing to the policy of His Majesty's Government the job is now at an end and there is nothing more that I can do.'[89] The Foreign Office attributed this outburst to a fit of pique and saw it as a further example of Cripps' lack of experience as a diplomatist. Cadogan wrote to Eden, 'One doesn't want to be unnecessarily argumentative with Cripps, but if he is not occasionally pulled up I don't know where he will get us to.'[90]

The Prime Minister took Cripps' resignation threats very seriously. In 1941 Churchill had had few successes and his fortunes were at a low ebb. There was much talk of replacing him by a younger and more vigorous leader. His colleagues were becoming increasingly annoyed by his impulsiveness and bored by endless monologues. There was general agreement that he handled the House of Commons badly. Many feared that his health would fail. The appointment of his son-in-law, Duncan Sandys, as his special liaison with the Home Defence and Air Raid Precautions, was very unpopular. For all his outstanding abilities he seemed to be living too much in the past, and his Government appeared to lack clear direction and purpose. Eden was becoming increasingly disenchanted with him, although as yet he resisted suggestions that he should make a bid to become Prime Minister.[91] Sir Stafford Cripps was widely felt to be the obvious choice to replace Churchill. No one doubted his abilities. He was not a party man. Most important of all he was associated in the public mind with the partnership with the Soviet Union which Churchill had failed to exploit to the full. Most people found Cripps a more congenial leader of the pro-Soviet forces than Beaverbrook, the other contender. Some people on the left however were suspicious of the motives of those who wanted to get rid of Churchill at this stage of the war. D. N. Pritt felt that the move to replace Churchill by Cripps was part of a reactionary plot master-minded by Sir Thomas Moore, who had been a leading figure in the pro-Nazi Anglo–German Association, in order to secure a compromise peace with Germany and leave Cripps to 'hold the baby'. Pritt felt that Cripps could also appeal to the right because he had

> Exactly the attitude of the more progressive type of Tory: 'We don't like them; but we shall have trouble with them later; but they are absolutely anti-Nazi and we should be foolish to forego the help they can give us. We must not quarrel with them, but we must do what we can to ensure that the world is reshaped on our lines and not on theirs.'[92]

Pritt probably had not heard of Maisky's rather bizarre suggestion that Sir Thomas Moore should go to Moscow to act as a liaison between the British Military Mission and the Soviet Government, an idea which Christopher Warner at the Foreign Office described as 'an appalling proposal'.[93] Sir Thomas was later to be appointed a vice-president of the Communist dominated 'National Council for British–Soviet Unity', but few eyebrows were raised at a time when enthusiasm for the Land of the Red Dawn was so widespread, and

few shared D. N. Pritt's fear that Sir Thomas Moore was in a position
to sell out to Nazi Germany.

Churchill saw the danger, and was determined to fight Cripps. In
a draft letter to the Ambassador, which was in fact rejected by the
Cabinet, Churchill begged him to stay in the Soviet Union and issued
a clear warning to his rival:

> I hope you will believe that I give you this advice not from any
> fear of political opposition which you might raise over here by
> making out we had not done enough, etc. I could face such
> opposition without any political embarrassment, though with much
> personal regret.

Churchill went on to say that he was prepared, if necessary, to destroy
Soviet arguments in the House, and thus to ruin the alliance. He
fumed that Britain had wrecked her tank and aircraft programme for
the sake of the Soviet Union, and had lost twice the number of pilots
and machines than were lost in the Battle of Britain in the attempt
to hold German airpower in the west.[94]

Shortly before writing to Cripps, Churchill received a letter from
Stalin which argued that there were two main reasons why Anglo–
Soviet relations were so strained. In the first place there was no
definite understanding on war aims and plans for the post-war
settlement. Secondly, there was no agreement on mutual military
assistance against Hitler.[95] Cripps saw this as an excellent opportunity
to settle the outstanding differences between the two countries. He
saw no reason why the Russians should be interested in talking to
either Wavell or Paget since both generals had appointments in the
east and were not intimately acquainted with the situation at home.
But the central issue was that Cripps wanted to discuss post-war
planning, while Churchill wanted to leave all such questions to the
peace conference.[96] Writing to the Foreign Office, Cripps said,

> It tends to support my view that now in their hour of uncertainty
> and adversity, the Soviet Government would prove more amenable
> in the discussion of post-war European settlement than they would
> be later, if they succeed in stemming the German tide.[97]

The Foreign Office felt that it was impossible to have any clear idea
of the post-war world, and that sending Wavell and Paget to Moscow
was sufficient to begin the talks on military cooperation. At this stage

of the war Eden was not particularly concerned with political issues, and felt that military assistance to the Soviet Union was the key to the situation. He resented the stubborn attitude of the Chiefs of Staff and their refusal to do anything significant to help Russia, and he was equally annoyed with the pig-headed attitude of the Military Mission in Moscow. He believed that the only way to get anything from the Russians was for the British to do something themselves, and that it was incumbent on the Chiefs of Staff to come up with that something.

The delight over the signing of the Moscow Protocol was thus soon forgotten. The Soviets continued to demand some large-scale operation which would relieve the pressure on their rapidly retreating forces. The British deeply resented these repeated requests, complained of Soviet secretiveness, and seemed to have little to offer but what Churchill called 'KBO' (Keep Buggering On). The situation was further complicated by the fact that support for the Soviet Union was becoming an important factor in British domestic politics which posed a real threat to Churchill's position as Prime Minister. But there was some light on the horizon. 'Enigma' decrypts indicated that the German offensive in the Soviet Union was running out of steam and that the Russians would survive the winter. There was also hope that the 'Crusader' offensive in North Africa might turn the tide and give the British a firmer position from which to approach her relations with the Soviet Union.

4 First Attempts at Cooperation

British forces were never involved directly in the campaign in Russia, and the only example of Anglo–Soviet military cooperation during the war was the curious expedition to Spitzbergen. In the middle of July 1941 Molotov told Cripps that he would welcome a joint attack on Spitzbergen and Bear Island which might be combined with an attack on northern Norway to drive out the Germans and secure the sea lanes to Murmansk and Archangel. Cripps was enthusiastic about the idea, and his only concern was whether the Norwegians, who did not have diplomatic relations with the Soviet Union, would agree to the scheme.[1] The Foreign Office supported the idea of occupying Spitzbergen and Bear Island, but were very doubtful whether anything would come of the proposal to attack northern Norway. They did not think that the Norwegians would object, but they doubted whether the British military authorities would be prepared to spare the men and material for such an attack. Support for the Spitzbergen expedition also came from the Ministry of Economic Warfare which wanted to stop the Germans from getting any coal from the island.

The planners were quick to respond to this proposal. The initial reaction of the Chiefs of Staff Committee was that the Royal Navy could provide cover for the establishment of a Soviet garrison on Spitzbergen, but that men and material could not be spared for a joint attack on northern Norway. The War Cabinet's Joint Planning Staff agreed with this assessment. They stressed the strategic importance of Spitzbergen and Bear Island, and argued that the Russians should occupy the islands because they were better suited to withstand the rigours of the climate than the less hardy British troops. A rather more serious consideration was that Spitzbergen lies some 650 miles from Murmansk and 1300 miles from Scotland. On the question of an attack on Norway the Planning Staff agreed that it was out of the question at that stage of the war.[2] The Foreign Office hoped that the Norwegians would be prepared to accept a Soviet garrison on

Spitzbergen, and suggested that if they objected the Chiefs of Staff should consider a joint Anglo–Norwegian expedition. The Chiefs however objected to this latter proposal, saying that they were unable to equip the Norwegian soldiers. In other words they hoped that the Foreign Office could settle the political differences between the Norwegians and the Russians and that the Russians would provide the troops.

Eden, who had not yet seen the paper from the Chiefs of Staff, was under considerable pressure from Maisky to get moving with the expedition and saw it as a valuable opportunity to further the cause of Anglo–Soviet cooperation.[3] He therefore discussed the plan with the Norwegian Foreign Minister, Trygve Lie, who favoured a joint Anglo–Soviet–Norwegian expedition with a token Norwegian force of some fifty men. Maisky found this suggestion acceptable.[4] The Joint Planners' new report, which was approved by the Chiefs of Staff, now rejected the idea of a joint expedition as being impractical but the Foreign Office, who saw considerable political advantages in the scheme, went ahead regardless. Collier, who was appointed Ambassador to the Norwegian Government-in-exile, had lunch with Lie who announced that he was 'somewhat taken aback' by the idea of Soviet troops on Spitzbergen, and that his colleagues in the Norwegian Government were strongly opposed to the suggestion. Norwegian nationals had been expelled from Moscow one month before the German attack on the Soviet Union, and this had caused much bitterness. Lie suggested a compromise solution: there should be a joint Norwegian and Soviet attack on the island, with full guarantees of Norwegian sovereignty.[5] The Norwegian Government was not prepared to support a joint expedition until diplomatic relations with the Soviet Union returned to normal. The Soviets were obliging, and by the end of July their outstanding differences were settled.

The Ministry of Economic Warfare kept up its campaign in favour of the expedition, stressing the importance of Spitzbergen for communications with Archangel which would become absolutely vital if the Japanese were to close off the route through the Pacific. Cripps continued to press for the expedition on political grounds. Relations between the Norwegians and the Soviets had now improved to the point that they were no longer a matter of concern to the Foreign Office. But although there was general agreement that a joint expedition was politically desirable, the planners began to raise the question of whether Spitzbergen was really worth the effort.

Cavendish–Bentinck, speaking for the Joint Intelligence Committee, argued that it was ice-bound from November to May, and since it was in continuous darkness from 26 October to 7 February it was of no use to anyone but polar bears. The Ministry of Economic Warfare thought that this reasoning was absurd. The island produced one million tons of coal per year, and an expedition to destroy the mines would deny the Germans use of this valuable source of fuel.[6] Meanwhile the Navy decided that Spitzbergen would be valuable as a fuelling station and therefore strongly endorsed the proposal to land allied troops on the island. Gradually the idea of sending Soviet troops was dropped. The Foreign Office pointed out that it was absurd to send British ships to Russia, load them up with Soviet troops and then go all the way back to Spitzbergen. The political advantages of cooperation with the Russians were outweighed by the reluctance of the Norwegians to allow a Soviet garrison on their island. Pushed by the Prime Minister, and assuming that the Navy wanted Spitzbergen as a fuelling station, the Chiefs of Staff Committee of Portal, Phillips and Pownall drew up a new plan. They suggested that a small force of two battalions of Canadians should be sent to secure a base on the island. The Canadians were eager to see some action, and maybe the Chiefs of Staff felt that coming from the Cold North they were as well suited as the Russians to withstand the Arctic cold. Orme Sargent did not like the proposal to send the Canadians and said that they had been useless in Iceland. Eden, however, saw no objection, and pointed out that there were 'only polar bears this time'.[7]

Within a week the Navy changed its mind. A study of the map showed that the harbour on Spitzbergen was unsuitable as a refuelling station, and as the mouth of the harbour was five miles wide it would be extremely difficult to protect against submarine attacks. Another more suitable location was felt to be too vulnerable to air raids. The Chiefs of Staff therefore proposed 'Operation Gauntlet': a small task force would destroy the mines and the German meteorological and radio stations. The 2000 Russian miners and the 700 Norwegians on the island would be evacuated.[8] As there were no Germans on the island this was hardly a very risky operation.

On 12 August the Foreign Office hosted a meeting with Maisky, Admiral Kharlamov, the Norwegians, Portal, Phillips, Pownall and Ismay to discuss 'Operation Gauntlet'. Maisky suggested that the Russian miners should be given arms and left on the island. The Norwegian Prime Minister, Nygaardsvold, was horrified at this proposal and argued that it would be much better if the mines were destroyed. The Chiefs of Staff pointed out that without the coal the island was of no use to the Germans, and that an armed force could easily be bombed and would probably die of exposure. The fate of the miners was not decided at this meeting, but three days later Maisky told Eden that his Government agreed that they should be evacuated.[9] The Foreign Office then suggested that a Soviet official should go to Spitzbergen with the expedition to explain to the miners why they had to leave. Maisky sourly replied that he could not spare anyone for this duty, but eventually he relented.

With full agreement between all parties involved, Force 'A' left Scapa for Spitzbergen on 19 August and landed six days later.[10] The expedition was a disorderly affair. According to the Foreign Office 'the behaviour of the Canadian troops left a great deal to be desired'.[11] Apparently a Russian settlement was burnt to the ground for no reason at all, and Mr Lie complained to Eden that the Canadians had looted Norwegian property. The behaviour of the Russians was no better. The miners discovered a stock of eau de cologne which they proceeded to drink and then went on the rampage. The Soviet consul who travelled with the Canadians was so incapacitated by drink that he had to be taken back on board ship on a stretcher. Whether this resulted from an over-indulgence of eau de cologne or of a more conventional intoxicant, is not recorded in the official report. Maisky tried to claim that the miners had been ill-treated, but was unable to give any precise details, no doubt because the Consul had a rather dim recollection of what actually happened. As the miners loaded 200 tons of communal property on board the British authorities felt that they had no real cause for complaint. The Norwegians claimed that excessive damage had been done and asked for compensation, but the Army Council felt that their claims were grossly exaggerated and refused to offer any compensation.[12] It then appeared that amidst all the confusion a group of Norwegian trappers had been left behind. The Foreign Office regretted this oversight, but pointed out that at least they had plenty of coal to keep them warm. The report by CIGS to the Prime Minister was enthusiastic and contained an unintentional pun: 'Brigadier Potts reports that throughout the operation all ranks under his command worked with the greatest energy and that the spirit shown was excellent.'[13]

The BBC was even more glowing in its account of the operation, describing it as 'daring' and as a 'big campaign'. Cripps was furious at such exaggeration and worried about the effect it would have in the Soviet Union. He wrote to the Foreign Office, 'In view of their recent pressure on us to do something big in the west, this will be taken as an elaborate and stupid attempt to magnify a simple and safe operation into something large and important and will either be resented or laughed at.'[14] Eden told Maisky that Orme Sargent described the expedition as 'another glorious evacuation', and reported that the ambassador was 'mildly amused'.

Churchill felt that Spitzbergen should be permanently occupied and asked the Chiefs of Staff 'How was it that we did not think it worthwhile to remain in occupation of Spitzbergen when the Germans evidently do? ... Why was it necessary to burn all the valuable coal stores and quit the island?'[15] In a further message to the Chiefs he ordered that 'The use of Spitzbergen was to be continuously and effectively denied to the enemy.'[16] The Chiefs of Staff felt that Spitzbergen was not worth all this fuss, and repeated their view that an occupying force would be too vulnerable to air attack. Supplies for the garrison would also be a major headache.

While the Prime Minister and the Chiefs of Staff argued about the future of the island it was reported that the Germans had returned in Junkers 52s and 88s.[17] They set up a radio station, but this was bombarded by HMS *Harrier* and put out of business. The Russians then decided to set up a meteorological station of their own on Spitzbergen, and asked the British to get permission from the Norwegians. The Norwegians also wanted to send a small expedition to Spitzbergen to keep the mines from being destroyed by the Germans. The Chiefs of Staff felt that a permanent garrison was impractical since Spitzbergen was as big as Scotland, and the force would have to be very large to be of much use. It was decided that the meteorologists and the Norwegian troops on the Island should be highly mobile so as to keep out of trouble with the Germans. It was also suggested that the Germans should be kept at bay by naval vessels disguised as fishing boats. The Chiefs of Staff Committee agreed that a further limited expedition might by useful.[18] In May 1942 Naval Intelligence reported that the German meteorological station was working again. In June a party of ten Norwegians landed, but they were attacked by the Germans and six of the men were wounded. A small force was eventually established on Spitzbergen, but in September 1943 the *Tirpitz* and a number of support ships attacked the island. A commando force was landed and the weather station destroyed. Further damage was also inflicted on the mines, fuel dumps and water supply.

The Spitzbergen affair was hardly a glorious example of Anglo–Soviet cooperation, but at least it had been possible to come to some sort of agreement on a common policy and friction had been minimal. Eden had welcomed it as a golden opportunity for a common effort, and was furious at the Chiefs of Staff for 'blowing hot and cold' over Spitzbergen.[19] In the end he got his joint venture with Soviet support, and this unique if somewhat comic episode was perhaps better than nothing. It did show that it was possible to work with the Russians and solve a politically sensitive issue, but the Defence Committee's hope that by agreeing to the Spitzbergen expedition a political answer could be found to the impossible Soviet demand for 25 Divisions was completely unfounded.

The German attack on the Soviet Union also made possible an Anglo–Soviet agreement on the future of Iran. Unlike the raid on Spitzbergen, which was carried out after close consultations between the two governments, the infinitely more important invasion of Iran comprised two separate operations and the British had only the vaguest notion of what the Russians were doing. After the German attack in June 1941 the Soviets were determined to chase the Germans out of Iran, for there they posed a direct threat to the Caucasus and the vital supply route to the Persian Gulf. The British Government had long wanted to expel the Germans from Iran, but they lacked the troops and had been reluctant to further damage relations with the Soviet Union by pursuing a too-strenuously anti-German policy in the area. The Germans were very active in Iran, for they knew full well how important Iranian oil was for the British war effort. They had encouraged the Shah's frantic and ill-considered efforts to modernise the country, and had supplied him with many of the outward trappings of a modern state, including aircraft and other military supplies. The Shah was duly impressed by Germany's military triumphs and believed that they would be ideal partners in his efforts to rid the country of British and Soviet influence. After the launching of Operation Barbarossa German subversive activity in Iran increased. *Abwehr* agents were sent to reconnoitre Soviet Transcaucasia and to prepare for a German invasion of Iran from the north. Contacts were established with the Kurds, Bakhtiaris and Quashgais to prepare for sabotage actions. Major Schultze-Holthus was to prove quite successful in leading these anti-British tribesmen in raids on the British lines of communication, even after the Anglo–Soviet invasion. Another ambitious but unsuccessful scheme was 'Operation Armina': a plan to destroy the Abadan oil refineries.[20] British Military

Intelligence, although not fully aware of the scope of German activities in Iran, did not think that they posed any serious threat. Only if the Soviet Union collapsed would Iran be open to German domination.[21] On the other hand the British were anxious to forestall any repetition of a pro-Nazi rebellion such as that which had occurred in Iraq. They were therefore ready to agree to the Soviet proposal to invade.

Under the terms of the Russo–Iranian Treaty of 1921 the Soviets had the right to send troops into Iran to remove any foreign forces that threatened the security of the Soviet Union. On 8 July 1941 Cripps informed the Government that Stalin was pressing for a joint action against the Germans in Iran and Afghanistan, insisting that they were preparing the ground for an attack on Baku, thus giving the Soviet Government a pretext to act within the terms of the 1921 treaty.[22] According to Cripps, Stalin stated 'that no doubt the Shah, whose unpopularity he appreciated, would attempt to play each of us off against the Germans and that therefore some form of combined action was necessary'. The Soviets suggested that economic sanctions should be applied against Iran to force the Germans out, while Cripps wanted a military demonstration on the northern border. Eden however preferred to use diplomatic pressure. On 19 and 20 July the British and Soviet Ambassadors delivered notes to the Iranian Foreign Minister to the effect that their Governments were only prepared to preserve the independence of Iran if the Iranian Government freed itself from German influence, and a demand was made that certain specified Germans should be expelled forthwith. Strong hints were made that if the Iranians did not act on these demands economic sanctions and military pressure would be applied.[23]

The Iranian Government, faced with this united and forceful action, agreed that the number of Germans in the country should be reduced but, when the German Government informed them that if their nationals were expelled they would break off diplomatic relations, they did nothing. The Iranians were thus caught in a hopeless situation and could do little but stall for time in the hope that military developments on the Russian front would obviate the need to make such a painful choice. Meanwhile the Turkish Government viewed this Anglo–Soviet pressure on Iran with increasing alarm. They felt that the two countries were deliberately exaggerating the number of Germans in Iran as an excuse to pursue their imperialist aims.[24]

Repeated requests to the Iranians to expel the Germans met with no response other than an insistence that proper respect should be shown to Iranian neutrality. Since the British Government was determined to secure their access to the Iranian oilfields, economic sanctions could not be contemplated. The British Ambassador in Iran, Sir Reader Bullard, suggested a massive propaganda campaign blaming the chronic food shortages in Iran on German rapacity, but this policy had little chance of success. The British and Soviet Governments therefore saw no alternative to a joint invasion of Iran. C.-in-C. India was told that the aim of British policy was to throw out the Germans and to control the communications system in Iran.[25] In fact the overriding concern of the British Government was to secure the Iranian oilfields, and the Petroleum Department gave the military a detailed brief on which oilfields to seize.

It is hardly surprising that one of the strongest advocates of intervention in Iran was the Minister of Economic Warfare, Hugh Dalton. As a neutral country Iran allowed non-military goods to be moved on the railway to the Soviet Union, but Dalton wanted an Anglo–Soviet condominium over the railway so that military material could be sent to Russia.[26] The Foreign Office felt that intervention would be very risky and that it would be unwise to rush things, although Eden took a somewhat tougher line and tended to agree with Dalton. He was strongly influenced by Cripps' despatches which supported Stalin's arguments about the danger of a German fifth column in Iran and the threat to the Caucasus. He was also constantly egged on by Maisky who made the preposterous claim that there were 10 000 Germans actively engaged in subversive activities in Iran.[27] C.-in-C. India was obsessed with the danger which the German presence in Iran posed to the security of India and also repeatedly requested firm action.[28]

On 19 July Eden told Maisky that he had asked the Chiefs of Staff to look into the military aspects of the Iranian problem, adding that after the experience of Abyssinia he did not believe in economic sanctions. His main concern was the effect that an Anglo–Soviet invasion of Iran would have on Turkey.[29] Oil rather than Germans continued to be the main concern in London. Most of the Germans were in northern Iran, and although it was known that the Russians were exaggerating their number, it was conceded that they had some justification for their concern. For the British the activities of German agents in northern Iran were trivial compared with the security of oil supplies which could become critically important if the Russians were defeated in the Caucasus. Only Wavell was really concerned about the Germans in Iran. He complained to CIGS that 'The complaisant attitude it is proposed to adopt over Iran appears to me incomprehensible.' He insisted that it was essential for the defence of India to get all the Germans out of Iran.[30] On 18 July the Chiefs of Staff discussed Iran and decided that an invasion posed no serious problems if only the Russians were prepared to cooperate.

The main problem for the British was that they had no idea what the Russians were planning. A War Cabinet Committee on Iran was formed, with Sir John Anderson in the chair, but it had no information about Soviet intentions.[31] The most that was achieved was that Eden and Maisky agreed that once the invasion of Iran begn it would be desirable to exchange small military missions to keep each side informed of the other's moves.[32] Although the British told the Soviets about their plans they got no information in return. Mason-Macfarlane told the Foreign Office that the Russians had not even made up their minds when the attack should begin, but a few days later Maisky asked Eden to postpone the invasion until 25 August. This offhand agreement on the date for the operation was the sum total of the military cooperation between the two powers over Iran.

On 25 August Soviet troops crossed the northern frontier of Iran and British troops moved up from the south. Apart from some sporadic sniper fire the Iranians were unable to offer any resistance. Two days later it was reported that the Iranian Government had resigned. Although the Iranians had given up the struggle the Soviets continued to bomb Teheran until the Shah accepted the Anglo–Soviet ultimatum on 2 September. All German citizens were to be expelled, the Iranian forces were to be withdrawn to designated areas and the Iranian authorities agreed to assist in the transportation of supplies from the Gulf to the Soviet Union.

The Shah did little to carry out these demands and continued to stall. This placed the British in a somewhat awkward position. They felt that the Shah would have to go and some reforms begun to undo some of the worst consequences of his mismanagement, but it was feared that the Russians would want to become involved in the reorganisation of Iran, and this the British wanted to avoid at all costs. The British laboured under the illusion that the Iranians would welcome the British and ask for their support against the Russians, and that the ordinary people would be won over by shipping food supplies to a hungry population.[33] Although the British did not want to become too closely involved with the Russians in Iran the fact that there was no liaison between the two forces further complicated the situation. Bullard told the Shah that he hoped that the Russians would not occupy Teheran, but he did not have the faintest idea whether they would. The Ambassador told the Shah that he fully understood his concern about the Russians, but added rather unkindly that there was still a large area of Persia that had not been occupied where he could flee.[34] A further difficulty was that since the Anglo–Soviet forces had entered Iran ostensibly to secure the country's neutrality, it was not legally possible to evict the German legation. Churchill characteristically suggested that the German Minister should be kidnapped and used as a hostage to secure the release of Sir Lancelot Oliphant, the British Ambassador to Belgium who had been captured by the Germans on 2 June 1940. But Cadogan, speaking for the Foreign Office, objected strongly to such 'monkeying about'.[35]

Sir Reader Bullard was horrified at the spectacle of Soviet troops swarming all over northern Iran, but Churchill told him to use the threat of a Soviet occupation to force the Shah to toe the line. He added that if the Shah did not cooperate 'his mismanagement of his people will be brought into account'.[36] The Prime Minister was not in the least bit concerned about the Soviet troops in Iran. He told Eden that if necessary they should be invited to Teheran 'to get the Germans in our hands', and added that 'your Minister at Teheran does not seem to be at all at the level of events'. Churchill also told Cadogan that Bullard 'has got a worn outlook, and wants toning up'.[37] The Prime Minister decided to do the toning up himself and wrote to Bullard, 'Dismiss from your mind any idea of a generous policy towards the Germans to please the Persians or anyone else.' He told the Ambassador to use the threat of a Soviet occupation of Teheran to get his way with the Shah, and further ordered him to secure the capture of the Mufti 'dead or alive'.[38] All this was very unfair to Bullard. British policy was never properly defined and the Ambassador was receiving very ambiguous and often contradictory messages from the Foreign Office. Oliver Harvey called the attack on Iran an act of 'naked aggression', and wrote that both Churchill and Eden were rather ashamed of themselves.[39] At the end of August the Chiefs of Staff defined the strategic aims of the occupation. Defence of the oilfields was made the top priority, and the other main objectives were to establish a strategic position against a possible German attack from the Caucasus, to join hands with the Russians and to establish secure lines of communication, and to strengthen the naval forces in the Gulf.[40] The political aspects of the operation were never systematically tackled, no agreement was reached with the Soviets, and the Ambassador was left to do the best he could without proper guidelines.

Bullard felt that Churchill's understandable desire to get the Germans out of Iran and to establish the supply route to the Soviet Union was blinding him to the danger posed to British interests by the Soviet presence in Iran. He told the Foreign Office that for the moment the Russians were busy requisitioning private motor cars and arresting potentially dangerous persons, but they might soon try to bolshevise northern Iran.[41] Sir Stafford Cripps, who had been one of the strongest advocates of joint military intervention in Iran, also began to share some of the Ambassador's concerns. He suggested that it was dangerous to allow the Soviets to occupy the Caspian littoral as it might prove extremely difficult to get them out again after the war.[42] Eden would not listen to the objections. He resented the attacks made in the press about Britain's havering and dilatory policies in Iran and wrote to Churchill, 'personally I consider the Persian affair to have been a neat piece of joint military and diplomatic action. In its way it is a minor classic.'[43] Churchill and Eden felt that the Soviets were a useful stick with which to beat the Shah, and they gave little thought to the consequences. British and Soviet troops entered Teheran on 17 September and the Shah abdicated in favour of his son.[44]

The Foreign Office did not agree with Stafford Cripps' misgivings about long-term Soviet intentions in Iran. They believed that all efforts should be concentrated on improving the Iranian railway and moving supplies to the Soviet Union from the Gulf. It was felt that the Soviets would want to avoid trouble in Iran so that supplies could be moved without hindrance. Only if the local Communists got out of control would there be any serious difficulties. The British were in no position to complain about the Soviets, for they had stepped well outside the agreement made with them that the aim of the intervention was to intern the Germans, to say nothing of the claim that the two powers were simply acting to preserve Iranian neutrality. British forces were also occupying territory beyond the agreed demarcation line.[45] The main worry for the British was that authority had collapsed in Soviet-occupied Iran resulting in a state of near-anarchy. It also seemed that the Soviets were exploiting this situation to encourage movements for local autonomy and might possibly be preparing the ground for absorbing parts of Iran into the Soviet Union. Churchill tried to discourage this tendency by drafting a telegram for Stalin in which he wrote, 'Our object should be to make the Persians keep each other quiet while we get on with the war.'[46] The much-maligned Sir Reader Bullard was perfectly correct in his assessment of the situation when he pointed out that the Soviets held all the trump cards. The British found themselves having to work through the Persian ruling class which the Ambassador found to be 'worthless', while the Russians had the 'common people' on their side.[47] But for the time being these concerns were put aside. With minimum friction Britain and the Soviet Union had achieved their objectives. The Germans were rounded up, apart from a few stray *Abwehr* agents who continued to work with the tribesmen, and the vital route from the Gulf to the Soviet Union was secure. On 26 January 1942 the Iranian parliament, the Majlis, accepted the tripartite treaty and the Iranian intervention appeared to be crowned with success.

Stalin's note to Churchill of 13 September requesting twenty-five to thirty divisions suggested that these troops could be sent to Persia and then sent to southern Russia. Although the Foreign Office realised that the numbers suggested were absurd, it was felt that it would be politically desirable to send some troops to the Caucasus. Christopher Warner suggested that 'it would undoubtedly improve our relations with the Russians if we could send troops to the Caucasus', but he added that it would have to be a substantial force.[48] Cadogan was adamant that there was 'nothing sensible we can do', but Cripps continued to insist that troops should be sent to Russia. He told the Foreign Office,

So far as the political side is concerned I have found the Soviet Government uniformly helpful, though there has been an element of distrust creeping in again since the last message of the Prime Minister, in which he pointed out the impossibility of giving actual military help on any other front for the present.[49]

Cavendish-Bentinck was also a strong advocate of sending British troops to the Caucasus, insisting that this would have a far greater effect on Soviet morale than sending supplies, which were still only a drop in the bucket. Cadogan, echoing the sentiments of the military, felt that it would only be possible to send a token force and that there was a very serious danger of further dispersing the very limited manpower resources. Eden refused to take sides in this debate and commented that he found the discussion 'interesting'. Armine Dew of the Northern Department warned that 'Our continuing inability to take any action to relieve the pressure on the Russian front can only provide ammunition to any persons in the Soviet Union who may be advising the conclusion of some agreement with the Germans.'[50] The Minister of Supply claimed that all the Soviets really wanted was war material and that the whole issue of the second front was irrelevant. Churchill argued that if British troops were sent to the Caucasus it would clog up the Iranian railway system and make it all the more difficult to send supplies to Russia.[51]

Faced with the growing problem of the Soviet presence in Iran and the insistent demands for British troops in southern Russia, Churchill tried to solve both issues at once. He suggested to Stalin that British troops should relieve the five Soviet Divisions in Iran. There was little chance that this ploy would be successful. Stalin was growing increasingly impatient with the British. He wanted British troops in the Ukraine where there was heavy fighting, and not in the Caucasus where there was none.[52] Cripps put the suggestion that British troops should relieve the Soviet forces in Iran to Molotov, and was not in the least bit surprised to get an unenthusiastic response. Writing to the Prime Minister, Cripps pointed out that if British troops were to replace Soviet troops in Iran it would look as if an attempt were being made to gain control of the entire country. Similarly, British operations in Libya looked to the Russians as if the British were pursuing their imperialist aims in Africa while the Soviets were left to fight the Germans. He reminded Churchill that the Russians were obsessed with the idea 'that we are prepared to fight to the last drop of Russian blood'.[53]

The feud between Cripps and Churchill was to rage on, but this exchange marked the end of the proposal to send troops to southern Russia, although similar proposals cropped up at later stages of the war. The campaign in North Africa and the increasing Japanese threat to British positions in Asia meant that it was impossible to send a large force to the Soviet Union. Even if it had been possible to spare two divisions Churchill felt that the Russians would find such an offer insulting and it would hardly have altered the over-all military situation. There were two RAF Hurricane squadrons at Murmansk, but with the approach of winter they would soon be unable to continue operations. Churchill therefore suggested that they might be sent to the south where they could still fight. He felt that at least eight squadrons should have been sent to Russia 'which would have gained great fame, destroyed many German aircraft, and given immense encouragement all along the front'. Portal excused the size of the force by saying, 'At the time it was decided to send them we had no idea how successful the Russian resistance to the German invasion would be.' The Air Ministry wanted the men withdrawn, and argued that it was too late for them to get used to fighting in a new theatre. It was pointed out that the Soviets had agreed that the men should be withdrawn at the onset of winter. Cripps was vehemently opposed to withdrawing the men, and Air Vice Marshall Collier reluctantly suggested that if the men had to stay in Russia they should remain in Murmansk.[54] At the beginning of November the Foreign Office informed Cripps that it had been decided to withdraw the airmen and to hand over their planes to the Soviets.[55]

Another curious episode in which the British offered their assistance to the Soviet Union involved a plan to demolish the oilfields in the Caucasus. There had been discussions of schemes to destroy the oilfields in the early stages of the war, when the Soviets were supplying oil to the Germans. Now it seemed possible that the Germans might seize the oilfields, and the British were afraid that the Russians would let them fall into their hands undamaged. In May 1941 the Joint Intelligence Committee assumed that the need to secure oil supplies was one of the main motives for the forthcoming German attack on the Soviet Union, and it was calculated that they would overrun the area very quickly.[56] MI3 felt that bombing the airfields would be a 'tedious experience', and that the best way of denying them to the Germans would be to send an SOE demolition team.[57] Wavell, under whose command any such operation would fall, suggested that Armenian Dashnak bands, with whom British Military Intelligence had been in touch for some time, would be ideal for the job. It was even imagined that the Soviets would allow the Armenians a degree of regional autonomy after the war in gratitude for demolishing the oilfields and denying them to the enemy.[58]

Such ideas, however romantic, were quite impractical. Apart from the obvious difficulty of getting Soviet consent to demolition squads wandering around the Caucasus, the demolition of an oil well is a highly skilled and difficult task that can only be performed by specialists. It so happened that a group of demolition experts were standing by in the Middle East. In Romania in 1940, fearing that the Germans might soon invade, a group of some twelve civilian engineers under the command of Commander Watson RN, formed a demolition squad in the hope that it might prove possible to destroy some of the oil wells before they fell into German hands. They had no opportunity to test their skills, for they were suddenly given twelve hours to leave the country by a Romanian Government anxious to appease the Germans. Most of the men found their way by devious and adventurous routes to the Middle East where they were reorganised to form Mission 131, an expert demolition team ready to go to the Caucasus.

At the beginning of July the War Cabinet instructed Sir Stafford Cripps to test Soviet reactions to the proposal that a British demolition team should destroy the oil wells in the Caucasus if they were in any danger of falling into German hands. The Ambassador was told that the British Government would make up any losses of oil in kind.[59] Eric Berthoud, a BP executive working for the Ministry of Supply, was sent to Moscow to discuss the scheme with the Soviet authorities. He realised that the only way to allay the understandable Soviet fears of the scheme was to make a firm guarantee that alternative oil supplies would be forthcoming, and such a guarantee could only come from the United States' Government. Berthoud therefore went to Washington on a brief visit and got the guarantee he required, although some felt that the wording of the guarantee was uncomfortably vague.

Cripps was opposed to the suggestion when it was put to him by Berthoud, arguing that the Russians would never agree to it and that the American guarantee that they would do their best would be unlikely to convince the Russians.[60] The Chiefs of Staff also felt that the Soviets would be most unlikely to welcome the demolition team, given their excessive suspicions of British motives, but they agreed that the mission should be kept at the ready in case the Soviets agreed. After further discussion Wavell's suggestion of using the Dashnak bands was rejected on the reasonable grounds that as they were both anti-Soviet and anti-Turk they would be a serious political liability. No mention was made of the fact that these stalwart nationalists were also incapable of carrying out such a technically difficult operation.[61] Berthoud returned to Moscow in September with the Beaverbrook–Harriman Mission, and agreed with Cripps that the Russians were unlikely to welcome the demolition experts, but he urged that Mission 131 should be ready to move if they changed their minds.[62]

Mission 131 was thus held at the ready, with Wavell fretting about the problem of finding some roubles to give them. 16G(R) Mission of some 100 men, which had been formed to sabotage oil installations behind the German lines, was disbanded as unlikely to be effective.[63] Then, much to everyone's surprise and astonishment, Vyshinskii suddenly announced that his Government would welcome Mission 131 and suggested that they should travel at once to Baku. The Mission was given no proper guidelines and the Foreign Office was less than enthusiastic. Cavendish–Bentinck of the Joint Intelligence Committee wrote, 'We have a mania for offering the Russians advice and technical experts, neither of which they want, and which only arouses their suspicions.'

In fact Mission 131 was a remarkable and unique piece of wartime cooperation between Britain and the Soviet Union. After an inauspicious start when the leader of the Mission, Colonel Fairwell, was injured in a car crash, they arrived in Baku under the capable command of Major Gwynne Elias who, as a civilian engineer in Romania, had been part of the original group. The importance of the Mission to the Soviets was underlined by the fact that they were welcomed by Beria's senior henchman, Merkulov. He was People's Commissar for State Security and Beria's deputy. As such he played a key role in the Katyn Massacre and in the deportation of civilians from the Baltic States and vigilantly and ferociously rooted out persons of anti-Soviet leanings and other counter-revolutionary agitators. He was also considered to be a leading expert on scorched earth policy. He proved to be a charming host, plying the members of Mission 131 with seemingly endless supplies of caviare and vodka and creating an atmosphere of somewhat excessive conviviality. Meanwhile, Merkulov's experts translated the Mission's handbook into Russian and tried out the suggested demolition methods with complete success. Within 48 hours Merkulov told the Mission that their methods were excellent and would be used if necessary, but that he intended to move all the oil installations rather than destroy them. The professional engineers in the Mission were greatly impressed by the extraordinary efficiency with which the Soviets tackled the problem of moving vast quantities of equipment from the installations at Maikop and quickly realised that Merkulov had not been indulging in a vain boast.

Having given the Soviets the information they needed there was little for the Mission to do but to enjoy the lavish hospitality of their hosts. After a few weeks the Mission returned to Cairo. The victory of the Red Army at Rostov had removed the sense of urgency which had prompted the Soviets to forget their resentments and suspicions and to welcome the help they badly needed and which they were so efficiently given.[64]

5   The Anglo–Soviet Treaty

British public opinion strongly favoured the closest possible cooperation with the Soviets, thus making the Russian card a tempting one
for ambitious politicians to play. Shortly after the German attack
the British Institute of Public Opinion conducted a survey on the
question 'Do you feel that Britain has taken or has not taken full
advantage offered by the German attack on Russia?' The replies
were: Has taken 29%; Not taken 49%; Don't know 22%.[1] The Home
Intelligence Weekly Reports, based on an extensive survey of public
opinion, continued to show concern that Russia was fighting the war
for Britain with insufficient help. One such report stated that 'People
realise that every Russian killed is one Englishman less to die, and
they are not only thankful, they are grateful.' There were also
widespread complaints that there was not nearly as much enthusiasm
at the top to help the Soviet Union as there was among the working
class.[2] Another report spoke of annoyance at 'persons in high position
who are not one hundred per cent in favour of assisting the Russians'.
It was pointed out that such people still refused to sit on the
same platforms as Communists even though the Soviets were now
comrades-in-arms.[3] At least until the end of October 1941 there was
a strong desire for a second front to be opened as soon as possible.
One report stated that 'The feeling seems to be gaining ground that
our capitalists will hold up help to Russia in the hope that both
Germany and Russia will exhaust themselves.' Remarks by Lord
Moyne and by Halifax about the folly of attacking in the west were
denounced as an encouragement to Hitler to move more troops to
the Russian front.[4] The publication of Lord Gort's dispatches during
the Dunkirk evacuation did much to dampen enthusiasm for a second
front in the west. They showed how badly equipped the BEF had
been, and brought home the fact that the invasion of France would
lead to terrible losses.

The arch-villain in the public mind was the Minister of Aircraft

Production, Colonel Moore-Brabazon, who had said at a private meeting that it was a good thing that Britain's two greatest enemies were now at each others' throats. Trades Unionists were present at this meeting and the Minister was denounced by the president of the AEU at the Trades Union Congress in September. Churchill's support for Moore-Brabazon was widely criticised, and when he was dismissed from the War Cabinet in February 1942 the move was widely acclaimed. In a subsequent election in his safe Conservative seat of Wallasey the Labour candidate, George Reakes, supported by Sir Richard Acland and his Forward March movement, won a tremendous victory. It was perhaps a sign of the times that the Conservative candidate hoisted the red flag over his committee rooms and was supported by the Communists who decorated their headquarters in red, white and blue. Such antics were not enough to wipe out the stigma of anti-Sovietism which attached to Conservative candidates.[5]

The heroes of the day were Cripps and Beaverbrook, particularly Beaverbrook because of his widely applauded efforts at the Moscow conference. His popularity did much to move public opinion away from a demand for an offensive in the west in favour of feeling that more arms for Russia was a better solution.[6] Beaverbrook had not yet placed himself at the head of the second front movement. This feeling was reflected in a public opinion survey in October which reported that 'The news of better Christmas dinners is met by the remark: "We want guns for Russia, not butter."'

This popular enthusiasm for the USSR placed the propaganda specialists at the Ministry of Information in a somewhat difficult position. A Viennese refugee, who had adopted the sturdily English name of Smollett, was responsible for handling propaganda to and about the Soviet Union. His aim was to show that the two countries were quite distinct and separate, but united in a common effort to destroy Hitler. No attempt was made to attack the Communist system of government, and it was hoped that it might be possible to present a fair and accurate picture of the Soviet Union while at the same time stealing some of the thunder from the left. To this end the Ministry of Information sponsored a Penguin Special '100 Questions About Russia', but the answers were so favourable that the book did nothing to halt the leftward drift. A major problem was that it proved extremely difficult to find anyone who was not on the left who was willing to speak about the Soviet Union or to write pamphlets for the Ministry. Died in the wool anti-Communists were discredited and were quite unsuitable to help forge a united front. Public opinion was moving to the left, and enthusiasm and admiration for the Soviet Union was widespread. Smollett's section was under-staffed and had an inadequate budget, and was thus forced to rely on prominent figures on the left, such as lecturers and writers on Soviet affairs. Far from stealing the thunder from the left, the Ministry of Information did much to strengthen the impression that the Soviet political system was partly responsible for Russia's successes in withstanding the Nazi attack. This in turn helped to increase the popularity of the Communist Party which loudly demanded all-out support for the Soviet Union and the opening of the second front.

This increasing enthusiasm for the Soviet Union had little effect on the policy makers. Neither the War Cabinet nor the Foreign Office was swayed by public opinion on matters of foreign policy or military strategy. But there was growing concern that this understand-able sympathy for the Soviet Union might lead to a growth of Communism at home. Churchill ordered the Ministry of Information to 'consider what action was required to counter the present tendency of the British Public to forget the dangers of Communism in their enthusiasm over the resistance of Russia.' R. H. Parker, the director of the home division of the Ministry, felt that 'Close liaison between the Ministry and the Soviet Embassy will greatly assist us in dealing vigorously with the English [sic] Communist Party since the attitude of the Soviet Government is almost cynically realist about the war position.'[7] That Maisky and his staff were seen as the best guarantee against the spread of Communism in Britain is testimony to the virtual impossibility of the task at that particular juncture.

The Foreign Office gave financial support to the Anglo–Soviet Public Relations Committee, a broadly-based organisation which, it was hoped, would keep Russophiles out of the Communist camp. The Committee was short of funds and about to collapse and was saved at the last moment by an injection of public funds. Lord Horder, the King's physician, presided over the committee and gave it an air of unimpeachable respectability. Its prominent members were typical representatives of progressive and enlightened opinion: Sir Richard Acland, Aneurin Bevan, H. N. Brailsford, Harold Laski, Low, Kingsley Martin, J. B. Priestly, Eleanor Rathbone, Mervyn Stockwood, H. G. Wells, Tom Wintringham and Leonard Woolf. It is doubtful whether the Foreign Office got good value for their money. The Committee published laudatory articles by the Cambridge Communist economist Maurice Dobb on the virtues of the Soviet

Constitution of 1936, and Leonard Woolf announced that Soviet democracy was 'no less magnificent than liberal democracy'.[8]

Communist and fellow-travelling organisations flourished. The Society for Cultural Relations with the USSR, a fellow-travellers' front, was widely used by the BBC as well as Government departments. The Joint Committee for Soviet Aid, and the Russia Today Society were directly controlled by the Communists. It was an easy matter for the Communists to cash in on the wave of popular enthusiasm for the Soviet Union and their efforts were blessed by bishops, financed by the Government and given musical accompaniment by Guards' bands. Pamphlets on the glorious achievements of Stalin's Russia found a ready market, and Sidney and Beatrice Webb's frightful 'Soviet Communism: A New Civilisation' was republished without the question mark at the end of the title. By 1942 almost everyone seemed to be something of a fellow-traveller. Even an impeccable conservative like T. S. Eliot refused to publish George Orwell's *Animal Farm* at Faber and Faber, arguing that such an anti-Soviet satire was politically undesirable.[9] Perhaps the best summary of such views is Beaverbrook's speech given in New York in 1942 and broadcast coast-to-coast:

> Communism under Stalin has won the applause and admiration of all western nations.
>
> Communism under Stalin has provided us with examples of patriotism equal to the finest in the annals of history.
>
> Communism under Stalin has produced the best generals in the world.
>
> Persecution of Christianity? Not so. There is no religious persecution. The church doors are open ...
>
> Racial persecution? Not at all. Jews live like other men. There are many races in the Soviet Union and not even a colour bar.
>
> Political purges? Of course. But it is now clear that the men who were shot would have betrayed Russia to her German enemies.[10]

Such was the temper of the times that an enthusiastic capitalist and unrepentant anti-Communist could give what his biographer describes as 'the most enthusiastically pro-Soviet speech ever delivered in the United States'. Beaverbrook knew that without the support of the Soviet Union Britain could never win the war, therefore every effort had to be made to ensure that relations between the two countries should be as close and harmonious as possible. But speeches such as these gave powerful support to those who argued that the extraordinary achievements of the Soviet Armed Forces were due in part to the inherent virtues of Communism. There was a spectacular growth in membership in the Communist Party from 12 000 members in 1941 to 65 000 by September 1942, but it still remained something of a sect and there were very few people, even within the party, who wished to turn Britain into a carbon copy of the New Civilisation. In political terms admiration for the Soviet Union meant a demand for more nationalisation, all-out war on the Blimps and the Moore-Brabazons, greater workers' control of industry, and above all arms for the Soviet Union and a second front as soon as possible. In 1945 it was ironically the Labour Party, whose leadership had been consistently critical of the Soviet Union throughout the war – far more so than the Conservatives – who were to gain most from the popularity of Russia.

By October 1941 the situation on the Eastern Front further deteriorated and Moscow was in serious danger. The last week of September had been designated 'Tanks for Russia Week' by Beaverbrook, all production to go to the Soviet Union. Workers worked overtime to produce 'Another for Joe'. Mrs Churchill launched her Aid to Russia Appeal which met with a remarkable response. *Ci-devant* interventionists and enthusiasts for the struggle of the Finnish people against Muscovite expansionism now outdid one another in singing the praises of the heroic Red Army. In a remarkable gesture of solidarity with the Soviet Union in her moment of peril the Athenaeum elected Maisky a member.

As the Germans prepared their assault on Moscow the Diplomatic Corps was evacuated to Kuibyshev, a town which the British journalist Philip Jordan described as 'a monument more to the Russian skill in improvisation than to their passion for the more modern of the amenities'.[11] The train journey was made even more unpleasant when Cripps' dog 'Joe' was violently sick. Joe, like his master, was a vegetarian. He remained in the Soviet Union when Cripps returned to London and the new Ambassador, Sir Archibald Clark Kerr promptly fed him meat which hastened the unfortunate animal to an early grave. Cooking facilities on the train were almost non-existent, and SOE's George Hill ingeniously used a stove designed to heat ladies' curling irons to do some modest cooking. In spite of the fact that the Bolshoi Ballet had also been moved to Kuibyshev and a special gastronomic store was opened for foreigners life was terribly dull. There was little to do but eat caviare, drink champagne, and browse through ancient copies of 'The Tatler' at the British Embassy. Mason-Macfarlane tried to learn a little Russian, George Hill continued his experiments mixing vodka with other drinks, and everyone lamented their fate at being stuck in a town of 200 000 inhabitants with two hotels, no baths, and only two vice-commissars for foreign affairs to whom to report. Cripps and his staff were cut off from the Soviet Government who remained in Moscow. It was not until the beginning of December that the Soviets were able to push back the Germans from Moscow in a brilliant but costly campaign which saved the capital.

With the Soviet Union fighting for its very existence relations with Britain deteriorated still further. The British offer to relieve the Soviet troops in Iran was rejected out of hand. Churchill regarded the repeated Soviet requests for 25–30 Divisions as a 'physical absurdity'. Cripps called for more aid, and was locked in battle with the Prime Minister. Meanwhile, in London, Maisky pressed for a British declaration of war on Finland, Romania and Hungary as a gesture of solidarity with the Soviet Union.[12] Four days after this initial request Maisky bitterly remarked to Eden that if the British were unwilling or unable to give any material support to the Soviet Union at least they could help politically by a declaration of war on these three countries.[13] Within a week Maisky was back again to see Eden, who told the Ambassador that the War Cabinet saw no advantage in declaring war on these countries unless it was possible to back up these gestures with action. He tried to stall Maisky by pointing out that the Dominions would first have to be consulted.[14] Maisky continued to keep pressure on Eden but to little effect. He therefore requested British troops for the Russian front. He told Eden that before the war there had been a number of people who felt that Germany should be given a free hand against the Soviet Union, and now these same people were trying to stop a second front. He called for immediate action to dispel these suspicions. Christopher Warner commented on the Ambassador's outburst,

> The fact of the matter is that to the Russians who for close on five months have been fighting, as they feel, alone, the lack of British military action, whether in Europe or elsewhere is becoming suspicious.[15]

On 21 November Churchill told Stalin that he would give Finland another two weeks before declaring war. But this message was hardly sent when the American journalist Kuh, one of Maisky's familiars, published a story that the Soviet Union was calling for a declaration of war on Finland, Romania and Hungary and that the British Government was reluctant to comply. The Foreign Office was convinced, quite rightly, that Maisky was once again up to his tricks, and another black mark was awarded to Kuh and his friend Andrew Rothstein.[16]

Churchill saw no point in declaring war on these three states but he felt obliged to give way in order to placate the Russians. On 28 November he sent a message to General Mannerheim warning him that if he did not cease hostilities he would have to declare war out of loyalty to the Russians. The letter was most conciliatory, Churchill saying,

> My recollections of our pleasant talks and correspondence about the last war lead me to send this purely personal and private message for your consideration before it is too late.

The United States Minister in Finland was informed that 5 December was the deadline for a positive reply from the Finnish Government.[17] Similar notes were sent to Romania and Hungary. The effect of the British ultimatum to Finland was somewhat undermined by a strongly pro-Finnish and anti-Soviet talk which was broadcast by the BBC. The Anglo–Russian Parliamentary Committee promptly informed the Soviet Embassy, thus causing considerable embarrassment to the Foreign Office at what they termed an 'idiotic broadcast'.[18] Britain declared war on Finland, Romania and Hungary at midnight on 5 December 1941 but this did little to improve relations with the Soviet Union.

Stalin's message to Churchill on 8 November had brought up the question of war aims and the post-war settlement which Stalin felt were the principal causes of the friction between the two countries. He had told Churchill that there was no point in sending military experts to Moscow to discuss strategy until these major political questions were settled. Christopher Warner felt that Stalin had some understandable reasons to be suspicious of the British. He pointed out that Stalin clearly thought that the British wanted the Soviet Union to be 'crippled in crippling the Germans and to be of no account in the peace settlement'. It was not wholly unreasonable of Stalin to think that the British and Americans were far from open with him. After all, the Soviet Union had been excluded from the discussions which led to the publication of the Atlantic Charter, there was no second front, and material support from Britain was still very modest. Warner argued that Britain needed the Soviet Union far more than they needed Britain. The cooperation of the Soviet Union was needed in Iran and Afghanistan, and could very well be critical in the event of a war with Japan. Most important of all, if the Soviet Union collapsed nothing would stop Hitler from launching a full-scale invasion of England. He suggested that this need for Soviet support was so great that it might prove impossible to avoid the issue of war aims.[19]

The War Cabinet discussed Stalin's message at length. The Prime Minister said that he had already told Maisky that he could not go beyond the terms of the Atlantic Charter and that as the Russians were clearly not at all interested in seeing Generals Wavell and Paget at least a week should elapse before a reply was sent. Eden repeated Warner's view that the Russians were afraid that the British and the Americans were thinking of making a deal behind their backs, and suggested that they should be given every assurance that this was not the case. He also came up with the extraordinary idea that if he were to tell Maisky that an immediate reply to the telegram from Stalin was not possible he might create the impression that Stalin's message had been misunderstood, and that this might make the Soviet authorities somewhat more forthcoming. Acting strictly on Cabinet instructions, Eden told Maisky that his Majesty's Government was 'surprised and pained' at the tone of the letter and that a reply was not possible for the moment. Eden then telegraphed to Cripps at Kuibyshev saying that there could be no question of discussing peace terms with the USSR because the British Government had already agreed with the Americans not to do so. Both the United States and Britain were bound by the Atlantic Charter and therefore could not make a bilateral agreement with the Soviet Union about post-war frontiers. Eden added that he was prepared to go to Moscow with some top military advisers in an attempt to improve the situation.[20] This message from Eden was in reply to an angry note from Cripps saying that either the Chiefs of Staff and the Secretary of State should come to the Soviet Union, or he should be given full authority to settle all outstanding issues, otherwise he would resign.

On 18 November Cadogan, Sargent, Law, Strang, Harvey and Ronald held a conference at the Foreign Office to discuss relations with the Soviet Union, which seemed to be rapidly deteriorating. It was agreed that Stalin's great concern was that he might be excluded from the peace conference at which a settlement would be reached by the Americans and the British to the detriment of Soviet interests. Stalin badly needed British help after the war when Britain would be strong and the Soviet Union hopelessly weak, and therefore wanted a formal agreement before the end of the war. But above all it was felt that Stalin was very anxious about Soviet security after the war. It was felt that disarmament and an international police force to enforce the peace would do the job and provide an effective alternative to Soviet annexation, which might well result from her need to protect her frontiers. The Foreign Office had heard from Harriman that the United States Government favoured an agreement that would cover the post-war period. Thus the Foreign Office felt that an agreement with the Soviet Union on the post-war settlement would solve most of the outstanding problems between the two countries and would not antagonise the Government of the United States. The Foreign Office thus disagreed with the Prime Minister, who wished to put off all discussion of a post-war settlement until after the war. Moreover, they had no real idea what they wanted by way of a post-war settlement, and had even less of a clue what the Russians had in mind.[21]

Churchill did not reply to Stalin's letter until 21 November.[22] He told the Soviet leader that he had issued an ultimatum to the Finns, and suggested that Eden should go to Moscow with top military experts to discuss outstanding military and political issues including the possibility of sending some troops to the Caucasus. Stalin's reply was prompt and unusually friendly. He welcomed the idea of Eden going to Moscow and insisted that

> the differences of the state organisation between the U.S.S.R. on the one hand and Great Britain and the United States on the other hand should not and could not hinder us achieving a successful solution of all the fundamental questions concerning our mutual security and our legitimate interests.

Encouraged by Stalin's brief homily on the virtues of peaceful coexistence the War Cabinet agreed that Eden should go to Moscow as soon as possible and that Wavell and Pownall should travel with him as military advisers. The Chiefs of Staff were requested to draw up an *aide-mémoire* on the possibilities and the limitations of military aid to the Soviet Union.[23] The Foreign Office prepared a position paper for the Foreign Secretary to help him in his forthcoming discussions with the Soviet Government. The central issue was that of post-war frontiers:

> They want us to approve their annexation of the Baltic States and Eastern Poland, and to help them secure special rights with regard to Finland, the Dardanelles and access to the Persian Gulf, and an icefree-port in northern Norway. It will be difficult at this stage to give the Soviet Government much satisfaction on these points, and presumably we shall have to decline for the present to go beyond the first and second clauses of the Atlantic Charter.[24]

This approach to the problem of the post-war settlement was certainly in accord with the views of the War Cabinet, but it overlooked one of the main causes of friction between Britain and the Soviet Union during the war. It was clear from the outset of hostilities with Germany that the Soviet Union would continue to be deeply suspicious of the British Government as long as there was no agreement on the post-war frontiers of the Soviet Union, particularly in the Baltic. A major reason why the Soviet Union had reached an agreement with Nazi Germany, and had remained a faithful partner for the first two years of the war, was to secure the Baltic States and eastern Poland. Even at a time when it seemed that the Soviet Union might be defeated at any moment, Stalin continued to press for recognition of the 1941 frontiers by the British Government. Now, as he prepared for the great counter-offensive around Moscow, he was unlikely to change his tune. Cripps had insisted all along that the Baltic States should be sacrificed in the interests of the Anglo–Soviet alliance, the Foreign Office wavered, and the Prime Minister was firm in his opposition to any discussion of the post-war settlement until the fighting had stopped.

Stalin was also becoming deeply suspicious that the British were considering a separate peace with the Germans. He could not get it out of his mind that the Hess mission was part of a scheme to forge an anti-Soviet Anglo–German alliance. It was pointed out in the War Cabinet that it was essential to convince Stalin that the British Government would never contemplate a separate peace with Germany, even if Hitler and his gang were overthrown by dissident generals. Churchill strongly disagreed, arguing that it might be a very good idea to negotiate with a Germany controlled by the generals.[25] Stalin's suspicions were thus not wholly unfounded, and as Sir

Stafford Cripps never tired of pointing out, the British Government gave much for his suspicious nature to brood on.

The War Cabinet issued their final instructions to Eden on 4 December. He was told not to allow himself to be drawn into discussions of post-war Soviet frontiers and also to avoid any commitments on post-war economic policies. The War Cabinet felt that the best way to help the Soviet Union was to press home the offensive in Libya and to supply Russia with war materials. Eden blandly announced that he intended to tell Stalin that the second front was in Libya, thus showing how little he understood the Soviet position on this extremely sensitive issue. It was pointed out to the Prime Minister that he had virtually promised to send British troops from Iran to the Russian front, and had repeated this offer in his recent letter to Stalin, but Churchill suggested that the Soviet victory at Rostov changed the situation completely and the Red Army no longer needed the support of British soldiers.[26] It thus seemed to the British that Stalin's conciliatory message to Churchill removed the need for bridge building, and the British Government was slipping back into the disastrous habit of regarding the Soviet Union as a junior partner in the war against Hitler whose demands for help were tiresome, impertinent and untimely. Soviet successes in the battles for Rostov and Moscow reinforced this attitude by removing the sense of urgency from discussions of how best to assist the Soviet Union.

Shortly before Eden left for Moscow, Cripps sent a warning that this was no time to relax efforts and that, on the contrary, it was an appropriate moment to get down to brass tacks with the Russians. The Polish Prime Minister, Sikorski, had recently talked to Stalin who had told him that he 'profoundly distrusted the British Government'.[27] Sikorski felt that his suspicions were mainly due to the failure to concert military planning. In November there had been some concern at the Foreign Office about brass tacks. Cadogan was beginning to think that the time had come to begin discussions about the post-war settlement. Eden agreed, adding that it was vitally important to treat the Russians as equal partners and to cooperate fully with them 'or this war may have been fought in vain'.[28] Armine Dew, whose thinking was very close to that of Stafford Cripps, wrote,

> The Soviet Government are no doubt worried about the situation in which the U.S.S.R. will find itself at the end of the war if America and ourselves have not sacrificed men and material to

the same extent as the U.S.S.R. and if the consequent peace is likely to be dictated rather by the U.S.A. and ourselves than by the Soviet Union.[29]

This sense of concern seems to have been lost as Stalin showed himself more forthcoming, the Red Army won some significant victories and the British pushed forward in the desert. The Soviet Union would clearly survive the winter. On 5 December it was learnt that Hitler had ordered an Air Corps from Russia to North Africa thus providing further evidence for those who supported the far-fetched notion that the 'Crusader' offensive in the desert marked the opening of a true second front. In such circumstances and in spite of the strong reservations of the Foreign Office, Eden was easily persuaded by his Cabinet colleagues that he should take a tougher line with the Soviet Union in the forthcoming negotiations. It was all too easy to forget that Soviet demands and concerns, however tiresome and ill-mannered they might appear in Whitehall, had rational and legitimate foundations.

Eden's trip to Moscow was not a success. He travelled by sea to Murmansk with Maisky on the same ship. Some indication of what awaited him might have been gained from the curious behaviour of the Soviet delegation. They remained totally isolated from the British throughout the voyage. From Murmansk they travelled by train to Moscow, and on 16 December Eden had his first meeting with Stalin. It became immediately obvious that the post-war settlement was uppermost in Stalin's mind. He began the discussion by presenting Eden with the draft of an agreement on Soviet frontiers.[30] The main points were the recognition of the 1941 frontiers in the Baltic States and Finland, the annexation of Petsamo and Memel, a modified Curzon line as the frontier with Poland and the transfer of East Prussia to Poland. To Eden's astonishment Stalin spoke at some length and with considerable authority on such matters as reparations from Germany, the separatist movement in the Rhineland, the strategic significance of Scandinavia, the Netherlands and Belgium and the future status of the Dodecanese Islands. Eden replied that it was impossible for him to agree to these requests or even discuss such a wide range of problems until they had been examined by the War Cabinet. Molotov then put forward two drafts on mutual military assistance and on post-war issues to which Eden could agree. The first of these was a mutual undertaking not to make a separate peace with Germany, and the second spoke rather vaguely of the principles of the Atlantic Charter, and of non-aggrandisement and non-interference.

Stalin agreed to meet Eden again the following evening at his favourite hour of midnight. He was even more blunt and accusatory than he had been at their first meeting and Eden was shocked and stunned by his behaviour. He demanded an agreement on the Baltic States and Finland. Eden rather lamely told him that 'there are no independent Baltic States and that in fact they do form a part of the U.S.S.R.', but the British Government was unable to grant *de jure* recognition to this undoubted fact because of an agreement with the Americans not to discuss post-war boundaries in Europe. Stalin was furious at what he regarded as ridiculous hair-splitting. He told Eden, 'We are in the midst of the greatest war in history and I think these nice formulae about *de jure* and *de facto* etc., are rather out of place.' This remark triggered off another lengthy wrangle, with Stalin threatening to postpone the signing of the general agreements, and Eden trying to explain the position of his Government to a man who would not or could not understand.

The two men met again the following evening for a third and final round of talks. Stalin was more moderate in his language but he would not modify his position. It was agreed that no agreements should be signed on this occasion as the War Cabinet had instructed Eden not to make any pledges to the Russians on frontiers. Discussions of the military situation were much more satisfactory. Stalin said that he was not 'in the least hurt or offended' at the British inability to establish a second front, given the serious situation in the Far East. He did not press his request for British participation in an attack on Petsamo, and Eden in return let drop the British plea for support against Japan. The meeting ended in a reasonably cordial atmosphere when Stalin agreed to issue a full communiqué rather than sign an agreement, a suggestion which, had it been made by Eden, would probably have been denounced by the Soviet leader as hair-splitting. The talks now completed, the visit ended with a typically mammoth feast which lasted until five the next morning. Stalin tried, with only partial success, to unnerve the suave Eden by giving him Georgian pepper vodka, which he claimed was whisky specially provided for the Foreign Secretary. Eden drank this noxious brew in all innocence believing it to be Scotch. With superhuman effort he managed to preserve his sang-froid, but observers noted that his face turned an alarming shade of puce.[31]

Eden had stood up quite well against Stalin at his most intransigent, and he probably did not lose any points for doing so. He found the experience most taxing, reporting to the Foreign Office that he found the Soviet attitude 'deplorable'.[32] Cadogan, who travelled with Eden to Moscow, gained a more favourable impression of Stalin, finding him 'restrained and quiet' and looking 'rather like a porcupine'.[33] At least Eden realised that Stalin's request that the USSR and Britain should 'work for the reconstruction of Europe after the war with full regard to the interests of the USSR and the restoration of its frontiers violated by Hitlerite aggression' implied a recognition of the 1941 frontiers.[34] But Stalin's tactics paid off, for when Eden returned to London he argued in favour of recognising the 1941 frontiers. Eden may have hoped to get some political boost from his visit to Moscow, but he was disappointed. Beaverbrook, who had returned from the Soviet Union as a popular hero and was to resign from the Government in February 1942 to champion aid to the Russians and the opening of the second front, was the most outspoken advocate of an alliance with Russia. His resignation strengthened the popular view that the Government was not doing all it could to help the Soviet Union and made it even more difficult for Eden to gain any political advantage from supporting Soviet claims to the 1941 frontiers and maximum possible support for the Soviet war effort.

Churchill's position on the frontiers remained unequivocal. From the United States, where the Prime Minister was 'reclining in the mellow sunlight of Palm Beach', resting on his doctor's advice after the strain of his visits to Washington and Ottawa, he telegraphed to Eden saying that these frontiers 'were acquired by acts of aggression in shameful collusion with Hitler'. He insisted that recognition of these frontiers would be 'contrary to all the principles for which we are fighting this war and would dishonour our cause'. He showed no sympathy for the Soviet position, saying that the Russians 'entered the war only when attacked by Germany, having previously shown themselves utterly indifferent to our fate, and, indeed, they added to our burdens in our worst danger'. Since after the war the Soviets would need the British more than the British would need them, it was important to stick to the principles of the Atlantic Charter and allow the future of the Baltic States to be decided by 'freely and fairly conducted plebiscites'.[35]

Eden ignored this outburst and set about trying to square the Soviet demand for recognition of the 1941 frontiers with the Atlantic Charter, and then trying to sell the whole package to the Americans. He argued that the Russians might possibly win the war largely on their own, and would then be able to establish Communist regimes in Europe, seize German industrial machinery and thus not be dependent on Britain for post-war reconstruction. If Russia were left exhausted by the war then she would be dependent on Britain, but in either case Eden suggested giving in to the Russians on the 1941 frontiers and getting some quid pro quo. In early 1942 it never occurred to anyone that Britain might be destitute after the war and in no position to help anyone, and it was also not at all clear what Russia could offer in return. Perhaps the Soviet Union would agree to British military bases on the Continent, as Stalin had suggested to Eden. Perhaps there should be an agreement not to interfere in the affairs of other countries. Maybe the Soviet Union would agree to a confederation in the Balkans, or the unification of Poland and Czechoslovakia, or perhaps they would agree to cooperate in a major effort for European reconstruction. In short, Eden felt that Britain should give way on the frontiers but get something in return, and he was annoyed at being stuck between the 'exaggeratedly moral' United States, and the 'amoral' Soviet Union and found it exceedingly difficult to steer a middle course.[36]

The more Eden thought about the frontiers the more he realised that there was very little that Britain could do, and therefore the wisest course of action was to come to terms with the Soviet Union. In a draft memorandum for the United States Ambassador he wrote that it was impossible to convince the Russians of British goodwill unless the British Government recognised the 1941 frontiers in Finland, the Baltic States, Bessarabia and the Northern Bukovina. He insisted that a strong Russia would be needed after the war as a guarantee against a resurgence of Germany, and that these frontiers would leave the Soviet Union strong, powerful and secure, equal to the task of restraining Germany. His main point, however, was that 'It must in any case be borne in mind that we shall not be able to effect the issue at the end of the war by anything we do or say or refuse to say.'[37] Eden was deeply concerned that if the Soviet request for recognition of the 1941 frontiers were turned down, Anglo–Soviet relations would be in ruins. Indeed he believed that Stalin had a justified case, had shown considerable restraint during their talks in Moscow, and could have asked for more. He told Halifax that the main problem was to convince the United States Government.[38] But this was also no adequate solution, for if the Soviets heard that the British and the Americans were discussing their post-war frontiers they would immediately feel that a deal was being done behind their backs. Maisky bluntly told Eden that he saw no reason why the United States should be dragged into the talks, and Eden rather feebly replied that he of course attached much importance to the wishes of the United States Government.

In his first report to the War Cabinet after his return from Moscow, Eden told his colleagues that he found it utterly impossible to understand Molotov's mental processes, and that his overriding impression was that the Soviets were deeply suspicious of the British. There was nothing exceptional in these remarks, and the only real piece of information he had to offer was that Sir Stafford Cripps was fed up and wanted to come home.[39] It was not until the Prime Minister returned from the United States, having nearly been shot down by 6 Hurricanes from Fighter Command who mistook his aeroplane for an enemy intruder, that a discussion of the Soviet frontiers took place in the Cabinet.[40] Beaverbrook, recently appointed Minister of War Production and on the point of resigning from the Cabinet, argued strongly in favour of accepting the Russian borders of 1941. He said that recent events had wiped out everything that had happened between the two countries up to that date. The Soviet Union needed these areas for her security and protection. Russia had contributed far more to the war effort than the United States, to whom the British were constantly making concessions. Britain had not acceded quickly enough to the Russian requests for military aid, and had dragged her feet over the declaration of war on Finland. Beaverbrook believed that Romania and Finland, by fighting on the German side, had lost all right to any consideration and that the Baltic States were the 'Ireland of Russia' that had to be under the strategic control of Moscow. Eden countered this opening salvo by arguing that the important thing was to reconcile the demands of the Soviet Union with the objections of the United States. He suggested that the Russians might be given bases in the Baltic States if the United States would agree. Attlee objected strongly that this line of argument was 'wrong in itself and inexpedient'. He was convinced that one concession of this sort would only lead to others, and he was in any case strongly opposed to the idea of strategic frontiers. Herbert Morrison suggested that there should be limits to the principle of self-determination, as this had led to so many difficulties after the last war, and he stressed the vital importance of establishing friendly relations with the Soviet Union. The Secretary of State for Air said that since the Russians would be firmly established in the Baltic States at the end of the war, and since there was nothing the

British could do to get them out, the Government might as well accept the fact and gain their goodwill. Churchill would not listen to any of these arguments and remained adamant that all such questions should wait until the peace conference as it was still quite uncertain how the map of Europe would look after the war. He felt that a 'balanced presentation' of the question should be made to the United States Government.

Several ministers felt that the Prime Minister was simply trying to avoid the issue and pointed out that an approach to the United States would merely prompt them to ask what the British Government intended to do about the Baltic States. Ernest Bevin enquired whether Stalin's demands in Finland, the Baltic States, and Bessarabia were final. Eden replied that they were. At the end of this extensive debate in the course of which all the main arguments about the future of the Baltic States had been put forward, the Cabinet agreed to the Prime Minister's proposal to send a 'balanced statement' to the United States Government. It was also agreed that the Dominion Governments should not be informed. Thus Churchill once again got his way, and Eden offered very little resistance. It was an uneasy compromise which hardly satisfied Attlee who had threatened to resign from the War Cabinet if Russia were to be condoned for annexing the Baltic States, and it infuriated Beaverbrook who championed the recognition of the 1941 borders. On 9 February Beaverbrook offered his resignation, having announced that he would leave the Government if Stalin's claims were not accepted.[41]

Some three weeks later Churchill told the Cabinet that Roosevelt hoped to deal directly with Stalin and that personally he welcomed this prospect. Some Cabinet members felt that this was a serious mistake which would further harm British relations with the Soviet Union, and others suggested that the President was far too optimistic about his chances of success in dealing with Stalin.[42] The advantage of handing the entire problem over to the Americans was that the British Government did not have to make up its own mind about the frontiers and thus avoided, for the time being, any further discussion of such a tendentious issue which had already resulted in the resignation of a prominent minister. The disadvantage was that the Government had no real policy, and nothing was done to assuage Soviet suspicions and fears.

The question of the Soviet frontiers was very closely tied to an estimate of the effectiveness of the Soviet armed forces. The Foreign Office from the outset of the war had a higher opinion of the Soviets' ability than the Service Departments, and therefore thought that sooner or later the British Government would have to give way to the Russians over their demand for recognition of their claim to the Baltic States. At the end of 1941, by which time the Red Army had amply shown its ability in combat with the Germans, Cadogan wrote, 'We should realise, by retrospect, that our staff have throughout underestimated Russian strength to a highly misleading degree. (I am not quite sure that even now they have not rid themselves of this error.)' Eden appended his favourite marginal note: 'I agree.'[43] Liddell Hart had the temerity to suggest in the *Daily Mail* that the Germans were not on the run in Russia, and Eden was so angry that he referred to him as 'this creature'. With the Germans back in Benghazi and the Japanese in Singapore the British were in no position to demand anything of the Russians. Warner felt that a tough and businesslike approach to the Soviet authorities was the only attitude that was likely to be successful, and Orme Sargent complained that endless flattery of the Russians was a 'minor form of appeasement'. Bruce Lockhart suggested that the Russians were suspicious by nature, and that it was important to treat them as normal human beings and not as criminals. Eden wistfully remarked, 'I should find my task easier if we could occasionally have a military success.'[44]

By early 1942 the Foreign Office began to think of the possibility of an early Soviet victory in the east. In spite of his reservations about appeasing the Russians, Orme Sargent felt that the only way to have a hold on the Russians was to 'build up a store of goodwill and confidence to be drawn upon when relations with the Soviet Government become difficult'. He suggested that the Red Army might soon defeat the Germans and that a treaty was needed which would include concessions on the Baltic States and 'other matters'.[45] The prospect of a Soviet victory before the British were back on the Continent was most alarming to the Foreign Office. Cadogan wrote that he hoped very strongly that the Russians would not be too successful in the summer of 1942. Eden pointed out that the further the Russians advanced the greater would be the difficulties. In a letter to Halifax, Eden suggested that if Germany were defeated Russia would be by far the strongest power in Europe. If Britain were not on good terms with the Soviets they might be tempted to make a deal with the Germans. He also warned that it would be unwise to bank on the Soviet Union needing Britain's help after the war, as they would be able to make use of German plant and machinery. A victorious Soviet Union would have enormous power and prestige and would be able to establish Communist regimes in many European countries. It was therefore essential to establish good relations with them at this stage of the war, before it was too late.[46] Cadogan did not agree with Eden and thought that he was giving way to Stalin's bully-boy tactics. He did not think that it was wise to give way over the Baltic, Finland and Romania, particularly as President Roosevelt wanted to leave all these issues until after the war.[47] Eden thus found himself stuck between Churchill who wanted no concessions on the frontier question, and Beaverbrook who gleefully quoted Churchill's words in his speech on 22 June 1941: 'The Russian people are defending their native soil. The Russian soldiers are standing on the threshold of their native land.' But the Foreign Office was beginning to think that the Soviets might advance well beyond the threshold of their native land, and Armine Dew quoted the Marquis de Custine for the edification of his colleagues, '*en dépit des prétentions inspirées aux Russes par Pierre le Grand, la Sibérie commence à la Vistula*'.[48]

In early 1942 the first rumours began to circulate that peace talks were beginning between the Soviet Union and Germany.[49] The Foreign Office discounted these reports, and the story was published in *The Times*, attributing it to German propaganda.[50] Such rumours persisted in the following weeks, but they were never taken seriously. The Foreign Office was perfectly correct in refusing to believe these rumours, for it was not until the Spring of 1943 that there was any real indication that the Soviets were trying to sound out the Germans about a possible peace settlement. Christopher Warner suggested that any hints from the Soviet Union of a separate peace, such as Stalin's widely discussed 'Order of the Day' to the Red Army on 23 February, which spoke of the war as one for the liberation of Russian territory rather than as a struggle against Nazism, were designed to prod the United States and Britain.[51] The Foreign Office therefore decided to use the same trick. It was suggested to Lord Halifax that if the United States Government refused to cooperate fully with the Russians they might be tempted to begin separate peace negotiations.[52] Thus the rumours about peace feelers were used by the Foreign Office to put pressure on the Americans to make concessions over the Soviet frontiers. But with both the Prime Minister and Eden uncertain about which policy to pursue, those in the Foreign Office who hoped to conciliate the Soviet Union could do little but hope that Roosevelt would come to their rescue. This hope was vain, for the President continued to insist that all questions of frontiers should be left until the fighting had ceased.

The Foreign Office never doubted for a moment that the issue of the Baltic States was vitally important to the Soviet Union. This question has been partially responsible for the breakdown of the talks with the Soviets in the Summer of 1939 and was the price the Germans had been prepared to pay to secure Soviet support in the early stages of the war. It was therefore apparent that as long as this problem was not settled Anglo–Soviet relations would never be very satisfactory. If the Red Army were victorious the Soviets would almost certainly seize the Baltic States and present the British Government with a *fait accompli*. Alternatively there was always the remote possibility that if the British Government continued to be stubborn the Soviets might be tempted to come to an understanding with the Germans. If the Soviet Union were defeated then the whole issue would be of no significance.

Eden suggested in March 1942 that the Russians thought that the British and Americans were trying to fight their own war and that 'They suspect that we are interested in co-operation with themselves solely to the extent that such collaboration will keep them fighting hard against Germany, while in their view we are not pulling our weight in the war.' He therefore suggested that unless every effort was made to break down these suspicions the Soviets were likely to pursue entirely selfish aims, both during and after the war. Apart from the Beaverbrook–Harriman Mission nothing much had been done to deal seriously with the problems of supplies and shipping, and as the Anglo–Soviet protocol expired at the end of June this was a serious consideration. The Foreign Secretary suggested that a tripartite conference should be held in Moscow to iron out these problems.[53] A further complication was that Beaverbrook had promised Stalin a 50 per cent increase in supplies after June 1942 and a 100 per cent increase after December. With Britain involved in a war in the Far East it was virtually impossible to meet these figures. It had already taken a major battle to secure the priority of the Moscow protocol over other demands for munitions and raw materials, and it was realised that as long as the question of the frontiers was not settled the Foreign Office felt that the protocol was the key to Anglo–Soviet understanding.

The Minister of Supply, Oliver Lyttelton, disagreed strongly with Eden on this issue. He pointed out that the Russians refused to divulge any details of their supply situation, and that shipments to the Soviet Union might leave British forces seriously short of supplies so that Britain would be unable to play her full part in the war. Lyttelton argued that nothing could be done to overcome the Russians' suspicious nature, and that at any future conference the British delegation would be forced to make excessive commitments simply so as not to come home empty-handed.[54] Eden refused to accept these arguments and insisted that all outstanding problems could be aired at a tripartite conference.

British policy over the Baltic States was further hampered by the Prime Minister's inability to make up his mind on the question which was central to any improvement of relations with the Soviet Union. He was anxious not to strain his friendship with the United States over an issue which seemed to be so important to them, but he was still torn between the idea that the Russians were perfidious aggressors in the Baltic and that they were protecting their legitimate national interests. On 7 March Churchill wrote to the President that since the Russians had agreed to the Atlantic Charter at a time when they were already in possession of the Baltic States this issue should not stand in the way of making a treaty with them.[55] The message overlooked the fact that Soviet possession of the Baltic States was at that stage of the war purely theoretical.

Churchill's understandable concern to avoid having to choose between the United States and the Soviet Union accounts for his hesitations and changes of tack. The Foreign Office was similarly divided on this question. Cadogan argued that it was essential to consult the United States before signing any treaty with the Soviet Union. Stalin was likely to make further demands and to drive a very hard bargain, and therefore a firm understanding with the Americans was vital. Warner felt that the British Government might have to go it alone, and he objected to Churchill's remark to Stalin in his telegram of 3 March that the British Government had asked the President to approve an Anglo–Soviet agreement on frontiers after the war. Eden, who usually followed Cadogan's advice, was uncertain which side to take in this argument, but he accepted the responsibility for the wording of the Prime Minister's note to Stalin. At the same time the Foreign Secretary was getting increasingly annoyed with the Americans. He wrote in the margin of a report of Roosevelt's discussion of the frontier question with the Soviet Ambassador, 'A dismal tale of clumsy diplomacy. President Roosevelt has shown no consideration for our views, and has increased our difficulties.' The

Americans had an equally low opinion of the British approach. Sumner Wells wrote,

> The attitude of the British Government is not only indefensible from every moral standpoint, but likewise extraordinarily stupid. I am confident that no sooner will this treaty have been signed than Great Britain will be confronted with new additional demands for the recognition of the right of the Soviet Union to occupy Bukovina, Bessarabia and very likely eastern Poland and northern Norway.[56]

Britain was in no position to offer the second front which the Russians demanded, and supplies were still insufficient to meet the demand, therefore the British Government agreed to a Soviet proposal for a treaty between the two countries. Stalin told Churchill that Molotov would visit London on his way to Washington to 'dispose of all the matters which stood in the way of signing an agreement'.[57] The War Cabinet felt that the treaty should not actually be signed during Molotov's first visit for fear of giving offence to the Americans, but it was hoped that full agreement could be reached on a final text before Molotov went to Washington.

Preliminary meetings between Eden and Maisky were far from encouraging. Maisky went on at great length about the bitterness and resentments of the Soviet people at the inadequacy of British support for their superhuman efforts against the Hitlerite invaders, and raised his price at each meeting. Eden constantly repeated that the Americans would have to agree to the terms of the treaty, but the Soviet Ambassador was not impressed by this argument. The British had four principal objections to the Soviet proposals. They contained no provision for the emigration of the inhabitants of territories overrun by the Soviet Union, a clause which the British felt might help allow the United States to accept the annexation of the Baltic States. The Soviets demanded a clear-cut and definite statement by the British on the question of the Baltic States which the British, looking over their shoulders towards the Americans, were reluctant to give. The British request to be involved in the settlement of the Polish frontier question was refused, and any mention of the allies in the United Nations was studiously avoided.[58] Having made the British position clear, Eden preferred to wait for Molotov's arrival, and the War Cabinet postponed any further discussion of the treaty.

On 21 May Churchill and Eden began their discussions with
Molotov. From the outset it was clear that the main stumbling blocks
would be the Soviet demand for a second front and their insistence
that the question of the Soviet–Polish frontier should be settled
directly between the two countries. On the following day Eden
proposed a completely new treaty on a different basis in order to
break the deadlock. He suggested a 20-year pact of mutual assistance
which would leave aside the vexed question of frontiers and affirm
Britain's desire that 'Russia, as our ally be strong and secure'.[59] Once
he realised that his proposals for a political treaty were quite
unacceptable both to Britain and the United States, Molotov agreed
to Eden's proposal, but he still wished to continue discussions of the
Soviet draft. After further fruitless discussions, which were not helped
by the presence of the United States Ambassador, Winant, Molotov
finally agreed to telegraph Eden's text to Moscow for approval. On
26 May the treaty was signed. It committed the two powers to mutual
help and assistance during and after the war, and both countries
agreed not to enter into any negotiations with Nazi Germany without
consulting the other. No mention was made of frontiers or the post-
war territorial settlement. It thus fell far short of Soviet expectations,
but there can be little doubt that it was a step forward even though
it did not go all the way to relieve the Soviets of their continuing
suspicions of British motives. For the British it was something of a
triumph, for the master stone-waller, Molotov, had backed down
and accepted a satisfactory compromise.

To celebrate the signing of the treaty the Foreign Office com-
missioned Frank Salisbury to paint a picture of the ceremony. Eden
was horrified at this suggestion, and described Salisbury as an
'excruciating artist'. Sir Kenneth Clark was asked to give his opinion
and spoke grimly of Salisbury's 'ghastly efficiency'. The resulting
picture was felt to be so awful that it was not released to the press.
Salisbury got his commission, a handsome sum, but had hoped that
his picture would be widely reproduced and used for propaganda. In
fact it was given to the Russians whose aesthetic sensibilities were
felt to have been so numbed by years of socialist realism that they
were unlikely to be offended.[60] Apart from this artistic débâcle,
Molotov's visit was a success, although there were reports from the
lobby of the House of Commons that there were a number of
complaints about another Munich and talk of 'acquiescing in an
aggression'.[61]

During Molotov's visit Churchill made an attempt to clarify the
British position on the second front. He invited Molotov to a meeting

attended by Attlee, Eden and the Chiefs of Staff. The visitor opened the proceedings by demanding an immediate attack on western Europe by at least 40 Divisions. Churchill, showing an unusual degree of self-control, replied that a landing would only be possible in areas where the British had control of the air, and that this narrowed the choices to the Pas de Calais, the tip of the Cherbourg peninsula and the area around Brest. He told Molotov that plans were being made to land a force in one or more of these areas in the course of the year, adding that this would only be possible if sufficient landing craft were available, and that he doubted that this would be the case until 1943. In the meantime it was hoped that German forces might be drawn from the eastern front, and the British would continue to engage a large part of the Luftwaffe. He tried to impress upon Molotov the enormous difficulties of mounting a cross-Channel invasion, pointing out that Hitler had desisted from attacking England even though the British army only had 100 tanks, 200 field guns, and a handful of ill-equipped troops after the retreat from Dunkirk. He assured Molotov that he was totally committed to the idea of a second front but repeated that there were enormous difficulties and risks involved in such an operation. It is doubtful whether any of this made much impression on Molotov, although it is possible that the promise of a second front, even in such vague terms and with so many provisos, helped to speed the signing of the treaty. Certainly Stalin was pleased with the treaty, and it would be nice to think that the reason why Molotov kept a pistol under his pillow when staying at Chequers was that he could not break the habits of his revolutionary past, rather than that he harboured sinister suspicions of his hosts.

Questions of the second front and the Soviet frontiers were thus left open, but at least a treaty had been signed. Both Churchill and Eden were convinced that relations with the USSR were now on a completely different footing.[62] Churchill wrote a memorandum for the War Cabinet which called for selected raids on the Continent and for plans for a landing on the Continent in August or September 1942, the availability of landing craft being the main limiting factor. He envisaged a full-scale invasion with the Americans in 1943.[63] Reports from Moscow indicated that although the Russians were still pushing for a second front they were delighted with the treaty.[64] But this fund of goodwill was soon exhausted and the issue of the second front continued to bedevil Anglo–Soviet relations, particularly after the Anglo–American decision to invade French North Africa rather than northern France, a suggestion which Churchill made to Roosevelt during his visit to Washington in June.

6 Churchill Meets Stalin

In February 1942 Stafford Cripps entered the War Cabinet as Lord Privy Seal having finally resigned from his post as Ambassador to the Soviet Union. Although he had wide popular support, particularly from the disaffected left, it was soon apparent that he was no serious threat to Churchill. The House of Commons found his prim and high-minded tone distasteful. The austerity measures he introduced did nothing to increase his popularity, particularly as he seemed to positively relish cutting the petrol ration, imposing a five shilling limit on restaurant meals and reducing the number of sporting events. Cripps and austerity became almost synonymous. Jokes at his expense were widespread and popular. One wit said of him, 'You can just see the home-made lemonade boiling in his veins.' Another had Churchill saying of the Libyan desert, 'There are miles and miles of nothing but arid austerity. How Cripps would like it!'[1] His unsuccessful mission to India in March 1942 further weakened his popularity, although some Conservatives began to appreciate his centrist position. His pleas for a consideration of policies for post-war reconstruction and his endorsement of the ideas of Beveridge and Keynes horrified the far left but did much to maintain his position as one of the dominant figures in British politics. He was still a challenge to Churchill, but not nearly as dangerous as he had seemed some months before.

It would be difficult to find a more striking contrast to Cripps than the new ambassador to the Soviet Union, Sir Archibald Clark Kerr. Compared with the austere and idealistic Cripps, Clark Kerr was positively flamboyant. The teetotaller Cripps was replaced by a man never known to refuse a drink, a point distinctly in his favour as far as the hard-drinking Stalin was concerned. Some memorable drinking bouts would take place between the two men, with the Ambassador reduced to insensibility by his world-class opponent. Clark Kerr had previously been Ambassador to China where he had lost his wife to the American military attaché and developed a taste for Confucian philosophy. His wife, a much younger South American woman of exceptional beauty, having abandoned him, he reaffirmed his homosexual proclivities. He had little liking for his fellow diplomats and preferred the company of journalists and intellectuals. He insisted on writing his witty dispatches with a quill pen. For all his eccentricities, affectations and light-heartedness he was a highly competent diplomatist and a shrewd representative of his Government. Churchill respected him and described him as 'a personal friend of many years standing'.[2] Of all the Ambassadors in Moscow he was probably the closest to Stalin, although this did not amount to very much, and certainly not as much as Clark Kerr fondly imagined.

Clark Kerr was anxious to meet Stalin when he arrived in Moscow in March, but he wisely felt that there was no point in seeing him unless he had something to offer. The Foreign Office could not think of anything to say to Stalin. The Prime Minister had told Stalin that he was thinking of 'other measures' short of the second front to help him out, but no one could find out what these were. It was felt that it might present a bit of a problem to the new ambassador if Stalin were to ask for details. After much head-scratching Eden left it to Clark Kerr's discretion whether or not to pay a visit to the Soviet leader.[3]

The garrulous Ambassador soon found himself almost as frustrated as his predecessor, even though he soon managed to meet Stalin and their encounter was, in his view, a success. He wrote a long letter to Cripps telling him of his difficulties: 'I came here prepared to offer a hell of a lot – all I had. But there is no one to take it! What is a fellow to do?' He confessed that 'A fellow like myself needs I won't say an audience, but a sympathetic readership on the part of others to turn over and have a look at what he has to offer.' He felt that

With Vyshinskii I have established a happy enough relationship. We manage to laugh over our little problems and thus they solve themselves. But with Vyshinskii nothing fundamental can be done. And I feel that what is needed is something fundamental. That bootfaced Molotov made me the most fervent promises of close cooperation and with Stalin I like to think that I clicked. We fraternised over pipes and we were amused by each others jokes. Indeed I found him to be just my cup of tea.

Yet in spite of these jolly meetings with Vyshinskii and Stalin he closed his letter by saying, 'I am only puzzled and uncomfortable and fretful.'[4] He reported to Eden that he was getting on splendidly with

Stalin, adding that 'Probably it was no more than a juxtaposition of two old rogues, each one seeing the roguery of the other and finding a comfort and harmony in it.' Stalin, he added, 'seduced rogue no. 2 with a present of pipe tobacco'.[5]

Apart from his inability to get anywhere with 'that football faced Vyacheslav Mikhailovich Molotov', whose visage never showed the slightest glimmering of an emotion, these convivial rounds continued. It was not until July 1943 that Molotov won over Clark Kerr by presenting him with a tommy gun, which the Ambassador described as 'shining bright and browned in a way that might well out-Purdy Mr. James Purdy' and which not only gave him enormous pleasure but also increased his admiration for the Soviet armaments industry.[6] His pleasure in this gift was enhanced by rogue no. 1 pretending to mow down the assembled ministers and generals who, not sharing the Ambassador's appreciation of his playfulness, were visibly terrified. He got so catastrophically drunk with Vyshinskii that he could not remember a thing of the film he was shown after dinner. Although he strongly objected to the shape of Stalin's pipe, the stem of which 'described a sort of Regent Street quadrant', he enjoyed chatting to him about pipe-smoking. To the Foreign Office he reported that there was 'much talk on a technical level far beyond the reach of the cigarette smoker Molotov'. Stalin's smile he found 'engaging and disarming', and in an extraordinary simile he likened him to a possum. 'A possum that you would get very fond of (against your better judgment), but would have to keep a sharp eye on, lest he nip you in the buttocks out of sheer mischief.' The possum's stomach was given to growling stupendously. 'I mean really on the dictator level.'

All this was entertaining stuff and no doubt relieved much of the routine tedium of work in the Foreign Office, but Clark Kerr's initial enthusiasm for Stalin paid no political dividends. The Ambassador was convinced that only the opening of a second front would relieve the tensions which remained beneath this outward bonhommie. He knew that the Anglo–Soviet Treaty, although a major step forward, was not enough and he reported to the Foreign Office:

> The Treaty was stupendous. I was bowled over by its decency and straightforwardness. It is an immense stride forward and it is full of promise of solid long-term stuff and its value may be incalculable if it is followed up by the something else which all Russians from Vladivostok to the front line trenches are fit to burst for want of.[7]

Pressure for a second front was a natural response to German successes with their renewed offensive. By the end of May they had occupied most of the Crimea. At the end of July Rostov finally fell and the way was open for the critical advance towards Stalingrad. The Germans had regained the strategic initiative after the set-backs of the winter campaign. With the war in the Far East going strongly in favour of the Japanese, and with the relative ineffectiveness of the British air offensive against Germany it seemed doubtful that the British could do much to relieve the pressure on the Soviet Union.

These reverses served to increase Soviet intransigence over the Baltic States. Clark Kerr was convinced that since there was no way of getting the Soviets out of the Baltic States once they were there, it was best to accept this fact and come to terms with them. Churchill felt that such a view was 'full of dangerous admissions'. He also knew that there was strong opposition to any treaty over the Soviet frontiers and did not want 'to face a bunch of resignations'. Sir John Simon turned Clark Kerr's argument around and suggested that as the Soviet Union would get the Baltic States anyway there was no need to sign a treaty which would only serve to antagonise the United States.[8] But as the German campaign in the Soviet Union reached a critical point the second front dominated Anglo–Soviet relations and the issue of the Baltic States seemed somewhat academic.

Having signed the Treaty Molotov travelled to Washington to discuss American plans for the second front. He then returned to London with a communiqué which had been agreed upon in Washington which stated that, 'In the course of the conversations full understanding was reached with regard to the urgent tasks of creating a second front in Europe in 1942.' The British Government had not been consulted about the wording of this communiqué and were naturally concerned that it might be interpreted by the Russians as a firm commitment to open the second front that year. On 9 June the Chiefs of Staff prepared an *aide-mémoire* for a further meeting with Molotov, who was described in the document, as 'Dr. Cocktail'.[9] Although it was full of caveats and contained no promises, it was a somewhat ambiguous statement of the British position. It stated that planning was being undertaken for continental landings in August and September 1942 and that the shortage of landing craft was the main limiting factor. When Molotov arrived in London he was given a note which repeated the arguments presented to him on his first visit, and which spoke of a major Anglo–American operation on the Continent in 1943 with raids in 1942.[10]

The ambiguities contained in these two memoranda were not dispelled when Eden told Molotov that the British Government would accept the wording of the Washington communiqué simply because it could be used to deceive the Germans. Molotov sourly remarked that there should be 'no deception among friends' and Eden blandly agreed. The situation was further confused when Eden repeated the statement on the second front in the House of Commons without offering any comment on its exact meaning. Molotov therefore returned to Moscow with statements from both the American and the British Governments which could be used to exert strong pressure for a second front. The British were angry when they realised that they had been manoeuvred into a very awkward situation, and there was a sigh of relief when Molotov flew home. Eden was furious when Maisky asked him to see Molotov off at midnight, and Cadogan commented on this request, 'What savages!'[11]

Reporting to the War Cabinet on these discussions of a second front, the Prime Minister announced that time constraints on a September raid were such that he had recommended that the idea of a 'three or four days' raid be abandoned in favour of a small hit and run operation'. Although he did not give any details, Churchill presumably had the Dieppe raid in mind, planning for which had begun in April and which was to be launched on 18 August. In Moscow, Molotov told Clark Kerr that he was greatly impressed by Churchill's frankness about the second front, but he persisted in interpreting the communiqué as a solemn pledge that a second front would be opened in 1942. Although this interpretation was clearly unjustified and was obviously designed to push the British into action, there can be little doubt that the British Government failed to make its position perfectly clear. That Molotov could be given an *aide-mémoire* on 9 June which envisaged the possibility of a second front in 1942 and that Churchill could tell the Cabinet two days later that a small raid was all that could be expected, shows that the Government had been somewhat disingenuous.[12]

Molotov refused to listen to Clark Kerr's repeated assertions that no hard and fast promises had been made, and the Soviet authorities continued to insist that the communiqué was a guarantee that the second front would be opened in 1942.[13] The Foreign Office repeated to the Ambassador the arguments which Eden had presented to Molotov that

the passage in Anglo–Soviet communiqué relating to second front was included at express wish of Molotov to correspond to similar passage in United States–Soviet communiqué and we concurred since it would tend to disquiet the Germans. But you will see from the above that we have made no promise of any kind that operations will be undertaken this (repeat this) year.[14]

This argument was simply seen by the Soviets as an attempt to wriggle out of a commitment and a further example of British bad faith.

Additional strain on Anglo–Soviet relations in the summer of 1942 was caused by arguments and mutual recriminations over the Murmansk convoys. German battleships, submarines and shore-based aircraft were deadly in the almost perpetual daylight and with the convoys forced to sail close to the shore because of the danger of ice. The Russians probably did what they could with their limited resources, but were unable to provide any proper protection for the convoys either by air or by sea. Losses were so heavy that the First Sea Lord came to the conclusion that 'the whole thing is a most unsound operation with the dice loaded against us in every direction' and wished to cancel convoys PQ 16 and 17 which were to sail on 18 May and 3 June.[15] Churchill was under considerable pressure not only from the Russians but also from Roosevelt who was determined to clear the backlog of supplies destined for the Soviet Union. He told the Cabinet that the convoys would have to sail 'as a matter of duty'.

PQ 16 was a success, with only seven of the fifty ships lost, the Russians doing their best to provide air cover and submarine escorts. This fortunate outcome, in spite of Pound's dire predictions, plus the slight improvement in Anglo–Soviet relations after the signing of the treaty meant that it was unthinkable that PQ 17 should not be sent. The result was a disaster in which 23 ships were lost out of a total of 34. The British Government therefore decided to cancel PQ 18, for it was agreed that if a large escort were provided from the Home Fleet losses might very well be so heavy that the Germans would gain control of the Atlantic, thus placing Britain in mortal danger. Churchill therefore sent a message to Stalin on 17 July cancelling any further convoys during the period of perpetual daylight.[16]

The reaction of the Soviets was brutal and unfair. Maisky claimed that the PQ 17 disaster was a deliberate ploy designed to show that it was impossible to send convoys, and was supported by Vansittart who told him that Admiral Dudley Pound was a 'poltroon and a sluggard' known on the lower deck as 'don't do it Dudley'. Admiral Kharlamov, the head of the Soviet military mission, claimed that there had been no need for the escort to disperse as the *Tirpitz* could never have caught up with the convoy.[17] Stalin's reply was equally harsh. He wrote to Churchill,

> I received your message of 18 July. Two conclusions could be drawn from it. First, the British Government refuses to continue the sending of war materials to the Soviet Union via the northern route. Second, in spite of the agreed communiqué concerning the urgent tasks of creating a second front in 1942 the British Government postpones this matter until 1943.

He was highly critical of the decision to disperse PQ 17 and refused to accept the arguments for cancelling PQ 18. The War Cabinet decided to ignore this telegram and it was agreed that Maisky should be told why his charges were unwarranted. This made little impression on the Soviet Ambassador who promptly mounted a counter-attack by claiming that the British bomber offensive was dropping off at a time when the Red Army was fighting for its life.

These attacks from the Soviet government were deeply insulting, for the British had sacrificed a great deal in the attempt to live up to the commitments made in the protocol on supplies, but the British knew how serious the situation was in the Soviet Union and tried to think of some way to offer immediate help. The Air Ministry suggested that once Rommel was defeated it would be possible to send 20 squadrons to southern Russia.[18] Maisky tried to convince Eden that the supply situation was so critical that a second front was essential, for Soviet losses might become so great that the Germans would be able to move more troops to the west which would make a landing in France impossible. Churchill reacted to this pressure by calling for a landing in France as well as in French North Africa, both invasions to take place in 1942. Almost in desperation he wrote to Roosevelt,

> We must establish a second front this year and attack at the earliest moment. As I see it this second front consists of a main body holding the enemy pinned opposite SLEDGEHAMMER and a wide flanking movement called TORCH (hitherto called GYMNAST).

Roosevelt replied that planes should be sent to southern Russia immediately and that Stalin should be promised a second front in 1942.[19]

All this was mere wishful thinking. Auchinleck had stopped Rommel's advance into Egypt at the first battle of El Alamein, but the Germans had yet to be defeated in North Africa. Operation Torch could not be launched until November and would make it impossible to even consider a landing in France. But something had to be done to help the Russians. As Clark Kerr wrote,

What the U.S.S.R. wants is some tangible evidence that we realise that the time will come when great and costly efforts will have to be made so far as land fighting on the continent of Europe is concerned. As I see it they are not yet convinced that we understand this, or that we are yet taking the war seriously. They set up their own enormous losses against our (by comparison) trifling losses in men and material since the close of 1939.[20]

The Foreign Office endorsed Clark Kerr's assessment and pointed out to the War Cabinet that British help to the Soviet Union, even though it involved a considerable sacrifice, was merely 'a modest percentage of the material she has used and is using'. A military solution to the immediate problem was almost impossible. Even if the British offensive in North Africa coupled with the Torch landings led to the defeat of the Germans in the desert it was still doubtful whether this would bring much relief to the Russians. There could be no further convoys until September, and no aircraft could be spared until the successful completion of the North African campaign. In such circumstances the only hope of mending the alliance was some dramatic political initiative.

For some time Clark Kerr had been anxious that Churchill should meet Stalin and on 28 July he sent a telegram to Eden suggesting that the Prime Minister should go to Moscow. At that time Churchill's main concern was with the situation in the Middle East and he had decided to go to Cairo to have a close look at the Eighth Army and make sure that they went on the offensive as soon as possible. Eden strongly supported Clark Kerr's suggestion, and felt that it was even more important that Churchill should go to Moscow than to Cairo. Eden gave the Ambassador's letter to the Prime Minister on 30 July and Churchill promptly canvassed the opinion of the War Cabinet. The Cabinet was very concerned about the state of Churchill's health and safety and it was agreed that a final decision should be made at a meeting with Anderson, Cripps and Churchill's doctor, Sir Charles Wilson. Churchill brushed aside all objections to the trip, and on 31

July Cadogan telegraphed Clark Kerr telling him that the Prime
Minister would visit Stalin after going to Cairo. It had been hoped
that the meeting could be arranged in Astrakhan, but Stalin insisted
that he could not leave Moscow. President Roosevelt was consulted
and gave his blessing to the mission, and it was agreed that Averell
Harriman should travel with the British delegation as a gesture of
American approval.[21]

Churchill was keen to go to Moscow, but he knew that his task
would be very difficult. He told his doctor, 'We may go to see Stalin.
He won't like what I have to say to him. I'm not looking forward to
it.'[22] The reason was obvious. In spite of the exchange of telegrams
with the President he knew that he had to tell Stalin that there would
be no second front in 1942, and, judging from previous experience,
the Soviet leader's response was liable to be extremely unpleasant.
In spite of all these misgivings preparations were immediately made
for the trip to Moscow, codenamed 'Operation Bracelet'.

After his visit to Cairo, Churchill arrived in the Soviet Union on
12 August. His plane landed at a military airfield outside Moscow
and was met by a large crowd which included, in Clark Kerr's
account, 'Molotov and his gang, Marshal Shaposhnikov (specially
dosed, poor old man! for the occasion and hardly able to stand on
his feet), the American Ambassador and all his guys, I and mine
and innumerable photographers'. Churchill had some difficulty in
extricating himself from the machine, as the door was underneath
rather than at the side. The British Ambassador described the scene:

> The first glimpse I had of the P.M. was a pair of stout legs dangling
> from the belly of the 'plane and feeling for *terra firma*. They found
> it and then came the plump trunk and finally the round football
> head, and quite a normal hat. All this stooped under the machine,
> but it scrabbled successfully out and drew itself up. It was like a
> bull at the *corrida* when it first comes out of its dark pen and stands
> dazzled and bewildered and glares at the crowd. Like the bull's
> the P.M.'s eyes were bloodshot and defiant and like the bull he
> stood and swayed as if uncertain where to make the first charge.
> But the charge came from the crowd, headed by Molotov, and the
> bull was lost to sight in a wild scrum.

Churchill arrived in Moscow without his entourage. Cadogan,
Wavell, Brooke and Tedder were in a second Liberator which was
stuck in Tehran with engine trouble. They were highly alarmed at

what the Prime Minister might do in Moscow without their restraining influence, but they had no grounds for concern. Clark Kerr gave him excellent advice, and managed a difficult situation and a truculent Prime Minister with considerable skill.

Repairing to Stalin's own dacha which had been prepared for him, Churchill asked the Ambassador what the Russians wanted. Clark Kerr replied that there was only one thing: a second front in Europe and quickly. Churchill grunted that they were not going to get it, at least not until the following year, and that he had come to Moscow to tell this to Stalin. He added that there was to be a full-dress Anglo–American invasion of French North Africa combined with commando raids on France. He asked what Stalin's likely response to this alternative to an immediate second front would be. Clark Kerr replied that Stalin would be very disappointed, but if it were put to him forcefully this might be followed by consolation and even by pleasure.

After a large meal and considerable quantities of drink, Churchill went off to meet Stalin in the Kremlin. The meeting lasted for about three hours and was, as Clark Kerr wrote, 'full of ups and downs. But in the end the ups prevailed.' Churchill told Stalin that he was preparing for a very great operation in 1943. Stalin suggested a demonstration in the Pas de Calais. Churchill replied that this would be 'a waste of seed corn'. Stalin countered that there was not a single German division in France of any value. Churchill replied that there were 25 Divisions and that 9 of them were first class. Stalin objected that German divisions only consisted of two Regiments and added a cruel gibe that 'a man who is not prepared to take risks could not win a war'. He was not at all impressed by Churchill's promises to help him meet the German offensive in the Caucasus and the Caspian, but at least he agreed that it was necessary to bomb the Germans into total submission. It would also seem that Stalin accepted Churchill's arguments in favour of Operation Torch.[23]

The meeting was conducted in a curious atmosphere. Stalin constantly leaped up to stuff cigarettes into his pipe, and Churchill shuffled around in an attempt to stop his trousers sticking to his chair. Clark Kerr was delighted that this first session ended in 'much apparent understanding and goodwill', and Churchill returned to his dacha at 11 o'clock in excellent spirits. The Ambassador was relieved that everything had gone so well, his only peeve being Harriman's distressing tendency to 'bumsuck' the Prime Minister and Churchill's obvious pleasure at such treatment.

The next morning Clark Kerr found Churchill in a querulous mood due, he felt, to an excess of Caucasian wine the previous evening. At luncheon Harriman continued to be as sycophantic as ever, infuriating the British Ambassador with such 'sustained bumsucking'. Churchill complained of a headache and lay his head on the table like a small child. Taking Harriman by the hand he said, 'I'm so glad, Averell, that you came with me, you are a tower of strength.' While Harriman consoled the Prime Minister, Clark Kerr was rewarded with hostile glances from his temperamental and difficult guest. After luncheon Clark Kerr went for a stroll in the garden with Sir Charles Wilson who told him that there was no accounting for his patient's black bile, but that it was unfortunately a frequent manifestation. Their only consolation was that Churchill had been pleased with his first encounter with Stalin and had remarked to his doctor, 'I want that man to like me.' They hoped that the Prime Minister would recover from his unfortunate mood and be on his best behaviour when next he met Stalin.

Churchill's first appointment that day was with Molotov who immediately demanded a second front and ignored any reference to Operation Torch. While the Prime Minister was engaged with Molotov, Clark Kerr went off to meet the rest of the British delegation who were due to arrive from Teheran. Shaposhnikov, drunk again, welcomed them on behalf of the Soviet Government. Clark Kerr was furious with the bad manners of the soldiers who refused to speak to the Russians, and spent all the time fussing about their luggage and chattering among themselves. Finally the Ambassador cornered Wavell, who spoke Russian, and forced him to make some effort to be polite. Alan Brooke reminded him of a rabbit. 'Not the quick white scutted little animal that dashes out of the bracken to be shot, but the hutch rabbit, the Belgian hare, that placidly nibbles bottom leaves and makes a hell of a stink because he can't help it.'

After a most unsatisfactory meeting with Molotov, Churchill was handed a note from Stalin on the second front. It pointed out that a second front had been promised in the Anglo–Soviet communiqué of 12 June 1942. It went on to claim that the Russians were doing most of the fighting and that there was no serious German military presence in France. Churchill's reply repeated all the familiar British arguments.

The meeting with Molotov and the note from Stalin should have been sufficient warning that the Russians were beginning to get tough, but Churchill was confident that his meeting with Stalin that evening would go well. He told Tedder that he considered Stalin to be a peasant whom he could handle without any difficulty.[24] Clark Kerr was not included in the party which set off for the Kremlin that evening, but it is uncertain whether this was out of spite as he thought, or because Cadogan had now arrived. The meeting was a disaster. The interpreters, Dunlop and Pavlov, were very poor, and that added to the difficulties. Stalin began by repeating the arguments he had used in the message he sent to Churchill earlier in the day, accusing the Allies of bad faith and saying that although there were sound military arguments in favour of Operation Torch it would do nothing to help the Russians. He insisted that supplies were failing to reach Russia not because of enemy action, but because of the low priority given to them by the British and the Americans. He asked that six to eight Divisions should be landed on the Cherbourg Peninsula as soon as possible. Churchill replied that this 'overlooked the existence of the Channel'. Most insulting of all, Stalin told Churchill that the main reason why the British refused to open the second front was that they were frightened of the Germans. Churchill replied furiously that he found no 'ring of comradeship' in anything Stalin said. The meeting ended at 12.45 a.m., leaving Churchill most upset. He felt that he had established a good rapport with Stalin at their first meeting, now he realised that this simple peasant was not quite so easy to manage as he had imagined. Harriman tried to comfort him by saying that this was typical Stalin treatment: first he was nice and then he got nasty. He and Beaverbrook had experienced exactly the same thing in 1941.[25] Harriman stayed with Churchill until 3 a.m. in an attempt to calm him down, but with little success.

Clark Kerr went round to the Prime Minister's dacha the following morning to find everyone 'scuttling about like startled hens'. He was told that Stalin had been 'obstinate and truculent', and no one seemed to know why. Clark Kerr believed that he had been a little carried away by the Prime Minister's masterly presentation of Operation Torch at their first meeting, and was now trying to divert Torch from North Africa to France. Churchill wandered around the dacha 'like a wounded lion', dressed in a vivid dressing gown and denouncing Stalin in 'ponderous Gibbonesque periods'. He announced that he was damned if he was going to dine with Stalin that night. The Ambassador was furious that the 'champion bumsucker' Harriman, 'that footling Commander Thompson' and the 'nice and apparently intelligent Rowan', were all 'subscribing to the P.M.'s indignation and to the imprudent things that it prompted him to say'. Clark Kerr was livid that nothing was done to calm Churchill, and he felt that 'at Luncheon the P.M. was at his bloody worst and his worst is really bloody'. He came to the conclusion that what Churchill really deserved was 'a good root up the arse'. Then, much to everyone's intense relief, the 'good doctor', Wilson, managed to persuade Churchill to go to bed for his afternoon nap.

In spite of his protestations, Churchill agreed to dine with Stalin that night, but he went off to the Kremlin in a foul mood. Stalin put on a lavish banquet for Churchill, with more than one hundred guests assembled in a room which had at one time been Catherine the Great's bedroom, a venue which greatly appealed to Clark Kerr. The Prime Minister arrived at dinner wearing

> a dreadful garment which he claimed to have designed himself to wear during air raids ... It looks like a mechanic's overalls or more still like a child's rompers or crawlers. All the bourgeois Bolshevists, in uniform or in their prim black bourgeois suits, stared in amazement.

The splendour of the occasion did nothing to improve Churchill's temper, and he was utterly impervious to Stalin's determined efforts to charm him. Clark Kerr was very annoyed with the soldiers for making no attempt to be sociable. The one exception was Tedder, 'who got on hugging terms with no. 1 Gestapo Chief Beria, who was very drunk'. The taciturn Wavell, in spite of his knowledge of the language, was true to form. Brooke, who disliked this 'semi-Asiatic race with innate bargaining instincts' and who 'got so bored and disgusted at looking at food', gave curt answers to Voroshilov's questions, but never asked any of his own.[26] At 1.30 a.m. Churchill stormed off with Stalin running after him, prompting Clark Kerr to wonder whether grumpiness and bad manners were the key to Bolshevik hearts. Back at the dacha Churchill announced that he would leave without seeing Stalin again. At quarter to four he climbed into bed, put on his black eye-shade and prepared to sleep, determined to leave Moscow as soon as possible.

The unfortunate Clark Kerr arrived at the Prime Minister's lodgings on the morning of 15 August to find an even more chaotic scene than on the previous day. Churchill stuck to his decision to pack his bags and leave, announcing that he had had more than enough of Stalin, and was damned if he would see him again. Cadogan, fortified by an excess of vodka, had tried the previous evening to make the Prime

Minister see reason, but had failed miserably. Now he asked Clark Kerr if he was willing to make one final attempt. Preparing for what he knew would be a frightful ordeal, the Ambassador wandered around a raspberry patch to collect his thoughts. Among the raspberry canes he discovered Dr Wilson, also deep in thought. Wilson told Clark Kerr that Churchill was convinced that Stalin was trying to make the visit a complete failure in an attempt to bring down his Government. How Churchill managed to get this extraordinary idea is unclear, but he was in a mood to believe almost anything. Wilson did much to strengthen Clark Kerr's resolve, insisting that this was the last chance to overcome the breach between the two statesmen.

At this point Cadogan appeared on the scene and announced that the 'minotaur was ready for his next victim'. Clark Kerr asked to see the Prime Minister alone. He found him 'lowering and sullen', but he managed to persuade him to go for a stroll. Churchill put on his 'preposterous ten gallon hat', armed himself with a stick, and marched off onto the terrace with Clark Kerr following in his wake. The Ambassador warned him of the consequences if his mission to Moscow were a failure, both to Churchill's position at home and to Russia's prospects in the war. He insisted that he should not allow himself to be offended 'by a peasant who didn't know any better'. Churchill listened in silence, then returned to the dacha leaving Clark Kerr outside. Shortly afterwards Cadogan called him to Churchill's room. Churchill told Cadogan that Clark Kerr thought the whole situation was his own fault, and then he began to chuckle. Clark Kerr had succeeded.

A very bibulous luncheon followed at which Churchill was in an exhilarated mood. He delivered a spirited harangue in defence of the aristocracy, denouncing the 'pedlars of Brummagum and the filthy iron works from which the Baldwins had made their money'. At six o'clock a message arrived from the Kremlin asking Churchill to visit Stalin at seven. The Prime Minister set off in high spirits, 'declaring that he would not leave the Kremlin until he had Stalin in his pocket'. Accompanied by a new and excellent interpreter, Birse, a Scotsman educated in Russia, he arrived at the Kremlin determined to do his utmost to make the visit a success.

When the two statesmen met it soon became obvious that it was Stalin who was in a bad mood and Churchill who was cheerful. It took more than an hour for the ice to break and for Stalin to invite Churchill to stay for dinner. Back at the dacha Clark Kerr and Cadogan dined with General Anders, the Commander-in-Chief of the Polish Army in Soviet territory. At 1.30 a.m. Clark Kerr slipped away and fell asleep on a sofa, to be awoken at about 3 o'clock by the noisy return of the Prime Minister's party. After exchanging a few words with Anders, Churchill flung himself on a sofa, kicked his legs in the air and told the assembled company what a splendid evening he had enjoyed, and what a pleasure it was to work 'with that great man'. He then yelled for his man to draw him a bath and began to tear his clothes off. With a huge cigar clamped in his mouth he stood in front of the Ambassador half-naked. 'From under his skimpy vest penis and a pair of crinkled creamy buttocks protruded.' He talked warmly of Stalin, apologised handsomely to Clark Kerr for his behaviour, and then departed to take his bath to refresh himself for the flight home which was due to leave at 5.30 a.m.

Churchill's dinner with Stalin was quite an affair. Mounds of food were produced: suckling pig, two chickens, beef, mutton and various types of fish. Stalin attacked the pig, scooping out the brains with his knife, then slicing the cheeks and eating the flesh with his fingers. Stalin's daughter Svetlana made a brief appearance, and Churchill was much impressed by this red-headed well-favoured girl, and took this visit as a sign that Stalin was welcoming him into his family. A somewhat discordant note was introduced into this friendly conversation when Stalin dismissed the liquidation of ten million kulaks with the remark, 'What is one generation?' Stalin endorsed Churchill's plan for an attack on northern Norway and Petsamo in November 1942, codenamed 'Operation Jupiter', although Churchill knew full well that the British and American staffs were not at all enthusiastic about the scheme. Stalin was not at all interested in 'Operation Velvet', a plan to send an Anglo–American air force to the Caucasus.[27] On the personal level Stalin said of Maisky, 'He talks too much and cannot keep his tongue between his teeth.' This was the first indication that Maisky's days as Soviet Ambassador in London were numbered.

Talks held between the British and Soviet military were inconclusive. Voroshilov said that the German forces in the south of Russia posed a real threat to India, even though Stalin had denied this on the 13th, and that a second front was the only way to secure the Middle East and India. Voroshilov also announced that he had no intention of authorising the building of airfields in the Caucasus and neither Brooke nor Tedder could give any indication of the number of aircraft that would be available for Operation Velvet. There was also no agreement on the exchange of technical information. Mutual suspicion and a reluctance to share any secrets made any such arrangement impossible, and the Soviets had to continue to rely on their agents and spys in Britain to extract the information they required.

Looking back on Churchill's visit to Moscow, John Reed of the Moscow Embassy wrote to Clark Kerr that his masterly handling of the Prime Minister caused him to recall 'distant memories of nursery governesses reconciling fractious little boys', but he gave Churchill full marks for suffering 'with good grace the sycophantic and quite exceptionally silly conversation of the American Ambassador'. He described Cadogan as a 'rather wan, formalistic gentleman', and he complained bitterly of the Generals who distinguished themselves 'by their bad, or rather inadequate manners'. John Reed thought that Stalin was drunk at the Kremlin banquet and he made two or three toasts to the British intelligence officers present, reminding them grimly of the dangers of their work and the horrible penalties it might entail. This had caused the unfortunate Admiral Miles to go bright red. Stalin also announced that the one good thing about Molotov was that he knew how to drink. Frank Roberts had felt that the behaviour of Churchill and Stalin was 'disconcertingly reminiscent of the wayward gambols of cats amusing their future dinners'.[28] Cadogan used a somewhat similar analogy in a letter to Eden in which he said of the relationship between Stalin and Churchill, 'The courtship of the larger and more temperamental mammals presents some puzzling features.'[29] Churchill had amused himself with a zoological simile when told that his dacha was bugged by saying of his hosts, 'They are lower on the scale of nature than the orang-outang. Now let them take that down and translate it into Russian.'[30]

It is difficult to assess the importance of Churchill's first meeting with Stalin. Nothing concrete was settled, and the Soviets still refused to accept the British arguments about the difficulties of a landing in France. Clark Kerr had managed to persuade Churchill to meet Stalin again, and thus avoided a rupture which could have had disastrous consequences. Churchill now believed that Stalin was his friend, but this was not a view shared by all of the British delegation. Colonel Jacob, a sound judge of character, remarked that making friends with Stalin was like making friends with a python, and he was unable to forget the story that General Anders had told him. When Anders asked Stalin what had happened to some 8000 Polish officers who had been imprisoned in 1939 he shrugged his shoulders and suggested that they had all run away.[31] The discovery of the mass grave at Katyn in April 1943 was soon to reveal the grim truth. The British delegation were also unable to decide who was really in charge in the Soviet Union. Desmond Morton told Dalton that he was convinced that Stalin was merely the tool of the Politburo, and Churchill frequently put this view forward whenever he wished to explain away some of Stalin's more outrageous behaviour. The British were thus as mystified as ever by the behaviour of the Russians, and the attempt to explain their behaviour by thinking of them as a bunch of peasants who had not had the good fortune to be educated at either Eton or Harrow did little to clarify the situation. 'Operation Bracelet' was thus in no sense a turning point in Anglo–Soviet relations.

7 Fronts and Frontiers

In the summer of 1942 the Ministry of Information reported that there was growing impatience about a second front.[1] As the German advance continued, public opinion tended to feel that the second front might be too late, and there was a suspicion that Britain was leaving Russia and Germany to fight it out because the Government did not want Russia to come out of the war too strong.[2] When the battle for Stalingrad began in September there was an extraordinary wave of sympathy for the Soviet Union and a widespread conviction that Stalingrad would fall unless something dramatic was done to relieve the pressure on the Russian front. Sympathy for the Soviet people in their life and death struggle did not necessarily involve an uncritical attitude towards Soviet society. In the words of one report,

> The recollection of eulogy and anathema rapidly succeeding one another, often in the same quarters, has produced considerable cynicism as well as an appreciable devaluation of the organs of opinion in the public mind.

The question of religious freedom in the USSR was a matter of considerable concern. The Soviet Union was still seen as a police state, and the GPU represented in the public mind everything that was most brutal and unattractive about the Soviet Union. There was a general questioning of the long-term aims of Soviet policy, but the Moscow show trials and the pact with Nazi Germany had been largely forgotten. The jovial pipe-smoking Stalin with his taxi driver's cap was in charge and the Soviet Union was seen as a mighty ally badly in need in every possible help.

With the beginnings of a British offensive in North Africa demands for a second front began to die down, but there was still a deep concern, particularly among the working class, that relations with the Soviet Union needed considerable improvement. There was tremendous admiration for the courage of the Red Army which became symbolised in the resistance of the men at Stalingrad.

141

Although Soviet society was not seen as a blue print for a future society, many people felt that a number of useful tips would be gained from the Soviet system when it came to rebuilding Britain after the war.[3] Enthusiasm for the Soviet Union probably reached its height when the Germans were defeated at Stalingrad. Ministry of Information reports indicated that there was a 'deep-seated sympathy' for the Soviet Union, which was seen as 'the true country of the ordinary people'.[4]

Sympathy for the Soviet Union, the desire for closer ties between the two countries, and the growing public demand for sweeping domestic changes in post-war Britain all helped to revive Eden's ambitions to make a bid for supreme office. Oliver Harvey egged him on, but unlike Beaverbrook, Eden was reluctant openly to attack Churchill and his policies. But by September Eden told Harvey that he would like to be Prime Minister during the war, and not wait until it was over. He even started thinking about possible cabinet appointments.[5] Eden planned a Conservative–Labour coalition, with the Communist Party in opposition, which would be firmly committed to post-war reconstruction and to close ties with the Soviet Union. Churchill's fortunes were at a low ebb. The heroic summer of 1940 when the Prime Minister had his finest hour was beginning to fade in the memory. There had as yet been no real military success. Churchill's visit to Moscow had done little to improve relations between the two countries. He still refused to turn his mind to post-war reconstruction. His attitude to the Soviet Union was curiously ambivalent for, as Oliver Harvey wrote, 'He hates Russia and all that it stands for, though he will do his utmost to help her win the war.'[6] At least Churchill wanted a second front rather more urgently than the Chiefs of Staff, who were prepared to send some arms to Russia until the Germans were worn down and then attack the 'exhausted animal' in 1944. Both Churchill and Eden were strongly opposed to this attitude in 1942, although as far as the Soviets were concerned it was precisely the policy which the British government adopted.[7] The victory of El Alamein abruptly shattered Eden's day-dreams and, as the church bells rang throughout the country, he once again resigned himself to playing the role of heir apparent.

Meanwhile, Churchill returned to London and told his colleagues in the War Cabinet that he was greatly impressed by Stalin and 'had formed the highest opinion of his sagacity'.[8] The Prime Minister did not need Maisky's constant promptings to be reminded that help for the Soviet Union was a top priority. In a memorandum for Brigadier

Hollis of the Chiefs of Staff Committee he pointed out that keeping Russia supplied was 'one of the three or four most important vital objects before us'. He suggested that this could either be done by resuming the PQ convoys or by his pet favourite, 'Operation Jupiter', designed to clear the Germans out of northern Norway. He hoped that if the French supported 'Operation Torch' it might be possible to spare troops for 'Jupiter'. He was strongly critical of the pessimistic analysis of the possibilities of 'Jupiter' given by General McNaughton, the Canadian Commander-in-Chief in England. Stalin had offered to support 'Jupiter' with an offensive near Petsamo, although he knew all too well that if 'Torch' and 'Jupiter' both went ahead there could be no question of a landing in France ('Operation Round-Up') until 1944.[9]

Once again Churchill was swept away by his enthusiasm for a pet project. He wrote to Roosevelt suggesting that if 'Torch' went well the Allies should consider launching 'Jupiter' rather than an attack on Sicily, Sardinia or even Italy. 'Jupiter' would, he felt, do something to counter Stalin's disappointment at the postponement of 'Round-Up' and the cancellation of further convoys, possibly until 1943. Perhaps in an attempt to check his own enthusiasm for the project, he warned that there was no guarantee that 'Jupiter' would be successful.[10] Churchill then wrote to Stalin suggesting that General McNaughton, whom he described as 'a man of very great ability and independence of mind', should go to Moscow to discuss 'Jupiter'.[11] Two days later he again wrote to Roosevelt saying that it was doubtful if 'Torch' would leave enough shipping available for 'Jupiter' and expressing his grave concern that relations with the Soviet Union had reached a critical juncture. He suggested that it was vitally important to find out exactly what Stalin thought of 'Jupiter' and how important it was to him.[12] Churchill then asked Mackenzie King, the Canadian Prime Minister, if McNaughton could be sent to Moscow. This was a curious choice, for Churchill knew of McNaughton's reservations about 'Jupiter'. Perhaps it was designed to convince Stalin that much as the British Government supported 'Jupiter' it was not militarily sound at that time. On 7 October Churchill drafted a letter to Stalin in which there was vague mention of an attack on northern Norway, but in the context of the letter it was clear that this was hardly a serious offer. He also said that he hoped it would be possible to resume regular convoys in January 1943.[13] 'Jupiter' was soon forgotten, and PQ 18 in September had not been a total disaster, although losses had been serious in spite of the fact that it was the most heavily defended convoy ever to sail the Arctic route. Without 'Jupiter' to clear the airfields, any future convoy would still be dangerously vulnerable to air attack. Churchill therefore told Stalin that the only possibility was to send isolated ships at 200 mile intervals on moonless nights.

With the convoys cancelled and 'Operation Torch' making it impossible to consider 'Operation Jupiter', the only immediate possibility of helping the Russians was to send an air force to the Soviet southern flank. Enthusiasm for a second front in France had dwindled considerably after the heavy casualties suffered during the Dieppe fiasco. Churchill made this offer in his message to Stalin on 7 October and proposed sending 5 bomber and 9 fighter squadrons from the RAF and one transport and one heavy bomber squadron from the USAAF to arrive in the Soviet Union early in 1943. The project was given the code name 'Operation Velvet'. Churchill felt that this operation was politically desirable, as he liked the idea of British airmen fighting alongside the Russians. In November Air Marshall Drummond went to Moscow to discuss placing these squadrons in the Caucasus, but the Russians were less than enthusiastic. On behalf of the Soviet air force Falalaev told Drummond that he would welcome the aircraft, but had no need of the crews. Stalin did not bother to answer Churchill's note for almost a month, and on 5 November he accepted a repeated offer from the Prime Minister. By now the Soviet position in the Caucasus had strengthened greatly, their counter-stroke at the end of November removed the immediate danger so that the need for reinforcements was no longer so acute. On 13 December Molotov turned down the 'Velvet' proposal, arguing that it would interfere with the flow of supplies from the Persian Gulf.[14] Drummond left Moscow on Boxing Day having spent almost six weeks in fruitless discussions. There was no longer any serious threat to the Caucasus or to British positions in the Middle East, so that traditional Russian suspicion of foreigners on their soil reasserted itself, and there could be no question of that 'genuine spirit of comradeship in arms' for which Portal had hoped.

While the British Government still waited for reactions to 'Operation Velvet' the War Cabinet discussed the parlous state of Anglo–Soviet relations. Various suggestions were made as to why they had deteriorated so badly. Was the Soviet regime under popular attack for the terrible losses suffered by the people, and were they therefore trying to put the blame on the Allies? Was the military now playing a more important role in the affairs of state? Were the Soviets afraid that they might be cheated out of the fruits of such a costly victory by the British and the Americans acting in concert? No answers were offered to these speculations and the Prime Minister suggested that the best way to improve relations with the Soviet Union was to follow up the victory at El Alamein with the total destruction of Axis forces in North Africa. He imagined, mistakenly as it turned out, that this would be a tremendous boost to Soviet morale.[15]

British military successes in the desert did nothing to improve relations with the Soviet Union for the time being, although the Soviet press did give some coverage of the North African campaign. At the end of October, Churchill told the War Cabinet that it was vitally important to open the second front in 1943 as Stalin 'had prompted him' on this point during his visit to Moscow.[16] A few days later the Prime Minister wrote to Stalin announcing that Rommel was defeated, 'Operation Torch' was imminent (in fact the landings began three days later) and he repeated the offer to send aircraft to the Caucasus, this time increasing the number to 20 squadrons. Stalin replied that he needed the squadrons as soon as possible, but as the situation on the eastern front improved he changed his mind once again.[17]

By the end of 1942 it seemed that there had been a slight improvement in Anglo–Soviet relations. Summing up the experiences of the past year, Cadogan suggested that the way was open for closer cooperation with the Soviet Union. He felt that if the Russians were fully informed of British military planning, schemes for a post-war settlement and of any other matter in which Soviet interests were involved, then they would be much more forthcoming. Cadogan argued that the British Government had not always been fully frank with the Soviets. Perhaps a New Year's resolution to this effect would improve matters.[18]

In January 1943 it was suggested that a senior scientific adviser, Sir Henry Tizard, should head a mission that would go to Moscow in order to discuss the exchange of technical information.[19] Eden complained to Churchill that the Russians were not giving much military information, but he suggested that 'in the interests of the common war effort' the British should not withhold information from them which might be of operational value. A major problem was to find an adequate definition of technical information. The Russians, for example, were asking for details of the manufacturing process of plywood. Plywood was widely used in vehicles and aircraft, but was it essential to the war effort? The suggestion that Tizard should go to Moscow prompted a swift and violent reaction from his arch-rival, 'Prof' Lindemann, now Lord Cherwell. Cherwell told Churchill that as the Russians refused to divulge any of their military secrets he saw no reason why the British should give them any of theirs.[20] Eden objected strongly to the idea of using technical information as a bargaining tool and wanted to help the Soviet Union as much as possible without necessarily asking for anything but goodwill in return. Lyttelton, the Minister of Production, agreed with Eden. After considerable wrangling a compromise was reached whereby it was agreed that Tizard should be furnished with a supplementary list of technical information which would only be disclosed if the Soviets were cooperative.[21] A draft 'Charter for the Exchange of Intelligence between Soviet and British Staffs' was then drawn up which called for the exchange of operational intelligence, enemy intelligence, tactical information and general war experience. The British military attaché in Moscow, General Martel, was to be given a personal letter from Churchill to Stalin in support of this agreement, and it was hoped that this would mark the beginning of a new era in Anglo–Soviet cooperation.

In spite of this inspiring talk of a new era, the Chiefs of Staff continued to be opposed to the idea of sending any information to the Russians that was not absolutely necessary. They also insisted that all such information should be channelled through the British Military Mission in Moscow and not through the Ambassador.[22] Eden and Cadogan agreed that Clark Kerr should be given all the information possible which he could use to improve his position with Stalin. Christopher Warner felt that the arguments put forward by the Chiefs of Staff that there should be an absolutely equal exchange of information with the Soviets was prompted by their desire to 'avoid letting their skeletons out of the cupboard'. Clark Kerr rejected the Chiefs' arguments in a forceful dispatch, and Orme Sargent agreed that the Ambassador should be given 'all possible straw with which to make his political bricks in the Kremlin'. The Chiefs of Staff were unmoved by these arguments, and Hollis informed Sargent that they refused to change their minds.[23] The Foreign Office tried to get the Chiefs of Staff to produce a military survey on the second front which might have helped Clark Kerr in his arguments with the Soviet authorities, but they flatly refused. The Air Ministry also turned down a Foreign Office request to open a regular direct flight to Moscow.[24]

Faced with the intransigence of the Chiefs of Staff, Eden began to waver, suggesting that if military information were filtered through the Military Mission in Moscow it might upgrade its importance, but he agreed to wait on further developments. In spite of his friend Cherwell's objections, Churchill supported the idea of the Tizard mission which was to include two distinguished scientists, Cockcroft and Blackett. Churchill told Cadogan that 'we are too much in these people's debt already on account of their vigorous fighting'.[25] But this encouragement from on high did little to change the situation. Tizard fell ill and the offer to send the mission had to be postponed. At the end of April 1943 the Soviets were finally informed of the proposal to send the scientists to Moscow, but the British received no reply. By mid-June Churchill had to agree with the Chiefs of Staff that the mission should be cancelled for there was still no answer from the Russians. Almost a month later Clark Kerr mentioned the mission in the course of a conversation with Molotov who promptly announced that he was enthusiastically in favour of receiving the mission, saying that he greatly valued any information that Tizard might bring.[26]

While they waited for the Russians to make up their minds whether they wanted the Tizard mission to come, the British discussed what technical information should be withheld from the Russians. It was agreed that they should not be given any information about high frequency radar, the latest radar-controlled bomb sights, radio proximity fuses, impulse signalling and the radar-jamming device 'Window'. It was agreed that the Russians could be given radar equipment that was already being used, but that they should not be given any details of research and development. Further complications were caused when the United States Government objected to any exchange of technical information on the extraordinary grounds that the Russians might hand over the information to the Japanese. The Americans tried to stop the British giving the Russians any information on jet propulsion, heated wing de-icing, pressurised cabins for fighter aircraft and a number of similar items. Under such circumstances it is hardly surprising that the Russians were less than enthusiastic to welcome Tizard, and by late 1943 the Americans suggested that a tripartite agreement on the exchange of technical information might be the best way to get something out of the Russians. This suggestion was strongly supported by Sir Stafford Cripps.[27]

Since the Allies were so unwilling to share technical information the Soviets decided to resort to espionage. The national organiser of the Communist Party and the man who recruited Kim Philby into the NKVD, Douglas Frank Springhall, managed to get information on 'Window' from a Mrs Sheehan who worked for the Air Ministry which he passed on to the Russians. Springhall was tried in camera, found guilty and sentenced at the Old Bailey to seven years' imprisonment. One Captain Oren was also cashiered for passing on information to Springhall.[28]

Stalin had been invited to join Churchill and Roosevelt at Casablanca in January 1943, but he had declined. He had little reason to be pleased with the outcome. The Americans had agreed to the British proposal to invade Sicily prior to an invasion of France, and this meant that there could be no question of landing troops in France until 1944, unless there were a sudden and unexpected German collapse. Stalin was not convinced by the arguments in favour of this Mediterranean strategy. For him the second front was synonymous with the invasion of northern France. On returning to England from Casablanca, Churchill wrote to Stalin saying that such an invasion might be possible as early as August 1943, the major limiting factor being the shortage of landing craft. Stalin, who was by now familiar with the argument about landing craft, correctly took this to mean that there would be no invasion of France until 1944 and complained bitterly at the lack of urgency in tackling this central issue.[29]

Continuing difficulties with Stalin lent some credence to the theory that he was fighting a strong opposition group within his own Government. As Churchill put it in a letter to Eden, there seemed to be two Stalins: 'a) Stalin himself, personally cordial to me. b) Stalin in council, a grim thing behind him, which we and he have both to reckon with.'[30] When Clark Kerr returned to Moscow after his leave in February he was asked to find out what substance lay behind these rumours. He was unable to find any satisfactory answer, although since he found Stalin personally most attractive he tended towards the view that his power was limited by another group hostile to the Western Allies.

After the victories at Stalingrad and El Alamein and the successful conclusion of the North African campaign, there was growing concern about the shape of the post-war world. At the top of the list of those who thought that Russia was hell-bent on expansion in Europe was Clement Attlee. In January, 1943 he told Dalton that the Soviet Union would take over all the Slav states and that it would therefore be necessary to be harsher on Germany than after the last war.[31] Within the War Cabinet it was Beaverbrook who had most strongly opposed such views. He had tried to stop the appointment of Attlee as Deputy Prime Minister on the grounds that he consistently tried to block any sensible and cooperative policy with Russia, and he had threatened to resign from the Cabinet over the issue of the recognition of the Baltic States. Beaverbrook claimed that Attlee's persistently anti-Soviet attitude had been one of the main reasons for his resignation from the War Cabinet.[32] Having left the War Cabinet, Beaverbrook became the leading spokesman for full cooperation with the Soviet Union. In February 1943 he told the House of Lords,

> If Russia should win the war in Europe, if Russia should 'pull it off' every sensible person in the British Empire will rejoice and rejoice greatly ... For my part, I welcome the growing influence and expanding power of Russia.

He confessed that he was 'tremendously impressed by the Stalin philosophy', with the significant difference that he was still an unashamed enthusiast for profit and private enterprise, and he looked forward to the day when Europe would be controlled by a consortium of the Soviet Union and Britain.[33] Beaverbrook saw supplies as the key to an understanding with Russia, and continually complained that they were insufficient. In February he wrote to Eden,

> Certainly we have been parsimonious in the supplies we have sent to Russia. We produce, say, 7000 airplanes a month. We send 400 to Russia – about 5 per cent of the total output. So the Russians do 90% of the fighting and get 5% of our – U.S.A. and Great Britain, output of planes.[34]

While Beaverbrook was pressing for increased supplies for the Soviet Union the Foreign Office was beginning to think that they should be reduced. American supplies to Russia were increasing, the output of Soviet factories grew steadily, and with planning beginning for the invasion of Europe it was felt that a thorough review of supply policy was badly needed.[35] The Foreign Office remained convinced that the key to a better understanding with the Soviet Union lay in an agreement over the post-war settlement. Churchill seldom addressed his mind to such problems, and when he did he indulged in vague ramblings which infuriated the Foreign Office. In February 1942 he had written,

No-one can predict with certainty that the victors will never quarrel among themselves, or that the United States may not once again retire from Europe, but after the experiences which all have gone through, and their sufferings, and the certainty that the third struggle will destroy all that is left of the culture, wealth and civilisation of mankind and reduce us to a level almost of wild beasts, the most intense effort will be made by the leading powers to prolong their honourable association, and by sacrifice and self-restraint win for themselves a glorious name in human annals.[36]

This was hardly the sort of thing on which a consistent policy could be based, and subsequent statements from the Prime Minister were similarly vague. The Foreign Office therefore decided to go it alone, and to keep Churchill in the dark about any schemes to discuss the post-war world with the Russians.

Eden believed that it might be possible to settle in advance at least the outline of the peace settlement by means of discussions between the three great powers. Clark Kerr was therefore instructed to make some soundings in the hope that such discussions would improve relations between Moscow and London. Stalin's reply to the Ambassador's *démarche* was somewhat surly, but it did open up the possibility of tripartite talks, even though the Foreign Office felt that such talks were premature, not least because they had a good idea what the Prime Minister's reactions to such a suggestion would be. As Warner wrote to Clark Kerr,

> The Secretary of State had approved your instructions, but nothing had been said about them to the P.M. The latter on seeing the telegram emitted a series of most vicious screams from his sickbed [Churchill was suffering from a bout of pneumonia] and ordained that the whole subject of post-war matters should be dropped at once like the hottest of hot bricks.[37]

To the Foreign Office it seemed that an excellent opportunity to improve Anglo–Soviet relations had been missed.

Churchill was gradually coming to accept the fact that the Soviet Union would play a major role in the post-war world. In April 1943 he wrote, 'The overwhelming preponderance of Russia remains the dominant fact of the future.' He concluded that since neither Britain nor the United States would maintain large continental armies after the war, France would have to be built up as the main defence against the Soviet Union. Churchill warned that Russia would be the only continental country able to use force 'and that to a measureless and unlimited extent'.[38] The Prime Minister repeated this concern to Stimson and Sumner Welles, pointing out that since it was an alarming prospect that there would be no powerful country between the Soviet Union and Britain, France would have to be greatly strengthened.[39]

In early 1943 the British Government thus refused to take any political initiative towards the Soviet Union, and it also proved impossible to send any further convoys on time. Heavy losses of shipping in the Atlantic and the concentration of the German fleet in northern Norway made it impossible to meet the requirements for a satisfactory escort for a future convoy without seriously endangering the vital Atlantic route.[40] President Roosevelt agreed that the time had come to tell Stalin that there would be no further convoys until August or September.[41] The major problem was that no one knew exactly where the German fleet was positioned, and thus it was agreed to wait and find out before unloading the convoy which was preparing to sail. The situation was made even more tense by the attitude of the Soviet authorities who first demanded that the two squadrons of Hampden torpedo bombers designated by the RAF for northern Russia should be placed under Soviet operational control. Then they insisted that radio jamming equipment at Murmansk, Polyarnoe and Archangel should be closed down. Admiral Miles of 30 Mission complained that the Russians had 'passed the bounds of mere irritation and [were] prejudicing the safety and operational control of [the] convoys.[42]

British public opinion was still enthusiastic for the second front, but there was a growing concern about the Soviet Union's post-war intentions. There was widespread questioning why the Soviets had not been present at Casablanca in January. Appreciation of the contribution of the Soviet Union to the war was perhaps never as strong as it was while the battle for Stalingrad still raged. A report in January 1943 stated that, 'People are beginning to run out of adjectives to express their admiration for the Russian offensive.' It was asked whether enough was being done to help the Russians at this critical stage of the war, and when Kharkov fell to the Germans demands for a second front were more vocal than ever. But such admiration was not uncritical. Stalin's order of the day to the Red Army of 23 February, in which he insultingly claimed that the Soviet Union was fighting alone, was bitterly resented. There was also a mounting fear that the Russians might defeat the Germans before the second front was opened, and that they might not stop at their frontiers but would march on to absorb much of eastern Europe.

Even the strongest supporters of cooperation with the Soviets were continually frustrated by their attitude. Oliver Harvey summed up the feelings of many members of the Foreign Office when he confided in his diary, 'The Russians are very tiresome allies, importunate, graceless, ungrateful, secretive, suspicious, ever asking for more, but they are delivering the goods ... They are winning the war for us.'[43] It was a constant frustration to the Foreign Office that the Service Departments refused to accept the fact that the Russians had shown exceptional military prowess, and that they continued to treat them as if they were junior partners, and often scarcely as partners at all. There was also growing concern that the Americans might begin to push for 'bulwarks against Bolshevism', which would inevitably lead to further divisions in the post-war world.[44] This desire to have the best possible relations with the Soviet Union in no sense implied an uncritical attitude towards Soviet society. Everyone involved in Soviet affairs found the authorities maddening and frustrating. An unfeeling and insensitive bureaucratic machine seemed to be hell bent on making life as difficult as possible for everyone. In a sense the ludicrous and heartless refusal of Soviet officials to allow the Russian wives of British subjects to leave the country did as much to undermine Anglo–Soviet relations as did fundamental questions such as the future frontiers of Poland. Such irritations increased as the war progressed and did much to destroy feeling of sympathy and admiration for the Soviet Union.

With the victory at Stalingrad the Soviet Government turned its attention once again to the frontier question and made demands on Poland which resulted in a steady worsening of relations between the Soviets and the Polish exile government in London. Churchill was very concerned about this situation, but there was very little that he could do. The British war effort did not impress the Russians who were unlikely to listen to protestations on behalf of the Polish government. Churchill, for all his sympathy for Poland and his admiration for the Poles who had fought so valiantly for the allied cause, thought that the London Poles were a tiresome bunch of intriguers, with the notable exception of the Prime Minister, General Sikorski. Sikorski, who had managed to establish remarkably good relations with Stalin under exceptionally difficult circumstances, knew that he would lose the support of the Polish underground army if he made any concessions to the Soviets. The Polish Government therefore demanded the restoration of the frontiers of 1 September 1939, and protested vigorously against the enforcement of Soviet citizenship on Polish nationals, which resulted in them being conscripted into the Red Army, and denied exit visas. But by this time both the British and the American Governments were prepared to accept the Curzon Line and the Soviet claim to the Baltic States, with compensation for Poland in East Prussia and Silesia. The problem was thus how to make the Polish Government come to terms with reality, while at the same time getting the Soviets to modify their harsh, inhuman and intransigent attitude towards the Poles.

At the end of March 1943 the Foreign Office wrote to the Prime Minister suggesting that he should tell Maisky in no uncertain terms that there had to be a significant improvement in Soviet–Polish relations, and that the Soviet Union was largely to blame for this unfortunate state of affairs. Churchill was in no mood to embark on a crusade on behalf of the Poles and replied that he wished to wait until Eden returned from Washington, and until General Anders' Polish Army Corps went into action. Churchill told the Foreign Office that Anders was anxious to get exit visas for the wives and families of Polish subjects who were in the Soviet Union, but was unable personally to do much to support the Poles as 'my influence is not supported by sufficient military contribution to the common cause to make any representations effective'. At the same time he complained bitterly of the 'usual fissiparous and subversive agitation' by the Poles which was a constant headache to him.[45] Churchill was also concerned about Soviet attempts to incite the Poles to premature action against the Germans, which he felt would only lead to disaster.

The War Cabinet discussed Russo–Polish relations and agreed that the situation was extremely serious. Eden suggested that Clark Kerr should begin discussions of the outstanding problems in Moscow. Churchill felt that as a first step towards improving relations the families of Polish troops in the Middle East should be allowed to leave the Soviet Union.[46] There was no time to act on either of these suggestions, for the following day the German Government announced that they had discovered a mass grave at Katyn, near Smolensk, in which were found the bodies of 10 000 Polish officers who, the Germans claimed, had been murdered by the Russians. Churchill's immediate reaction to this news was to tell Sikorski that this was an obvious propaganda move by the Germans, and Eden told the War Cabinet that the whole affair was designed to sow discord between the Allies and should be ignored as much as possible, otherwise the Russians would not allow the Poles in the Soviet Union to leave.[47]

The Poles were in no mood to ignore this frightful crime whatever its effects on allied unity. Clark Kerr reported from Moscow that,

> The Polish Ambassador of course believes what the Germans say is true. In a horrible way it seems to fit in with the Poles' story of the disappearance of 8300 officers. Then anger and unconvincing terms of Soviet denials suggests a sense of guilt. This is disturbing, for it is uncomfortable to reflect upon consequences of an enquiry which might show that guilt was there. I feel therefore that to pursue the proposal made to the International Red Cross might be to court something a little short of disaster.[48]

On the same day Churchill received a note from Stalin claiming that the Polish press 'avidly fanned' German propaganda and that General Sikorski had delivered a 'treacherous blow to the Soviet Union to serve the cause of Hitler's tyranny'.[49] In his reply to Stalin the Prime Minister agreed that the Katyn affair was 'terribly effective propaganda' and, taking Clark Kerr's advice, he strongly opposed the idea of the Red Cross making an investigation of the site under German auspices as 'such investigation would be a fraud and its conclusions reached by terrorism'.[50] The attitude of the British Government was that the Katyn massacre was acutely embarrassing and should be ignored as much as possible. Oliver Harvey summed up this attitude in his diary. 'The Poles have fairly upset the applecart. They will need very firm treatment if they are not to upset the peace settlement and wreck Anglo–Russian unity.'[51] In his masterly fictional reconstruction of the war years Anthony Powell allows the odious Widmerpool to expound at some length on the Katyn massacre.

> In any case [said Widmerpool] whatever materializes, even if it does transpire – which I sincerely trust it will not – that the Russians behaved in such a very regrettable manner, how can this country possibly raise official objection, in the interests of a few thousand Polish exiles, who, however worthy their cause, cannot properly handle their diplomatic relations, even with fellow Slavs? It must be confessed also that the Poles themselves are in a position to offer only a very modest contribution, when it comes to the question of manpower. How, as I say, can we approach our second and most powerful Ally about something which, if a fact, cannot

be put right, and is almost certainly, from what one knows of them, the consequence of administrative inadequacy, rather than wilful indifference to human life and the dictates of compassion? What we have to do is not to waste time and energy in considering the relative injustices war brings in its train, but to make sure we are going to win it.[52]

Colonel Widmerpool here speaks the authentic language of official England.

Having sent his cautious reply to Stalin, Churchill spoke to Maisky. He pointed out to the Ambassador that if Sikorski were forced to resign over the Katyn affair he would almost certainly be replaced by someone even more hostile to the Soviet Union, for Sikorski was constantly under attack for being too conciliatory towards Russia. Churchill repeated these arguments in an impassioned letter to Stalin in which he said that whatever the Russians might think of Sikorski at least he was not pro-German, and he warned of the terrible consequences if the Soviet Government were to break with the Poles over Katyn, emphasising that there were six million Poles in the United States who were not without political influence. Stalin replied harshly that he had already broken off relations with the Polish Government. Churchill was almost in despair. He wrote to Roosevelt, 'We must work together to heal this breach. So far it has been Goebbels' show.'[53]

The War Cabinet discussed these alarming developments on 27 April. It was agreed that Sikorski should be restrained from reacting too strongly to the break with Moscow and that any discussion of future Russo–Polish frontiers should be avoided. The Ministry of Information was instructed not to allow the British press to discuss Russo–Polish relations, and that a policy should be formulated governing the censorship of journals published by foreign governments in Britain so as to keep the Poles quiet.[54] While the British Government tried to defuse Dr Goebbels' skilfully placed bomb, Clark Kerr reported from Moscow that he feared the Soviet Government would use the crisis in order to establish a puppet Polish Government on Soviet soil. Eden shared this view, and passed the Ambassador's letter on to Churchill. The Prime Minister's impatient reaction was that 'there is no use prowling round the three year old graves of Smolensk.'[55] But he also knew that the graves would not go away, and therefore resolved to write once more to Stalin in an attempt to patch up the differences between the London Poles and

Moscow. Clark Kerr rejected the first draft of this letter, saying that it was far too apologetic in tone, and suggesting that something tougher was required if Stalin were to change his mind. The message was re-written, and although it was very carefully worded brought a howl of protest from Molotov that the whole affair was a 'libel put out by German propaganda and fostered by pro-Hitler elements among the Poles'. Maisky tried to pour some oil on the troubled waters by announcing that the Soviet Government had no intention of setting up a new Polish Government in the Soviet Union.[56]

In a conversation with Eden a few days before, Maisky had made no such categoric denial, and merely stated that the Soviet Union was 'unlikely' to encourage the formation of an alternative Polish Government. Eden replied that were this to happen it would be 'extremely serious'. Suspicions that the Soviet Government intended to set up a puppet Polish regime prompted the War Cabinet to suggest to the Prime Minister that it might be necessary to settle the Polish frontier question before the end of the war in order to stop Stalin from taking such drastic action.[57] The major problem was that it seemed most unlikely that the United States Government would agree, for they would almost certainly claim that it was inconsistent with the Atlantic Charter.[58]

Rather than set up a new Polish Government, Stalin urged Churchill to force Sikorski to change the personnel of the London Exile Government. Eden pointed out to Churchill that the Poles would never give way to such pressure as they could not accept the Soviet claim that anyone who was born east of the 'Molotov–Ribbentrop Line' was automatically a Soviet citizen. The War Cabinet drafted a reply to Stalin's request which said that although Sikorski's government was 'susceptible of improvement' this could not be done as a result of foreign pressure.[59]

Neither Churchill nor Eden took much notice of the War Cabinet's support for the London Poles. Three days after the Cabinet meeting the Prime Minister wrote to the Foreign Secretary, 'My feeling increasingly is that we must not be too tender with these unwise people. I trust you will be successful in inducing Sikorski to reconstruct his government.' Churchill also called for a rigorous censorship of the Polish press in London to ensure that they did not publish anything that might offend the Soviet Union.[60] As Eden told Maisky, the problem was to get the Poles to change their Government without it seeming that it was imposed on them. Eden agreed with Churchill that Sikorski should remain in office but that the whole of the rest of the government should be changed.[61] It is impossible to tell whether Sikorski could ever have been persuaded to change his entire government for on 4 July he was killed in a plane crash while returning from a visit to Polish troops in the Middle East. His death was a very serious blow to the British Government, for he was an outstanding statesman who alone could have achieved a degree of compromise sufficient to save the situation from deteriorating further. A new government was formed under Mikolajczyk, with Romer responsible for foreign affairs, and the outspokenly Russophobe General Sosnkowski as Commander-in-Chief. This line-up did not augur well for the future of Russo–Polish relations, but it was difficult to think of any capable men who might provide a viable alternative government.

After their victory at Stalingrad and as their armies moved west the Soviets were in a more confident mood, and once more demanded an agreement on frontiers and nationality. The Foreign Office wished to avoid any discussion of these issues. Clark Kerr was told not to speculate about the future of East Prussia, on the grounds that this might be taken up by the Germans and used to considerable propaganda effect.[62] Eden wrote to Molotov pointing out that the British Government wished to avoid making any agreements with countries which had exile governments. The Soviets took the view that there was nothing in the Anglo–Soviet Treaty of 1942 which precluded making treaties and agreements on post-war matters. The best that the Foreign Office could hope for was that the Soviet Government would agree to a 'self-denying ordinance' on this matter; but this was only possible if Anglo–Soviet relations improved greatly, and such an improvement did not seem to be imminent.[63]

The Foreign Office was greatly encouraged by the announcement in May 1943 that the Comintern had been abolished. They felt that this was a significant step away from revolutionary Communism and towards a genuine accommodation with the capitalist world. They therefore considered that the Labour Party was being extraordinarily silly in denouncing the whole thing as a purely tactical move designed to conceal the true intentions of the Soviet Government.[64] The War Cabinet, largely in deference to the views of the Labour members, felt that it was unwise to comment on the abolition of the Comintern. It was agreed that if questions were asked in the House, Eden should stick to purely factual replies.[65] The Labour ministers were convinced that the whole thing was part of a plot to infiltrate the Trades Unions and the Labour Party and refused to agree to a Government statement welcoming the decision to disband the General Staff of the world revolution. Oliver Harvey wryly commented, 'I only hope Stalin isn't going to abolish Communism itself next and instead put a crown on his head.'[66]

In fact the Foreign Office made little attempt to work out the significance of the abolition of the Comintern. It was felt that the Comintern was obsolete, moribund, inefficient and an embarrassment to the coalition, and that its abolition was in large measure due to a resurgence of old-fashioned nationalism which had little use for the internationalist pretensions of the Comintern.[67] This was as plausible an explanation of what had happened as any other, and left the Foreign Office far less confused than some of the Communist parties who were being ordered to abandon their revolutionary hopes and subordinate everything to the selfish political ambitions of the Soviet state. Stalin now no longer had to bother about the reaction of any international organisation, even one which, like the Communist International, had been bullied, purged, and murdered to the point of abject and terrified submission.

Since the Foreign Office had no specialists on the Soviet Union, and no one whose Russian was fluent, they relied to a considerable extent on the reports produced by the Foreign Office Research Department (FORD) for interpretations of the arcana of Soviet policy. FORD was run by Brigadier Skaife, a Russophile who knew pre-revolutionary Russia well and who admired many of the achievements of the Soviet Union. The undoubted star of the organisation was the young Marxist historian, Christopher Hill, who skilfully recycled Soviet propaganda into position papers acceptable to the Foreign Office and who was soon to become the Northern Department's leading authority on Soviet affairs. There was nothing at all odd about such a state of affairs, for this was a time when the bands of the Brigade of Guards played fanfares to the glory of Marshall Stalin, John Gielgud appeared at the Royal Albert Hall as the 'voice of Moscow Radio', and the Seatonian Prize, awarded at Cambridge for a poem on a sacred subject, was given to a poem on 'Holy Russia'. Whitehall was crawling with Communists, fellow-travellers, and boudoir bolsheviks and only the most Blimpish reactionary complained, usually from the depths of a well-stuffed chair in a club smoking room.

Typical of the FORD approach was a handbook on Soviet affairs: a joint effort, edited by Skaife. There was a glowing section on labour conditions in the Soviet Union, in which Stakhanovism was described merely as rationalisation which was accepted by all Soviet workers without question. The enormous progress which had been made in Soviet agriculture was also stressed, but there was some mild criticism of Soviet chauvinism and anti-Semitism. The historical section of the handbook argued that the Soviet Union believed that the western powers were determined to embroil her in a war with Germany and thus asserted her neutrality in the Nazi–Soviet Pact. It was also claimed that the Soviet Union wanted a common front against aggression, had been let down at Munich, and therefore had no alternative but to make a pact with Hitler in order to buy time. Armine Dew, reviewing the draft of the handbook for the Foreign Office, commented that this tendentious document was 'on the right lines'.[68]

Although sympathy and admiration for the Soviet Union was widespread, there was always a concern that the Germans might be able to conjure up the bogey of Bolshevism and use it as an effective propaganda weapon. The Foreign Office and the Ministry of Information agreed that the best way to counter such a threat was to stress Soviet contributions to the arts and sciences, the increasing freedom given to the religious communities, and the respect shown to small businessmen and small investors. In this romanticised version the Soviet Union had become a state of managers and small entrepreneurs rather than of revolutionaries, and since the demise of the frightful Trotsky it had no desire to export its revolution. Red terror was dismissed as being merely a harsh but necessary response to Nazi terror.[69] Given this conviction that the Soviet Union had abandoned its revolutionary tradition, it was hardly surprising that Geoffrey Wilson, who worked in the Northern Department after he returned to London with Sir Stafford Cripps in 1942, when discussing whether the Western Allies should attempt to get into eastern Europe as quickly as possible and before the Russians got there, pointed out that the social revolutionary movements in Europe were autonomous and natural local movements which had nothing to do with the USSR, even though the Soviets would almost certainly try to work through them and dominate them. It was in Britain's interest to keep on the right side of such movements, and it would be a serious mistake to see them as part of a monolithic Communist bloc.[70] Subsequent developments were to show that Wilson was perfectly correct, but no one was to foresee how ferociously Stalin was to crush any independent movements in all areas occupied by his armies.

It would be a mistake to imagine that FORD was merely an uncritical mouthpiece for Soviet propaganda. It had more than its fair share of Communists and fellow travellers, but its work was seldom totally uncritical. The War Office Weekly Intelligence Review, which was largely produced by FORD, was passed on to the United States, but not to the Soviet Union, because it contained some highly critical material on the Soviet Union. One of FORD's pro-Communists leaked this material to the *Daily Worker*, and the issue was promptly brought up by the fearless defender of Stalin's Russia, D. N. Pritt, during Question Time in the House of Commons.[71] Pritt was particularly irate over the references to the 'boring monotony' of Soviet demands for a second front.

A marked increase of interest in the Soviet Union coupled with the obvious lack of experts on the topic prompted the Foreign Office to push strongly for an increase in funds for Russian studies at the Universities, and it was also suggested that there should be a regular system of student exchanges established as soon as the war was over. The Foreign Office was also beginning to think about trade in the post-war world. An Interdepartmental Committee on Post War Trade with Russia was established later in 1943 with representatives from the Foreign Office, the Board of Trade and the Treasury.[72]

In July the Soviet Government recalled Maisky, who was replaced by Gusev, a man described by Clark Kerr as 'like a sea calf and apparently no more articulate'.[73] Geoffrey Wilson found the new Ambassador 'uncouth', and had a low opinion of both his abilities and character. Armine Dew remarked that he had 'the appearance of having come from a collective farm after a short course of GPU training'. The replacement of a man of unusual ability by this inexperienced thirty-eight year old who gave all appearance of lacking either brains or charm was a calculated insult to the British Government which Eden found 'disquieting'. Clark Kerr did not agree. He told the Foreign Office that Gusev was probably the best man they had for the job and that it was 'poverty more than anything else that has obliged the Soviet Government to make this inadequate appointment'. The precise reason for this change in a key diplomatic posting is unknown, although it is usually suggested that Maisky was recalled for having failed to secure the second front. This was certainly the version which Mrs Maisky liked to give to visiting British friends after the couple had returned to Moscow.[74]

Gusev arrived in England after yet another acrimonious exchange between Churchill and Stalin on the subject of the second front. Writing to Clark Kerr in June, Churchill said,

Nothing will induce me in any circumstances to allow what at this stage I am advised and convinced would be a useless massacre of British troops on the channel beaches in order to remove Soviet suspicions. I am getting rather tired of these repeated scoldings, considering that they have never been actuated by anything but cold-blooded self-interest and total disdain of our lives and fortunes.

Stalin replied disdainfully to Churchill's concerns about the losses that would be sustained in an invasion of France by pointing out that losses of 100 000 out of one million was not very impressive to a country that had suffered as many casualties as the Soviet Union. He followed this up with a long list of what he claimed were broken promises of a second front. In his covering letter with Stalin's reply, Clark Kerr wrote,

Our weakness lies not in our ability to open the second front but in our having let him believe we were going to ... My slight experience of him tempts me to the view that he would conceive that he had marshalled his complaints with moderation ... I know you are not to me a submissive man but I think it would be a mistake to take amiss such stuff as this when it comes from a man as rough and as green and as bad mannered as Stalin.

The Ambassador advised the Prime Minister not to break off his correspondence with Stalin in a fit of deserved pique, but to persevere in trying to reach an understanding with him. Churchill's reaction to this advice was to tell Maisky that Clark Kerr was always standing up for the Soviet Union and that he hoped that he was doing the same for England.[75] It is just possible that Maisky had stood up for England, but it is very doubtful whether Gusev, who arrived in London shortly after this conversation, ever did. Gusev neither earned nor deserved the hospitality and the friendship that many had extended to Maisky who, exasperating though he could be, was always regarded as a worthy representative of his country.

In August 1943 Churchill met Roosevelt at Quebec in order to discuss their joint plans for 1944. Churchill was still angry with Stalin for his endless jibes about the second front and had no desire to have him at the Quebec meeting, although a very half-hearted invitation had been sent to him. Churchill also knew that the Americans supported the Russian insistence on a cross-channel invasion, and he was determined not to be outvoted two to one on this issue. He went to Quebec hoping to convince the Americans to move on from Sicily, which had been invaded at the beginning of July, to Italy and then to cross the channel to northern France in May 1944. At the Quebec meeting Churchill once again got his way so that he was now prepared to agree to a Big Three meeting. He wanted this to take place as soon as possible, and Eden agreed. Stalin appeared to be enthusiastic, although he said that he would not be able to leave the country as he had to pay frequent visits to the front. He also requested that an agenda should be agreed upon prior to the meeting so as not to waste time.[76] Stalin suggested Astrakhan or Archangel as a meeting place, but Churchill and Roosevelt preferred Fairbanks, Alaska. After considerable further haggling it was agreed that the Foreign Ministers should meet in Teheran. Eden was greatly relieved when this was all settled, for he was becoming increasingly concerned about Churchill's anti-Soviet feelings and feared that the meeting might not take place at all because of his growing impatience with Stalin.[77]

Anglo–Soviet relations were further strained in the Summer of 1943 by the actions of the Allied troops in Italy. With the capture of Sicily and large areas of southern Italy civil administration was left to the AMGOTS (Allied Military Governments – although there was a widely-believed rumour that it was the Turkish word for shit). General Montgomery had a very low opinion of these institutions. In a letter to Sir James Grigg, the Secretary of State for War, on paper which he had confiscated from the local Fascist headquarters and which was decorated with Fascist insignia and quotations from Il Duce, he wrote, 'It is my own opinion that they have a very poor lot of chaps in AMGOT; old school tie, the peerage, diseased Guardsmen, etc., etc.'[78] The Foreign Office was much less concerned about the personnel of the AMGOTS than they were about the fact that the Soviets had not been consulted about the administration of a defeated enemy country. The formation of the Free Germany Committee in the Soviet Union, made up of pro-Communist German prisoners of war, was seen as an attempt by the Russians to retaliate after this exclusion from Italy. Those in the Foreign Office who wanted to have a general discussion with the Soviet Union about the future of Europe saw this as further evidence for their point of view that if such talks did not take place the alliance would gradually fall apart into two hostile camps.[79]

It was not long before signs came from Moscow which indicated that such fears were justified. At a lecture in the Central Park of Culture and Rest in Moscow the speaker argued that the aim of

Allied policy in Italy was to set up 'Anglo–American Quislings' and referred to the 'Anglo–American *Gauleiter*' in the AMGOTS.[80] Stafford Cripps wrote to Eden complaining that the Soviet Union had not been consulted over Italy. One Foreign Office official asked how the British Government would react if the Russians signed an armistice with General von X without any prior consultation, the way the British had done with Badoglio. Bruce Lockhart felt that this was all complete nonsense and that there was no reason whatever to fear the Russians, pointing out that 'we should remember that Stalin's avowed aim, as opposed to Trotsky's, was to give every Russian a dinner jacket and a white shirt'. He was convinced that Russia would need British support after the war in order to achieve this praiseworthy goal. Eden was not very impressed with the dinner jacket argument and wrote to the Prime Minister suggesting that the Government should address itself to the question of Russia's western frontier which, as the Allies would soon be back in France, was becoming a question of some urgency.[81]

A further problem with the Russians was the familiar issue of convoys. Shortly after the Quebec conference Churchill wrote to Eden, 'There is, of course, no question of being able to resume these convoys in the near future on account of the manner in which the operations in the Mediterranean have broadened out.'[82] But it was not merely the shortage of shipping which was the problem. The Defence Committee met in September and agreed that convoys could resume in November, but that 'resumption of the convoys would be dependent upon a settlement, satisfactory to us, of outstanding grievances regarding the treatment of our personnel in North Russia'.[83] The Foreign Office had little sympathy for the Service Departments' view that the best way to get anything out of the Russians was to be tough with them, and therefore told the soldiers that

> In view of the decision taken at Quebec to omit from the instructions of H.M. Ambassador any offer to furnish the Russians with a full analysis of the reasons for not re-starting convoys, any explanations that may have to be given to the Russians here will be confined to general terms and based on the present enemy dispositions and on other operational commitments.[84]

At the beginning of October the Prime Minister wrote to Stalin saying that it would be impossible to send any convoys while the Battle of the Atlantic still raged, while Allied forces were being built up in Italy and while the war against Japan continued to use up vast numbers of men and material; but he ended his letter with another of those vague promises which Clark Kerr found so objectionable, this time that it might be possible to send a convoy in November, or December, or January, or February ... This in turn would only be possible if British personnel in northern Russia were increased, and Churchill repeated the complaints which had been voiced against the Soviet authorities.[85] The situation was so bad that the crews of a number of merchant ships refused to sail unless they got a guarantee that they would be treated properly. Most of the grievances could easily have been rectified, and showed a singular lack of goodwill on the Soviet side. A major complaint was that the Soviet authorities refused to hand over mail that was sent to the British personnel in northern Russia, and when it was eventually given to them it had been so heavily censored as to be almost unreadable. Eden decided to discuss the convoy question with Stalin during his visit to Moscow in October. He soon realised that he was wasting his time. Stalin told him that he bitterly resented the fact that the British regarded convoys for Russia more as a favour than as an obligation, and he flatly refused to allow any more British personnel to go to northern Russia, adding that there were enough there already and all they did was make a nuisance of themselves.[86] Nothing was done about the mail. The naval authorities in northern Russia wrote to the Admiralty, 'The Christmas bag of 19 bags which arrived December 20th is spending the festive season in hands of Russian censors. This fact is not exactly conducive to good will to all men.'[87] No doubt the Soviets were angry that there were no convoys until December, and British personnel was bored with the drab restrictive routine of life in the Soviet Union, but things could all too easily get out of hand. Two merchant seamen charged with smoking in a restricted area and then assaulting a Soviet official were given 5 and 3 years' imprisonment. In England they would have got fourteen days or a £10–£15 fine.[88]

The Foreign Office was prepared to try to reach an agreement with the Soviets on the frontier question, but in the summer of 1943 Churchill had no interest in such matters and the United States Government was still anxious to postpone the whole issue until after the war. The British Government had effectively accepted the Soviet claim to the Baltic States in the Anglo–Soviet Treaty. The future frontier with Finland had not been discussed, nor had the British raised the question of the Polish frontier with the Soviets, although they had informed the Americans that they accepted the Curzon

Line. The Foreign Office also saw no objection to the Soviets taking Bessarabia and the Northern Bukovina, although the question of Romania had not yet been discussed with the Soviet Government. Thus the Foreign Office was prepared to accept the Curzon Line, with the Poles keeping Lvov and compensated with Danzig, East Prussia and Upper Silesia. Feeling that a settlement of the frontiers might dramatically improve relations with the Soviet Union, and frustrated by the Prime Minister's refusal to address the problems of the post-war settlement, the Foreign Office hoped to persuade the American Government to agree to these proposals. The instructions sent to the British Ambassador in Washington were delightfully frank in admitting that such a proposal was a flagrant violation of previous agreements,

> Your Excellency will appreciate that in advocating such a settlement of Russia's western frontier we should be driving a coach and horses through the Atlantic Charter. We should hope that the President would be prepared to join us on the box, but you will obviously not need to take the initiative in raising this point with him.[89]

The Foreign Office thus wanted to settle the whole question of Soviet frontiers with the Americans before the next meeting with the Soviets. Eden then put these proposals to the Prime Minister, hastily adding that it might be expedient to avoid an actual agreement with the Russians before the fighting stopped. Churchill's only comment was to pen a large question mark in the margin.[90]

Clark Kerr felt that such an approach was quite wrong. Maisky told him that difficulties with the Russians were caused by the fact that the Soviet diplomats were callow and inexperienced. The Ambassador silently agreed, but he felt that the root of the matter was that the British refused to treat the Russians as equals as they did the Americans. He told the Foreign Office, 'We *consult* Washington and we *inform* Moscow ... We shall have to learn not to be snobs and still more not to be fools.'[91] In July of 1943 the foreign missions had moved back to Moscow from Kuibyshev and Clark Kerr was delighted to be back in the capital where the chances of contacts with high Soviet officials were so much better. He was also anxious to meet the Turkish diplomat whose visiting card had given him such amusement: His Excellency Mustapha Kunt.[92]

In September it was finally agreed that a 'Conference of Foreign

Office Representatives' should meet in Moscow, and that the Big Three should then meet in Teheran. Preliminary discussions of the agenda indicated that the Soviets wanted to make a discussion of measures to shorten the war the main topic for the Foreign Ministers' conference. The British wanted to avoid endless wrangles about the second front and therefore proposed that the conference should concentrate on the treatment of Germany. Churchill was in a belligerently anti-Soviet mood, and on 5 October he told the War Cabinet that after the war Germany would have to be strengthened and used as a bulwark against Russia, a suggestion which was warmly supported by General Smuts who was attending the Cabinet meeting. Eden began to suspect that this was the beginning of an attempt by the Prime Minister to wriggle out of his commitment to the second front in 1944, and he was prepared to resign if he did. It was the fear that the second front would be postponed again, rather than the suggestion that it might be desirable to build up an anti-Soviet western bloc which would include Germany, which really disturbed the Foreign Secretary.[93] Churchill was determined to avoid making any commitments to the Soviet Union on the frontier question. He told Eden that a

treaty with SU on her western frontiers would split H of C. I think we should do everything in our power to persuade the Poles to agree with the Russians about their eastern frontier, in return for gains in East Prussia and Silesia. We could certainly promise to use our influence in this respect.[94]

This was mere wishful thinking. After Sikorski's death there was no hope whatever of the Poles reaching an agreement with the Soviets on their common frontier.

In spite of Churchill's anxieties that the Moscow conference would rapidly get bogged down in questions of Soviet frontiers and denunciations of British inaction over the second front, the meeting was something of a success. The Soviets were unusually conciliatory. They did not push the question of frontiers and appeared to be satisfied with the explanations given for the delays in the invasion of France. General Ismay, who accompanied Eden to Moscow, explained that the invasion plans for 1944 were subject to certain conditions, which included the availability of landing craft, the size of the German air force in northern France, and the strength of the German reserves. Churchill persistently telegraphed to Eden protesting at the idea of making any commitment to the Soviet Government on the precise date of the invasion of France, telling him that OVERLORD should not be allowed to jeopardise the operations in Italy, and warning him not to become entangled in any 'lawyer's agreement' over the date of the invasion. Such talk convinced Eden that Churchill wanted a further postponement of OVERLORD.[95] When Eden screwed up his courage and told Stalin that OVERLORD might be postponed until the summer of 1944, he was surprised and gratified to be granted a benign hearing.

The Soviets were deeply suspicious of the Turks, and urged that Turkey should be forced to join the allied cause so as to keep an eye on them. Eden appeared to be successful in persuading Molotov that the British were not supplying arms to Turkey so that they might eventually be used against the Soviet Union. He also managed to counter Soviet arguments that Sweden should join the war against Germany, and succeeded in getting the question of support for the Yugoslav partisans taken from the conference agenda, for he knew that this would only lead to further discord.

Eden was undoubtedly the dominant figure at the Moscow conference. The Russians were conciliatory, the Americans inexperienced and Eden carried the show. He devoted much of his energy to securing agreement for his proposal for a European Advisory Commission which was designed to co-ordinate the efforts of the three powers in the liberated countries and in Germany. Neither the United States nor the Soviet Union was enthusiastic about this suggestion, but eventually they agreed and it was decided to establish the Commission in London. Eden paid a high price for Soviet agreement. He accepted the Soviet suggestion that the 'self-denying ordinance' or wartime treaties should not stand in the way of a treaty between the Soviet Union and Czechoslovakia. This was to enable the Soviets to establish a precedent which was to prove extremely useful as they set about strengthening their grip on eastern Europe. A separate Allied Advisory Council was designed to deal with the problems of Italy. At Soviet insistence it was agreed that the aim of the three great powers was to wipe out all remaining vestiges of fascism in Italy, although Eden argued rather lamely that it was difficult to find experienced and competent anti-fascists after twenty years of Mussolini's dictatorship.

There was also general agreement with the British memorandum on general principles for the liberation of occupied countries. The avowed aim of the document was to secure the self-government of the liberated countries as soon as possible, although it was stressed that a period of military rule by the Allies would be necessary in order to restore some semblance of normality after the upheaval and destruction of war. It was agreed that as far as possible all collaborationists, and those who had been hostile to the allied cause, should be excluded from important positions in the liberated countries. The three governments also declared that they would not seek to establish spheres of influence in Europe and that their principal concern was with the interests of Europe as a whole. Molotov did not like this last proposal, and argued that it was a purely negative statement which was quite unnecessary given the fact that the powers had already agreed to work together to secure the peace of the post-war world, nor did he wish to make any definite commitment about the future of Germany. Molotov did not bother to torpedo the statement, but he made certain that it was not published. On the future of Germany the only point of agreement was that Germany should not be left with more than her territories prior to the *Anschluss* of Austria.

The conference ended with a declaration which was signed by the Chinese ambassador on the final day of the conference to make it a four-power declaration. It was a rather empty and overblown statement which pledged cooperation between the signatories to prosecute the war and to establish a 'general international organisation, based on the principle of the sovereign equality of all peace-loving States . . . for the maintenance of peace and security'. It was also announced that the European Advisory Commission and the Advisory Council for Italy would be established, full independence would be granted to Austria, and democracy would be restored to Italy. Churchill, Roosevelt and Stalin signed a further declaration that all Nazi criminals should be tried in the countries where they had committed their atrocities and that they would be tried according to local law.[96]

The British were delighted with the outcome of the Foreign Ministers' Conference. Eden had been very worried that the Soviet demand for 'such urgent measures in 1943 that will ensure a second front' meant that the Russians would be satisfied with nothing less than a guarantee that the second front would be opened that year. But they did not press this demand, and Eden could telegraph to Churchill, 'There may of course be snags later but for the moment we are in unexpectedly smooth waters.'[97] Eden had been able to head off the Soviet move to get Sweden and Turkey to support the Allies, his basic argument being that it was not worth the effort.

Above all, he had got his European Advisory Commission, although it was a somewhat toothless affair. The response in the Soviet press to the conference was unusually enthusiastic. Clark Kerr was delighted. In his report on the conference he wrote,

> For the first time the Russians felt that they had been admitted freely and on terms of complete equality to the most intimate councils of ourselves and the Americans from which, as they saw it, they had been hitherto largely excluded.

The fact that Eden and Hull had gone to Moscow had stirred their vanity, and there was no doubt that Eden, rather than the somewhat passive Hull, had been the star performer.[98]

Eden was enormously encouraged by the discussions in Moscow. He felt that the ice had really begun to melt and that the time had come for some generous British initiative. He suggested to Churchill that a Soviet officer should be attached to the Combined Chiefs of Staff. He pointed out that the Russians had invited Ismay and that they had been most cooperative, and he concluded his argument by saying that it was essential that the Russians should not feel left out.[99] This suggestion was very badly timed. Churchill had already written to the President saying that he did not want a Russian officer attending meetings of the Combined Chiefs, pointing out that none of their senior men could speak a word of English and that the man would not be given any authority. Worst of all 'He would simply bay for an earlier second front and block all other discussions.' Churchill was convinced that anything short of top-level discussions between the Big Three was a waste of time, and these were due to begin in Teheran in a few weeks' time. He therefore fired a hasty reply to Eden to nip the idea in the bud. He briefly repeated the objections he had already raised in his letter to Roosevelt: 'triple conference is excellent, but an irresponsible Russian observer at a conference on the conduct of purely Anglo–American operations would be most injurious'.[100] Ismay, predictably, supported the Prime Minister. In his memorandum on the Moscow Conference he wrote that it would be a 'farce' to be saddled with Russian and Chinese observers. They would have no authority and would be only concerned with specific theatres of war.[101] But even Ismay was affected by the good feeling engendered by the Moscow Conference. He told the crew of HMS *London* that Stalin 'has an infectious laugh and a nice sense of humour'. Churchill was not in the least bit impressed by all this, and continued to speak of 'The suspicious Bruin'.[102]

8 Teheran and its Aftermath

While the Foreign Office felt that the successful Moscow Conference should be followed up by an imaginative political initiative or a generous gesture of good will, the Combined Chiefs of Staff took the opposite view. They felt that the time had come to make some demands on the Russians. To the Combined Chiefs the Moscow Conference was yet another exercise in appeasement. Their view was that

> At the Moscow Conference the United States and British representatives were primarily engaged in explaining and defending their own position. In future the United States and Great Britain should make specific requests of the Soviets.

These requests included air bases in the Russian zone of operations for shuttle bombing; a Soviet air offensive; adequate air routes from Britain, the United States and Teheran to the Soviet Union; meteorological information; military co-ordination with OVERLORD; detailed discussions about the future of Italy and Japan; and the co-ordination of propaganda efforts.[1] In 1943 General Mason-Macfarlane was replaced by General Giffard Martel to head the British Military Mission in Moscow. Eden was convinced that this was a deliberate ploy by CIGS to annoy the Russians, and wrote that Martel was 'something of a calamity' and that the Military Mission was as tactless and incompetent as ever.[2] Perhaps there was something in Eden's suspicions, for CIGS wrote in his diary that Martel was furious when he was told that he had been posted in Moscow as he regarded himself as the greatest tank man in the British Army.[3] Martel had a distinguished war record and the Foreign Office thought that he was at least an improvement on Mason-Macfarlane. Churchill built him up, and Stalin was quite nice to him at their first meeting. He was offered KV-1 and T-34 tanks for shipment to England. He was treated to a visit to the Front. The Russians appeared to be more forthcoming with technical information. But soon this honeymoon period was over. Martel, like most soldiers, believed that the only way to get anything out of the Russians was to be tough, and he told Clark Kerr, 'I do not associate myself with these "good will" methods when dealing with the Soviet Government.' In his memoirs he gives an example of how he dealt with a Soviet general who was far from forthcoming when persistently pressed for information on the Red Army's dispositions.

> This ... was the moment for the tough stuff! Trying to look very angry I spoke out strongly and said: 'Do you imagine that I have come all the way out from England to put up with tomfoolery of that sort. I have never been so insulted before in my life. I certainly do not propose to put up with that kind of treatment for a moment.'[4]

The Soviets did not warm to this sort of treatment, nor to his claim that the Soviet victory at the battle of Kursk was due in part to the advice he had given the Red Army on tank tactics. He also bored the Russians at social occasions by endlessly repeating his tiger-shooting story about his chum 'Fattie' Gort. Not even the genial Admiral Kharlamov could stop him with his remark that the Russians were more sporting: they used a plywood shield, and when the tiger sprang they nailed his claws to the inside. The Russians got their own back on Martel when only three of the thirty people invited to a reception in his honour actually turned up. Martel obviously had to be recalled, and on his return to London he complained to all and sundry that his mission had failed because the Foreign Office had refused to allow him to be tough enough. The Foreign Office felt that Martel was pompous and humourless, constantly pestered the Russians for information without bothering to say why it was needed, and as a crowning insult his report of the activities of the Red Army in 1943 was unbelievably complacent and patronising.[5]

Martel was succeeded by General Brocas Burrows who was determined to be tough with the Russians and not to toady to them. On the other hand Burrows was far less abrasive than Martel and spoke excellent Russian. Cavendish-Bentinck was perfectly correct when he surmised, 'I have a feeling that General Burrows will not enjoy his sojourn in Muscovy.' His patience soon began to wear thin and in September 1944 Stalin complained to Clark Kerr that Burrows had referred to the Russians as savages. Clearly Burrows had to go.

It is almost certain that Burrows in fact made such a remark, although it may well have been picked up by the NKVD from the bugs they planted in his office. Major Salt of the Military Mission complained to the Foreign Office that his colleagues 'hated the Russians and do not conceal their antipathy'.[6] The Foreign Office felt that Burrows had at least tried to do his best, but were disgusted with the violently anti-Russian attitude of the CIGS and the service chiefs. Warner complained that one hundred years of bad relations with the Soviet Union was

> surely altogether too heavy a price to pay for the prejudices of C.I.G.S. and the inability of a comparatively small number of British officers to exercise self-restraint under provocations which the youngest diplomat is expected to practice.[7]

Geoffrey Wilson thought that Soviet talk of 'nests of fascist opposition' was not a bad way to describe the Chiefs of Staff and the Post Hostilities Planning Staff, 'given the necessary allowance for Soviet terminology'. Eden and Orme Sargent found it necessary to give the Chiefs of Staff a lecture on the harmful effects of their anti-Soviet stance. All they got in return was a lecture from Portal that the Soviet Union intended to absorb a united Germany, and the Chiefs insisted that the only way to deal with the Russian threat was to make sure that Germany was divided.[8]

Burrows was recalled in October 1944 and he was not replaced. Admiral Archer was left in charge of the Military Mission. The Foreign Office was not particularly upset. They had been immensely bored by his reports, and preferred to read the lurid accounts of gigantic drinking sessions which were sent by the naval attaché. They also felt that no soldier in Moscow was better than another disastrous appointment. No doubt the members of the Military Mission had been sorely tried, but certainly no worse than the diplomats who at least managed to preserve their professional dignity in uncongenial surroundings. The attitude of the British military was truly extraordinary. 'Bomber' Harris told the Chiefs of Staff in October 1943 that the only reason why the Russian army had succeeded in advancing was because of the bomber offensive.[9] But perhaps the situation was best summed up by Conrad Collier, the air attaché in Moscow, when he wrote, 'What did I join the RAF for – to argue with four letter Russians or shoot bloody Huns?'[10]

The Service Chiefs were thus still determined to be tough with the Russians, the Prime Minister was deeply suspicious of Soviet motives, but the Foreign Office hoped to build on the foundations laid at the Moscow Conference. A major problem which had been avoided at Moscow was the question of Poland. The nearer the Red Army came to the Polish frontier the more acute the problem became. Eden hoped that the Poles would also benefit from the improved relations between the three great powers which had been achieved at Moscow. He assured the Polish Ambassador that 'M. Molotov had shown no desire to dominate or absorb Poland when liberated and that I was convinced that the Soviet Government had no intention of setting up a pseudo-Soviet Government in Warsaw.'[11] The Foreign Secretary suggested that it might be possible to do a deal with the Soviets on the Polish frontier and that this might well be underwritten by the United States. Otherwise there was a very real danger that Poland might face a *fait accompli* with the Red Army firmly established in the country.

The London Poles did not need any such warnings. They were already deeply concerned that the Russian troops would establish a puppet Communist government in Poland, and they were also afraid that they would take reprisals against the Polish patriots. Eden was still convinced that the Curzon Line, including Lvov and with compensations in East Prussia, Danzig and Silesia, was the best that the Poles could expect, and he pointed out that at least it was a slight improvement on the Molotov–Ribbentrop Line. But the Polish Government was still unwilling to negotiate, and the Polish Prime Minister told Eden that he pinned his hopes on an uprising that would coincide with the arrival of the Russian army on Polish soil.[12] Eden took this suggestion up with Molotov and proposed that arms should be sent to the Polish resistance. Molotov replied portentously that arms should only be given into safe hands, adding that he doubted whether there were any safe hands in Poland. He told Eden that the Soviet Union wanted an independent and friendly Poland, but said that the London Poles could hardly be described as friendly. It was doubtful whether any truly independent Polish government would ever be regarded as friendly by the Soviets, and the stage was being set for the tragedy of the Warsaw uprising.[13]

As Churchill prepared for his meeting with Stalin and Roosevelt in Teheran his main concern was not with Poland but with Italy. It seemed that he was positively obsessed with what Harry Hopkins called 'his bloody Italian war'. In a memorandum to the Chiefs of Staff Committee, Churchill wrote,

> The Germans have been able to withdraw several divisions from Italy, including one from the south of Rome in order to meet the needs on the Russian front. We have therefore failed to take the weight of the attack off the Soviets.

The offensive in Italy was going very badly, and the Yugoslav partisans were managing to engage as many divisions as the British and the Americans together. Churchill was seriously worried that the campaign in Italy had run out of steam and was leading to acute differences with the Americans. He was also annoyed by the lack of concern shown by the Chiefs of Staff who argued that as the Germans had only withdrawn three of their twenty-three divisions it was unfair to say that the Allies had not taken some of the heat off the Russians.[14] The Americans suspected that Churchill's obsession with Italy was part of a move to secure a further delay of OVERLORD, but in fact the main reason was that Churchill was painfully aware that he was going to meet Stalin with a very poor hand to play. Had the campaign in Italy been more successful his position would have been quite different, and he was determined to finish the job in Italy as quickly as possible. He told his doctor, 'Because the Americans want to invade France in six months' time, that is no reason why we should throw away these shining, gleaming opportunities in the Mediterranean.'[15]

Churchill arrived in Teheran tired, frustrated, badly prepared and heading for a serious illness. Roosevelt seemed unwilling to get to grips with the real issues, and still believed he could win over his friend Uncle Joe. Stalin, as always excellently briefed, had a far surer command of the overall military and political situation and had no difficulty in dominating the conference. There were great moments. Stalin was visibly moved when Churchill presented him with the sword of Stalingrad on behalf of King George VI. Stalin told Churchill, 'you are pro-German, the Devil is communist, and my friend God is a conservative'. Churchill proposed a toast to the proletarian masses. Stalin replied by drinking to the Conservative Party. Cadogan had little patience with such goings-on. He wrote to his wife, 'Winston and Joe and the President have bibulous parties, which I dare say will result in something concrete and useful, but at present it's a pretty woolly conference – all over the place.'[16] In his diary he confessed that he did not know what was going on at the conference and that he was very bored.

The only man who really knew what was going on was Stalin. His objective was to make sure that France was invaded as soon as possible. The Americans, spurred by Stalin's promise to declare war on Japan once the fighting in Europe ended, and who had always been enthusiastic second fronters, supported Stalin. Churchill, with his obsession about Italy and the Balkans, appeared to be the obstructionist. Stalin wanted a definite date for the invasion so as to prepare the Red Army for a fresh campaign and to soften the blow if there were any further delays.

At Teheran the decision taken at the Cairo conference that the invasion should take place in May 1944 was reaffirmed. It was agreed that the invasion might have to be postponed until June at the latest because only the first few days in May had suitable tides. If landing craft were available the invasion of northern France would be coupled with an invasion in the south (operation ANVIL). The Combined Chiefs hoped that the Soviets would agree to launch an offensive to coincide with the invasion, and they also hoped to work out a common policy for the Balkans. Nothing concrete came of these discussions.

On the question of the Polish frontiers there was tacit agreement that the Curzon Line should be the eastern frontier, and Churchill said that it would not break his heart if Lvov were to go to the Soviet Union. With the help of three matches Churchill demonstrated to Stalin how Poland would have to move westwards, a demonstration which pleased Stalin immensely although he would have liked to push Poland even further west.

Stalin told Churchill that he feared that Germany would go to war again within the next twenty years, and he emphasised that the Germans were a very clever, industrious and cultured people, and therefore extremely dangerous. Stalin and Roosevelt were both strongly in favour of splitting up Germany in order to render her hopelessly weak. Churchill did not think that this was an important issue. He believed that the trouble with Germany was Prussia and Prussian militarism which could be solved by allowing the Soviet Union and Poland to absorb Prussia, and by stringent controls on any revival of German military power. Stalin and Roosevelt disagreed, saying that there was no difference between Prussians and South Germans. Stalin said, 'They all fight like devils.' Stalin added that after the war at least 50 000 Germans would have to be executed. Churchill replied that he would 'not be a party to any butchery in cold blood. What happens in hot blood is another matter.' Stalin would not listen to this objection and insisted that 50 000 Germans had to be shot. Churchill grew increasingly angry and Roosevelt, who was greatly enjoying the sport of Churchill-baiting, suggested a compromise whereby only 49 000 Germans should be killed. At this point Churchill stormed out of the room, only to return when he had been mollified by Stalin.[17]

In retrospect it is amazing that the Teheran Conference achieved anything. The place was inconveniently situated, and a teeming Middle-Eastern city presented extraordinary security problems. The American delegation was hospitably lodged in the Soviet embassy, where no doubt their conversations were carefully monitored. The excuse given was that there were Nazi assassins on the loose and that the embassy was the only safe place for the Americans. In spite of Stalin's insistence no agenda had been prepared for the conference. Serious differences between the British and the Americans had arisen during their preliminary meeting in Cairo, and Roosevelt unwisely went to great lengths to stress these differences during his first meeting with Stalin. Stalin exploited this situation for all it was worth, but with his deeply suspicious mind he was still not convinced that the British and the Americans would honour their commitment to the second front. Churchill's handling of the Polish question was so off-hand that he must have given Stalin the impression that he did not really care what the Soviets had in mind. Teheran convinced the Soviets that the Western Allies recognised their right to establish what they euphemistically called 'friendly governments' in eastern Europe, and the glowing accounts of the conference which appeared in the Soviet press were a clear indication that Stalin felt he had secured a major victory.

After Teheran the second front was no longer a major issue. Stalin might continue to be suspicious, delays might occur, but a firm commitment had been made. The tremendous victories of the Red Army in the summer of 1943 against Army Group Centre removed the sense of urgency from the situation. With the second front issue out of the way Anglo–Soviet relations were now dominated by the question of the post-war settlement, and here the greatest problem was still the future of Poland. On his return to London from Teheran, Eden told the War Cabinet that he thought the Curzon Line was 'defensible' and that Stalin would probably agree to it. He felt that the Soviet proposal that the Oder should be the western frontier of Poland was 'extreme', but he felt that the Poles would be wise to 'close on this'.[18] The Foreign Office set about trying to get the Polish Government to agree to these frontiers, and hoped that the Russians would not wish to risk damaging Anglo–Soviet relations by refusing to accept such a reasonable solution. On 23 December Eden entertained the Polish Foreign Minister and Ambassador to dinner and outlined these proposals, although he studiously avoided mentioning the Soviet demand for Königsberg for fear that the Poles might suspect a plan by the Russians to encircle Poland.[19] In a subsequent meeting with Mikolacjzyk, Churchill repeated the argument that the Poles should settle with the Russians before the Red Army overran the country and was in a position to dictate terms. Mikolajczyk told the Prime Minister that he could not accept the Curzon Line as four million Poles lived on the other side of it, but Churchill warned him that there was very little room for negotiation.[20] Churchill was getting increasingly impatient with Polish intransigence. He wrote to Eden,

I rather contemplate telling the world that we declared war for Poland and that the Polish nation shall have a proper land to live in, but we have never undertaken to defend existing Polish frontiers, and that Russia, after two wars which have cost her between twenty and thirty millions of Russian lives has a right to the inexpugnable security of her western borders. ... They [the Poles] must be very silly if they imagine we are going to begin a new war with Russia for the sake of the Polish eastern border.[21]

Churchill wrote to Stalin saying that he hoped he would be able to get the Poles to see reason, and he wrote again to Eden that

If they [the Poles] do not come to terms the advancing Russian armies will set up their own men to run the country from which will certainly result in dissension, bloodshed and great evils to Poland. I think that we can do much with Mikolajczyk, Romer and Raczynski. I am told that the obstructionist is the President, though he has always seemed a weak creature to me.[22]

The more frustrated the Prime Minister got with the Poles the greater was his sympathy for the Russians. He told Eden,

The tremendous victories of the Russian armies, the deep-seated changes which have taken place in the character of the Russian state and government, the new confidence which has grown in our hearts towards Stalin – these have all had their effect.[23]

It soon became obvious that this confidence in Stalin and his regime was premature, for the Soviet Government made it perfectly plain that they did not want any discussions with the Poles, and demanded an acceptance by the Poles of the Curzon Line. It was even questionable whether they were prepared to deal with the London Poles at all. The Foreign Office reported that Beneš had told the Australian chargé d'affaires in Moscow that the Soviets wanted a drastic reconstitution of the Polish Government before they would be prepared to treat with it.[24] A few weeks later Molotov told the Australian Minister that the Soviet Union would only deal with a Polish Government elected by 'democratic' Poles in Britain, the United States and the Soviet Union.[25] As the Soviets stepped up the pressure on the Poles the British despaired of ever reaching a satisfactory settlement of the frontier question. Eden wrote, 'The Poles will be mad if they don't try to come to terms with the Russians; unhappily signs are they are mad.'[26] In a lengthy memorandum Orme Sargent wrote,

> Stalin no doubt is convinced that however much we may protest, in fact the Russian armies are going to reach Warsaw one of these days, and when they do he will be able to set up a Polish Government which will negotiate a settlement giving the Soviet Government full control of Polish territory up to the German frontier. For this, I feel sure, is what Stalin is determined to have. He knows he could never get this from the present Polish Government, and as he does not intend to be rebuffed he prefers to wait until he can ensure full and prompt acceptance of his demands by dictating his terms in Warsaw.

His conclusion was that there was no point in having a headlong collision with Stalin when there was no hope of winning.[27]

A Soviet note on the Polish question delivered in January prompted a violent reaction from the Poles. The Polish Government flatly refused to accept any declarations about the frontiers until after the war. Eden told the War Cabinet that he 'had made it clear to the Poles that if they took this line they would forfeit the sympathy of British public opinion and that they would put themselves in a position in which we would not be able to help them'.[28] The British

Government managed to get the Poles to tone down their reply, but this had no effect on the Soviets who were not interested in any discussions.[29] The Foreign Office, although urging the Poles to negotiate, were disgusted with the attitude of the Soviet Government, not only for their intransigence over the Polish question, but also because they were accusing the British of negotiating with the Germans for a separate peace. Cadogan was so incensed at this charge that he wrote of the Russians, 'They are the most stinking creepy set of Jews I have ever come across. ... They are swine.'[30] Churchill said,

> Trying to maintain good relations with a Communist is like wooing a crocodile. You do not know whether to tickle it under the chin or to beat it over the head. When it opens its mouth you cannot tell whether it is trying to smile or prepare to eat you up?[31]

At a discussion of the Polish question in the War Cabinet on 25 January Churchill pointed out that he was faced with a major problem in that whatever the outcome he would be charged with violating the Atlantic Charter. On the other hand if a settlement was not reached the Russians would enter Warsaw and have a plebiscite to set up a government that would be in full accord with their views. He added, 'Nor ought we to ignore the fact that only Russian sacrifices and victories hold out any prospects of the restoration of a free Poland.' Eden was also determined to reach a settlement 'since the bargaining position of the Polish Government would worsen rapidly as the Russians advanced over Polish territory'. The War Cabinet decided that the only hope was for the Prime Minister to deal directly with Stalin over the Curzon Line.[32]

A further complicating factor in the Polish situation was the attitude of the Polish underground army. As the Russians approached the Polish frontier they were soon likely to go into action. The British Government welcomed their determination to 'kill Huns', in Churchill's phrase, but were naturally anxious about the reaction of the Soviets. Eden was encouraged when he was informed in early January that the Polish authorities were prepared to co-ordinate their military efforts with the Soviet Union, and he hoped that this would end Stalin's virulent accusations against the underground army.[33] Shortly afterwards Mikolajczyk handed Eden a copy of a Soviet order which read in part:

On the instructions of Comrade Nozenko all partisans are ordered
to disarm Polish detachments. Those resisting are to be shot
on the spot. All Polish underground organisations are to be
exterminated and their leaders executed.

The Polish Prime Minister told the Foreign Secretary that a number
of Poles had already been shot and that others were reported
missing.[34] Yet in spite of this grim report the British continued to
support Polish plans for a 'general rising' against the Germans. It
was hoped that 150 000 men could be armed and that guerilla activity
could be stepped up. The major problem was the difficulty of dropping
supplies to the Polish underground army, for SOE reported that
supplies were still woefully inadequate. The Foreign Office decided
that nothing should be said to the Russians until the Poles had been
properly supplied and were prepared for an uprising, and that military
co-ordination could then be carried out through the SOE detachment
in Moscow.[35]

Reporting to the Prime Minister at the beginning of February Eden
said that Romer, the Polish Foreign Minister, had assured him that
the Poles would attack the Germans as soon as the Russians crossed
the border. Eden supported this plan on the grounds that it would
show that the Poles were on the same side as the Russians – an
argument which overlooked the fact that many of the members of
the underground army were as fiercely anti-Soviet as they were anti-
German.[36] Churchill was keenly aware of this problem and told the
War Cabinet that he was seriously worried that the Poles might soon
start fighting the Russians, thus making the situation even more
intolerable.[37]

With the perceptible hardening of the Soviet attitude towards
Poland and with the Poles showing no willingness to compromise,
the British Government thus found itself in an almost impossible
situation. On 28 January Churchill wrote to Stalin warning him that

the creation in Warsaw of another Polish Government different
from the one we have recognised up to the present, together with
the disturbances in Poland, would raise issues in Great Britain and
the United States detrimental to that close accord between the
three Great Powers upon which the future of the world depends.[38]

In reply Stalin lectured Clark Kerr on Poland for two hours, the nub
of his argument being that he saw no reason why the British
Government should not get rid of the Commander-in-Chief and

President elect, Sosnkowski, the Minister of Information, Kot, and Kukiel, the Minister of War.[39] The War Cabinet discussed this response and Churchill suggested that an effort should be made to remove the 'intransigents' from the Polish Government and that the whole matter might then be settled through direct negotiations with the USSR. The Minister of Information announced that he was going to cut off supplies of paper to the Polish opposition press which did nothing but provide the Russians with ammunition to use against the London Poles and to embarrass the British Government.[40]

There was no doubt in Eden's mind that the Soviet Union would get the Curzon Line and would be able to restructure the Polish Government and that there was precious little that the London Poles could do about it. He wrote to Churchill that the British Government would have to 'accept a considerable degree of responsibility for the practical execution of the bargain', but that at least this would enable the Poles to make a 'leap in the dark'.[41] Churchill then invited Mikolajczyk, Romer and Raczynski to Chequers in an attempt to get them to accept Stalin's terms. It soon became obvious that the Poles were not prepared to do any leaping in the dark. Mikolajczyk told the Prime Minister that he was grateful to him 'for all he had done, but he could not go so far as was proposed without abandoning Poland's moral right and losing the support of his people'.[42] Churchill reported to the War Cabinet that he was left with the impression that the Poles were more likely to accept changes in the Government than they were to accept the Curzon Line.[43] Thus a solution was as far off as ever.

The Polish Government found a staunch supporter in the British Ambassador to Poland, Sir Owen O'Malley. He told Churchill that the British Government was obviously not prepared to quarrel with the Russians over Poland and that 'if this view is a true one, H.M.G. would have eventually, even if not immediately, to bear the odium of what the Poles call "A second Munich"'. Cadogan on reading this memorandum felt that

> the Polish Government certainly have a terrible choice before them. They look like choosing to safeguard their own honour at the expense of their country. Whether that is right morally I don't pretend to say. ... What *are* we going to do?

Churchill had no patience with such talk. He felt that the Soviet demands on Poland were perfectly justified and that there was no question of them being morally wrong.

They are in my opinion no more than what is right and just for
Russia, without whose prodigious exertions no vestige of Poland
would remain free from German annihilation or subjugation. . . .
If of course the view is adopted that Russia is going to present
herself as a new Nazi Germany ideologically inverted, we shall
have to make what head we can against another tyranny, and this
would have to be borne in mind when considering the position
which a chastened Germany would occupy.

That the Poles should start talking about another Munich particularly
infuriated the Prime Minister, for they had 'jumped on the back of
Czechoslovakia in the moment of agony and helped to rend her to
pieces'. Churchill felt that the Curzon Line had been good enough
in 1920 and therefore should be acceptable in 1943. In his view the
Poles were being utterly unreasonable in not seeing this simple fact,
and should be made to see sense.[44] Churchill therefore told the War
Cabinet that the Poles should be persuaded to accept the Curzon
Line, and if they still refused the British Government should inform
the Russians that they would support their claims against Poland at
the peace conference.[45] This was hardly a solution to the problem,
for the Poles were unlikely ever to accept this frontier and the
Russians did not appear to be interested in making a deal with
anyone.
    Clark Kerr had another interview with Stalin about Poland at the
end of February. Stalin wasted no time on diplomatic niceties. He
demanded the acceptance of the Curzon Line and the reconstruction
of the Polish Government. He flatly rejected Churchill's offer
to mediate. Reporting this interview to the Foreign Office, the
Ambassador suggested that it was very unlikely that the London
Poles had much support in Poland and that if that were indeed the
case then the British Government should reconsider supporting them.
Churchill, who saw all his hopes of reaching a compromise shattered,
was furious with Clark Kerr and minuted, 'I don't much like this
stuff. He would give up everything to appease Stalin.'[46]
    Churchill was certainly in no mood to appease Stalin. The more
intransigent Stalin became the more the Prime Minister sympathised
with the Poles, particularly as Stalin showed no understanding of the
exceedingly difficult situation in which the British Government was
placed. Churchill told the War Cabinet that if Stalin was going to
make the going rough for him he would stand up and fight and show
the world that the British Government supported the London Poles.[47]

He then wrote to Clark Kerr telling him that his support was still for the London Poles, that he would not put up with Stalin's bullying tactics, and that the War Cabinet was 'solid and stiff'.[48]

Stalin continued to attack the British Government, accusing them of leaking one of his telegrams to the press and for backing down on the Teheran agreement over the Curzon Line. The British were convinced that the leak came from the Soviet Embassy in an attempt to embarrass the Government, but there was also a widespread feeling in Government circles that the Poles were being deliberately tiresome and were doing serious harm to the alliance with the Soviet Union. Eden told the War Cabinet that the Government should make a statement that they had done everything possible to bring about an agreement between the Soviet Union and the Poles, but that they had failed through no fault of their own. The only possible hope still seemed to be that the Poles could be convinced that the Russians would accept the Curzon Line and that this was the best possible deal they could get.[49]

Churchill felt there was little chance of this policy being successful, for it had already failed miserably and the Poles showed no signs of changing their minds. He believed that it was pointless to argue with the Russians and his main concern now was that they would start murdering the Poles. He was utterly disgusted with the Russian attitude towards the Polish question and he wrote, 'Although I have tried in every way to put myself in sympathy with these Communist leaders I cannot feel the slightest trust or confidence in them. Force and facts are their only realities.' He even began to worry that the Russians might 'tip the wink to the Germans and let them move troops west when we get on the Continent'. Eden did not share this bleak view. He felt that Poland was the one great exception and that otherwise the Soviets still recognised the British *locus standi* as mediators in the settlement in Eastern Europe. Churchill still could not believe that this unfortunate situation was Stalin's fault, and he agreed with the Foreign Office that he was being pressured by his victorious generals who wanted to keep the British out of Eastern Europe.[50]

In January 1944 the question of responsibility for the Katyn massacre again came to the forefront, making any agreement between the London Poles and the Soviets almost impossible. The Soviets appointed a 'State Commission for the Investigation of German Fascist Atrocities' and invited British and American journalists to visit the Katyn woods. Bruce Lockhart reported from Moscow that most of the reporters found the Soviet account of the massacre singularly unconvincing. Their entire case rested on providing that the men had been killed after July 1941, and many felt that the medical evidence in support of this theory was inadequate. One brave Pole in Moscow told some of the reporters that the men were alive in the Summer of 1941, and many were impressed by his testimony.[51]

The Soviet report on the Katyn affair was sent to FORD for analysis. The FORD team, in which Christopher Hill was a leading figure, on the whole supported the Soviet version, using the highly dubious argument that 'the Soviet evidence is not conclusive in certain important respects. This fact tells against the accusation that the evidence was simply manufactured by the G.P.U.' The Poles stuck to their version of the story and insisted that the Soviets had taken about 181 000 Polish prisoners of war of whom about 10 000 officers had disappeared. They believed that these officers had been murdered between March and April 1940 and pointed to the dates on the papers found on the bodies as evidence for this approximate date. The Poles pointed out that when they had asked the International Red Cross to examine the graves, Molotov had written to Romer claiming that the Poles had 'treacherously stabbed the Soviet Union in the back' and that they were preparing the ground for a pact with Hitler. The Soviets then broke off diplomatic relations with the London Poles who saw this move as tantamount to an admission of Russian guilt.

The London Poles had a firm champion in O'Malley who pointed out that none of the families of the missing officers had received any messages after May 1940, although the Germans did not reach Smolensk until the summer of 1941. The Polish Government had never been given a satisfactory reply to their requests to the Soviet Government for information about what had happened to the officers. The Ambassador was also fiercely critical of the British Government's attempts to play down the affair. He wrote to Eden, 'We have in fact perforce used the good name of England like the murderers used the conifers to cover up a massacre' and he added a quote from Headlam Morley: 'What in international affairs is morally indefensible generally turns out in the long run to have been politically inept.'[52]

When the Soviet report was published, and in spite of FORD's acceptance of the general line of argument, O'Malley returned to the fray. He pointed out to Eden that the Soviet version asked people to believe that 10 000 prisoners stayed in a camp from April 1940 to July 1941 without a single man escaping or getting word to the outside. Turning to Polish reactions to the report he remarked bitterly, 'Affliction and residence in this country seem to be teaching them how much better it is in political life to leave unsaid those things about which one feels most passionately.' Eden was not entirely convinced by this line of argument, and told the Prime Minister that 'the evidence is conflicting and whatever we may suspect, we shall probably never know'. Churchill felt that the Katyn affair was a nuisance and an embarrassment and replied, 'This is not one of those matters where absolute certainty is either urgent or desirable.'[53]

The Foreign Office also hoped that the Katyn affair would not prejudice Anglo–Soviet relations and therefore tried to play it down as much as possible. Geoffrey Wilson minuted:

> The Russians were certain to set up their own commission of investigation some time, and its report will come in handy in the dispute with the Poles. To avoid any new outburst of recrimination it would be useful if the British press could be induced to give the report, when it appears, the minimum of publicity.

Frank Roberts added:

> It is perhaps worthwhile recalling in this connection that the chances of smoothing things over at the time of Katyn were seriously prejudiced by the Prime Minister's tactics in dealing with Marshall Stalin. Sir A. Clark Kerr twice 'jibbed' against delivering messages in terms drafted by the Prime Minister but the latter insisted.[54]

The Foreign Office therefore decided to ignore the affair as much as possible and to invite experts to examine the relative merits of the German and Soviet reports. Unsolicited advice was not slow in coming, including a report from Professor D. L. Savory, charmingly addressed to the 'Primate Minister'. Cadogan reached the frustrating conclusion that '*All* evidence from *both* sides is faked,' but a paper by the historian B. H. Sumner was felt by both Wilson and Warner to seriously undermine the Soviet argument. O'Malley's passionate paper was deemed by Warner to be 'brilliant but not quite objective'. The Foreign Office's legal adviser, Sir William Malkin, examined the reports and called for a suspension of judgement. The view was readily accepted by the Foreign Office.[55]

The Polish question thus plagued Anglo–Soviet relations in early 1944, and an attempt to improve the exchange of technical information did nothing to improve the situation. The British and the Americans discussed the question of sending technical information to the Russians in a fresh round of talks in early 1944. It was agreed that the two countries should pool their technical information and then decide what to give to the Russians. The War Office was in a slightly more generous mood than usual, and decided to give the Russians information on radar, including production methods and technical characteristics. The Americans were even more secretive than the British, and there was a great deal of information they wished to withhold. The British favoured the idea of a tripartite agreement on the exchange of technical information, as the existing arrangement meant that elaborate excuses had to be found why certain information was not given, and this often placed them in a very awkward situation. Furthermore the Americans had quite often vetoed the sending of material which the British were prepared to send. The Americans would not agree to the tripartite system as they were deeply suspicious of the Russians and wanted to avoid making any definite commitments. The British assumed that the Germans would be defeated by the end of 1944 and that the Russians would then go to war with Japan. They therefore argued that the Russians should be provided with as much modern equipment as possible so as to make them fully prepared for war with Japan in January 1945 and help bring the war in the Pacific to a swift conclusion. The main concern of the British was thus to work out a new agreement that had a satisfactory escape clause. The Americans were obsessed by the idea of reciprocity which, given the much lower level of Soviet technology, would make any agreement almost impossible.[56]

Although the British still preferred a tripartite agreement, the Chiefs of Staff were prepared to accept the American idea of a monthly 'shopping list' of requests to the Soviet Union. But the Soviets continued to withhold information to such an extent that the hardliners in the War Office were provided with ample ammunition to support their case that no concessions should be made to the Russians. The Soviets refused to say which German divisions they were facing at the front and would not release a Panther tank which the British were particularly anxious to examine. The British were getting very tired of this endless haggling and Cavendish-Bentinck wrote: 'The Russians are Asiatics and cannot be judged by European standards.'[57] Although the Foreign Office felt that helping Russia was an end in itself they began to feel that it was not unreasonable to expect something in return. They sympathised with the Russians in as much as they found the intransigent attitude of the British Military Mission in Moscow intolerable, and they felt that the Service Departments could show more generosity and goodwill towards an ally who was fighting so well, but their patience was beginning to wear a trifle thin. The Soviets showed no interest whatever in the proposed technical mission, and given the mutual feelings of suspicion and often of downright hostility, no workable solution could be found for these problems.

Almost the only hopeful sign of a possible improvement in Anglo–Soviet relations at this time was provided by the Soviet–Czechoslovak Treaty of 11 December 1943, for it was hoped that this might provide a model for a settlement of the Polish question.[58] In retrospect Churchill's admiration for Beneš, whom he called 'Beans', and the hope that the Czechs would be able to mediate between the Soviets and the Poles, seems truly extraordinary. Of all the exile governments in London the Czechs were the most consistently pro-Soviet and anti-British, and Beneš showed an astonishing degree of gullibility in his dealings with the Russians who disguised their amazement at his political innocence with rich doses of flattery and elaborate hospitality. While in Moscow Beneš spoke disparagingly of the London Poles and suggested that the only solution to the Polish question would be the formation of a new government in Poland once the country was occupied by the Red Army. In the vain delusion that he would be able to 'swallow and digest' the Communists, he told his Soviet hosts that he would be happy to accept a Communist Premier of Czechoslovakia after the war.

Eden at first thought that the Czechoslovak–Soviet Treaty was a serious mistake that would isolate the Poles and lead to the division of Europe, a view that was held by the United States' Government. Frank Roberts believed that the Treaty placed Czechoslovakia firmly in the Soviet camp and marked a radical break with Masaryk's policy of close ties with the West. But having been bombarded by eulogies of Beneš, Eden changed his mind and wrote of American opposition to the Treaty, 'The Americans don't help themselves but are always ready to criticise the efforts of others.'[59] From Cairo Lord Killean reported to the Foreign Office,

President Beneš is greatly pleased at results of his visit to Moscow. He found them all, from Stalin downwards, free from their old suspicions and frankly delighted to be treated on a footing of complete equality by Great Britain and America. ... He has spoken very frankly to Stalin about Poland and the Polish fear of being Bolshevised. Stalin had denied any such policy as being idiotic and not his intention.[60]

John Balfour, writing from the Moscow Embassy, was even more expansive. He told the Foreign Office that Stalin was determined

> to grant the liberated peoples of Europe the full right and freedom to decide for themselves the question of their form of government. ... Quite apart from the change in mental outlook as compared with the self-assertive ideology of the earlier revolutionary epoch, past experience has in any case taught the rulers of this country that international communism is a weapon of dubious value, whether for furthering the larger aims of Soviet Russia as a world power or for promoting the sympathy of sister Slav states situated near home. The road which has of late been travelled is marked by such conspicuous milestones as the dissolution of the Comintern last May and the publication in December of the new National Anthem.[61]

The British had no idea what actually went on during Beneš' visit to Moscow, and the situation was not made any clearer by his disingenuous reporting of his experiences. The terms of the treaty were vague, but Beneš' reputation as a statesman was enhanced. The British knew that they were clutching at a straw when they hoped that Beneš had found a solution to the problem of how to come to terms with the Russians, but they had no idea how thin this particular straw was to prove. Far from helping to reach a compromise over Poland, Beneš' visit strengthened Stalin's determination to find a Czechoslovakian solution to Poland. In other words Poland was to be reduced to a state of fawning submission disguised as statesmanlike realism. As Frank Roberts wrote:

> Time will show whether the new Czech realism, which seems to consist of an absolute faith in the unqualified support and good intentions of the U.S.S.R. (equalled only by their previous faith in France and the League of Nations) is in fact anything more than a façade of realism.[62]

Secure in the knowledge of Beneš' compliance the Soviets began to press for a more active resistance movement in Czechoslovakia in which the local Communists would win fresh laurels in the anti-fascist struggle. The NKVD hoped to get SOE support for this plan, but SOE thought that the proposal was absurd. After the murder of Heydrich, which had been planned by SOE, there had been terrible reprisals, of which the massacre at Lidice was the most ghastly example, and the Czech underground had been virtually destroyed. German security forces were so efficient in Czechoslovakia that it was almost impossible for allied agents to survive for more than a few hours after being dropped into the *Reichsprotectorat*.[63] When the Slovak uprising began in late 1944 the British only sent medical supplies, for the Chiefs of Staff ruled that Slovakia was in the Russian sphere of operations as they did not want to become involved in another disaster as terrible as the Warsaw uprising. SOE operations in the *Reichsprotectorat* were also wound down and the whole of Czechoslovakia was considered to be the responsibility of the Soviets. All requests from the Czechoslovak resistance were to be channelled through Moscow. SOE protested that this policy would result in Czechoslovakia being taken over by the Communists. The Foreign Office felt that this would probably happen anyway and adopted a fatalistic attitude, and the Chiefs of Staff did not want to do anything that might lead to a general uprising which the Germans were likely to crush with the utmost brutality.

In early 1944 the British were obliged to address a problem which was to become increasingly difficult and which has subsequently become the object of bitter criticism and recrimination.[64] Cavendish-Bentinck of the Joint Intelligence Committee reported that there were about 470 000 Russians either in the German army or working in some capacity for the military.[65] The Foreign Office hoped that it might be possible, in Sir A. Noble's words, to spread 'alarm and despondency' among these Russians, and it was felt that this could be done without getting the Soviet authorities involved. Bruce Lockhart argued that the best possible form of propaganda would be to promise them good treatment if they surrendered to the Allies. From the outset of these discussions Geoffrey Wilson pointed out the central dilemma. It was known that these men could expect no mercy from the Soviets, that the Soviets would demand them back after the war, and that it would be very difficult not to comply with such a request. In these circumstances it was obvious that the promise of good treatment would be essentially an empty one. In April 1944 Wilson wrote, 'I think we could ignore Russian criticism of our broadcasting to those men but I do not see how we could refuse to hand them over to the Russians after the war if we were pressed to do so by Moscow.'[66] Bruce Lockhart replied that British propaganda should therefore include a promise that the men would not be handed over to the Soviet authorities otherwise it would have no effect. The problem was therefore whether to concentrate on the short-term question of undermining the morale of the Russians in the German armed forces, even at the risk of making promises that were certain to be broken, or whether to look more carefully at the moral, human and political consequences of such an action.

The branch of Military Intelligence responsible for Germany, MI3(c), estimated that there were about 200 000 Russians with the German forces in France and they insisted that they would fight well against the allied forces in Normandy. The Foreign Office felt that this estimation of their fighting ability was grossly exaggerated, but they agreed with Military Intelligence that these Russians were an excellent target for political propaganda. According to British intelligence reports General Andrei Vlasov's 'Russian Army of Liberation' did not include members of the 'minor nationalities'. These were organised by the Germans into legions with German officers and NCOs. A large number of Soviet POWs were also used for construction work in *Organisation Todt*. Others were sent to anti-aircraft units. Cavendish-Bentinck had a very low opinion of all these units, including Vlasov's army which was regarded as something of an élite force. Subsequent experience was to prove his assessment perfectly correct.[67]

It was obviously absurd to imagine that a massive propaganda campaign could be directed against these Russians without the Soviets finding out about it. In May 1944 SHAEF therefore asked the Russians to agree to a general amnesty for Soviet deserters from German units. This amnesty was to take the form of a general declaration published immediately after D-Day.[68] This proposal was forwarded to the Soviets by the British Military Mission in Moscow who got a prompt reply that the whole idea was quite pointless as there were so few Soviet POWs in the West. This ridiculous argument left the British in no doubt that the Soviets would never cooperate with any propaganda efforts of this sort. They were therefore left with three possible courses of action. They could make promises to the Soviet POWs and then break them. They could postpone any action until they got an assurance from the Soviets that the prisoners would be well treated on their return to Russia, but it was most unlikely that the Soviets would ever agree. Lastly, the British could accept full responsibility for the Soviet prisoners and refuse to hand them over to the Soviet authorities unless they misbehaved. The Foreign Office still felt that a propaganda offensive was the best course of action. Christopher Warner suggested that the Russians should be told that their good deeds would be counted in their favour and that they should expect no mercy if they were found actively cooperating with the Germans. SHAEF however were afraid that any such appeal would simply prompt the Germans to take counter-measures and would thus be self-defeating. Warner continued to argue that the Russians should be promised good treatment if they handed themselves over, and asked whether it might not be possible to refuse to hand them over to the Soviets. At the same time he suggested that the Soviets might still be persuaded to change their minds. SHAEF replied that the whole affair was not worth the risk of a major row with the Soviets and therefore it should be dropped. Eden, who knew that the Soviets would never agree to offer an amnesty, felt that nothing should be done unless the Chiefs of Staff felt that it was really worthwhile. They did not, and therefore nothing more was done about it. An exchange of notes between Clark Kerr and Molotov on the POWs indicated that the Soviets had no intention of changing their minds.

The first intelligence reports that came in after the D-Day landings indicated that the Russians were terrified of being sent back to the Soviet Union as they were convinced that they would either be shot or sent to labour camps. Nobel suggested that perhaps these prisoners might be used in British labour camps in the Far East, but this proposal was rejected on the reasonable grounds that there was certainly no labour shortage in that part of the world. Interrogations of the first batch of prisoners confirmed that they were indeed terrified of being sent back to the Soviet Union but at the same time they had no desire to fight against the Allies. But what could be done with these people? Eden suggested that the British could use the Soviet POWs as cheap labour and suggested that the Soviets 'couldn't be so haughty about other peoples' Quislings'.[69] It was also suggested that the Soviet prisoners should be treated as émigrés and issued with Nansen passports, but Warner would not hear of this suggestion and argued that the prisoners could be used as bargaining counters to score points with the Soviets. Cadogan doubted whether this was a practical proposition and wrote, 'The Russians are Soviet soldiers taken prisoner by the Germans, who have, doubtless under duress, taken up arms in the service of the enemy. The Soviet Government would probably demand their return for execution.' Geoffrey Wilson thought that the Permanent Under-Secretary was being excessively morbid. He replied, 'I doubt if the Russians will shoot many – they are very hard up for labour and I expect their fate will be construction work in Siberia for a good many years.'[70]

A number of captured Russians were sent to England. At a camp in Devizes there were some 1000 Russians, 90 per cent of whom had been in the Red Army, and only two of them were classified as 'Whites'. All of them claimed that they had been forced to serve in the German army. The non-combatant Russians were held at another camp at Kempton Park, and they showed a much greater willingness to return home. The Soviet authorities were immediately informed of the presence of these Russians in England, and the Foreign Office hoped that a satisfactory agreement could be reached on their fate. The immediate reaction from the Soviets was a barrage of complaints that the Russians were far worse treated than the German POWs. Brigadier Firebrace of the Russian Liaison Group flippantly replied that the Germans had signed the Geneva Convention and the Soviets had not, so there was no reason for complaint. The Foreign Office felt that this was a joke in very poor taste.[71]

The presence of these Soviet POWs in England made the Chiefs of Staff more enthusiastic for a political offensive against the remaining Russians in the German armed forces. They suggested that SOE might use the prisoners to convince the Russians who were still fighting against the Allies to surrender. The Foreign Office agreed in principle, but insisted that any such programme should be carried out in cooperation with the Soviets. An approach was therefore made to NKVD, who took a long time to reply. Their answer showed a deep suspicion of British motives, but under the circumstances the Foreign Office felt that this was quite understandable.[72]

In September Warner reported that the War Cabinet had decided that the Soviet Prisoners should be handed over to the Soviet authorities, but that the Soviets should agree not to try or execute any of them before the cessation of hostilities in Europe. No such undertaking was forthcoming, but it was reported that the first batch of prisoners who were sent back to the Soviet Union via Iraq had been well treated. Each man had been issued with 50 cigarettes, they were shown movies, given hot baths, allowed to use the swimming pool and were taken on a sight-seeing tour of Baghdad. By November 1944 some 10000 men had been returned to the Soviet Union. It was not until the end of the year that a Major Cregeen reported that there had been no welcoming party for a shipload of prisoners when they arrived in Murmansk and that they had been rushed off to a prison camp under a heavily-armed guard. Geoffrey Wilson did not think that this was necessarily a cause for concern. He commented on the report, 'The armed guard is not in the least surprising ... I should like to know a great deal more about Major Cregeen.'

Thus by the end of 1944 the question of the Soviet POWs was hardly a matter of major concern. The British Government had tried to reach an understanding with the Soviets that the prisoners would be well treated, but they had failed. The British authorities were not particularly concerned about the Russians, for most of them had fought in the German army or worked in *Organisation Todt* and it was virtually impossible to tell in each individual case whether they could be excused by extenuating circumstances. Germany was still far from being defeated and the preservation of the alliance with the Soviet Union was of the utmost importance, particularly as the whole issue was first raised in the nervous weeks before D-Day. At such a time it was unthinkable that the Soviet POWs should be given émigré status, or British nationality. A legal adviser to the Foreign Office, Patrick Dean, stated that it was not possible for a soldier who was captured while serving in the enemy's forces to claim the protection of the Geneva Convention. It was not until the end of March 1945 that the Foreign Office learnt that the Americans did not agree with this legal interpretation and argued that forcible repatriation was against the spirit of the Geneva Convention. Proposals to use some half a million people in labour camps were hopelessly unrealistic and were therefore never discussed in any detail. From the British point of view the whole matter was a Soviet concern and it was hoped that one day a satisfactory agreement could be reached with the Soviets; meanwhile the last thing the British wanted was to be accused by the Soviets of harbouring traitors, fascists and counter-revolutionaries. The preservation of the wartime alliance had to take precedence over the fate of Soviet citizens who had been fighting for the Germans. It was not until this basic policy had been established that the British authorities began to find themselves in a cruel and politically insoluble moral dilemma.

9 The Beginnings of Post-War Planning

It was not until 1944 that the British Government began to think seriously about the problems of the post-war world and the probable tendencies of future Soviet policy. In April the Foreign Office prepared a lengthy document for the War Cabinet outlining its thinking about the likely effects on British interests of post-war Soviet policy.[1] It was felt that for ten years after the war the Soviet Union would be totally absorbed with the rehabilitation and reconstruction of its own territories and would present no threat to the Western Powers. Furthermore, since Stalin's victory over Trotsky the fixed point of Soviet policy had been the search for security against any power, or group of powers, which might threaten her while she was organising and developing her own domain. In the post-war years the Soviet Union's main concern would therefore be with the possible resurgence of German power. The most salutary effect of the war on the Soviet Union was that it had enabled her to get on terms of equality, confidence and cooperation with the principal world powers other than Germany and Japan, and to exorcise her fear of those two powers. Thus the Soviet Union would be able to devote all her energies to internal organisation and development without fear of aggression from without and, given the consolidation of the regime during the war, without fear of counter-revolution from within. Thus if the British Commonwealth and the United States were willing to cooperate, the post-war years were likely to be marked by a long period of peaceful relations between the three Great Powers.

The key to exorcising Soviet suspicions therefore seemed to the Foreign Office to lie in the treatment accorded to Germany and Japan. If Soviet demands, which would probably be very severe, were not met, the Soviet Union would probably suspect that the Western Powers were planning to combine with a revived Germany against her, and would thus become a highly disruptive force in Europe using all the weapons at her disposal: the sympathy of left-wing governments, political intrigue and power politics. If the experiment in post-war cooperation were to fail the Soviet Union would remain an immensely strong military power with enormous influence in the eastern hemisphere and would pose a particular threat to the British position in the Middle East.

The Soviet Union would emerge from the war as the strongest land power in the world, as a great Slav power, and with an impressive war record based on the achievements of a planned economy and socialism in one country, so that the Soviet state was likely to find sympathetic admirers in many quarters. But the Soviet Union would have to concentrate on the awesome task of reconstruction after the horrendous devastations of war, and this would be made all the more difficult by the probable increase in the demand for consumer goods coupled with a decreased capacity to meet such a demand. If the harsh restrictions on the consumer sector imposed by the five-year plans and by the exigencies of a war economy were relaxed recovery would probably be very slow. It was likely that the Soviet Union would seek economic assistance from the United States and Britain to help overcome the difficulties of post-war reconstruction. Provided that both these powers were willing to supply the Soviet Union on advantageous terms the Soviets were unlikely to do anything that might jeopardise the flow of goods, and both the Western Powers would thus be able to exercise considerable influence over the USSR. In the long term, however, the Foreign Office felt that trade considerations were unlikely to play a significant role in Soviet policy, and the Soviet Union would probably revert to her traditional policy of trying to remain as autarchic as possible.

The experiences of 1941 and 1942, when a country of 100 million fewer inhabitants than Russia overran in an incredibly short time a greater area than had ever been conquered since the campaigns of Alexander the Great, showed up the shortcomings and the inefficiencies of the Soviet system, and it had only been possible to stem the tide by staggering sacrifices of men and material. The recovery of Germany would therefore be the Soviet Union's principal concern in the post-war period. For this reason Stalin wanted the complete dismemberment of Germany and would never risk the possibility of a strong power, or combination of powers, which might grow up on the Soviet Union's western frontier and which might combine with Germany against her. Soviet demands were therefore certain to include the recognition of the 1941 frontiers, the total subjugation of Germany, and a guarantee that nearby European countries would be neither willing nor able to threaten her territory either alone or in combination. If the Soviet Union, Britain, the United States and China could agree on a scheme for world organisation and combine to resist any attempts by a resurgent Germany to undermine it, the chances for a long period without any major frictions or tension were good. A possible problem was that the United States might withdraw from the world organisation, but even then Soviet relations with Britain would be satisfactory if the European settlement was agreeable to the Soviets.

The aim of British policy should be to maintain regular consultation, cooperation, and mutual give and take with the Soviet Union in the post-war years, otherwise the Soviets would revert to their traditional suspiciousness. Even if the wartime alliance were to break down it was felt that it was unlikely that the Soviets would pursue an expansionist policy. They were likely to be passively uncooperative and tiresome rather than openly provocative and aggressive, particularly if the Anglo–American alliance remained close and strong. The Soviet leaders were realists and nationalists rather than ideologues, but they were still liable to exploit their role as champion of the world's proletariat, the downtrodden and the exploited in order to pursue their national goals. This would be particularly true in Eastern Europe where the new appeal of the Soviet Union was combined with the traditional appeal of Russia as the great Slav leader. It was felt that Bulgaria and Czechoslovakia were particularly prone to feel the pull of this attraction.

Having examined the probable thrust of Soviet policy, the paper then turned to the Soviet Union's interest in specific countries. The Soviets were determined that Germany should be dismembered and used as a source of reparations for the enormous damage inflicted on them. Soviet mistrust of Germany was such that they would probably not even welcome a Communist Germany, and the paper suggested that the Soviet Union was gradually abandoning Communism and therefore feared that a Communist Germany could very well take over the leadership of world Communism. Given these fears of Germany it was essential that the Western Powers should resist any temptation to combine with Germany, for this would mark the end of the Anglo–Soviet alliance.

As far as Poland was concerned the Foreign Office felt that the Poles should accept the proposals on frontiers made by the Soviets at Teheran, for they would never be able to secure a more satisfactory arrangement. If the Soviets were satisfied that Poland was not hostile to them they would probably tolerate a degree of genuine independence, although they would almost certainly demand a guarantee that Soviet troops could march through Poland to meet any future threat from Germany.

It was also felt that the USSR would have no serious objections to the revival of France as a great power which was an important aim of British policy. France would play a vital role in containing Germany and would thus help to relieve the Soviets' greatest fear. The French Right had been discredited by its connivance with the Germans and the post-war government of France was likely to be friendly towards the Soviet Union.

In the Baltic and Scandinavia the Soviet Union would be principally concerned with the protection of Leningrad and would thus incorporate the Baltic States and probably include Memel, Tilsit and Königsberg within her new frontiers. They would demand the 1940 frontier with Finland and probably annex the Petsamo ore fields. It was felt that they would make no territorial demands on Norway and Sweden.

In Romania the Soviets would demand Bessarabia and the Northern Bukovina, and probably require a share of the oil resources of the country and the right to maintain naval and military bases. Bulgaria would probably end the war under the 'moral domination' of the Soviet Union. The Soviets were unlikely to have any territorial demands on Turkey, but would prefer to see her as a fully independent power without an alliance with any great power. They would also require a revision of the Montreux Convention that would give them free access to the Straits.

In the Middle East the Soviet Union would probably show considerable interest, and this could become a source of friction with Britain were there to be a cooling off of the alliance. She might be looking for oil supplies from the Middle East and this could lead to a conflict with the United States and Britain. She might also be looking for a warm water port in the Persian Gulf in spite of the expense of such a route by road or by rail. The Soviets had reaffirmed their intention to leave Persia after the war, and they were likely to confine their activities in that country to supporting the democratic and constitutionalist Tudeh Party so as to be able to have considerable influence in Persia should Anglo–Soviet cooperation break down.

Afghanistan was unlikely to be a problem unless Anglo–Soviet relations deteriorated, and the same applied to India since the Soviets had ceased all their rhetoric about the world revolution. In the Middle

East the main cause of concern to the Foreign Office was that the regimes were based largely on the reactionary classes and were opposed by the younger and more progressive elements, and this was a weakness which might very well be exploited effectively by a Soviet Union alienated from Britain. In the Far East the main concern was with the questions of Outer Mongolia and Sinkiang and the attitude of the Kuomintang towards the Chinese Communists.

Thus the Foreign Office felt that the preservation of the Anglo–Soviet Alliance in the post-war world should be one of the main aims of British policy. They did not feel that Soviet territorial demands were likely to pose any serious threat to British interests. The Soviet Union was seen as a pragmatic and nationalist power legitimately concerned with its own security and concentrating on building up its internal power, having abandoned its role as the torch-bearer of the world revolution. With such a power the pragmatists of the Foreign Office believed cooperation was both desirable and possible. The two major problems that stood in the way of the achievement of this aim were the future of Germany and the post-war policies of the United States.

On the same day that Allied forces landed in Normandy the Post Hostilities Planning Sub-Committee produced a paper for the War Cabinet on the probable effects of Soviet policy on British strategic interests, having been instructed by the Cabinet that the aim of British policy would be 'to foster and maintain the friendliest possible relations with the USSR'.[2] The committee assumed that the Soviet Union would not attempt to dominate either Western Europe or the Continent of Europe. They isolated four vital British strategic interests: the oil supplies from the Middle East; communications in the Mediterranean; sea communications; and the concentrated industrial areas of the United Kingdom. The aim of British policy should be to secure the full cooperation of the Soviet Union in a system of world security; failing that the alliance with the USSR and British relations with the United States and China would have to be further strengthened. The key to such a policy would be to refrain from opposing any reasonable demands of the Soviet Union which did not conflict with Britain's vital strategic interests. In order to secure the oil supplies from the Middle East close cooperation with the United States would be necessary. Collaboration with the Western European states, particularly France, would help ensure that the Soviet Union would not fill the vacuum left in a Europe weakened by war. In order to meet any possible threat from the USSR and to secure both the sea communications and the industrial areas of Britain, the navy and the air force would have to be maintained at a high level of effectiveness after the end of hostilities. It was also felt that Britain's strategic reserves should be placed in the Middle East.

The Post Hostilities Planning Sub-Committee based most of their arguments on the Foreign Office paper drawn up in April, but in some cases went somewhat beyond it. They felt that the Soviet Union would have a predominant influence in Czechoslovakia, whereas the earlier paper argued that the Soviet–Czech Treaty of December 1943 was a satisfactory model for relationships between the USSR and her western neighbours. The paper also stressed the powerful influence that the Soviet Union would have over Hungary, Romania, Bulgaria and Yugoslavia. Yugoslavia was an area of particular concern to the committee who argued strongly that the British Government should resist any attempt by the Soviets to make permanent commitments in this country which might be prejudicial to British interests in the Mediterranean. On the other hand it was suggested that the British Government could support Soviet attempts to renegotiate the Montreux Convention of 1936, provided that a powerful air base was maintained in the Middle East and that the Royal Navy had access to adequate naval facilities in the Eastern Mediterranean.

The Committee made an astonishingly optimistic assessment of the probable internal developments in the Soviet Union after the war. It was felt that the Stalin constitution of 1936, which guaranteed on paper both personal liberty and the right to work, might lead to greater freedom and to a greater knowledge and appreciation of foreign social conditions. Indications of a move to decentralise certain functions to the constituent republics seemed to point to a certain relaxation of the dictatorship, and showed a determination to concentrate on reconstruction and rehabilitation and on improving the lot of the Soviet people. It was argued that the Soviet Union would concentrate on achieving a higher standard of comfort, liberty, culture and contentment for the people rather than pursue a policy of expansion and aggrandisement which might well involve her in another war and jeopardise her peaceful economic development.

In the event of the Soviet Union attempting to become a great naval power and also building up a strategic bomber force it would be essential for Britain to maintain strategic reserves of the highest order. The main concern would be to obtain well-placed bases to secure sea and air communications.

The Committee, whose brief had been to consider the worst

possible situation, was therefore sanguine about the future of Anglo–Soviet relations. Soviet demands for a post-war settlement seemed reasonable and did not pose a serious threat to British security. The only area of some concern was the Middle East, but the Committee was confident that a satisfactory counter-balance to any Soviet attempts to encroach on the area could be found. The report agreed with the Foreign Office that cooperation with the Soviet Union provided the best form of security but greatly exaggerated the power available to meet any future threat from the Soviet Union should the twenty-year alliance collapse. Britain in 1944 had a great deal of political influence and acumen, but her power had eroded drastically. It was one thing to plan a post-war settlement, but it was highly questionable whether Britain had the strength necessary to secure the implementation of such policies. Coming to terms with British weakness was a long and painful process, and those who tried were all too easily branded as appeasers.

The next major paper on future Soviet policy was presented by the Secretary of State to the War Cabinet in August.[3] Eden was on the whole optimistic about the prospects, but he could not accept the view of the Post-Hostilities Planning Staff that Britain would be able to meet the military challenge of the Soviet Union without the support of a powerful alliance. He argued that provided the Soviets did not think that Britain and the United States were trying to build up a combination of European states around a revived Germany in order to hold her in check, and was convinced that Britain intended to keep Germany weak, they would continue their policy of cooperation. He felt that it was most unlikely that the Soviets would take advantage of the chaos in Europe to unleash a crusade against capitalism and imperialism, and his paper was based on the assumption that they would not.

Eden stressed the uncomfortable fact that British financial power had largely disappeared, and that in future her influence in the world would depend on achievements in the social, economic, industrial, scientific, and intellectual fields and by standing for the traditional British values of progress, democracy and the struggle against autocracy. In other words Britain would have to offer an attractive alternative to Communism. Within the framework of the Anglo–Soviet Alliance, Britain should attempt to consolidate her position in Western Europe, Scandinavia and the Mediterranean. Britain should also make every effort to spread her influence as far as possible in Eastern Europe by building on the relationships established during the war and by exploiting the moral authority and esteem which had been gained as a result of the successful struggle against Nazi Germany. Eden believed that the Soviet Union would not stand in the way of legitimate British interests in Eastern Europe. Possibly he was encouraged in this optimism by Clark Kerr's report that Stalin had told him that 'Communism is no more fit for Germany than a saddle for a cow', and believed that Stalin would not try to harness other unwilling cattle.[4]

The arguments used to support the view that the Soviet Union was likely to be interested in cooperation with Britain in the post-war period were based on the Foreign Office's earlier paper and therefore do not need repeating. Eden's analysis of the likely policies of certain European states were, however, much more detailed and are of considerable interest.

De Gaulle's policy of cooperation with the Russians was taken as an encouraging sign by the Foreign Secretary, and he did not share the fears of those who felt that De Gaulle was attempting to loosen his ties with the Anglo–Saxon countries. Likewise he discounted the likelihood of a Communist regime in France after the war, and saw no evidence that the Soviet Union was attempting to interfere in the internal affairs of France. A Popular Front government, in which the Communists would play an important role, was the most likely outcome, and this was one which would probably lead to collaboration between France and the Soviet Union without in any way endangering the Anglo–French relationship. Indeed this situation would be one in which relations with both France and Russia would be on the same terms of mutual confidence and equality.

Although the British Government had initially opposed the idea, the Soviet–Czechoslovak Treaty was now seen as a very hopeful step.[5] The fact that Soviet relations appeared to be so satisfactory with Czechoslovakia, a country which Eden described as 'a "petit bourgeois" country with a capitalist structure of society and prosperous lower-middle class and peasantry,' led him to believe that the Soviets had no desire to impose Communist regimes on the Central European countries. He therefore believed that the treaty should serve as a model for similar treaties between the Soviet Union and Hungary as well as Austria. On Poland Eden wrote,

Large numbers of Poles have, unfortunately, pinned their faith in British and American support against the territorial and strategic demands which Russia will make of Poland. It would be fatal, not only to Anglo–Soviet relations and therefore to the future prospects of peace in Europe, but also to Poland herself if we encouraged the Poles to rely upon such support instead of staking everything upon achieving good relations with Russia.

Eden hoped that the Mikolajczyk Government, 'who represents precisely those solid democratic elements on which the future of Poland can best be built,' would be able to reach an accommodation with the Soviet Union by facing realities and showing a reasonable spirit of compromise. Other prominent figures in British politics were prepared to go much further than this. Hugh Dalton had, for example, written in March 1944, 'Poland, like Czechoslovakia, must go with Russia after the war if not right into the Soviet Union as a constituent republic, at least into a close alliance and an advanced stage of dependence.'[6]

In Hungary Eden saw the possibility of avoiding a clash between British and Soviet interests. Both countries were in favour of a far-reaching land reform and wanted a genuinely democratic regime. His great fear was that there would be repeat performance of the 'excesses of the Bela Kun regime after the last war'. But he felt that, 'In so far as Hungary is a country with a Western outlook and not a Balkan country, and a country with no affinities with the Slav world, the desired reforms can probably be promoted more effectively by British than by Soviet precepts.' Given that there was apparently a common interest in preserving an independent Hungary, with a democratic and progressive regime, and which renounced all claims to the Crown of St. Stephen, it might well be possible for the Soviet Union and Britain to work together and avoid any serious conflicts.

Eden's vision of the post-war world was thus one in which the Soviet Union, secure behind its new frontiers and with alliances with her western neighbours along the lines of the Soviet–Czechoslovak Treaty, would concentrate on reconstruction and economic and cultural development, and be happy to cooperate with Britain, for there would be no conflicting interests that would seriously threaten the twenty-year alliance. The Post-Hostilities Planning Staff however were far less optimistic and devoted their attention to the possibility of a hostile Soviet Union, producing a paper for the War Cabinet on security in Western Europe and the North Atlantic.[7]

The paper pointed out that with the development of air power and long range missiles the strategic position of the United Kingdom had seriously deteriorated and that a closer association with continental

Europe was essential. The two powers most likely to pose a threat would be the Soviet Union and Germany. With Germany disarmed and the USSR as the greatest land power in the world the traditional British policy of the balance of power would no longer be feasible. Britain would need powerful allies, depth of defences on the Continent and in the United Kingdom, and technical superiority in the application of science to warfare.

The Committee envisaged two possibilities for the post-war world. There would either be an effective world organisation, at the core of which would be the close association of Britain, the United States and Russia, or such an organisation would fail to materialise or prove to be ineffective. It was felt that the key to the success of the world organisation would be to take swift and effective action against any infringements by Germany of the restrictions placed on rearmament. A major problem would be to stop the Soviet Union playing a predominant role should the reoccupation of Germany become necessary.

The Committee believed that the USSR would not pose a serious threat for at least five years after the war. By 1955 she would become immensely powerful by developing her strategic air force and fleet and by strengthening her economic infrastructure. The Soviet Union was not susceptible to blockade, she had overwhelming superiority in land forces and could disperse her vital industries to protect them against air attack. Without some revolutionary development in weapons technology Britain would thus be faced with the prospect of a long war of attrition. Since the Committee probably knew nothing of the development of the atomic bomb, and even if they did there was no means of telling whether it would work, they insisted that defence against a Soviet threat would have to be based on a close military alliance of the Western European states, which if possible would also include western Germany. But this alliance would be of little avail unless the United States was prepared to supply the manpower and reserves needed to achieve superiority over the Soviet forces.

The main problem about forming a Western Bloc against a hostile Soviet Union was obviously the question of policy towards Germany. The report stated:

Any measures designed to secure for our benefit a revival of German power, which are inconsistent with the policy of preventing renewed German aggression, must inevitably tend to alienate our

Western European allies and antagonise the U.S.S.R. In any event, we could never be sure that German support would be reliable, nor should we have any confidence that it could be made effective in time. Neverthless, should circumstances arise which enabled us to obtain German co-operation, it would be of great value to us despite the fact that, after the defeat of the U.S.S.R., a strong Germany might again constitute a major threat to our own security.

Whatever happened, it was essential that Britain should not agree to evacuate her zone of Germany before the Soviet Union evacuated hers. The worst possible situation would be one in which the USSR and Germany actively cooperated, and this could best be stopped by the rigorous enforcement of measures designed to prevent the resurgence of Germany. No attempt should be made to build up Germany against the Soviet Union unless the Anglo–Soviet alliance had collapsed beyond repair.

The paper concluded by endorsing the Foreign Office's view that it was in the vital interests of Britain to remain on friendly terms with the Soviet Union, and that this was best achieved within the framework of the World Organisation. Should the Soviet Union ever pose a real threat it would be necessary to form a powerful western alliance and which would include the United States and members of the British Commonwealth and Empire, and would possibly include western Germany.

The Committee's report was thus considerably more pessimistic in tone than the papers produced by the Foreign Office, which the Chiefs of Staff felt were the product of a somewhat naïve optimism. Brooke was firmly convinced that Germany would have to be included in a western alliance designed to contain Russia, and complained that 'unfortunately this must all be done under the cloak of a holy alliance between England, Russia and America. Not an easy policy and one requiring a super Foreign Secretary.'[8] The chief stumbling block to such a policy was the attitude of the Foreign Office, and the Chiefs of Staff complained that the diplomats 'could not admit that Russia might some day become unfriendly'.[9]

A major problem facing the British in their assessment of the policies of the Soviet Union was that the country was seen as both the centre of World Communism and as a great power pursuing an essentially pragmatic policy. An assessment of the relative strengths of pragmatism and ideology was exceptionally difficult, and opinions often changed drastically in altered circumstances. No one was more changeable in his views than the Prime Minister. On the one hand he remained inflexible in his anti-Communism, on the other he admired Stalin as a statesman and was generous in his acknowledgements of the extraordinary achievements of the Soviet armed forces. The Chiefs of Staff stuck to their bleak vision of the future of Anglo–Soviet relations. The Foreign Office for the most part continued to emphasise the pragmatic aspects of Soviet policy. Considerable encouragement for such a view came from a report from the Polish-born American professor, Oskar Lange, who had spoken to Stalin and Molotov during a visit to Moscow and had been assured that the Soviet Government wanted a reasonable and fair settlement of the Polish frontier question. Warner and Wilson took this as evidence that the Soviets had no intention of communising Eastern Europe and that this was further indication that the abolition of the Comintern was a demonstration of a genuine Soviet desire to allow each country in Eastern Europe to go its own way. Both men agreed that the Soviet Union would be far too busy at home after the war to interfere in the domestic affairs of Poland.[10] Given this assessment of Soviet policy they felt that Anglo–Soviet relations were needlessly damaged by anti-Communist activities in Britain and the United States. Wilson wrote, 'A major source of irritation or worse will be removed if we can cut down the irresponsible anti-Soviet chatter which is all too common particularly among service personnel.' American officers were openly discussing the possibility of fighting the Russians and felt that the Alaska Highway provided an excellent route for an invading army to march towards Russian. The Poles were using British Government money for ceaseless anti-Soviet propaganda. These and similar activities made the Soviets understandably fearful of a united and anti-Soviet Europe, and it was this fear rather than any desire to expand which was felt to be the motivating force behind Soviet policy.[11]

Eden was greatly impressed by these arguments and he felt that the major obstacle to Anglo–Soviet cooperation was the lack of competent men among the Soviet élite which resulted in these people being terribly over-worked and unable to devote their time and attention to fostering the alliance. With his faith in the Soviet Union reinforced by these memoranda, Eden stopped the publication of an anti-Soviet tract which had been produced for the army educational service, ABCA. The Secretary for War, Grigg, also wanted to ban the pamphlet, but his reason was that he felt that it was too favourable to the Soviet Union. This minor incident clearly illustrates the difference between the Foreign Office and the War Office in their attitudes towards the Soviet Union.

Those, like Wilson, who took an optimistic view of Soviet postwar intentions, felt that the Soviet Union would press for popular front governments, and they did not think that any great harm would be done to British interests by such a policy. The more conservative diplomats felt that popular front governments were, in Orme Sargent's words, 'feeble, corrupt and inefficient', and cited the examples of Leon Blum's government and the Republicans in Spain. Sargent believed that Stalin wanted 'a strong autocratic government administering a system of state socialism and following a pro-Russian policy irrespective of the whims and prejudices of the population'.[12] A possible testing ground for such a policy, and one about which the British were very uncertain, was the Balkans. Churchill asked the Foreign Office,

> Are we going to acquiesce in the communization of the Balkans and perhaps of Italy? Mr. Curtin [the Australian Prime Minister] touched upon this this morning and I am of opinion on the whole that we ought to come to a definite conclusion about it and that, if our conclusion is that we resist the Communist infusion and invasion, we should put it to them pretty plainly at the best moment that military events permit. We should of course have to consult with the United States first.[13]

Eden replied rather lamely that the British Government supported Tito and also EAM in Greece and that 'it is an unfortunate fact that the Communists seem to make the best guerilla leaders'. But he did acknowledge that the Prime Minister had a point, and in another memorandum he wrote: 'We must think of the after-war effect of these developments, instead of confining ourselves as hitherto to the short-term view of what will give the best dividends during the war and for the war.'[14] Eden was far more concerned about Yugoslavia than he was about Greece. In May 1944 he had made an agreement with Gusev that Greece should be in the British sphere of influence, and Romania in the Soviet Union's.[15] The only problem about this agreement as far as Eden was concerned was that it conflicted with what he had said in the House of Commons about the British Government's repudiation of spheres of influence.[16] Fitzroy Maclean, who was Churchill's personal representative to the Yugoslav Partisans, did not feel that Eden needed to worry unduly about the future of Yugoslavia. He wrote to the Foreign Office saying that Tito would play the British and the Americans off against the Russians 'in the approved Balkan fashion' and that he had no intention of becoming a Soviet official. Maclean believed that the Soviets wanted a friendly but independent Yugoslavia and had no desire to exercise direct control.[17] Subsequent events proved that he was absolutely right about his friend Tito and altogether too optimistic about Soviet intentions. Churchill agreed with Maclean's views and referred to Yugoslavia as 'Titoland'.[18]

The Foreign Office's view of the future of the Balkans was summed up in a memorandum by Wilson:

> Russian desiderata on her European frontiers are stable governments friendly, or at any rate not hostile, to herself. Beyond that I don't believe she is interested. The strength of her position in the Balkans is surely that she has solved, or what is more important, is thought to have solved, the economic and social problems which the Balkan countries have not solved. That factor gives her an influence with 'progressive' forces which it is difficult for us to counter. As regards trade, the Treasury, though not the Board of Trade, are not particularly hopeful about dealing with Russia either. But if there is a vacuum in this area it will be filled, willy-nilly, by the Russians.[19]

This question of post-war trade with the Soviet Union began to engage the attention of the Foreign Office in 1944. It was hoped that Soviet demand for machine tools would continue into the reconstruction period, and that Britain would be able to exchange these goods for raw materials, particularly timber. Since 1941 military supplies had been sent to the Soviet Union on a lend lease basis, but for non-military supplies the Soviets paid 40 per cent in gold, and the remaining 60 per cent was given in the form of a five-year credit at 3 per cent. The Treasury suggested that half of the Soviet post-war debt could form the basis of a new short-term loan. The Treasury was strongly opposed to granting any long-term loans to the Soviet Union. Orme Sargent pointed out that Britain would have to get used to playing a new role, as she was no longer a creditor nation. He wrote, 'For the last 200 years we have displayed in our foreign relations the rich man's complex, and this has become so much a matter of course that we do not realise how far we have relied in our diplomacy on the *cavalière de St. Georges* in order to maintain and assert our influence in foreign countries.'[20] Clark Kerr kept pushing for a fresh round of trade talks with the Soviets, but got no response. In London Geoffrey Wilson was the strongest advocate of expanding trade with the Soviets. He combed the Soviet trade journals looking for evidence that this was a worthwhile pursuit, and he became increasingly outspoken in his criticisms of the Chiefs of Staff and the Service Departments for their obstructionist tactics.

Treasury figures showed that £36.9 million had been advanced to the Soviet Union by the beginning of May 1944, and it was estimated that this would reach £59.9 million by May 1945.[21] Eden was opposed to the idea put forward by the Treasury that these loans might be extended after the war. He wrote: 'I am afraid that I don't understand why we have to make any loan to the Russians at all. They are much richer than we are, and are fully able to pay cash for what they buy.'[22] Wilson disagreed with the Secretary of State and argued that such loans would be necessary in order to gain a foothold in a potentially lucrative Soviet market. Orme Sargent basically agreed with Eden, and wanted payment in gold, but he also supported the idea of one loan of £30 million – in other words half the sum the Soviets were likely to owe at the end of the war. At the Bretton Woods conference Keynes had pointed out that Britain's external debt would be £3000 million by the end of 1944, whereas the Soviet Union had a very small foreign debt and had actually managed to build up her gold reserves during the war. The Soviets however claimed that they were very badly off, and clamoured for huge long-term loans. By the end of 1944 even Wilson was beginning to get a little tired of such importunity and suggested that the Treasury and the Board of Trade should make it clear to the Russians that the British refusal to grant a large thirty-year loan was not a case of 'won't' but quite simply one of 'can't'.[23]

The Chancellor of the Exchequer was strongly opposed to giving the Soviets any special treatment, but the Board of Trade sympathised with the Foreign Office's flexible approach and argued that the Russians should be given certain advantages. Eventually agreement was reached that 50 per cent of the amount owing under the Civil Supplies Agreement could be offered as a further credit. Sir John Anderson, the Chancellor, insisted that given Britain's chronic balance of payments deficit this was the most that could be offered. A number of large British firms, headed by English Electric, were pressing for a long-term trade agreement, and there were indications that the Soviets were prepared to pay 60 per cent cash. In August

1944 the Treasury and the Board of Trade discussed the question of post-war trade and credits in some detail. It was agreed that the Russians should be given a loan of £30 million for five years and that they should be required to pay 30 per cent cash. Since they were granted 70 per cent credit this meant an effective credit of £100 million. The Treasury wanted 3 per cent interest on the loan, the Board of Trade 2 per cent or less. After much wrangling it was agreed to offer the Russians 2¼ per cent. This proposal was then put to the Russians who rejected it out of hand. This reaction was seen by the Treasury as another example of Soviet hard bargaining and of their predeliction for 'bazaar tactics'. The Soviets broke off their discussions with British firms, including English Electric, and demanded a loan of £60 million over twenty years at 2 per cent interest. The Treasury knew full well that £30 million was such a trifling sum that it was almost insulting to the Russians, but argued that they had no alternative and simply could not afford to offer more. By 1945 the question was no longer how much credit should be given to the Soviet Union, but whether the Russians would ever pay their debts. In May 1945 Keynes suggested an immediate stoppage of all supplies to Russia until they paid up, and he had the full support of the Prime Minister. As soon as the war was over the British began to take a hard line, cutting off supplies and demanding payment in full of all outstanding debts.[24] General Martel expressed the solid military view that the whole idea of trying to reach a satisfactory trade agreement with the Soviets was yet another pathetic example of the civilians 'licking the Bolshies boots until we are black in the face'.

It thus soon became plain that the Soviet Union could not be mollified by any trade agreement that the British were able to offer, and the Polish question was far from settled. The problem was put very clearly in one of the Foreign Office's draft general papers which pointed out that it would be impossible for Britain to help Poland and that

> We cannot fight Russia to re-establish her eastern frontiers. Placed between a hostile Soviet Russia and a defeated Germany, she could only lean on the Western Powers who would not fight for her, or follow a new Beck policy with Germany. We should then have Europe again divided, with Russia an uncertain factor, as after the last peace.[25]

At the end of March 1944 Wilson pointed out that the British Government recognised the Polish Government in London (a) because of their claim to legitimacy and continuity, and (b) because they controlled the Polish armed forces which operated under British operational command. Wilson argued that

> Reason (b) is a limited liability in that it will no longer be operative when Polish armed forces have ceased to be under our operational command. By that time there will almost certainly be another government in Warsaw which we shall sooner or later have to recognise and the more we use argument (a) now the more difficult it will be to disembarrass ourselves of it when the time comes.[26]

Orme Sargent agreed with this assessment, and the Foreign Office began to prepare themselves to abandon the London Poles as a lost cause and as a serious impediment to good relations with the Soviet Union.

At the end of May a meeting was held at 10 Downing Street between the Prime Minister, Eden, O'Malley, Mikolajczyk, Romer and Raczynski. According to the minutes 'Mr Churchill explained that it was perfectly useless for any Poles to suppose that their country could possibly exist as a powerful and independent state unless it were on friendly terms with Russia.' As a first step in this direction the Poles agreed to drop Sosnkowski, who was particularly objectionable to the Russians and whom Churchill called 'Sozzle-something'. Churchill objected to the idea of using the SOE mission in Moscow for liaison between the Polish underground army and the Red Army, although talks had begun between General Gubbins of SOE and the Poles about it. Eden and the Foreign Office supported the idea of using the SOE mission for this purpose, for they hoped that a Polish uprising could be fully co-ordinated with the advance of the Red Army.[27]

The Polish question was further complicated by the intervention of the United States Government. Eden and Churchill were convinced that the opening of the second front would greatly improve relations between the Western Allies and the Soviet Union and that this would make a solution of the Polish question much more likely. But in June the Foreign Office heard that Roosevelt had told Mikolajczyk that he could have Lvov, Tarnopol and the oil fields of East Galicia as well as Königsberg, East Prussia and Silesia. Such a promise was a clear violation of the Teheran agreements and Eden was furious, complaining that the Americans had left all the work on the Polish question to the British delegation, and adding, 'The poor Poles are sadly deluding themselves if they place any faith in these vague and generous promises.'[28] Roosevelt told Mikoljczyk that Stalin had no intention of sovietising Poland, and that the Poles should have faith in Soviet good intentions. Naturally the Poles did not believe a word of this nonsense, but they did take heart at the President's promises to support their territorial claims. Eden felt that Roosevelt's assurances would simply make the Poles more stubborn than ever without in any way altering the outcome of the frontier dispute. Eden wrote: 'Here again Polish attitude has stiffened. When Russian armies sweep forward they will repent the chances missed. Poor vain deluded people.'[29] By now the Foreign Office was convinced that the Soviets would find the government they wanted in Poland and all the British could do was to hope for the best. If the London Poles were cooperative and realistic it might be possible to avert a disaster, if not there was absolutely nothing that the British Government could do to help.

The British were becoming increasingly fatalistic about Poland, but Italy was seen as something of a test case for Communist intentions and a country in which the British were far better placed to frustrate their policies. Eden was however very concerned that the Communists in Badoglio's 'Government of all the talents' might take over the entire country 'while Mr. Macmillan drifts complacently about the Mediterranean'. He was convinced that the Communists were 'gate crashing' Badoglio's Government and were preparing to destroy the left and centre parties. Orme Sargent did not share these concerns and believed, quite correctly, that the Communists had no such aim in Italy. Eden could not be convinced by Sargent's arguments and wrote:

I should dearly like to accept this summing up for I share entirely his valuation of Anglo–Soviet understanding. But I confess to growing apprehension that Russia has vast aims, and that these may include the domination of Eastern Europe, and the Mediterranean and the 'communizing' of much that remains.[30]

Eden's pessimistic assessment of Soviet intentions seemed to be partially confirmed when in March 1944 the Soviets began to make moves to establish diplomatic relations with Badoglio's Government while at the same time vehemently denying that they were doing anything of the sort. The Foreign Office became very concerned that this was part of a Soviet plan to undermine the Control Commission and to increase their political influence in Italy.[31] Cadogan told Gusev that Italy was under the command of C. in C. Mediterranean, and that any question of diplomatic recognition of the Italian Government should be left until after the peace treaty. Eden was determined to take a strong line against the Russians in Italy. Wilson suggested that a Soviet request to land planes in Italy should be used as a bargaining counter to establish a proper air service to Moscow, and possibly even to make life a little easier for the British Military Mission in the Soviet Union. Eden flatly refused to allow the planes to land.[32] Eden's attempt to get tough with the Soviets had no effect. By late 1944 there were 12 YAKs and 12 CO47s in Bari, with 122 officers, 75 NCOs and 190 Yugoslav airmen. By November the number had been reduced to 40 officers, 20 NCOs and 122 Yugoslavs, but no restrictions were placed on their movements.[33] As the Soviets were remarkably conciliatory in their approach to Italy Eden's fears of a Communist take-over began to fade.

It was not long before Roosevelt heard of the deal which Eden had made with Gusev over Romania and Greece and which established British and Soviet spheres of influence. The United States Ambassador to Greece had heard about the agreement and had passed the information on to Cyrus Sulzberger Jr of the *New York Times*. There was thus a possibility that the agreement would be published and become a highly sensitive public issue.[34] On 11 June the President wrote to Churchill protesting about this unilateral diplomatic move. Eden complained that the whole affair was the 'outcome of P.M. butting in'. The President suggested a compromise whereby the deal should only last for three months and then be reviewed. Although Roosevelt was moderate in his language he made it quite clear that he was disappointed that the British had not consulted the United States on this important diplomatic initiative, and he clearly objected strongly to any state other than the United States having spheres of influence. Churchill was even more annoyed about the entire episode. In his reply to Roosevelt he pointed out that swift action was needed in Greece, and that the Soviets would do what they liked in Romania anyway. He asked the President, 'Why is all this effective direction to be broken up into a Committee of mediocre officials such as are littering about the world?' Roosevelt would not listen to these arguments and accused Churchill of doing a deal with the Russians behind his back. Churchill contained his anger and replied, 'The Russians are the only Power that can do anything in Romania. ... On the other hand the Greek burden rests almost entirely on us.' He warned that

It would be quite easy for me, on the general principle of slithering to the left which is so popular in foreign policy, to let things rip when the King of Greece would probably be forced to abdicate and EAM would work a reign of terror in Greece, forcing the villagers and many other classes to form Security Battalions under German auspices to prevent anarchy.

Carried away by the bright prospects for British policy if only the Americans would not interfere, Churchill even managed to convince himself that he might be able to get Tito to support the King of Yugoslavia.[35]

To Cadogan the whole affair could be explained by the fact that the Americans 'have an astonishing phobia about "spheres of influence"'. But Churchill disingenuously told Halifax that there was no question of spheres of influence, merely practical politics. In July he poured out his heart to Eden:

Does this mean that all we had settled with the Russians now goes down through the pedantic interference of the United States, and that Romania and Greece are to be condemned to a regime of triangular telegrams in which the United States and ourselves are to interfere with the Russian treatment of Romania and the Russians are to boost up EAM while the President pursues a personal pro-King policy in regard to Greece, and we have to try to make all things go sweet? If so it will be a great disaster. We could produce for the President exactly the results he wants in Greece, and the Russians will take all they want in Romania whatever we say.[36]

To help clarify the situation the Foreign Office produced a paper on the Balkans which was carefully vetted by Sargent, Cadogan and Eden. The central argument of this memorandum was that the Soviets were out to establish their influence in the Balkans, but they did not intend to 'communize' the area. British policy should therefore be to divide up the pie for the duration of the war, as had been done in the Eden–Gusev agreement, and then settle all outstanding problems at the peace conference. It was felt that since communism was almost non-existent in Romania and there was a strong traditional anti-Russian feeling in the country, the most the Soviets could hope for would be a friendly government. The Soviets would also want a friendly, though probably not a Communist government in Bulgaria. Tito was almost certain to win in Yugoslavia, but would probably look for some reassurances against the Russians. The paper suggested that if the Russians stuck to their agreement to allow the British to take the lead in Greece it should be possible to build up an Anglo–Greek–Turkish block to act as a counter-weight to Soviet influence over the rest of the Balkans. In spite of the belief that Communism was very weak in Romania and Bulgaria, the paper concluded that the Soviet Union hoped to 'establish a Balkan federation of Soviet republics after the war'. Christopher Warner, who denied that the Soviet Union was a Communist country, wrote of this idea of a Balkan Soviet Federation, 'I'm prepared to bet any money you like against this.' History does not record whether there were any takers.[37]

In spite of the deal over Romania and Greece the British were still concerned about Soviet policy towards the Communist-dominated ELAS/EAM. It was reported that the Soviet air detachment in Bari had dropped a military mission to ELAS without informing the British authorities.[38] Eden became very worried that 'Given Russian relations with EAM it might add Greece to the postwar Balkan Slav Bloc which now showed signs of forming under Russian influence and from which we were anxious to keep Greece detached.' The Foreign Secretary told the War Cabinet that a force of about 10 000 men with two to three squadrons of aircraft were being prepared to go to Greece to block any such move.[39]

Another problem for the British was that they had very little idea of what was going on in Romania and Bulgaria. In January 1944 Lord Moyne reported from Cairo that SOE had not yet been able to penetrate Bulgaria. The Foreign Office suggested to Colonel Talbot Rice of MI3(b) that Colonel Hill of SOE Moscow should begin talks with the NKVD in order to get their assistance in dropping British agents into Bulgaria. By March SOE reported that Major Thompson, an outstanding linguist, political activist, and brother of the historian E. P. Thompson, had established contact with the Bulgarian partisans. Shortly afterwards Thompson was captured by the Germans and shot, to live on in the memory of many Bulgarians as a hero of the resistance. A further British mission was also swiftly destroyed. These failures were attributed partly to the ruthless efficiency of the Germans, and partly to the weakness of the Bulgarian resistance movement.[40] With the sudden collapse of Bulgaria the situation changed dramatically, and the Foreign Office was informed that, 'There are far too many of these agents wandering about Bulgaria with the inevitable result that the Russians are suspicious.'[41] The British then decided to send an official military mission to Bulgaria under General Oxley, which would be sent without even informing the Russians, as a deliberate attempt to show the flag.

With the Red Army in Bulgaria the British were worried that the Soviets might be tempted to support the idea of an independent Macedonia, thus solving the Yugoslav–Bulgarian dispute, weakening Greece and taking the first step towards the formation of a Soviet-dominated Balkan confederation. There was also the problem of the armistice in Bulgaria. Molotov studiously avoided all Clark Kerr's questions on this matter, and the British were kept completely in the dark about what was going on in Bulgaria. As Geoffrey McDermott wrote in a Foreign Office minute:

> The Soviet Government let us and the Americans down badly by not telling us in advance of their intentions; there is very little we can do about it, just because we haven't the force in that quarter and secondly because we do not possess, in other ways either, the influence possessed by the U.S.S.R.[42]

The Soviets continued to strengthen their position in Bulgaria, and forced the Gibson Party of 7 SOE and 4 OSS operatives to leave Sofia. As a result of the Prime Minister's visit to Moscow in October the British position in Bulgaria was further weakened by reaffirming that Bulgaria was in the Soviet sphere of influence. Lord Moyne's hopes that the Russians would agree to senior British intelligence officers going to Bulgaria and Romania disguised as an advance military mission and as oil and mining experts, proved to be excessively optimistic.[43] Clark Kerr was repeatedly asked by the Foreign Office to find out what was going on in Bulgaria and the Balkans, but the Soviet authorities refused to give him any indication of their intentions.

The idea that a possible Balkan confederation under Soviet aegis could be offset by an arrangement between Britain, Turkey and Greece was similar to proposals put forward for a Western Alliance. From the outset there was a realisation that any such schemes might have exactly the opposite effect to that which was intended. Such alliances, rather than providing a counter-balance to similar Soviet arrangements, might provoke the Russians to such an extent that the wartime partnership would be in ruins. Gladwyn Jebb's Post-Hostilities Planning Committee had been careful to point out that a 'United States of Europe' should not be allowed to cause a Soviet breakaway.[44] This point was stressed by Duff Cooper, then serving as British Representative to the French Committee of National

Liberation, in a letter addressed to Eden. He wrote that 'Russia has never wanted either colonies or *Lebensraum*, and the true creed of Communism is peace rather than war,' but at the same time he warned that the Soviet Union presented a new danger which had nothing to do with the bogey of the 'Bolshevik menace'. He felt that there was no need for Britain to panic, but that it was necessary to be vigilant. In his reply Eden said that a Western Alliance was necessary, but it should not seem to be anti-Soviet. Such an alliance would be designed for defence against Germany, but it would also form the basis of a defence in depth against the Soviet Union should this be necessary.[45]

The Foreign Secretary's unsatisfactory reply was the result of the confusion about whether Germany was really likely to be a threat to British security having been totally defeated, or whether at least part of Germany should be incorporated into the Western defensive system. An answer to this question depended on assessments of Soviet post-war policy. Duff Cooper wanted the political and economic union of the Western European democracies, but Eden felt that such an idea was hopelessly impractical. Eden's main concern at this stage was that Germany should not become some sort of no-man's land, but he had no clear idea how the German question should be tackled and could only fall back on a dwindling hope that the European Advisory Commission might be able to come up with a satisfactory solution. The Military was much more prone to emphasise the possibility of using part of Germany in an anti-Soviet alliance, although Brigadier Jacob cautioned that it would be most unwise to do anything that might antagonise the Soviet Union, and that Germany should only be used by the Western Alliance if relations with the Soviets had deteriorated to such an extent that there could be no real alternative.[46] In August of 1944 the Chiefs of Staff produced a paper on hostilities with the Soviet Union which merely raised such salient questions as the strengths and weaknesses of the Soviet war economy, the areas of the Soviet Union which were most vulnerable to attack, her dependence on outside resources, the size and technical efficiency of the armed forces, the role of Stalin, and the probable future course of Soviet policy.[47]

Such speculation horrified the Foreign Office. Orme Sargent wrote to Eden:

When we were speaking to General Burrows on 15th August I mentioned to you the increasing signs that the Chiefs of Staff and their subordinate organisations are thinking and speaking of the Soviet Union as being enemy number one and even of securing German assistance against her.

The Post-Hostilities planners were abandoning all caution and were busy talking about securing Germany as part of the Western European group. The Deputy Under-Secretary of State continued:

> In fact Germany would be the key to the security of these islands in the future, and, however unpalatable the fact might be there might well come a time when we should have to rely on her assistance against a hostile Soviet Union.

Such ideas formed the background of discussions about the dismemberment of Germany. It was agreed that Germany was Britain's main enemy, but

> we feel that the more remote, but more dangerous, possibility of a hostile Russia making use of the resources of Germany must not be lost sight of, and that any measures which we now take should be tested by whether or not they help to prevent that contingency ever arising.

The dismemberment of Germany would probably be in Britain's best interests, for 'at least dismemberment would reduce the likelihood of the whole of Germany falling within the Soviet orbit and combining with her against us.' Sargent complained that this was no way to talk about a twenty-year ally. Eden minuted: 'This is very bad,' and went off to see Ismay who told him somewhat cryptically that this attitude was not due to the directions of the Chiefs of Staff.[48]

Geoffrey Wilson argued that the Military's view that the Russians were the only power which could pose a serious threat in post-war Europe, and that Britain should be prepared to use the manpower and resources of North-West Germany in order to be ready to meet the Soviet menace, was liable to be a self-fulfilling prophecy. The Soviets would instantly retaliate. Since it was agreed that the Anglo–Soviet Alliance was the corner-stone of Britain's foreign policy everything possible should be done to maintain the highest degree of cooperation, including military talks.[49] Meanwhile the Chiefs of Staff and their 'wild acolytes' engaged in anti-Soviet planning and accused the Foreign Office of being a collection of ostriches and appeasers.[50]

Frank Roberts joined in the chorus by insisting that European security was only possible with the Soviets and not against them.[51] Sargent agreed with these expressions of concern and reaffirmed his belief that the first priority should be the strengthening of the Anglo–Soviet Treaty. The Foreign Office was also worried because Fleet Street was well aware of the violent anti-Soviet feelings of the Service Chiefs who were giving their tacit approval to the Post-Hostilities Planning staff and their talk about a possible war with the Soviet Union. Gladwyn Jebb and Christopher Warner agreed that in such an atmosphere there was no point in Anglo–Soviet staff talks, as all they could do was to talk about defence against each other. Eden offered the rather unhelpful comment that the whole problem was that the military got on so badly with the Russians.

Differences between the Foreign Office and the Chiefs of Staff about the future of Germany became very clear in the course of preparations for the Dumbarton Oaks Conference in the Summer of 1944. The Chiefs of Staff wanted part of Germany in a Western Bloc, and the Foreign Office opposed this suggestion. At Dumbarton Oaks the idea that 'regional associations' could be formed was accepted in principle, and Eden underlined this point in a speech in the House of Commons in October. General Smuts made a widely publicised speech in which he said that Britain would have to form a Western Bloc in order to offset her weakness *vis-à-vis* the Soviet Union and the United States. Churchill had no sympathy for such suggestions and still saw Germany as Britain's great enemy. At that stage of the war the idea of having Germans as allies was repugnant to him. Eden was already beginning to have second thoughts. He saw certain advantages in a Western Bloc, for it would stop individual nations from being eaten up one-by-one and would also mean that the Western nations would not look to Russia for salvation. The San Francisco conference recognised the need for 'regional arrangements or agencies', and in November 1944 Molotov accepted British explanations that their schemes for Western Europe were within these terms of reference. The British therefore felt they could discount much of the denunciations in the Soviet Press and by western communist parties that Western Europe was to become an imperialist and anti-Soviet bastion.[52]

By November of 1944 the Post-Hostilities Planners felt that, in spite of Foreign Office warnings that a divided Germany would result in a massive Soviet military presence in East Germany and thus bring Soviet military power closer to the Western nations, the advantages of a divided Germany greatly outweighed the disadvantages. They wrote: 'We are unlikely to secure the help of a united Germany against the U.S.S.R. as the Russians will not permit us to do so.' At the same time the Chiefs of Staff declared that a hostile Russia was 'one of our basic assumptions', and that strategic assessments of an expansionist Russia should be undertaken as soon as possible. Britain's defences would have to be based on defence in depth in Western Europe which would give sufficient time for the Americans to deploy their resources.[53]

Summing up the situation Wilson wrote:

It is our policy to build up, even within the framework of a world organisation, a Western European security bloc which will involve close military collaboration with our European neighbours. There is every reason to suppose that the Russians will do the same in Eastern Europe. These two military blocks will be a danger to the peace rather than otherwise unless their two leaders – the Union of Soviet Socialist Republics and ourselves – are very closely linked together not only diplomatically but also militarily.

In his view the Service Chiefs' idea of building up part of Germany against Russia would make a clash inevitable.[54] Sargent felt that it was essential to get the Prime Minister interested in the subject, but there was little hope of this. Gladwyn Jebb, whose views on the post-war world were quite different from most of his colleagues in the Foreign Office, complained to Dalton that Churchill was not interested in the post-war situation, and that he was 'an old autocrat surrounded by his advisers.'[55] Without the intervention of the Prime Minister these major differences between the Foreign Office and the Service Chiefs could not be settled.

10 The Polish Question

The hopes that the successful invasion of Normandy would improve Anglo–Soviet relations and pave the way for a satisfactory settlement of the Polish question proved to be illusory. In July Eden felt that the Soviets were getting even tougher over Poland, and this was confirmed by Stalin's letter to Churchill on 23 July, in which he expressed his determination to use the Soviet-dominated Polish Committee of National Liberation in Lublin to govern liberated Poland, and which spoke of the London Poles in disparaging terms and referred to the 'so-called underground organisations' as 'ephemeral and devoid of influence'.[1] The London Poles promptly reacted to this message by denouncing the Lublin Committee as nothing more than a collection of Quislings and unknown Communists, but Churchill assured the War Cabinet that the Committee of National Liberation were neither Quislings nor Communists but genuine Polish patriots. In a letter to Roosevelt the Prime Minister expressed his hope that a fusion of some kind between the Lublin and the London Poles might be possible. Certainly such a solution had not been entirely ruled out in Stalin's note to Churchill.[2] Writing to Stalin the following day Churchill said, 'It would be a great pity and even a disaster if the Western democracies found themselves recognising one body of Poles and you recognising another.' Stalin replied promptly and in a conciliatory tone. Churchill was delighted and wrote to the President, 'This seems the best ever received from U.J.'[3] Stalin had agreed to Churchill's suggestion that he should receive Mikolajczyk, and for a moment it seemed that the way had been opened for some form of reconciliation between the Lublin and the London Poles. Then on 1 August Warsaw rose up against the Germans and events in Poland took a new and tragic turn.

The Polish Home Army had long been planning a national uprising to show, in General Bor's words, the 'existence of Poland', to establish the full legitimacy of the Polish Government in London, and to counter the effects of what many Poles called the 'Russian invasion'. On 23 July the Red Army entered Lublin and proclaimed the Polish National Committee of Liberation. On 27 July Mikolajczyk announced that he would go to Moscow if Stalin would agree to meet him, and Raczynski told Eden that an insurrection in Warsaw was imminent and asked for military assistance. Although the British had long supported the idea of a Polish uprising, the Chiefs of Staff felt that it was operationally impossible to give the Warsaw insurgents any material help, and they therefore turned down this request.[4] By this time the Red Army was advancing towards Warsaw, and the Germans appeared to be in disarray. On 29 July Moscow Radio broadcast an appeal to the population of Warsaw to rise up and join battle with the Germans.[5] Three days later the uprising began.

The British Government was determined to give every possible help to the insurgents, and realised that until the Soviets agreed to help this would have to come from aircraft based in Italy. On 3 August the Chiefs of Staff sent Air Marshall Slessor and General Wilson details of proposed dropping points in Warsaw. The following day Churchill wrote to Stalin saying that he hoped to drop 60 tons of equipment to help the Warsaw insurgents, adding that 'this may help your operation'.[6] The British Military Mission in Moscow was given instructions to keep the Soviet military authorities fully informed of British intentions. At this point the Chiefs of Staff had a change of heart. They accepted the argument that missions to Warsaw from bases in Italy would entail unacceptable losses. Aircraft would have to fly north of Zagreb in daylight and then fly over Poland in moonlight. The Chiefs of Staff felt that this was far too hazardous and ordered the Military Mission in Moscow to exert pressure on the Russians to find out what they were prepared to do to help the Poles in their struggle against the Germans.[7] Stalin's reply to the Prime Minister's note did not give any grounds for optimism. He wrote, 'I think that the information which has been communicated to you by the Poles is greatly exaggerated and does not inspire confidence.' He pointed out that the Polish claim to have captured Vilna was pure nonsense, and mockingly asked what a handful of poorly-armed Poles could do against four German Panzer Divisions, including the crack Hermann Goering Division.[8] Churchill was staying at Chequers when Stalin's reply arrived and did not wish to disturb the relative peace of the Prime Minister's country retreat and therefore refused a request from the London Poles for an interview.

In spite of the Chief of Staff's reservations about flights to Poland from Italy, Slessor reported that 13 aircraft had flown to Poland and made drops between Warsaw and Cracow. He added that it was far too dangerous to fly to Warsaw since it was necessary to fly over the city at 1000 feet in order to make a reasonably accurate drop, and he concluded his report by saying that he did not intend to send any further flights to Poland in full moonlight.[9] The Chiefs of Staff accepted Slessor's judgement as they were already very dubious about the wisdom of allowing flights from Italy, but the London Poles insisted that they had accurate reports that there were no anti-aircraft guns in Warsaw and therefore Slessor's concerns were ill-founded. The Chief of Air Staff then reported to the Prime Minister that there was nothing that could be done to help the Poles and that the Russians should accept full responsibility for helping them.[10] At the same time a United States intelligence report warned that the Russians would oppose any attempt to arm the Poles and added that the Americans had no transport aircraft available for missions to Poland.[11] At this point Retinger, Mikolajczyk's *homme de confiance*, asked if Polish flights could go from Bari, and added the unfortunate remark that the Poles were very annoyed with the British for doing nothing to help the Warsaw insurgents. Eden felt that the Poles were being quite unreasonable, but as the planes involved were Polish he saw no reason why they should not be allowed to try to drop supplies on Warsaw. Whereupon the Chief of Air Staff told Slessor that the Poles should be allowed to fly to Warsaw.[12] The Combined Chiefs were not very happy with this suggestion, feeling that sending supplies to Warsaw should be a British responsibility and should be organised by SOE. Polish crews in SOE aircraft had already gained some valuable experience flying missions over Poland to drop men and supplies to the Home Army. These Polish airmen had been based in Brindisi since January 1944. Their initial flights had sustained heavy losses. From January to March they flew 23 sorties, of which only two were successful; but from April to July they flew 318 sorties of which 174 were completed. In this last period 114 men and 219 tons of stores and equipment were dropped.[13]

From the very early stages of the uprising London had no clear idea what was going on. The central question was the attitude of the Soviet Union. The London Poles were convinced that the Red Army was deliberately holding back outside Warsaw so that the Germans could conveniently butcher the Polish patriots. Eden told the Prime Minister that this 'occurred to us', but added that the War Office claimed that the Germans were making a tremendous effort to stop the Russians from taking Warsaw. Eden commented, 'This if true does put Stalin in a slightly better light, although it is odd that he did not say so in his message to you.'[14] The Warsaw uprising was also the subject of a minute by one of the Foreign Office's rising stars, Guy Burgess. He condemned the uprising as an irresponsible and premature attempt by the Home Army to score points against rival factions in Poland. He also supported the view that the Home Army had not properly informed the British and American Governments of their intentions.[15] The two extreme views were thus that of the London Poles who believed that the Russians were deliberately allowing the Germans to exterminate the Home Army and its supporters, and the Soviet view that the uprising was a politically motivated act of irresponsible adventurism. The British Government tended to take a middle position, swaying at times towards either extreme as circumstances changed.

On 9 August Mikolajczyk had an interview with Stalin who announced that he had every intention of helping Warsaw.[16] The Foreign Office, and particularly Oliver Harvey, who played an important role in determining British policy towards Poland, hoped that Mikolajczyk would have some success in Moscow and that an accommodation could be reached which would help the situation in Warsaw. Harvey wrote:

If the less responsible members of the Polish Government in London can wreck M. Mikolajczyk's efforts in Moscow, they certainly will do so. The only hope is agreement being reached by M. Mikolajczyk with the Polish National Committee and Stalin. That will not suit Kot and the generals, but the interests of Poland are greater than those of factions. It is most unfortunate that M. Mikolajczyk still has so many millstones round his neck which he should have shed during the past months as we urged. It is not the fault of ourselves that the Polish Government are now in this awkward position.

Eden wrote that he agreed emphatically with this analysis, and argued that 'Mick' should stay in Moscow in an attempt to reach a full settlement of all outstanding problems.[17]

British support for the Warsaw uprising was handled by SOE whose liaison officer to the London Poles, Colonel Perkins, knew the details of the plan for an uprising and who felt that this information should have been forwarded to the Soviet authorities via SOE in Moscow.[18] General Gubbins of SOE was anxious that there should be a Soviet liaison officer in Warsaw, and it would seem that SOE was probably responsible for dropping this officer over Warsaw.[19] Unfortunately the Soviet liaison officer was killed shortly after landing in Warsaw.[20] SOE was strongly in favour of the highest possible degree of cooperation with the Soviets, for they were fully aware that without their support little could be done to support the Poles in their struggle.

By 10 August the Chiefs of Staff reached the conclusion that flights to Warsaw from bases in Italy were not feasible, and suggested that supplies could be dropped by American aircraft flying from Soviet air fields near Warsaw. The USAF told the Chiefs of Staff that much as they would like to help the Poles they needed all their aircraft to supply operation DRAGOON, the allied landing in the South of France.[21]

While these discussions were going on the situation in Warsaw was deteriorating. The insurgents were desperately short of supplies and were suffering frightful losses. On 11 August the Polish Government told Churchill that a mass drop by two to three hundred aircraft was the only way to overcome the crisis, and that given the intransigence of the Soviets these aircraft would have to fly from British bases.[22] A draft reply to this note was prepared for the Prime Minister which read in part:

> I do not think that your Excellency's letter gives sufficient weight to the fact that these operations in Warsaw were launched without any prior consultation with HMG who can hardly be expected to improvise at such short notice effective means of assisting such a rising.

But the British Government realised that help was essential if Warsaw was not to be destroyed, and that should this happen it would not only be a terrible human tragedy but also a political disaster of the first magnitude. On 12 August Churchill therefore sent another telegram to Stalin asking him to help the insurgents in Warsaw. The Chiefs of Staff also sent an urgent message to Wilson and Slessor in Italy:

> You should know, however, that we are concerned at possible effect on morale of Polish forces fighting under our orders all over the world and on future Anglo–Polish relations if fight in Warsaw collapses and is followed by large scale massacre which Poles consider inevitable unless extraordinary measures are taken.

Yet in spite of this appeal the Chiefs of Staff still felt that there was very little that could be done, and they continued to press the Americans for help, even though they had been turned down point-blank at their first attempt. The Chiefs of Staff telegraphed Washington asking that 15th USAF should be given orders to drop supplies for Warsaw in the Kampinos forest outside the city. Further instructions were sent to the British Military Mission in Moscow to ask the Soviets for help. Slessor, who was informed of all these initiatives, wrote to the Prime Minister pointing out that aircraft from 15th USAF could not fly from the Mediterranean to Warsaw without bomb-bay fuel tanks, and therefore he suggested that 8th USAF in England could fly these missions from Soviet shuttle-bases. He assured the Prime Minister that in spite of all the difficulties he would try to get some of his aircraft to Warsaw if the weather improved, the main problem being bright moonlight.[23]

Reviewing the situation on 14 August, Churchill wrote that he was 'satisfied that everything possible is being done'. His main concern was the attitude of the Soviet Union, and he instructed Eden to ask Molotov what the Russians were doing to help the Poles. He underlined the obvious fact that it was a 100-mile flight for the Soviets to Warsaw, but 700 miles from the British bases in Italy. In fact the round-trip from Italy was 1720 miles. Eden did not think that an approach to the Russians at that stage would do any good and he told the Prime Minister that he was 'anxious lest too many messages to Stalin should only irritate the Russians'. He also pointed out that military intelligence showed that the Red Army had suffered a serious reversal outside Warsaw, although this did not explain why they would not consider air-drops to help the Home Army.[24]

In spite of enormous difficulties the airmen under Slessor's command made 86 sorties to Warsaw between 4 and 15 August. Forty-six of these managed to reach Warsaw, and Slessor estimated that 50 per cent of the supplies actually reached the Poles. Fifteen aircraft were reported missing, and 3 were known to have been shot down. Slessor argued that such losss were unacceptably high, and that anti-aircraft fire over Warsaw, whatever the London Poles might say to the contrary, was very intense.[25]

Reports from Moscow were far from encouraging. Clark Kerr and Harriman had an interview with Vyshinskii who told them that the whole Polish affair was utterly irresponsible and that he would do nothing to help. Vyshinskii told his visitors that he was not in the least bit worried about the effects on public opinion of the Soviet decision not to help the insurgents as the Soviet Union was used to being insulted and maligned. Clark Kerr tried to explain away this extraordinary attitude by saying that he felt that the Soviet refusal to allow the Americans to use their air bases was due to the fear that the USAF would get all the glory for helping Warsaw.[26] Eden responded to this information by instructing the Ambassador to deliver a strongly-worded note to the Soviet Government saying that there was no excuse for their behaviour. The Soviets had urged the Poles to revolt, and now it was their duty to help them. Eden pointed out that 'HMG have always been guided by the principle that whoever fights the Germans should receive all the support which the more powerful among the United Nations can supply.' He felt that it should be made clear that the Soviet attitude was placing a great strain on Anglo–Soviet and Soviet–Polish relations, and that Stalin should realise that the Poles in Warsaw were holding down 4 Panzer Divisions which was of enormous military benefit to him however 'reckless' he might consider this 'adventure' to be. The note warned that 'If, however, the present negative Soviet attitude is maintained suspicions concerning Soviet good faith will be confirmed and may well receive public expression with result useful only to the enemy and highly damaging to Anglo–Soviet relations.'[27] Clark Kerr was told to continue to press the Soviets to allow American planes to use their bases for drops on Warsaw. Eden also suggested to Churchill that he might enlist Roosevelt's support in an attempt to get Stalin to change his mind.

Hopes that such an approach would be successful were further dampened when Stalin wrote to Churchill telling him that he had no desire to become involved in the 'Warsaw adventure'.[28] Vyshinskii used exactly the same language when he told Harriman that British and American aircraft would not be allowed to use Soviet bases 'since the Soviet Government does not want to associate themselves either directly or indirectly with adventures in Warsaw'. Eden found it impossible to accept this argument. In a note to Churchill he wrote that the Poles had told the British Government that they were planning an uprising and that they needed help, but they had been firmly told that they could expect none. The fact that the Warsaw insurgents had been able to hold out for two weeks against overwhelming odds showed that they had not been quite so badly prepared as Stalin argued. Having talked to the Soviet Ambassador, Eden reported that 'it seemed to me to become clear that what he called "slanders" put out by the Poles in London had played a not unimportant part in determining the mind of his government'.[29]

By 19 August there were clear indications that the Poles were nearing the end of their strength. It was reported that General Spaatz of USAF was 'straining at the leash' to run shuttle flights to Warsaw from Soviet bases, but 'must await approving signal from Russians'.[30] Churchill and Roosevelt now decided that the time had come to make a joint appeal to Stalin. The message was sent on 20 August and stressed that 'we are thinking of world opinion if the anti-nazis in Warsaw are in effect abandoned'. They insisted that the Soviets should either drop supplies on Warsaw, or allow the Western Allies to use their bases. Stalin's reply came two days later. It was even harsher in its condemnation of the Poles than any of his previous utterances, 'Sooner or later the truth about the group of criminals who have embarked on the Warsaw adventure in order to seize power will become known to everybody.' He insisted that these evil men were solely responsible for the murder of the people of Warsaw. This grim note served to confirm the report from the Polish Government that leaflets had been dropped on Warsaw saying that the Russians would relieve the capital, but that they would arrest the leaders of the uprising. Further reports indicated that the Soviets were making mass arrests of the underground army throughout liberated Poland.[31]

By this time the British Government was receiving regular and detailed reports of the fighting in Warsaw from RAF Sgt. John Ward who had escaped from a German POW camp and had been living underground in Warsaw for three years. Ward had established close contacts with the Home Army and his radio messages which were sent almost daily chronicled the desperate plight of the insurgents. He was one of the many thousands of brave men who did their duty towards the Poles with courage and efficiency, and his reports were of considerable value to the British authorities. The Warsaw uprising also electrified public opinion and became one of the great emotional issues of the war. The Foreign Office was flooded with letters criticising the Government for failing to give sufficient support to Warsaw.[32] But the Foreign Office felt that this wave of public support for the uprising, however understandable it might be, was both unjustified and dangerous.

By the beginning of September the Foreign Office, annoyed by constant proddings from the Poles and by the clamouring of what they felt was an uninformed public opinion, began to get increasingly sympathetic to the Soviet point of view. On 2 September Eden wrote:

> I must say that I think that Stalin comes pretty well out of the Polish record. Certainly his was a frank statement of fact and there is much in what he says of the ineffectiveness and inaccuracy of droppings from the air in such conditions.

Orme Sargent was even more outspoken:

> Indeed we ought I suggest to do all we can to prevent public opinion from getting out of hand over this Polish issue, for if it does it may well distort and endanger the whole of our relations with Russia in which our post-war policy in Europe is necessarily based, and we cannot afford to quarrel with Russia in present circumstances. It is a sobering thought that over Poland Russia and Germany have always been able to agree. Such a quarrel might well endanger the security of this country in the coming years either by driving the Soviet Union back into isolation or, still worse, forcing her into collaboration with Germany as soon as the occasion offers.

Sargent concluded that Britain needed the Soviet Union rather than vice versa, and that Stalin was well aware of this fact.[33] In a further memorandum Sargent was even more emphatic:

> We cannot surely suggest that the Russians should alter their plans of campaign in order to help Warsaw. Is not the Russian attitude about Warsaw exactly the same as General Eisenhower's about Paris?

He strongly opposed the Prime Minister's suggestion that all further convoys to the Soviet Union should be stopped in order to get them to cooperate, and Frank Roberts agreed with this argument saying that such a policy would 'prove a boomerang'.[34]

Churchill was strongly affected by public support for the Warsaw uprising and was deeply touched by the telegram which the women of Warsaw sent to the Pope. He had many fierce altercations with the Polish Government and was frequently irritated by their stubborn refusal to compromise, but his generous spirit went out to the people of Warsaw and his imagination was fired by their heroism. On 3

September he wrote to Roosevelt putting forward his suggestion that the next convoy should be cancelled unless the Soviets allowed the Western Allies to use their airfields to send aid to Warsaw.[35] The following day an official note was sent to Molotov saying that British public opinion could not understand why no help was being given to the Poles, and asking for facilities to be given to the USAF. On 5 September Churchill again wrote to the President informing him that intelligence reports indicated that the fighting in Warsaw was over. In fact these reports were premature.

The Soviets took almost a week to reply to the British Government's note. It appeared initially to be utterly uncompromising and opened with a litany of complaints: 'No command in the world, neither British nor American, can tolerate the fact that a rising is organised in a large city opposite the front line of its troops without the knowledge of that command and contrary to its operational plans.' They called for a commission of inquiry into the uprising which, they claimed, would show the complicity of the London Poles. They demanded to know why the British Government had not seen fit to inform the Soviets of the impending uprising. They claimed that the whole affair was a repeat performance of the slanders and lies put out about the Katyn massacre in 1943. But in the middle of this extraordinary diatribe Molotov calmly announced that the Soviets were now ready to organise a joint drop on Warsaw. Clark Kerr commented on the Soviet reply, 'This is an unexpected and remarkable climb down. That it is tucked away in the middle of a preposterous pi-jaw is true to Kremlin form. They are still not grown up enough to come clean when they know they have made a bad mistake.'[36] Eden was delighted with the Ambassador's comments, and used them verbatim in a note he sent to Churchill discussing Molotov's reply.[37]

With the Soviets now willing to allow the Allies to use their airfields to help the insurgents the Air Staff announced that they saw no point in sending any further flights to Warsaw. They argued that with the fighting going on from street to street it would be impossible to make accurate drops, and that given the intensity of anti-aircraft fire such missions would be far too risky. In the three weeks up to 5 September 182 sorties had been flown to Warsaw. One aircraft had been lost for every 2·5 that had got through. In the last mission of 7 aircraft, 4 had been lost. It was felt that flights from Britain would be far too dangerous, and the drops would have to be made from 10 000 feet which would make them hopelessly inaccurate.[38] 'Bomber' Harris claimed that 30 per cent of the aircraft would be lost flying over

Germany. The War Cabinet was convinced by these arguments and concluded that losses would be too high to outweigh the boost that might be given to Polish morale.[39] Even if the Soviets gave their full support the arguments about the accuracy of the drops and the intensity of anti-aircraft fire still applied. On 10 September the Soviets began to send their own flights to Warsaw. These missions were not a success, largely due to the fact that the parachutes failed to open. The Americans sent a mission to Moscow to discuss arrangements for the use of Soviet bases by the USAF, meanwhile on 18 September 11 heavy bombers loaded with supplies for the Poles flew from American bases in East Anglia to Warsaw. Nine aircraft were lost, and only 30 per cent of the supplies were actually dropped but with questionable accuracy. The weather did not allow for a repeat performance of this mission.[40]

With the Soviets in a slightly more cooperative mood, although it was now too late to help the insurgents in Warsaw, the Foreign Office felt that an appropriate moment had come to make yet another attempt to settle the Polish question. Eden pressed Mikolajczyk to drop Sosnkowski who was well known for his outspokenly anti-Soviet views. Mikolajczyk went straight to the Polish President who flatly refused to dismiss Sosnkowski. Eden then left for Quebec and O'Malley kept pressing the Polish President to drop Sosnkowski, who was as much disliked by the British Government for his public criticisms of the lack of British support for the Warsaw uprising as he was by the Soviets. Some members of the Foreign Office, particularly Orme Sargent, felt that Sosnkowski and the Home Army were all that stood in the way of an understanding with the Soviet Union. Others were less optimistic. Frank Roberts believed that the Russians were determined to break with the London Poles completely and that they would only tolerate Mikolajczyk if he was prepared to do everything that he was told. Mikolajczyk's position had been seriously undermined as a result of the failure of the Warsaw uprising, and most of his colleagues were demanding his resignation for failing to get enough support from the British.[41] Eden was reluctant to play too active a role in Sosnkowski's dismissal. He wrote, 'I should very much like to see Gen. S. go. But I would like the Poles to dismiss him. I don't want to ask for his head when he has abused us. P.M. does not share my view and considers we should ask for his dismissal. Maybe I am too squeamish.'[42] But Mikolajczyk and Romer, having failed to get the President to dismiss Sosnkowski, tried to get Eden to do the job for them.[43] On Eden's return from Quebec he realised that there was no alternative open to him and forced the President to drop Sosnkowski, who resigned on 30 September. General Bor-Komorowski, the commander in Warsaw, was appointed in his place. But by now the uprising was nearing its grim and bloody end. On 4 October General Bor's troops could fight no longer and surrendered to the Germans.

It is difficult to assess the damage done to Anglo–Soviet relations by the attitude of the Soviets to the Warsaw uprising. There can be no doubt that the British Government was convinced that the Red Army had not deliberately halted in front of Warsaw. Churchill assured Stalin of this during his visit to Moscow in October.[44] Reviewing the situation in March 1945, Cavendish-Bentinck said that he was convinced that the Russians could not have taken Warsaw, pointing out that this was also the view of the War Office and that 'they cannot be accused of pro-Russian bias'.[45] Oliver Harvey, who followed the Polish situation closely, wrote in his diary, 'As usual they [the Poles] impute sinister motives to the Russians such as that they are deliberately not helping and not pressing their assault on Warsaw, because they wish the Poles to be exterminated.' The Foreign Office was determined not to allow the Warsaw tragedy to damage Anglo–Soviet relations, and therefore turned a blind eye to the nastier messages that came from Moscow. Churchill was extremely irritated by the Soviet attitude, but he was equally angered by the London Poles, particularly Sosnkowski, for their constant complaints and attacks. At the same time the wave of public revulsion at the callousness of the Soviets could not be ignored. Right-wing Tory MPs were constantly bombarding the Government with stories of Soviet atrocities in Poland. Vansittart kept writing to Eden, saying, 'I hope you can give me some assurance that action really is being taken to avert this appalling tragedy,' and threatening to put a motion on the subject before the House of Lords.[46] On the left Eleanor Rathbone spoke up for those who wished to protest against Russian ill-treatment of the Poles. One of her speeches on this subject was widely praised for being 'manly'. She was given public support by such prominent figures as H. N. Brailsford, the Duchess of Atholl and Rose Macaulay. The Foreign Office sent Frank Roberts to Eleanor Rathbone to tell her, in effect, to shut up, since any criticism of this sort would only make the Russians more difficult.[47] For all his diplomatic skill Roberts failed to silence this outspoken woman. Mounting criticism also came from groups throughout the country protesting against the arresting, deporting, and even shooting of Poles loyal to their government in

London, and insisting that the British Government was morally bound to uphold the Atlantic Charter. British public opinion believed that the Russians had stopped outside Warsaw for purely political reasons in order to impose the Lublin Committee on Poland and to get rid of nuisances in the Home Army. There were some fears of Soviet imperialist aspirations, but the British public still wanted the Russians to get to Berlin as quickly as possible and to give the Germans the treatment they deserved.[48]

Even after the collapse of the uprising flights to Poland continued to supply the Home Army. The Foreign Office soon began to feel that this was rapidly becoming a political liability. Eden wrote, 'I don't like these flights. if the Poles want to carry them out it is their affair. But I would in no circumstances be prepared to ask – or even acquiesce – in British crews being engaged upon them in present Polish political circumstances.' He also wrote to Churchill saying that no more liaison officers should be sent to the Home Army as they were becoming politically embarrassing, like 'our liaison officers formerly with General Mihailovich'.[45] Although the Prime Minister had made an undertaking to the Poles to fly supplies to the Home Army, the Soviets refused to allow this. Frank Roberts concluded that, 'Quite clearly the amount of practical assistance we can give the Poles is not such as to justify a row with the Russians.' He suggested that Stalin was determined to starve out his political opponents in Poland and there was precious little that the British could do to help these unfortunates. Eden agreed with these sentiments.[50]

Thus for the London Poles the Warsaw uprising was as much a political disaster as it was a military defeat. The London Poles were never able to recover from this catastrophe, for everything had been risked and everything lost. Far from asserting the 'existence of Poland' the London Poles had become an even greater burden on the British Government who were now increasingly inclined to drop them in order to maintain the Anglo–Soviet alliance.

In spite of the striking success of the Normandy landings and the prospect that the war would soon be over, Anglo–Soviet relations continued to deteriorate. Events in Poland were certainly a major contributory cause but there was also uncertainty about spheres of influence in the Balkans and Eastern Europe. Churchill therefore decided to make a second trip to Moscow to show the Soviets that the British Government was anxious to reach a settlement of these issues and to show their genuine desire for cooperation within the terms of the treaty. At the beginning of October Clark Kerr informed the Prime Minister that Stalin welcomed his proposed visit.

Churchill arrived with Eden in Moscow on 9 October, and had his first conversation with Stalin at 10 p.m. that evening.[51] The discussion turned almost immediately to the major question of Poland. Churchill remarked that Sosnkowski had been sacked and added rather cruelly, 'as for General Bor, the Germans were looking after him'. He assured Stalin that he supported the Polish frontier which had been agreed upon at the Teheran conference. Stalin replied that he would try very hard to bring the London Poles and the Lublin Poles together. In reply to Churchill's remark that where there are two Poles there is one quarrel, Stalin said that one Pole would begin the quarrel with himself out of sheer boredom. Both men reaffirmed the deal they had made over Romania and Greece, and Churchill hastily added that it was 'better to express these things in diplomatic terms and not to use the phrase "dividing into spheres," because the Americans might be shocked'. The Prime Minister also told Stalin that he felt that the Montreux convention was 'inadmissible today and obsolete' and agreed to support Soviet efforts to get it changed.

Turning to Italy, Churchill remarked that he 'did not think much of them as a people, but they had a good many votes in New York State'. He asked Stalin to 'soft-pedal the Communists' in order to avoid civil unrest in Italy. Stalin gave the singularly unconvincing reply that 'Ercoli' (Togliatti) was an Italian, the leader of an independent Italian Communist Party, and could very well tell him to mind his own business. But Stalin hastily added that Palmiro Togliatti was a wise man, was not an extremist, and would not start any adventures in Italy. On the question of Bulgaria, Stalin insisted that it was a Black Sea country and he could not see why the British wished to become involved in its internal affairs. At this point Eden chipped in with the remark that Britain had been at war with Bulgaria for three years and wanted a small share in the control of the country after Germany's defeat.

On the question of Germany, Churchill said that the problem was how to stop Germany from getting on her feet again in the lifetime of their grandchildren. Stalin said he felt that the problem was one of denying to the Germans any possibility of revenge. Heavy industry would have to be destroyed and the state would have to be split up.

After a brief discussion of Japan the meeting closed. The main outcome of this first session was an agreement on spheres of influence. Churchill slipped a small piece of paper across the table to Stalin on which the following figures were written: Romania 90 per cent to Russia, Greece 90 per cent to Britain, Yugoslavia 50–50, Hungary 50–50 Bulgaria 75 per cent to Russia. Stalin's interpreter, Pavlov, hastily wrote the names of the countries in cyrillic. Stalin read the list, changed Bulgaria to 90 per cent and expressed his approval of the percentages with a tick of his blue pencil. [52]

This remarkable piece of hasty arithmetic was discussed the following evening by Molotov and Eden. Molotov requested a revision of the Hungarian figures to 75 per cent to Russia and 25 per cent to Britain. Eden agreed to look into this question, and then went on the attack over the issue of Tito making a deal with the Bulgarians which was unacceptable to the British Government. Bulgarian troops in Northern Greece, who were under Soviet command, had placed a number of British officers under house arrest. Eden demanded that this should stop instantly. Molotov agreed to have a word with Stalin about this matter. Eden tried very hard to get greater British influence in Bulgaria, but he was hampered by the fact that Churchill had accepted the amended formula of 90–10. In the course of some rather unsavoury horse-trading Eden tried to improve the Bulgarian percentages to 80–20 in return for a concession in Hungary of 75–25. Molotov countered this proposal by demanding a greater share in Yugoslavia which Eden resisted. It soon became clear that the problem of Bulgaria could not be settled at this meeting. Eden's remark that Britain had been at war with Bulgaria for three years, whereas the Soviets had only been at war for 48 hours made no impression whatsoever on Molotov. The meeting ended with Eden appealing for a settlement of the Bulgarian issue within 24 hours, and Molotov promising to do his best.

Molotov returned to the bargaining table within this time limit and suggested 80–20 for both Bulgaria and Romania and 50–50 for Yugoslavia. He told Eden that the Bulgarian troops in Greece had been instructed to treat British officers in the proper manner. After some further discussion, in which Molotov tried to change the Hungarian percentages, Eden agreed to these proposals.

After all this extraordinary haggling over abstract percentages it is hardly surprising that Churchill began to have second thoughts about the whole procedure. Before dining with Stalin on 11 October he therefore drafted a letter to the Soviet leader expressing the fear that these figures might 'be considered crude, and even callous, if they were exposed to the scrutiny of the Foreign Offices and diplomats all over the world'. He also expressed his concern about the differences between totalitarianism and 'free enterprise controlled by universal suffrage', and said that he felt that the dissolution of the Comintern showed that the Soviet Government did not want to precipitate bloody revolutions and warned that Hitler had been able to exploit the fear of 'an aggressive, proselytising Communism'. In another note written the same evening he thanked Stalin for declaring himself 'against trying to change by force or by Communist propaganda the established systems in the various Balkan countries'. But at the same time he agreed that fascism and nazism could not be allowed to exist anywhere, for they were forms of government 'which give the toiling masses neither the securities offered by your system nor those offered by ours but on the contrary lead to the build-up of tyrannies at home and aggression abroad'. He ended on an optimistic note: 'We have a feeling that, viewed from afar and on a grand scale, the differences between our systems will tend to get smaller and the great common ground which we share of making life richer and happier for the mass of the people is growing every year.'[53] Churchill decided not to send either note to Stalin, possibly because it was all too obvious that the Soviet Union would never accept the principle of non-intervention in the case of Poland.

After a successful dinner at the British Embassy, Churchill and Stalin had an informal discussion of Yugoslavia, Italy and Switzerland. Stalin agreed that the British had a vital interest in Yugoslavia since the Adriatic was part of the Mediterranean which in turn was Britain's lifeline. They agreed that a civil war had to be avoided at all costs if it were to involve the British backing one side and the Soviets the other. On the subject of Italy, Churchill remarked that he found the Italians 'harmless and friendly' and that they had been misled by their leaders. When pushed by Stalin and Eden, Churchill admitted that he 'held no brief for the Italian people', and merely wanted to make sure that they did not starve. Stalin said that he did not think that the economic situation in Italy was particularly serious. Turning the conversation to Switzerland, Stalin announced that he thought the Swiss were 'swine'. Churchill felt this view was somewhat exaggerated, and asked Stalin whether he thought much the same of Ireland as he did of Switzerland. Stalin replied that the only man who knew how to treat the Irish was Oliver Cromwell since 'force was the way in which to deal with such people'. Churchill raised some objections to Cromwell's Irish policy, but Stalin brushed them aside saying that the only reason why the British did not like Cromwell was because he was a dictator.

Churchill met Stalin again on 13 October at Spiridonovka House. Mikolajczyk and Romer were invited to attend the discussions which were to centre on Poland. Mikolajczyk opened the proceedings by presenting his proposals for a compromise solution to the Polish question. These included a coalition government which would include Communists, and an alliance with the Soviet Union. Churchill said that there were a number of points in this presentation which he liked. Stalin muttered that he had not noticed them, and complained that there had been no mention of the existence of the Polish Committee nor of the Curzon Line. Mikolajczyk replied that he was prepared to make some concessions over the Lublin Committee, but on the question of the Curzon Line he said that he was not prepared to give up 40 per cent of Polish territory and 5 million Polish citizens. Churchill told the Poles that he supported the Soviet Union's position on the frontier and added that it was unreasonable to expect the Soviets to tolerate an unfriendly Poland after all the blood that had been shed. He insisted that the British Government supported the proposed frontier not because Russia was strong and powerful, but because she was perfectly right in this matter. In spite of this pressure Mikolajczyk flatly refused to accept the Curzon Line and shouted at Stalin and Churchill that he had not come to Moscow to participate in yet another partition of his country. The meeting therefore ended without reaching any agreement.

Later that day Churchill and Stalin met delegates of the Polish Committee. Churchill told them that he was tired of the endless squabbles among the Poles and wanted unity and compromise. Beirut, on behalf of the delegation, replied that the blame rested squarely on the shoulders of the London Poles whose government was based on the anti-national and anti-democratic constitution of 1935 and whose policy was to sow discord between the Allies by claiming that the Soviet Union was as much the enemy of Poland as was Nazi Germany. The Committee having listed all of Mikolajczyk's evil doings, Churchill remarked that Mikolajczyk had a monopoly of crime and the Committee a monopoly of virtue. Morawski then added General Bor to the list of criminals to which Churchill replied that he had won the admiration of millions not by his wisdom but by his courage. After this rancorous exchange Beirut finally agreed that it might be desirable for the Committee to meet Mikolajczyk.

The following morning Churchill and Eden told Mikolajczyk what had transpired during the meeting with the Committee. Churchill argued that a golden opportunity had been missed earlier in the year to settle the frontier question, and Mikolajczyk's refusal to do so had greatly strengthened the hand of the Committee. Now was the last chance to establish working relations with the Soviet Government. Mikolajczyk replied that the three great powers had already decided the frontier question at Teheran, and he was now being asked to accept a *fait accompli*. Churchill replied that Poland had been saved at Teheran, and he went on to tell Mikolajczyk that unless he accepted the Curzon Line the Russians would sweep through Poland and his people would be liquidated. At this point Churchill completely lost his temper, yelled at Mikolajczyk that he ought to be confined to a lunatic asylum and invited him to go ahead and conquer Russia if he wanted to. Unable to control himself, Churchill stormed out of the room, but he soon returned in a more conciliatory mood. Further attempts were made to get the Poles to accept the Curzon Line, but they all failed, largely because of their refusal to agree that Lvov should go to the Soviet Union. When Eden asked Stalin to make a concession over Lvov he replied dramatically that he was an old man and could not go to his grave under the stigma of one who had betrayed the Ukrainians. Finally Mikolajczyk agreed to accept the Curzon Line as a 'line of demarcation' and Churchill proposed this compromise to Stalin who promptly rejected it. Mikolajczyk then said he would return to London and attempt to convince his colleagues to accept the Curzon Line.

On 18 October Stalin gave a farewell dinner for Churchill. At the supper table Churchill told his host that Hess was now completely mad, and that his relations with Hitler had probably been abnormal. Stalin proposed a toast to the British Intelligence Service for inveigling Hess into coming to Britain. Churchill protested at this calculated gaffe, and Stalin blandly remarked that the Soviet Intelligence Service frequently failed to inform the Soviet Government of its intentions, and only did so after its work was accomplished. In drinking Gusev's health, Stalin remarked that he did not understand the English but that he was learning. Stalin assured Churchill that the Soviet Union, first because it could not if it would and then because it did not want to, had no intention either now or at any time in the future to sovietise other countries. Russia had quite enough to do at home to keep the people busy day and night. He added that the British thought the Russians were stupid, but this was not so. Russians are of average ability, not too clever but also not too stupid. On the other hand the Russians thought the British were very clever and for that reason feared them. He did not want his people to be cleverer than other people, he wanted them all to be on much the same level. After these strange musings the two men parted and Churchill returned to London.

In spite of the intransigence of the Soviets over the Polish question, and the Polish refusal to reach an agreement, Churchill was delighted with the results of his visit to Moscow. Writing to Attlee from Moscow he glowed with enthusiasm:

> We have talked with an ease, freedom and a *beau geste* never before attained between our two countries. Stalin has made several expressions of personal regard which I feel were all sincere. But I repeat my conviction that he is by no means alone. 'Behind the horseman sits dull care.'[54]

In a note to Eden written on his return to London, Churchill said that the most important result of the Moscow conference was Stalin's promise to join in the war against Japan as soon as Germany was defeated. He added, 'We should not show ourselves in any way hostile to the restoration of Russia's position in the Far East, nor commit ourselves in anyway to any U.S. wish to oppose it at this stage.'[55] Churchill and Eden agreed that the deal they had made over Greece and the Black Sea was a good one, and they were convinced that Stalin was a man who would never break his word.

On 24 November Mikolajczyk resigned. He told Eden that he was unable to get any support for the acceptance of the Curzon Line and therefore found himself unable to continue in office. Eden promised him that the new Polish Government would be treated 'with correctitude' but it would not be possible for the British Government to have an 'intimate relationship' with them. He also told Mikolajczyk that the new Government would be required to hand over the cyphers used to communicate with the Home Army.[56] The War Cabinet was informed that Mikolajczyk and Romer had resigned because they were convinced that the Soviets were negotiating in bad faith. Churchill told the Cabinet that he did not intend to break off relations with the London Poles, but that he would 'adopt an attitude of complete detachment and frigidity and leave them to look after their own affairs'. In spite of all these difficulties Churchill still felt that the Soviet Union was 'ready and anxious' to cooperate with the British Government, and he warned that 'No immediate threat of war lay ahead of us once the present war was over and we should be careful of assuming commitments consequent on the formation of a

Western bloc that might impose a very heavy military burden upon us.'[57] He believed that the rapport he had established with Stalin during his recent visit to Moscow provided a secure basis for the improvement of Anglo–Soviet relations, and that nothing should be done that might lead to the division of the world into two hostile camps.

11   On the Eve of Potsdam

From the summer of 1944 the Post-Hostilities Planning Staff had devoted much of their attention to the idea of forming a Western bloc of France, Belguim, Holland, Denmark, Norway, Iceland and possibly Sweden, Spain, Portugal and even parts of Germany. Churchill was strongly opposed to this idea. In a note to Eden he pointed out that it would take five to ten years for France to build up her army, and added, 'The Belgians are extremely weak and their behaviour before the war was shocking. The Dutch are entirely selfish and fought only when they were attacked, and then for a few hours. Denmark is helpless and defenceless and Norway practically so.' Under such circumstances it would be virtually impossible to defend the Continent, and Britain's first priority would be to build up her own air and naval strength. For a Western bloc to be viable the British would have to provide 50 to 60 Divisions which was clearly absurd. Churchill asked Eden how such preposterous ideas could possibly be entertained in the Foreign Office and elsewhere.[1] Some members of the Foreign Office who were much taken by Gladwyn Jebb's ideas of a Western bloc wanted to argue it out with the Prime Minister, but it was felt that this might be unwise. They were encouraged to desist from bearding the lion by a report from Clark Kerr that the Soviets would probably be prepared to accept the idea of a Western bloc provided that it was seen as being anti-German. The Ambassador pointed out that the Russians were doing exactly the same thing in Eastern Europe, and after all it was anti-German feeling that was at the core of the Anglo–Soviet alliance. The Foreign Office replied by telling the Ambassador to inform Molotov that the Western bloc idea was nothing more than a suggestion for a scheme to contain and control Germany.[2]

Such talk as this could only strengthen Soviet determination to maintain a commanding presence in Poland. The Foreign Office still hoped that it might be possible to get Mikolajczyk back into office, for he was seen as the only man who might stop Stalin from imposing the Lublin Committee on Poland. Churchill was quite confident that a settlement was possible and that there was no need to quarrel with Stalin over Poland. He told Eden, 'Before we have a head-on collision he presumably would blow his whistle, as at present our relations are most friendly.'[3] In order to minimise the difficulties over Poland the Foreign Office made strenuous efforts to stop speculation about the Katyn massacre. Oliver Harvey complained that reports from Poland were being deliberately embroidered by the London Poles to work up opinion hostile to the Soviet Union in the Press and in the House of Commons. The Foreign Office therefore pressed SOE to send an intelligence mission to Poland, so that it would no longer be necessary to rely on the London Poles for information.[4] Eden suggested to Churchill that the Ambassador to Poland should be withdrawn and replaced by a chargé d'affaires.[5] Yet while the British were constantly downgrading the new Polish Government in London they were also determined not to be manoeuvred into recognising the Lublin Committee.[6] Churchill still hoped that he could reach a compromise, and that he could rely on Stalin's friendly feelings towards him to avert disaster. But it was rapidly becoming obvious that Stalin was in a very strong position and in no mood to negotiate.

The behaviour of the Soviets during the Warsaw uprising was disturbing even to the pro-Soviet Czechoslovakians. The Soviets gave very little support to the Slovak uprising, and there was a growing fear that the Soviets were intent on taking over the entire country. Czechoslovakia had always been seen as a test case for Soviet intentions, and Churchill found a careful memorandum by Frank Roberts outlining these concerns 'deeply interesting'.[7] From early 1944 the Czechs had been getting increasingly worried about the consequences of being liberated by the Red Army, and they wanted to get British and American troops into the country as soon as possible. Prompted by Masaryk, 'C' arranged for a number of drops of SOE and SIS agents into Czechoslovakia. The missions – 'Chalk', 'Sulphur' and 'Clay' – faced frightful difficulties. The Gestapo was everywhere, the agents found it extremely difficult to find safe houses and often could not even get any food. Many of them were quickly captured by the Germans. Frank Roberts remarked that 'The Czechs, like the Austrians, have the assurance of a good future with little exertion on their part and it must be confessed that their pre-war experiences did not encourage either race to risk their lives now.'[8] In spite of all these difficulties the Foreign Office was appalled to discover that SOE agents had exceeded their instructions to such an extent that they were leading Czech and Slovak resistance groups to believe that they would get massive support from the British for an uprising. The Foreign Office believed that this would simply lead to a repeat performance of the Warsaw tragedy. The Slovaks began to fight the Germans in August, but the British military authorities believed that they should be supported by the Russians as the uprising was within the Soviet field of operations.[9] At the beginning of October General Ingr requested a drop of arms and ammunition for 60 000 men within 10 to 14 days. The Foreign Office believed that this should be left to the Russians. An additional factor for British unwillingness to help was that Eden had an incredibly low opinion of Czech and Slovak resistance movements, and felt that support would be wasted on them. The Czechs for their part were becoming increasingly annoyed with the British for refusing to support them and thought that they were being delivered up to the Russians.

By the end of October the Foreign Office began to feel that the Czechs had good reason to be worried and thought that if they were not given sufficient aid they would be forced into the Soviet camp for lack of a viable alternative. But the Chiefs of Staff saw no justification for supporting the Slovak uprising. Hollis told the Foreign Office that the Slovaks were up against four German divisions and that the Russians were one hundred miles away. His report concluded: 'The Chiefs of Staff would like the Foreign Office to reconsider their proposals in the light of the foregoing comments, since they view with apprehension the prospect of being committed to supporting the rising which has every appearance of being abortive.' The Foreign Office was convinced by these military arguments, and withdrew their request for help.[10] SOE was also opposed to a general uprising in Czechoslovakia, but agreed to continue sending intelligence and sabotage teams to help the underground army. Since the Foreign Office did not believe that the Soviets intended to establish a puppet regime in Czechoslovakia, support for the insurgents was hardly a top priority. The fact that the military believed that a large-scale uprising would be quickly crushed merely confirmed this view.

The British thus believed that only the Red Army could liberate Czechoslovakia, and that a satisfactory arrangement could be made with the Soviets for the future of the country. In spite of mounting evidence to the contrary the same was true for Poland. Mikolajczyk having resigned, the Lublin Committee promptly invited him to join them, but there was little likelihood of him accepting this rather dubious offer. Clark Kerr felt that he should return to Poland to form a new government. He felt that if Mikolajczyk simply disappeared from the political scene the Lublin Committee would take over complete control, and that would lead to a bitter rift in the Anglo–Soviet alliance. Churchill felt that the Ambassador's view was 'excessive with apprehension' as his relations with Stalin after his visit to Moscow were 'most friendly'.[11] Churchill clung to the belief that Mikolajczyk's resignation would show Stalin that he was a man of compromise and that he would soon be able to make a come-back to head a united Polish Government. Stalin, however, soon let it be known that in his view Mikolajczyk was 'unable to help in the solution of Polish affairs'. Stalin accused the London Poles of engaging in acts of terrorism against the Red Army and insisted that the Lublin Committee should be recognised as the only legitimate government of Poland.[12]

The question of the Polish frontiers was also far from settled. Owen O'Malley wrote:

> Being peasant-minded myself, I want to emphasise the poignancy of the situation with which so many young soldiers are faced who on the one hand are ardently preparing themselves for battle but on the other hand are being required by the Soviet Government and His Majesty's Government to move their homeland like – in their own words – a tinker's van, from one part to another part of Central Europe.[13]

Few people in the Foreign Office shared this view, but the question was still open as to where the tinker's van would end up. By the end of December 1944 there was also a growing conviction that sooner or later the British would have to recognise the Lublin Committee as the Provisional Government of Poland. Oliver Harvey wrote:

> As regards Stalin recognising the Lublin Committee as the Provisional Government of Poland, I doubt if there is any more we can do. Both the Prime Minister and the President have urged him not to take further action. The Polish Government over here by their foolish wireless communications to Soviet controlled Poland, and M. Mikolajczyk by his fatal lack of forthrightness have played into the hands of the Committee.[14]

On the frontier question Wilson and Warner were strongly opposed to the Western Neisse, and felt that the Foreign Office would have to risk sounding pro-German on this issue. The British position on Poland's western border would have to be made unequivocally clear to the Soviets and to the Lublin Committee. Eden suggested that a three-power meeting might be necessary to deal with the question of Poland's western frontier.[15]

Orme Sargent went even further, suggesting that some compromise could be reached with the Lublin Committee. In a memorandum on the subject he wrote:

> However unrepresentative the Lublin Government may be, the fact that it is now recognised by Stalin, that it can count upon the material and moral support of Soviet power, both military and political, will I am certain attract to its banners large numbers who have hitherto been indifferent or hesitating ... Ought we not to try to 'penetrate' the Lublin Government by arranging for Mikolajczyk and other political leaders and groups who are prepared to work for Polish–Russian Entente to join with the Government while the latter are still prepared to welcome them on account of their knowledge and experience and influence which they can contribute?[16]

Stalin had formally recognised the Lublin Government on 27 December. The British Government continued to recognise the London Poles, but with a singular lack of enthusiasm.

Stalin's recognition of the Lublin Government did not affect British policy towards the Soviet Union. The Foreign Office reaffirmed Memorandum N. 1008 of 29 April 1944 which stated that:

> Co-operation with Russia after the war is of primary importance. To this end we must play our full part against future German aggression, remove all grounds for Russian suspicions that our friendship with the Soviet Union is half-hearted, and, while not obstructing a very considerable extension of Russian influence over the states on her Western borders, build up our influence in secondary states.

It was still believed that the Soviet Union would be so weak after the war that she would 'refrain from attempts to enhance its influence in foreign countries by methods and to an extent which would seriously indispose opinion here and in the United States of America'. Even Owen O'Malley, a staunch supporter of the London Poles and a man who was deeply suspicious of Soviet motives, felt that the

Soviet Union would be unable to dominate Eastern Europe. He wrote that 'Even Czechoslovakia, the eldest concubine in the Kremlin zariba will prove unfaithful to her lord', the 'Stubborn Magyars' would resist, and Poland would 'prove indigestible'.[17]

Quite how indigestible some of the Poles were prepared to be soon became apparent. The Foreign Office was horrified to learn that the London Poles were in a state of considerable excitement as a result of reports from General Anders and General Maczek that a number of senior British officers, both in Italy and on the western front, had suggested that once the Germans were defeated the war should be continued against the Soviet Union. Eden commented on this report, 'I don't believe our senior soldiers can have said this. Only some of the more foolish M.Ps.' Warner wrote, 'This is bad; and those who have given the Poles this advice bear a heavy responsibility.'[18]

The Foreign Office also felt that Mikolajczyk's refusal to join the Lublin Committee was a serious mistake. Cadogan wrote that he has 'missed the bus', but added that even if he had joined the Committee he would probably get thrown out eventually. By this time Cadogan had become reconciled to the idea that the British Government would sooner or later have to recognise the Lublin Committee.[19] Churchill was also getting very impatient about the constant wrangles over Poland. He told the War Cabinet that it might be possible to get Stalin to give up his claim to Lvov at the peace conference, but he would only agree to do this if he was not submitted to constant pressure. Churchill also told his Cabinet colleagues that he was not particularly concerned about the eastern frontiers of Poland as the country could easily be compensated in the west. Bevin was strongly opposed to this idea and said that the Labour Party believed that the Oder was too far west, and if it were to become the border of Poland 'Germany would not be able to live at all'. He also pointed out that such a frontier would leave far too many Germans living in Poland. Churchill replied that he saw no objection to moving millions of people around, remarking that the Russians and the Turks had done a very good job of this sort of thing in the past.[20] The Lublin Poles wanted not only the Oder but also the Western Neisse which would result in Silesia going to Poland. Churchill and Eden agreed that this was going too far and that the Government should avoid tying its hands at this stage. Churchill, however, felt that the Lublin Government could not possibly be stopped, and suggested that British recognition of the Committee could be used as a bargaining counter to get the best possible deal over Poland.[21]

As the British Government prepared to recognise the Lublin Committee, Eden felt that the main aim of British policy towards Poland should be to ensure that there were free elections with American and British observers. Eden wrote: 'This might be a tall order. But something of the kind we must get from the Russians if Poland is to be really independent and if Anglo–American–Russian relations are to be possible upon that basis of cordiality necessary for the future peace of Europe.'[22] Pressure for the recognition of the Lublin Committee by the British Government also came from SOE. Colonel Perkins, who used the Soviet term 'émigré government' to describe the London Poles, suggested on behalf of SOE that the Soviets might agree to the inclusion of some of the more moderate London Poles, including Mikolajczyk, in the Lublin Government. The grounds for this misplaced optimism were that the London Poles had issued instructions to their followers in Poland to resist a Soviet-dominated regime, and the Russians might therefore be willing to make this gesture to avoid a civil war.[23] This scheme was not deemed worthy of discussion by the Foreign Office for it was clear that the Soviets did not intend to make any compromises. News that the Czechoslovakians, in spite of their waning enthusiasm for the Soviet Union, had recognised the Lublin Government, was a further nail in the coffin of the London Poles.

On the eve of the Yalta Conference the British hoped that it might be possible to extend the Lublin Government to include some moderate Poles, and there was considerable opposition to the idea of Poland absorbing too much of Germany. The brief which the Foreign Office prepared for Eden at Yalta insisted that the aim of British policy should be to work for a completely new Polish government which would be based neither on London nor on Lublin.[24] There was general agreement that this was a desirable goal, but there were few who believed it could possibly be attained.

As the war neared its end and the ring tightened around Germany it became necessary to take another look at the cooperation between SOE and NKVD. The Foreign Office began to ask whether cooperation between the two organisations would continue after the war, and were concerned about the effects of their activities on post-war European politics. SOE was determined to reach an agreement with NKVD on activities in countries surrounding Germany. Warner was most alarmed at this prospect, and asked whether 'surrounding Germany' included France, Holland and Belgium, and whether these activities would continue after the cessation of hostilities. Colonel

Sporborg of the War Office told the Foreign Office that SOE and NKVD worked in advance of their respective armies so that as the Allies approached Germany they were bound to come into close contact. SOE's post-war plans were not yet clear, and would depend on the political situation. The Foreign Office found all this very disturbing, and wanted to avoid having NKVD agents tramping all over Austria, Yugoslavia and Italy. Oliver Harvey said that he doubted whether SOE did much good and that they were unlikely to provide much assistance in pushing the Germans out of Italy. He added that the Germans were in Italy either because they had run out of petrol, or because Hitler had ordered them to stay, and in either case SOE could do little to help the allied armies. That SOE was actively helping their Soviet counterparts at this stage of the war was also a matter of considerable apprehension, and there was much talk in the Foreign Office of 'Trojan horses'. In a further letter to the Foreign Office Sporborg wrote, 'The position is that S.O.E. has a "treaty" with N.K.V.D. under which we have certain rights and obligations. We also maintain a mission in Moscow which is in contact daily under the general supervision of the Ambassador with N.K.V.D.' The present aim was to renegotiate the 'treaty' in order to get more out of the Russians. The Foreign Office felt that in these circumstances it was vital that they should get proper political control over these sensitive operations and make sure that they were strictly limited in scope. In April Sporborg announced that Churchill and Eden agreed that SOE should continue its work after the war.[25]

A glimpse at the relations between SOE and NKVD came from reports from John Ward who was still in Poland, having survived the Warsaw uprising. He claimed that the SOE Mission in Poland had been arrested by the Russians and had been set off by cattle truck to Moscow. He also reported that 90 per cent of the NKVD officers in Poland were Polish Jews who were behaving in an exceedingly brutal manner. This was confirmed in further reports from two Canadian airmen who had escaped from a German POW camp, PO Hubert Brooks and PO Anderson. All three insisted that the Russians were behaving even worse than the Germans had done. Brooks had been arrested by the Russians and had been extremely badly treated. Members of the underground army were being arrested and shot, and the Russians were looting all over the country.[26]

None of this cast a shadow over the Yalta Conference which was conducted in a spirit of unusual cordiality. In retrospect the conference seems more like a typical committee meeting than a major summit conference. Difficult decisions were simply deferred to a later conference, and the three leaders seemed to be satisfied with vague generalities. Yalta confirmed what had already been decided, rather than mark any fresh departure. Neither Roosevelt nor Churchill were at the top of their form. Both men were in poor health, Roosevelt near death, and they did not take the trouble to be adequately briefed. They hoped that their much vaunted friendship with Uncle Joe would see them through, and Stalin, who knew full well that he held most of the trumps, played a masterly hand. Soviet hospitality was lavish with vast banquets, endless toasts, and the delegations housed in exotic palaces which were virtually without plumbing. Stalin was in an expansive mood. He told Churchill that he was bound to win the election, and toasted him by saying that in 1940 he had 'kept the banner of civilisation flying and we shall never forget it'.[27] Churchill replied to this mixture of false prophecy and hypocrisy by saying that every Communist who killed a German was his brother, adding 'Even Tito.' Stalin remarked that when he asked German prisoners who came from the labouring classes why they fought for Hitler they replied that they were only executing orders. He had such prisoners shot.[28] On the subject of France, Poland and Yugoslavia, Churchill said, 'The eagle suffers little birds to sing and is not careful what they mean thereby.'

It soon became obvious that Stalin minded very much what the Polish bird sang. Churchill announced that,

> Great Britain had no material interest of any kind in Poland. Our sole interest was one of honour, because we had drawn the sword to help Poland against Hitler's brutal onslaught. We could never be content with any settlement which did not leave Poland a free and independent sovereign state.

Stalin replied that for him the Polish question was one of national security. He said that the London Poles were hostile, regarded the Lublin Government as a collection of 'bandits and criminals' and they were organising anti-Soviet resistance in Poland, and that 212 Soviet troops had already been killed by the Poles. Roosevelt made matters worse for Churchill by chipping in that Poland had been a source of trouble for over 500 years. Churchill made a vain effort to stop Poland getting the Western Neisse and said, 'it would be a great pity to stuff the Polish goose so full of German food that it died of indigestion'. Stalin replied that the German population was no longer a problem as they had all run away. Roosevelt and Churchill suggested that a new Polish Provisional Government should be made up of representatives from London and Lublin and then a new government should be formed as the result of free elections. Churchill said that before the British could abandon their present position of continuing to recognise the London Government, and transfer their recognition to a new government, they would have to be completely satisfied that it was genuinely representative of the Polish nation. This could only be achieved by free elections. Stalin replied that he had no objections to elections being held within one month. He claimed that the Poles enthusiastically welcomed the Russians as liberators, in spite of the efforts of the London Poles to stir up anti-Soviet resistance, and that the Lublin Government was made up of men like Beirut who had stayed in Poland during the war and had not run away to the safety of exile. The land reform programme of the Lublin Government was extremely popular. On the frontier issue it was agreed that the Curzon Line should form the basis for the eastern frontier and that the western frontier would be decided at the peace conference.

Observing all these goings-on, Cadogan described Roosevelt as 'very woolly and wobbly' and told his wife that Churchill was a 'silly old man' who knew nothing about important matters such as the Dumbarton Oaks Conference. He was delighted to find that 'Uncle Joe is in great form, though, and in a quite genial mood.' He echoed the general feeling at Yalta when he wrote, 'I must say I think Uncle Joe much the most impressive of the three men.' Elsewhere he wrote, 'I have never known the Russians so easy and accommodating. In particular Joe has been extremely good. He *is* a great man and shows up very impressively against the background of two ageing statesmen.' Cadogan felt that they had 'got an agreement on Poland which may heal differences for some time at least, and assure some degree of independence to the Poles.'[29]

In spite of this British satisfaction with the Polish agreement there can be no doubt that the Soviet delegation got their way over Poland. It was accepted that a Polish Provisional Government which would be 'more broadly based' was now possible as Western Poland had been liberated. The Lublin Government 'should therefore be recognised on a broader democratic basis with the inclusion of democratic leaders from Poland itself and from Poles abroad'. This government should then call 'free elections as soon as possible on the basis of universal suffrage and secret ballot. In the elections all democratic and anti-Nazi parties shall have the right to take part and to put forward candidates.'[30] The Prime Minister informed Attlee that he found this to be a 'very good draft', and obviously overlooked the fact that the Soviets' ideas about the meaning of words such as 'democratic' and 'anti-Nazi' were rather different from his.

The British did rather better at Yalta than many had expected, and they had good reason to be pleased with the Conference. On Poland, which was by far the most sensitive issue, they got as much as they had hoped for. An extension of the Lublin Government which did not expressly exclude some of the Poles from London was the most that could be reasonably expected, and many of the British delegates had doubted whether the Soviets would be prepared to make even that concession. The London Poles, of course, thought otherwise. Count Raczynski, the Polish Ambassador, told Orme Sargent that the Yalta agreement handed the government of Poland over to the Lublin Committee, and that Soviet notions of 'democratic' and 'anti-fascist' would result in rigged elections. The Three-Power guarantee of the independence of Poland gave the Ambassador little comfort.[31] When Cadogan told Mikolajczyk and Romer about the conference he met with a similar response. He wrote in his diary: 'They of course exhibited no gratitude, and were merely critical and unconstructive – like all Poles.'[32]

Churchill was delighted with the outcome of the conference, and was convinced that he had established a real rapport with Stalin. He told the War Cabinet, 'As far as Premier Stalin was concerned he was quite sure that he meant well to the world and to Poland.' Stalin had told him that he had committed many sins in the past and that he was determined not to commit any more. The Prime Minister 'felt no doubt whatever that in saying that Premier Stalin had been sincere'. Stalin perfectly understood the British position in Greece, and the Communist emissary from Greece to the USSR had been placed under house arrest and then sent back. Churchill assured the Cabinet that when the Russians made a bargain they kept it.[33] Shortly afterwards he said, 'Poor Neville Chamberlain believed he could trust Hitler. He was wrong. But I don't think I'm wrong about Stalin.'[34] In the bar of the House of Commons he was less euphoric and cautioned realism: 'Not only are the Russians very powerful but they are on the spot; even the massed majesty of the British Army would not avail to turn them off the spot.'[35]

The Foreign Office did not get quite so carried away in their enthusiasm for Stalin and sensibly felt that the most that could be achieved in Poland would be free elections for the 'anti-Nazi' parties supervised by the powers. This was also the view of SOE who were responsible for collecting information on the situation in Poland. The news was not encouraging. Mr Pickles of SOE reported that British POWs were being treated worse than those of other nationalities in Soviet transit camps.[36] If the British were concerned about these alarming reports of Russian activities in Poland they were also annoyed with the London Poles whose attitude they found consistently negative. Cadogan wrote: 'I wish I was [sic] a Pole (in one respect) free to criticize everything and find objection to everything. With my civil service training I should be very good at it.'[37] The Prime Minister, however, still intended to recognise the London Poles until such a time as a satisfactory government had been established in Warsaw. But as he had already given what amounted to a *de facto* recognition of the Lublin Committee this was hardly likely to impress the Soviets.[38]

Early reports from Moscow were quite encouraging. Clark Kerr said that Molotov had agreed to allow British observers to go to Poland. Churchill told him to take this up immediately as he needed to know exactly what was going on in the country.[39] Obviously the reports from SOE were not entirely satisfactory and were no substitute for official observers. Clark Kerr felt that the best man to send to Poland would be Brigadier Hill, SOE's man in Moscow. The Ambassador said that Hill had 'drive and resourcefulness' and had excellent relations with NKVD.[40] At this point Molotov changed his mind and refused to allow any British observers to go to Poland, and also would not agree to allow Mikolajczyk to travel to Moscow. Molotov told Clark Kerr that the new Polish Government would have to be made up of democrats, and he obviously excluded Mikolajczyk from this category.[41] Churchill told the War Cabinet that the Government would have to work closely with the United States against the Soviet Union in order to uphold the Yalta agreements. But he still pinned his faith in Stalin. A few days later he sent his frightful telegram to Roosevelt: 'U.Jay: O.Kay: U.Kay.'[42]

Eden, in the draft of a letter to be sent by the Prime Minister to the President, suggested that for Molotov the Yalta agreements simply meant adding a few utterly harmless Poles to the collection of Russian puppets on the Lublin Committee.[43] Eden agreed with Churchill that it was still possible to exert some influence over Stalin, but that with Molotov it was impossible. Eden was getting increasingly impatient and frustrated and wrote to Churchill,

Is there any other way by which Russians can be forced to choose between mending their ways and the loss of Anglo–American friendship. This is the only method by which we can hope to obtain anything approaching a fair deal for the Poles. Finally: is it of any value to go to San Francisco in these conditions? How can we lay the foundations of any new world order when Anglo–American relations with Russia are so completely lacking in confidence?[44]

Churchill was in no mood to challenge the Soviets, largely because he was not at all certain how much support he would get from the United States. The President told him that Yalta was a compromise, but one which clearly favoured the Lublin Committee. But it did not mean that the Lublin Poles had an absolute right to veto any Poles who were brought in for consultation. He reassured Churchill that he had told Stalin that the aim of the Yalta agreement was to form a new Polish Government, and one that was not simply an extension of the Lublin Committee.[45]

Churchill began slowly to realise that he had been outwitted by the Russians and tried a direct appeal to Stalin. At the end of March he wrote,

No-one has pleaded the cause of Russia with more fervour and conviction than I have tried to do. I was the first to raise my voice on June 22, 1941. It is more than a year since I proclaimed to a startled world the justice of the Curzon Line for Russia's Western Frontier, and this frontier has now been accepted by both the British Parliament and the President of the United States. It is as a sincere friend of Russia that I make my personal appeal to you and to your colleagues to come to a good understanding about Poland with the Western Democracies and not to smite down the hands of comradeship in the future guidance of the world which we now extend.[46]

Churchill appealed to Stalin to allow British observers to travel to Poland and to stop the Lublin Committee exercising a veto on the London Poles, particularly Mikolajczyk whom he described as the 'outstanding Polish figure outside Poland'.

Stalin replied on 10 April that he would exercise his influence over the Polish Provisional Government to invite Mikolajczyk provided that he publicly stated that he supported the decisions made at Yalta on the future of Poland. On the question of allowing observers into Poland he wrote,

> You ignore the fact that if British observers were sent into Poland, the Poles would regard this as an insult to their national dignity, bearing in mind the fact, moreover, that the present attitude of the British Government to the Provisional Polish Government is regarded as unfriendly by the latter.[47]

Churchill found this reply encouraging and its tone more reasonable than he had expected. The previous week he had told visiting Commonwealth leaders who were attending a meeting of the War Cabinet,

> It was by no means clear that we could count on Russia as a beneficent influence in Europe, or as a willing partner in maintaining the peace of the world. Yet, at the end of the war, Russia would be left in a position of preponderant power and influence throughout the whole of Europe.[48]

A major reason why Churchill was somewhat apprehensive about Stalin's reply was that the Soviets had just learnt that the British and Americans were negotiating with the Germans in Switzerland for the surrender of the German troops in Italy. The Soviets had been excluded from the AMGOTs and now they were being excluded from surrender negotiations in a clear violation of the spirit, if not the letter, of the alliance.[49] Churchill therefore promptly set about convincing Mikolajczyk to make the declaration which Stalin required.[50]

Another reason why the Soviets were being a little more cautious than usual was because they now had to deal with President Truman whom they felt it was prudent to treat with slightly more circumspection than his predecessor. Truman was determined to make the Soviets respect the spirit of the Yalta agreement on Poland and was strongly supported by Churchill. The two men sent a joint telegram to Stalin to that effect.[51] Stalin had no difficulty in arguing that he was indeed upholding the Yalta agreement and added a thinly veiled warning that the 'question of Poland is for the security of the Soviet Union what the question of Belgium and Greece is for the security of Great Britain'.[52]

In the case of Poland the British Government was lumbered with a government which they found increasingly tiresome and with a sense of obligation which they were unable to meet. The situation with regard to Romania was quite different. At the beginning of December 1944 the Romanian Communist leader Gheoghui-Dej met the British Military Mission and told them that he devoutly hoped that King Carol would stay in his Brazilian exile. No doubt greatly to his surprise, the British delegation 'heartily shared that hope' and then went on to suggest that all peasant holdings in Romania should be collectivised. Gheoghui-Dej replied that Romanian peasants were extremely individualistic and he doubted whether collectivisation would work. He was then treated to a lecture by the British Military Mission on the virtues of collective farming and was reminded that it had worked very well in the Soviet Union. Gheoghui-Dej, having listened to this extraordinary paean to collectivisation by British officers, rather lamely replied that 'Romanian Communism was a local product to meet local national needs.'[53] A Foreign Office memorandum on Romania was true to the percentages agreement when it suggested that

> our policy must be based on the assumption that the Russians intended to carry out their undertaking to withdraw from Romania when the armistice period came to an end; meanwhile our line must be to encourage the Romanians to co-operate fully and frankly with the Russians and not to look to us or the Americans for support.[54]

At the end of February 1945 the Soviets sponsored a *coup d'état* in Romania which established a Communist government in place of the coalition government of General Radescu in which Communists had been included. The British Government was unable and unwilling to do anything about this for, as Eden pointed out to the War Cabinet, they had agreed to give the Russians a free hand in Romania in return for a guarantee that the Soviets would not interfere in Greece.[55] Churchill pointed out that the Soviets had been extremely scrupulous over Greece so it was impossible to do anything about the situation in Romania. It was also hoped that if the British turned a blind eye to Soviet behaviour in Romania it might be possible to negotiate a better deal in Poland. As Churchill wrote to Roosevelt:

> Since the October Anglo–Russian conversations in Moscow Stalin has subscribed on paper to the principles of Yalta which are

certainly being trampled down in Romania. Nevertheless I am most anxious not to press this view to such an extent that Stalin will say (quote) I did not interfere with your action in Greece, why do you not give me the same latitude in Romania (unquote).[56]

One Foreign Office official found this attitude very hard to accept and wrote: 'This by a simple process of calling black white, democracy "fascism" and "fascism" (of left) "democracy" a legend is being built up which unless challenged will soon be accepted as epitaph of an independent Romania.' This remark angered Eden who commented, 'Who is supposed to challenge it? We have more important fish to reply [sic]. And what would be the result of challenging it? Nil.'[57]

Although some officials were concerned about British oil concessions in Romania it was generally agreed that Soviet domination of the country was a fair price to pay for the licence to crush the left in Greece. The situation in Bulgaria was somewhat different, and the question of relative influence of the British and the Soviets had never been satisfactorily addressed. At the end of February 1945 the British Minister in Bulgaria, Houstoun-Boswall, reported to the Foreign Office, 'I am afraid we must reconcile ourselves to the fact that we cannot prevent the Russians victimising any Bulgarians they choose.'[58] This report was shown to the Prime Minister who minuted, 'What is it we want to do here? He seems very much worried.' Orme Sargent wrote, 'As in the case of Romania, so here too I should prefer to leave it all to the U.S. Government to take the lead.' He felt that if the Americans thought strongly that their reading of the Yalta agreement should be implemented then the British Government should back them up, but with the Russians firmly entrenched in Eastern Europe there was little that could be done. Both Eden and Cadogan agreed.[59]

Houstoun-Boswall's talk was not made any the easier by the fact that the Foreign Office refused to let him know what had gone on during the Prime Minister's visit to Moscow. He therefore knew nothing about the percentages agreement and his political directive read in part: 'Although during the armistice period, Soviet influence will be predominant, there can be no question of abdicating our claim to have an equal share at the peace settlement and in the post-war period, in all political questions affecting Bulgaria'.[60] Since his political instructions were totally contrary to what had been agreed at the highest level, it is hardly surprising that he kept insisting that something had to be done in Bulgaria, and the Foreign Office was at a loss quite what to tell him. The British Embassy in Washington was told that the British Government was not prepared to do anything in Bulgaria because the Soviets might object. Clark Kerr in Moscow was informed that,

> In view of the representations we are having to make concerning Romania, the moment would not be propitious for taking up the general question of Soviet policy in Bulgaria even if Mr. Houstoun-Boswall were less reluctant that the sources of his information should be quoted.[61]

Nothing could be done about Romania because the Soviets were being so helpful over Greece, and nothing could be done in Bulgaria until the more important question of Romania was settled. In such a situation the British Government had virtually no room for manoeuvre.

As in Romania, the new Bulgarian government was a coalition under the domination of the Communists, although this was concealed somewhat more subtly. The United States began to take an interest in Bulgarian affairs and was prepared to take a firm line to secure free elections. Houstoun-Boswall agreed that it was probably a good idea to have it out with the Russians so that all the cards were on the table and the Russians would not harbour any suspicions. He also believed that Anglo–Soviet cooperation and understanding were the keys to the situation, rather than the particular form of Government in Bulgaria.[62] The Americans pressed for three-power consultation on the elections in Bulgaria, but Houstoun-Boswall was convinced that the Soviets would never accept such a suggestion. He was perfectly correct. The Soviets promptly replied that there was no need to interfere in the Bulgarian elections any more than there had been in Finland.[63] The Foreign Office sent a minute to the Prime Minister reporting that according to their information 3000 Bulgarians had been condemned to death for political offences, and 30–40 000 had been killed without trial. Orme Sargent commented that this was most unfortunate, but nothing could be done to put a stop to this 'unpleasant procedure'.[64]

In Hungary the Soviets were at first somewhat more cooperative. The political directive for the British Mission to Hungary summarised British thinking:

> Soviet intentions in regard to Hungary are unknown to H.M.G. at

this stage. The facts that the Red Army is in occupation and that Hungary has become a Soviet theatre of war mean that the Soviet Government must play the principal role in enforcing the armistice. We do not, however, desire to see Hungary fall under Soviet control and you should resist any attempt by the Soviet authorities to encroach on Hungarian sovereignty or independence.[65]

On the other hand the British were concerned that if the United States Government made too many demands about Hungary the Soviets might retaliate by making similar demands in Italy. This could be most embarrassing, for the Western Allies had deliberately excluded the Soviets from influencing the political life of Italy by establishing the AMGOTs without their participation. They were therefore not in a particularly good position to complain about being kept out of Eastern Europe.[66] At the end of March the Allied Commission of Control in Hungary had its first meeting and the British delegation was delighted with the cordial atmosphere and helpful attitude of the Soviet delegation. But these feelings of goodwill soon dissipated. Gascoigne reported from Budapest that the Russians were making endless difficulties over billets for British personnel. He also loathed the Hungarian Premier, Gyöngyössi, whom he regarded as a Soviet puppet and a poor patriot. Yet in spite of such irritations the situation in Hungary was never as tense as in Romania and Bulgaria, and Voroshilov and his subordinates showed a little more sensitivity in dealing with their allies.

Stalin's genial behaviour at the Yalta Conference caused a degree of euphoria. But this rapidly began to wear off. By the beginning of April the Foreign Office began to call for a tough line against Soviet ambitions in Eastern Europe and an end to the apparent drift in British policy. Frank Roberts wrote from Moscow that things had been going badly since Yalta and that perhaps post-war Russia would become every bit as dangerous as Germany. He described the Politbureau as 'full of rough, tricky and untrustworthy personalities' intent on dividing Europe into two camps. If this were to occur, Roberts insisted that Britain should make sure that they were in the better and stronger camp.[67] In spite of this growing unease, the British were still loath to blame Stalin for the worsening of Anglo–Soviet relations. In a memorandum for the Prime Minister, Orme Sargent suggested that the hard line adopted by the Soviets might well be due to the activities of the Red Army Marshals in the liberated countries who wanted to run their own shows, rather than to a change of heart on the part of Stalin who had been so reasonable during the Moscow meetings and at Yalta. He suggested that Eisenhower and Montgomery should be made to get to work on the Marshals. Churchill thought this was a very good idea, but was at a loss to know how to set about doing it. He told the Foreign Office that he would have a word with Eisenhower and Montgomery, but then he forgot all about it. When reminded of this he growled that Eden should do the job for him. Eden wrote, 'I haven't the slightest idea what I am expected to do.'[68]

With this growing tension between Britain and the Soviet Union the Germans were not slow to turn it to their advantage. A political intelligence report from SHAEF pointed out the German policy of trying to turn the Western Allies against the Russians. By tricking the Allies into rebuilding Germany as a bulwark against the Soviet Union, Germany would be able to regain its place as a Great Power. Such ideas were, the report continued, supported by that 'repulsive ragamadolio General Franco'. In conclusion it was suggested that 'Germany's present leaders are already at work to gain for Germany the status of co-belligerent against Russia. They are working in reality to defeat the Allies in the hour of their victory.'[69] There were some in Britain who felt that the Hun was greatly preferable to the Bolshie and who welcomed the idea of an anti-Soviet crusade, but these people remained at the lunatic fringe and had no influence whatsoever on British policy.

Worsening relations with the Soviet Union in the period immediately after Yalta prompted the Post-Hostilities Planning Staff to take a closer look at questions of British security outside Europe. The main area of concern was the Middle East, where the Soviet Union could pose a very grave threat to oil supplies vital to a full war effort both by the British Commonwealth and by the United States.[70] The old argument was repeated that since a hostile USSR would constitute a very serious threat it was vitally important to retain her friendship and cooperation but it was enunciated with a marked lack of conviction, and was probably included to keep the Foreign Office happy. The paper argued that Britain needed defence in depth in Northern Europe, the assurance of American support, and the maintenance of highly mobile forces in the Middle East. Britain's predominant role in the Middle East should be clearly recognised and should be devoted to ensuring the integrity and peaceful development of the Arab States. The British position would be strengthened if Persia was established as an independent state, in fact as well as name, and if the French in North-West Africa would help to provide depth to British defences and help secure the air and sea routes to the Middle East. Ties with Greece and Italy should be strengthened and a watchful eye should be kept to prevent the growth of Soviet influence in Turkey. Measures should also be taken to reduce Britain's dependence on Middle-Eastern oil.

Faced with this possible Soviet threat the British began to have serious reservations about any revision of the Montreux convention, in spite of the encouraging remarks which had been made to the Russians in Moscow and Yalta. It was agreed that it was contrary to British interests to allow the Soviet Union unrestricted right of passage for warships through the Straits, but it was also reasonably certain that the Russians would occupy the Straits at the outbreak of war. A revision of the Montreux Convention would have the undesirable effect of enabling the Soviet Union to build up a serious submarine threat in the Mediterranean.[71]

The more the British position in the Middle East was examined the weaker it seemed. It was highly doubtful whether the Persian oilfields could be defended against a Soviet attack and there were only slender prospects of maintaining the integrity of Iraq. It would be extremely difficult to build up Turkey as a military power without arousing Soviet suspicions. It was considered doubtful whether the possible advantages of a close military alliance with Turkey would be worth the offence likely to be given to the USSR. Palestine and Transjordan would have to be kept firmly under British control in order to provide bases for the British military presence in the Middle East. Lower Egypt was deemed to be the most suitable area for the deployment of an Imperial Strategic Reserve and for the principal administrative base. Naval operations would be directed from Alexandria, and air bases would have to be maintained at Malta, the Canal Zone, Palestine, Transjordan, Southern Iraq and Aden. As it seemed highly probable that in the event of war with the Soviet Union both Persia and Iraq would be lost, and with them 16 per cent of oil requirements (53 million tons), it would be of the highest strategic importance to ensure ways and means of making good that deficit.

Having looked at the problems of the Middle East the Post-Hostilities Planning Staff turned their attention to India.[72] It was assumed that at least until 1960 India would meet all her obligations towards the Commonwealth, even if she had in the meantime achieved Dominion status, and would thus continue to be a major military base, and a source of industrial war potential and manpower.

The Soviet Union was the only power liable to pose a threat to India, therefore it was considered essential that British influence in Persia and Afghanistan should be greater than that of the Soviets, and also that stable and genuinely independent governments should be established and maintained in those countries. Air defences in India would have to be strengthened, and an adequate system of civil defence developed so as to minimise the effects on morale of air attacks on crowded and highly inflammable buildings. The defence of Indo–China, Siam and Malaya was also seen as an integral part of the defence of the Indian Ocean area, since by holding Indo–China and Siam it would be possible not only to limit the threat to Burma but also to secure India from the more serious menace which would result if the Soviets were to overrun the Malay Peninsula.

In June 1945 all these papers on the threat posed by the USSR to British interests in specific areas were brought together in one paper printed for the Cabinet.[73] The paper stressed that the Soviet Union, provided she was able to maintain her political cohesion and military strength, could present an extremely grave threat to the British Empire. It was argued that the Soviet Union might begin hostilities with a limited objective, such as the seizure of the Middle Eastern oilfields, but that in a full-scale conflict she would seek a decisive result in Western Europe and also attempt to disrupt Britain's vital Atlantic communications. The Soviets might even attempt an airborne assault on the United Kingdom. An attack on the Middle East was considered almost a certainty, and the Soviets would also be able to contain large British forces in India and the Indian Ocean without a great expenditure of effort. It was felt that a Soviet threat in South-East Asia and the Pacific was remote.

The Planners felt that the USSR would not be susceptible to blockade, her industries and raw materials would be safe from attack by land and comparatively immune to decisive aerial bombardment, and it was unlikely that the British would be able to disrupt her internal communications by offensive action. Therefore the only hope of defeating the Soviet Union would be to fight a long and protracted war of attrition.

The paper argued that, 'The need for a Western European Group of Allies has already been stressed in connection with the prevention of German resurgence. Such a group would be of even greater value as a means of providing depth of defence against a hostile U.S.S.R.' It was felt that Germany should not be included in this group until relations with the Soviet Union were beyond repair. The defence of

Western Europe would be wholly dependent on swift support from the United States. Without such help the Soviet Union would be invincible. To aid in the defence of Western Europe, Britain would need bases in Eire, Iceland, Portugal and if possible Spain and Italy. Turning to the Middle East the planners remained convinced that Persia and Iraq could not be defended, but felt that it should be possible to hold on to the Suez Canal area. In such circumstances it was felt to be imperative that the strategic importance of the Middle East as a source of oil, as a communications centre and as an administrative base should be reduced.

In South-East Asia and the Pacific it was deemed essential that the great potential resources of China in man-power and raw materials should be made available to the USA and Britain rather than to the USSR. The planners argued that it should be possible to take those measures necessary to insure against any potential threats from a hostile USSR without at the same time endangering British relations with the Soviet Union, by pointing out that they were designed purely to meet any possible danger from a rearmed Japan.

The tone of this paper was quite different from the earlier studies. In all the previous papers it had always been stressed that the best defence against the Soviet Union was to maintain friendly and cooperative relations with her, whether out of conviction or in deference to the views of the Foreign Office is not easy to determine. Now this argument had been dropped, and the possibility of a global conflict with the Soviet Union was taken very seriously. The Soviet Union was seen as Britain's greatest enemy, and Germany was now a potential ally in the defence of the Empire against Soviet Imperialism.

The Post-Hostilities Planners went much further than Churchill although he was getting increasingly angry and frustrated as he saw the Soviet Union tightening its grip on Eastern Europe. On 18 May Churchill entertained Gusev for luncheon at Number 10. The conversation was supposed to be off the record, as Churchill was forming a new caretaker Government. He asked his guest how the Russians were facing the new situation in Europe, and without waiting for a reply answered the question himself:

By dropping an iron screen across Europe from Lübeck to Trieste behind which we had no knowledge of what was happening. All we know was that puppet governments were being set up about which we were not consulted, and at which we were not allowed to peep. ... All this was incomprehensible and intolerable. The Prime Minister and H.M. Government objected in the strongest terms to being treated as if they were of no account in the after-war world. They felt that they still counted for something and they refused to be pushed about. Their determination not to see this happen had moved them to postpone the demobilisation of the Royal Air Force.[74]

Clark Kerr, when told of this outburst, told the Foreign Office that he felt that the Prime Minister had gone too far. In his view the Russians intended

> to secure their own essential interests, and in particular to buttress the Russian frontiers against any possible renewal of German aggression by bilateral treaties, such as the Soviet–Czechoslovak Treaty, which bind the minor Slav countries firmly to Russia. In fact in this, as in other matters, Soviet policy is based upon the most realistic considerations. It tends to show scant regard for our own position or for our relations without allies in Eastern Europe. But this should not I think be interpreted as a sign of hostility to the west or as a danger signal for the future.[75]

Thus at the end of the war there were two distinct views of Soviet policy. Most of the Foreign Office believed that the Soviet Union was obsessed with her own security, and that although her methods in Eastern Europe were brutal and her disregard for the feelings of her allies reprehensible, her policy was understandable and did not pose a real threat to British interests. On the other end of the scale were the Post-Hostilities Planners who saw the Soviet Union as a potentially deadly enemy which posed a real threat to the British Commonwealth and against whom every possible defensive measure should be taken. Between these two extremes many people, including the Prime Minister, moved uneasily and uncertainly, turning towards one or the other view as circumstances changed. But there can be no doubt that as the war ended the view of the planners was gaining the upper hand as the outlines of the Cold War were beginning to form. Even the soldiers, most of whom loathed the Soviet Union and everything it stood for, were alarmed at this dramatic swing in British policy. On 24 May General Brooke wrote in his diary, 'This evening went carefully through the Planners' report on the possibility of taking on Russia should trouble arise in our future discussions with her. We were instructed to carry out this investigation. The idea is, of course, fantastic and the chances of success quite impossible. There is no doubt that from now onwards Russia is all-powerful in Europe.'[76] Churchill suddenly thought he had found the solution to all his problems in the atomic bomb. Brooke knew that there would be all kinds of problems of production and delivery of the bombs, and also that sooner or later the Soviets would build their own bomb, but Churchill 'had at once painted a wonderful picture of himself as the sole possessor of these bombs and capable of dumping them where he wished, thus all-powerful and capable of dictating to Stalin'.[77] Behind all this foolish talk was the uncomfortable realisation that the Soviet Union was a great power which could, if it so wished, dominate Europe. Britain, however, had ceased to be a great power, and although she had considerable influence it was becoming increasingly difficult to make that influence felt.

As the war drew to a close the British and Soviet authorities continued to tangle over the question of the prisoners of war. By the middle of November 10 000 of the 19 500 Soviet nationals in the United Kingdom had been returned to the Soviet Union. The Combined Chiefs wanted to get the Russians repatriated as quickly as possible to avoid problems with the Soviet Government. The only factor slowing down the return of the prisoners was the shortage of shipping. The main problem with the Soviet repatriation commission was that the British did not accept the Soviet definition of nationality, and much to the fury of the Soviets refused to regard Balts and Poles as 'Soviet nationals'. The Soviets insisted, on the contrary, that anyone born within the Frontiers of the Soviet Union in September 1939 should be considered a Soviet citizen.[78] To the British these prisoners of war, whether or not they were Soviet citizens, were a nuisance and a drain on already seriously strained food resources. They did not want to be 'burdened with any more Soviet nationals liberated on the continent', and agreed with the Combined Chiefs that they should be sent back to Russia as quickly as possible.[79] Orme Sargent told Hollis that the Foreign Office regarded the prisoners as a nuisance and an expense and wanted them repatriated as soon as possible.[80]

It soon became obvious that more was involved than the return of some tiresome prisoners of war to their homeland. Reports began to come in about the ghastly fate that awaited these men on their return to the Soviet Union, and these reports were augmented by gruesome stories that circulated the camps. The Home Office told the Foreign

Office that 'At a camp in Newcastle it appears that rumours have been spread abroad by the British orderlies that Soviet prisoners who are repatriated to Russia are ill-treated and in some cases shot.' A British officer who was acting as an interpreter had advised them to escape, and a number of prisoners acted on this advice.[81] A number of British officers did what they could to save the Russians. Brigadier Firebrace of the Soviet liaison group saved one man at the dockside who claimed to be a White Russian who had fought with Wrangel and who had lived in France for 22 years. But few of the prisoners were so fortunate.

The Soviet prisoners of war were not simply returned because there was no room for them, but mainly because the British were determined to stand by the Yalta agreement on the exchange of prisoners. In this they differed from the Americans. In March 1945 the British Government learnt that Soviet citizens who were captured wearing German uniforms and who demanded to be treated as German nationals, as they were entitled to do according to one reading of the Geneva Convention, were not repatriated by the Americans. No attempt was made by the British to inform such Soviet citizens of their rights under the Convention, although it might be argued that as the Soviet Union was not a signatory to the Convention this did not apply to them, and in any case the Foreign Office did not accept this reading on the Convention. Thus the fate of men who were, in Sargent's phrase, 'a nuisance' was not allowed to have an adverse effect on Anglo–Soviet relations, and the British in any case felt bound by the agreement made at Yalta which in turn merely confirmed what had already become established practice.[82] None of this applied to those who were not, in British eyes, Soviet citizens. This greatly angered the Soviet mission, headed by General Ratov, which was responsible for the repatriation of Soviet prisoners. The Soviet Embassy demanded the right to question anyone claiming to be a Soviet citizen, and complained bitterly that they were not being kept properly informed of the number of Soviet prisoners of war under British control. But, as Geoffrey Wilson wrote to the Aliens Department, 'We ... have no intention, of course, of handing over to the Soviet authorities individuals whom we do not regard as Soviet citizens.'[83]

Clearly such a situation was bound to cause a lot of ill-feeling on both sides. There were a number of cases where Soviet officials abducted men who were not Soviet citizens and who had never served in the Soviet armed forces. Many POWs claimed to be Poles and were handed over to the Poles who discovered that many of these claims were false. Such men were then handed over promptly to the Soviets. A report from SHAEF said that many of the Soviet prisoners of war in France were guilty of murder, rape, theft, wanton destruction of property and drunkenness. The Western Allies had no desire to be saddled with such criminals.[84] The Foreign Office suspected that Soviet citizens who did not wish to be repatriated had guilty consciences and were probably collaborators, although this was certainly not always the case, and the term 'collaborator' was used very widely. Military intelligence reported that it had been common practice of the Germans to ask Soviet prisoners of war to raise their hands if they did not wish to fight against Bolshevism. Few dared to do this for fear of being shot, although many volunteered in the hope of getting better food.[85] Obviously men who claimed to have been press-ganged into the German army could not claim to be treated as German citizens under the terms of the Geneva Convention. Wilson made the Foreign Office's position on this question perfectly clear in a letter to the International Red Cross in which he wrote:

The Soviet citizens who have fallen into our hands while wearing German uniforms have insisted that they had been conscripted into the German forces against their will, and they are therefore being treated as liberated Soviet citizens in accordance with the Agreement – the terms of which have been published – which was concluded with the Soviet Government in the Crimea.[86]

The Foreign Office was not seriously concerned about the fate of the repatriated prisoners of war. Christopher Hill wrote, 'I do not believe the Russians will shoot many of those who fought for the Germans – except enthusiasts for collaboration – if only because of Soviet shortage of manpower.'[87]

It was not until June 1945 that the Foreign Office received first hand reports that Hill's judgement of Soviet manpower requirements was incorrect, and the true meaning of Stalin's remark to Churchill at Yalta that those who had agreed to fight for the Germans could be dealt with on their return to Russia was given its true meaning. A British officer who accompanied a group of repatriated prisoners who had expressed reluctance to return to the motherland had been shot in a dockside warehouse within fifteen minutes of disembarkation in Odessa. Others were sent off to 'Educational Labour Camps'.[88] The Foreign Office's response to this grim news was to insist that every possible care should be taken to ensure that only those men who were covered by the Yalta agreement should be repatriated. In other words, in every case Soviet citizenship should be clearly established. The Foreign Office was now in a cruelly difficult situation. Should they allow Soviet POWs to escape? If they did, would the Russians take reprisals against British POWs who had fallen into their hands? Soon it appeared that these fears, which had seemed very real, were misplaced. British POWs returning to Britain reported that although conditions in Soviet camps were extremely primitive they had been reasonably well treated in most cases, although there were frequent complaints that they had had their watches stolen.[89] This did not, however, wholly remove the fear that the Soviets might begin to treat British POWs badly in the future if the British did not stick to the letter of the Yalta agreement.

A large number of non-Soviet prisoners were allowed to escape from the POW camps. Thus a group of Latvians who were denounced by the Soviet authorities as deserters from the Red Army, and who were being held in a camp pending the outcome of their case, were allowed to disappear.[90] Other cases were decided on political grounds. Sir Patrick Dean intervened personally to stop one Andronov being sent back to the Soviet Union. He had fought in Vlasov's army and would therefore almost certainly have been executed.[91] At the other end of the scale Buchaev, a Polish Communist, was forcibly returned, even though he was clearly not a Soviet citizen. Buchaev had escaped from a German prison camp in Poland and after 22 June 1941 had made his way to the Soviet Union where he was trained in intelligence work and parachuted into occupied France. He had been captured and tortured by the Gestapo, but had again managed to escape from the Germans and made his way to England with his Polish mistress, who had also escaped from a German camp in Poland and had managed to make her way to France to join her lover. Buchaev knew that since he had been unable to contact the Communist underground in Paris after his escape, as he had been ordered to do in such an eventuality, he would be shot for desertion. Brigadier Firebrace felt that it was perfectly fitting that he should be looked after by the 'appropriate local authorities', and commented that 'his record would seem to entitle him to preferential treatment in the nether regions of the Workers' Paradise'. Since he was regarded as a dangerous Communist and adventurer he was hastily dispatched back to Russia in spite of the fact that he was married with a son born in England, and his wife threatened to commit suicide if he was forced to return.[92]

Another Soviet POW was more fortunate. His wife gave birth to a child in a camp in Retford, but as he was neither a Communist nor an adventurer, and although he was a Soviet citizen, his case was taken up by Eden and Cadogan who argued successfully that as the father of a British subject he had a right to remain in England.[93]

A skilful attempt has been made to argue that the Foreign Office staffed by a collection of starry-eyed socialists and enthusiasts for Stalin's Russia, were in effect accessories to the murder of countless innocent Soviet POWs.[94] It is perfectly true that many innocent victims suffered frightful ordeals and even death, because of the Yalta agreement, but in the final analysis it is difficult to see what else the British authorities could have done. That they should have welcomed millions of Soviet citizens who had actively or passively collaborated with the Nazis, and some of whom were guilty of dreadful crimes, in the name of a lofty humanitarian ideal that is divorced from the harsh realities of the current situation, is altogether too much to ask. That innocent men were butchered indirectly in the cause of preserving the Anglo–Soviet alliance is a most frightful tragedy. But two overriding British concerns cannot be dismissed lightly. There was a genuine fear during the initial stages of the repatriation programme that reprisals might be taken against British prisoners of war in Soviet camps, and as Eden told the War Cabinet on 4 September 1944, the Soviets would simply not be able to understand purely humanitarian arguments. Even more important was the fact that the Yalta agreement also gave the British Government a free hand to crush communism in Greece, and Stalin gave a tacit guarantee that the Italian and French Communists would not cause any trouble. Stalin was true to his word, and the British did far better at Yalta than they had expected. The issue of the Soviet POWs was not going to prejudice these achievements. Statesmen who have to deal with countries like Stalin's Russia, and who have to negotiate from a position of weakness, are constantly faced with choosing the lesser evil. The victims of Yalta were the victims of such a choice, and those who mourn their fate should also remember the millions who were saved from the terrible fate of living the rest of their lives in satellite states of the Soviet Empire.

Conclusion

When the Third Reich had been reduced to a pile of rubble and the Great Powers assembled at Potsdam to decide the future of Europe, the British regarded their Soviet comrades-in-arms with apprehension but without hostility. British policy was dictated, to a large extent, by the realisation that her power had declined to such an extent that the Soviet Union would have to be treated as a difficult and regrettably crude partner rather than as an expansionist power that would have to be contained at any cost. Earlier illusions that the Soviet Union would be economically dependent on Britain for post-war reconstruction were shattered by the realisation of the parlous state of Britain's finances. Militarily Britain was hopelessly inferior, and even the news of the successful testing of the atomic bomb did not, in the view of most responsible military leaders, radically redress the balance of power, even though Churchill, in his wilder moments, imagined that it did. But above all there was the widespread fear that the Americans would withdraw from Europe leaving the western European states virtually defenceless. Yet in spite of all these problems the British Government was not unduly concerned. The Soviet Union appeared to be pursuing its legitimate security interests, albeit in an often heavy-handed way. The magnificent contribution of the Soviet armed forces to the defeat of Nazi Germany was acknowledged, although sometimes somewhat grudgingly. The actions of the Soviet Government did not give any fundamental cause for complaint. When Eden asked the Foreign Office to draw up a list of examples of Soviet bad faith, which he hoped to use to strengthen his bargaining position at Potsdam, his colleagues were only able to produce a few examples of uncooperative behaviour, evasion and stalling. The Foreign Office had to admit that the Soviets had clearly stuck to the letter, if not always to the spirit, of all the agreements they had made. The fear of the communist menace was far from men's minds. The Soviet Union was seen as a pragmatic and autocratic power, obsessed with its security, and bent on attaining traditional Russian goals. It was widely believed that the Soviet Union had outgrown its youthful ideological fervour and revolutionary zeal and had finally reached political maturity. It was now a great power whose voice could not be ignored, whose legitimate desires had to be satisfied, and which had to be treated as an equal. For the British this state of affairs gave little grounds for optimism, but also no reason for despair.

In 1939 the situation was totally different. In the early months of the war the Soviet Union was seen as a nuisance rather than a threat, as the slavish ally of Nazi Germany and squarely in the enemy camp. After the disastrous performance of the Red Army in the early stages of the Finnish war military observers no longer took them seriously and no one regarded the Soviet Union as a significant military power. There were some who imagined that air raids on the Caucasus oil fields would quickly bring the Soviet Union to her knees, and by thus destroying her greatest ally Germany would soon be defeated. Calmer heads prevailed. Experts pointed out that bombing the oil fields would be extremely difficult, and it was doubtful whether a sufficient number of aircraft could be spared for this risky mission. But the most important restraint on such drastic and foolhardy action was the hope that it still might be possible to reach a political agreement with the Soviet Union. Britain also needed to keep up her trade relations with the Soviet Union, especially to ensure an adequate supply of timber, and trade talks were enthusiastically supported by those who hoped that they might also lead to a comprehensive political agreement. The Soviet invasion of Poland and the Baltic States, and even the war against Finland, did little to change this attitude. They were seen as essentially defensive moves which were likely to place additional strain on the Nazi–Soviet Pact, and some even hoped that they might lead to war between these two allies.

The crushing defeat of France put paid to any hopes the Soviet Union might have had for a balance of power in Europe. They certainly did not want to see the Germans getting any stronger, but they could not afford to do anything that might antagonise them. The British Government was in no position to exploit this situation. They could not make an offer that would seriously tempt the Russians, and they were far too weak to make any meaningful threat. Stafford Cripps had gone to Moscow as Ambassador with high hopes of reaching an understanding with the Soviets, but he was soon frustrated and anxious to return home. Eden's appointment as Foreign Secretary in December 1940 strengthened the Foreign Office's determination to open the lines of communication to Moscow, but the Soviets did not respond except with a few guarded hints and innuendos.

When Germany invaded the Soviet Union some doubts were expressed as to the wisdom of an alliance with the Russians, for it was feared that this might have an adverse effect on American opinion, but Churchill had no doubts whatsoever. His overriding concern was to defeat Nazi Germany and he had long hoped that the Soviet Union would be forced to join him in this struggle. He remained as antipathetic as ever to the Soviet regime, but he learnt to respect Stalin and tended to exaggerate the cordiality of this peculiar friendship. 22 June 1941 did not mark quite so radical a new departure as has so often been assumed, for the foundations both for the Anglo–Soviet alliance and for future conflicts and misunderstandings had already been laid. Cold War hostilities between Britain and the Soviet Union have led to a serious distortion of the historical record both with respect to the extent to which the British hoped to win over the Soviet Union even at the cost of accepting her frontiers in 1940, and also an exaggeration of the extent to which the British Government felt duped and betrayed by Soviet Actions in Eastern Europe in the final stages of the war.

Although the signing of the Anglo–Soviet Alliance was seen as a significant new departure, the two countries continued to fight two separate wars and there was a minimal degree of cooperation between the two allies. The joint invasion of Iran and the small-scale invasion of Spitzbergen was all that passed for joint military action. In spite of the reluctance of the military, Britain sent supplies to the Soviet Union and suffered grievous losses in the process, but these amounted to such a small percentage of Russian war material that they were received with very little gratitude. It is also doubtful whether the intelligence information gleaned from Ultra, which was passed on to the Soviet Government via the military mission in Moscow, made any really significant difference to the Soviet war effort.

Whereas the British were mainly concerned with sending supplies to the Soviet Union that would enable them to withstand the German invasion, and with attempting to establish more satisfactory military liaison, the Soviets' main concern, even in the early stages of the war, was with the post-war settlement. Some diplomats, particularly Cripps and Clark Kerr, felt that the British Government should seize the opportunity and reach an agreement on post-war Europe while the Soviet Union was still weak and fighting for her very existence. Churchill, who claimed that he had constantly to look over his shoulders at the Americans, refused to discuss any such matters, and insisted that they sould be left for the peace conference.

British public opinion was strongly pro-Soviet and enthusiasm for Russia's heroic struggle against the Nazi invader led many people to feel that the Soviet state might well have something to offer Britain in the task of post-war reconstruction. This pro-Soviet attitude was also strengthened by the markedly leftward trend in British politics during the war of which the Labour Party, most of whose leaders were immune to the siren call of the New Civilisation, was the principal beneficiary. Conditioned as we are by decades of the Cold War it is difficult to imagine how few people were untouched by this enthusiasm and the open expression of socialist sympathies was commonplace even in Whitehall. In such an atmosphere it was easy for the NKVD's British recruits, who were obliged to be somewhat more reticent, to remain unsuspected and to work their way into positions of considerable importance. A close watch was kept on the Communist Party, but the fellow-traveller was the man of the hour, his organisations given government subsidies, and staunch anti-Communists like Cripps and Beaverbrook joined in their hymns of praise to the Soviet Union.

Champions of the Soviet cause echoed the demands for a second front which issued forth from Moscow in increasingly strident tones. British commitment to the Mediterranean strategy made an early invasion of France impossible, and as long as the Soviet Union continued to fight it hardly seemed a matter of great urgency or one that justified the risk of heavy losses. Massive bombing raids on Germany, although they were known to be of dubious military value, were continued in part to placate the Russians. Supplies were still sent in large quantities, but as the Soviets reorganised their war production and achieved very impressive levels of output they were even less forthcoming with their gratitude. The Russians remained deeply suspicious of the British and felt that they were being left to do most of the fighting. This attitude served to make the British military, who neither respected nor appreciated the Soviet armed forces, even more hostile to the Soviet Union. Frustrated by the inability of the British military mission to get anything out of the Russians, in spite of the fact that they were unwilling to give very much themselves, constantly badgered to open the second front, and taunted for their inability to hold down large numbers of German divisions, the British military came to the conclusion that the Soviet Union was almost as much of a potential enemy as it was an ally.

Even people who took a more charitable view of the Russians and who felt that they had every right to guarantee their security after all the frightful losses they had sustained, still refused to treat them as an equal partner in the Grand Alliance. As Sir Archibald Clark Kerr put it, the British Government consulted Washington – although perhaps not quite as often as he imagined – but informed Moscow. In such a situation Soviet suspicions and complaints were not wholly unjustified.

After the Teheran conference the second front was no longer an issue and the question of the post-war settlement became the central concern of Anglo–Soviet relations. The famous percentages deal made by Churchill in Moscow in October 1944 was hardly the cynical act he imagined it to be, but was the result of a carefully-considered policy which had been agreed upon for months before. It was conceded that Soviet concerns for the security of their western border were perfectly legitimate, and that however much one might regret the fact, Eastern Europe would be within the Soviet sphere of influence. In return the British got a free hand in Greece and the Communists in Italy and France were ordered to toe the line. The Soviet Union liberated Eastern Europe the only way they knew how – by setting up governments similar to their own. The British and Americans did much the same thing in their spheres of influence, making short shrift of any opponents of capitalism and often seriously compromising the principles of liberal democracy for which, in their public utterances at least, they claimed to be fighting the war. Both the British and the Russians sent in the tanks to depose governments they disliked and crushed popular movements. At the time this caused few difficulties, for each side turned a blind eye to the other's misdeeds. After all the British were in no position to complain about Russian actions in Romania when they were doing the same thing in Greece.

Poland was a special case and was the cause of the most friction between the two countries. Britain had gone to war ostensibly to save Poland. The Poles had fought with great gallantry in most of the major campaigns of the war. The Polish Government in London had many supporters and well-wishers. But once the British Government accepted the Soviet demand for a friendly government in Poland, and had lost patience with the Poles' refusal to make any concessions, they almost guaranteed that the future government of Poland would be Communist. Free elections in Poland would never have returned a government friendly to the Soviet Union. Hundreds of years of history precluded such a result.

As long as the war against Germany continued none of this presented a really serious problem and the Anglo–Soviet Alliance, which was born of expedience and necessity, held together. When Germany was no longer a threat the alliance began to fall apart. The British began to think of the Soviet Union as an aggressive, brutal and expansionist power hell-bent on subjugating the world to an aggressive Communism. The Soviets began to think of the Western Allies as perfidious imperialists sucking the life-blood of the workers of the world and forcing them to serve and worship the capitalist Moloch. But it took years for this absurd and dangerous manichean world view to reach its mature Cold War form.

As the war drew to a close it was obvious for all to see that the Soviet Union was by far the strongest power in Europe. It was not in a state of economic collapse as so many experts had predicted, although it faced the awesome task of rebuilding the country after four years of total war. By now it was such a great military power that even the most patronising of the British generals viewed it with awe, respect and considerable alarm. There appeared to be two ways of dealing with this uncomfortable situation. The Foreign Office believed that the key to post-war security lay in establishing good relations with the Soviet Union, and that to treat her as a potentially hostile and expansionist power would be tantamount to making a dangerously self-fulfilling prophecy. The military, who had always felt that the only way to deal with the Russians was to be tough with them favoured the formation of a western bloc, which would probably include western Germany, which would bar the way to the Soviet Union's westward expansion. At the same time Britain would have to establish a formidable defensive position in the Middle East and modernise the armed forces. This view was skilfully articulated by the Post-Hostilities Planning Staff.

Even with the benefit of hindsight, which is never the best historical perspective, the argument continues. One side sees the military and their supporters as pragmatists and realists who clearly foresaw the nature of the Soviet threat and the onset of the Cold War. Others argue that it was precisely this attitude of mind which caused the Russians to become increasingly suspicious that the enthusiasts for an anti-Bolshevik crusade were gaining the upper hand, and that they therefore strengthened their own position in the face of what appeared to be yet another challenge to the very existence of the Soviet regime. Neither view is correct, for it ignores the concrete historical situation in 1945. Britain and the Soviet Union had been driven together by Hitler's lust for conquest, and for no other reason. With Germany totally defeated the old suspicions were bound to resurface. The British began to feel that they had been swindled at Yalta, when at the time they had realised that they had got a very good deal. Similarly the Russians began to suspect that the British might be tempted to continue the war against them, although this was never for one moment seriously considered by anyone in a position of responsibility. But if the origins of the Cold War go back to 1917 it is also obvious that the war drastically changed the situation. The Soviet Union could no longer be viewed as a distant country engaged in a peculiar, unpleasant and possibly dangerous social experiment. It was now a very great power which Britain could only match if she became part of a global alliance supported by the full might of the United States. It was clearly impossible to create such an alliance for years to come, and even then it was uncertain whether the Americans would be prepared to play their part. If there really was a Soviet threat, then it had now become a positive menace. If the world was to be rid of Communism and freed from Stalinist tyranny then it would take a terrible war in which the suffering would be almost inconceivable. In 1945 there was none of the absurd talk of it being better to be dead than red. On the contrary, there was a general agreement that Communists were greatly preferable to Nazis and that the peoples of Eastern Europe could reasonably expect a decent and dignified future, for the Soviet satellite system had yet to be fully implemented.

Was it the case that the British Government was not yet aware of the true nature of Stalin's Russia, or was an opportunity, however difficult and remote, to build on the foundations of the wartime partnership lost in the moment of victory? Such a question overlooks the fact that there were two partners in the alliance, neither side was blameless, suspicions and betrayals were mutual, and any policy, however shrewd and enlightened, depends for its success on the responses it meets. British policy makers did their best in an exceedingly difficult situation and it would be both foolish and unjust to condemn them for blindly appeasing an implacable enemy. They were operating with dwindling funds and diminishing returns and, like all men in similar situations, were powerless to alter the great decisions of history.

Notes and References

1 THE RUSSIAN ENIGMA

1. Sir Llewellyn Woodward, *British Foreign Policy in the Second World War*, vol. 1 (London, 1970) p. 11.
2. CAB 65–1, 13–7, 12 Sep. 1939.
3. CAB 65–1, 18–3, 17 Sep. 1939. Oliphant was Deputy Under-Secretary of State at the Foreign Office. In December he was appointed Ambassador to Belgium.
4. G. Biliakin, *Maisky: Ten Years Ambassador* (London, 1944) p. 288.
5. Martin Gilbert, *Finest Hour: Winston S. Churchill 1939–1914* (London, 1983) p. 44. War Cabinet Paper no. 52 of 1939, 'Notes on the General Situation' 25 Sep. 1939.
6. Ivan Maisky, *Memoirs of a Soviet Ambassador* (London, 1967) p. 32.
7. T. D. Burridge, *British Labour and Hitler's War* (London, 1976) pp. 32 and 54.
8. CAB 65–1, 18–3, report of Deputy CIGS to Cabinet 17 Sep. 1939.
9. CAB 65–1, 32–18, 30 Sep. 1939.
10. CAB 84, COS (39), 66 JP, 6 Oct. 1939.
11. CAB 84–8, Report of Joint Planning Committee September 1939.
12. CAB 65–2, 39–7, 6 Oct. 1939.
13. CAB 65–2, 109–5, 9 Dec. 1939.
14. Dalton Papers, II 3/2.
15. Dalton Diary 15 Sep. 1939.
16. CAB 62–1, 16–5, 15 Sep. 1939 and CAB 62–1, 19–14, 18 Sep. 1939.
17. CAB 62–1, 31–10, 29 Sep. 1939; CAB 62–1, 32–5, 30 Sep. 1939.
18. FO 837, 1121, Report of President of the Board of Trade 13 Sep. 1939. Dalton Diary 16 Sep. 1939.
19. CAB 62–1, 33–9, 1 Oct. 1939.
20. CAB 65–1, 30–6, 28 Sep. 1939.
21. FO 837, 1121.
22. Dalton Diary 18 Sep. 1939 and 25 Sep. 1939.
23. Beatrice Webb Diary 24 Sep. 1939.
24. Dalton Diary 18 Sep. 1939.
25. CAB 65–2, 67–17, 1 Oct. 1939.
26. CAB 62–1, 34–7, 2 Oct. 1939.
27. CAB 65–1, 38–10, 5 Oct. 1939.
28. CAB 65–1, 54–5, 20 Oct. 1939; CAB 65–2, 92–10, 23 Oct. 1939.
29. CAB 65–1, 58–9, 24 Oct. 1939.
30. FO 371, 24839.

31. FO 371, 23701.
32. FO 371, 23692.
33. Ibid. This conversation took place on 14 Oct. 1939 just before the Finnish mission returned from talks in Moscow in which they refused Soviet proposals for a pact along the lines of that between the Soviet Union and Estonia.
34. CAB 65–2, 39–7, 6 Oct. 1939.
35. CAB 65–2, 85–10, 16 Oct. 1939.
36. FO 371, 23692, Lascelles to FO 9 Oct. 1939.
37. FO 371, 23843, Maclean minute 28 Oct. 1939.
38. CAB 65–6, 82–6, 5 Apr. 1940.
39. CAB 84–8, Snow to FO 21 Oct. 1939.
40. CAB 65–1, 57–8, 23 Oct. 1939; CAB 84–8; CAB 65–2, 67–9, 1 Nov. 1939.
41. CAB 65–2, 67–11, 1 Nov. 1939.
42. CAB 65–2, 99–8, 30 Oct. 1939.
43. CAB 65–1, 39–11, 6 Oct. 1939; CAB 65–1, 51–8, 18 Oct. 1939.
44. Woodward, *British Foreign Policy*, vol. 1, p. 39.
45. CAB 65–2, 97–7, 28 Nov. 1939.
46. CAB 65–2, 91–10, 22 Nov. 1939.
47. CAB 84–9, COS memo. Nov. 1939.
48. CAB 65–2, 101–6, 2 Dec. 1939.
49. CAB 65–2, 103–12, 4 Dec. 1939.
50. CAB 65–2, 103–7, 4 Dec. 1939.
51. CAB 65–2, 104–7, 5 Dec. 1939.
52. CAB 65–2, 112–5, 12 Dec. 1939; CAB 65–2, 123–2, 27 Dec. 1939.
53. CAB 65–2, 118–3, 18 Dec. 1939.
54. Oliver Harvey Diaries, 24 Dec. 1939.
55. CAB 65–5, 3–6, 4 Jan. 1940.
56. CAB 65–2, 116–8, 15 Dec. 1939.
57. CAB 65–2, 108–9, 8 Dec. 1939.
58. CAB 65–2, 112–10, 12 Dec. 1939.
59. R. A. Butler, *The Art of Memory* (London, 1982) p. 38.
60. CAB 65–2, 108–9, 8 Dec. 1939.
61. CAB 65–2, 109–5, 9 Dec. 1939.
62. CAB 65–5, 7–9, 9 Jan. 1940.
63. CAB 65–5, 17–2, 18 Jan. 1940.
64. CAB 65–5, 9–6, 11 Jan. 1940.
65. CAB 65–5, 11–4, 13 Jan. 1940.
66. CAB 65–5, 16–6, 17 Jan. 1940.
67. CAB 65–5, 24–4, 26 Jan. 1940.
68. CAB 65–5, 10–2, 12 Jan. 1940.
69. Woodward, *British Foreign Policy*, vol. 1, p. 72.
70. CAB 65–5, 14–9, 15 Jan. 1940.
71. CAB 65–5, 15–11, 16 Jan. 1940.
72. CAB 65–5, 20–3, 22 Jan. 1940.
73. CAB 65–5, 21–3, 23 Jan. 1940.
74. CAB 65–5, 22–5, 24 Jan. 1940.
75. CAB 65–5, 29–4, 1 Feb. 1940. Cabinet agreed to send 12 Hurricanes,

30 Gladiators, 28 Gauntlets, 12 long-nosed Blenheims, 12 short-nosed Blenheims, 17 Lysanders and 33 Dive-Bombers.
76. CAB 65–5, 46–5, 19 Feb. 1940.
77. Hugh Dalton, *The Fateful Years: Memoirs 1931–1945* (London, 1957) p. 293. Dalton Diary 17 Mar. 1940.
78. *Tribune* 1 Dec. 1939.
79. FO 371, 24839, 31 Jan. 1940.
80. Ibid.
81. CAB 65–5, 46–5, 19 Feb. 1940.
82. CAB 65–5, 39–8, 12 Feb. 1940.
83. PREM 1, 408, 10 Feb. 1940. Eden to Chamberlain.
84. CAB 65–5, 44–4, 17 Feb. 1940. Harold Macmillan, *The Blast of War* (London, 1967) pp. 27–8.
85. CAB 65–5, 46–5, 19 Feb. 1940.
86. CAB 65–5, 43–5, 16 Feb. 1940.
87. CAB 65–12, 68–4, 14 Mar. 1940.
88. CAB 65–11, 37–5.
89. CAB 65–11, 45–1; 49–6; 50–8.
90. David Dilks (ed.), *The Diaries of Sir Alexander Cadogan 1938–1945* (London, 1971) 19 Jan. 1940.
91. CAB 84–2, 19 Feb. 1940.
92. PREM 1, 408.
93. Harvey Diaries, 14 Mar. 1940.
94. FO 371, 24845, 18 Mar. 1940.
95. CAB 65–11, 35–8, 29 Mar. 1940.
96. FO 371, 24845, 29 Mar. 1940.
97. CAB 84–2, 19 Feb. 1940.
98. WO 208, 1754. Reports by Major Kirkman and Colonel Hammond 6 Mar. 1940.
99. Beatrice Webb Diary 18 Mar. 1940.
100. FO 371, 24850.
101. Nikolai Tolstoy argues this at length in *Stalin's Secret War* (London, 1981) p. 163 seq. but is unable to produce any evidence in support of this contention.
102. CAB 65–11, 35–8.
103. CAB 65–6, 61–4, 6 Mar. 1940.
104. CAB 65–7, 127–13, 18 May 1940.
105. FO 371, 24845.
106. CAB 65–12, 68–4, 14 Mar. 1940, COS (40) 181 of 2 Feb. 1940.
107. CAB 65–6, 66–1, 12 Mar. 1940.
108. CAB 84–9, Ministry of Supply to FO 31 Oct. 1939.
109. CAB 65–6, 72–2, 19 Mar. 1940.
110. CAB 65–12, 68–4, 14 Mar. 1940.
111. CAB 65–6, 76–6, 27 Mar. 1940.
112. FO 371, 24845.
113. CAB 65–12, 68–4.
114. FO 371, 24839; CAB 65–6, 77–7, 29 Mar. 1940.
115. CAB 65–12, 68–4.
116. FO 371, 24843, Stockholm to FO 17 Feb. 1940.

117. Ibid. Maisky to Pares 13 Mar. 1940.
118. CAB 65–6, 93–11, 15 Apr. 1940.
119. CAB 65–6, 97–11, 19 Apr. 1940.
120. FO 371, 24840.
121. Ibid.
122. FO 371, 24839.

2   SIR STAFFORD CRIPPS GOES TO MOSCOW

1.   CAB 65–7, 146–13, 29 May 1940.
2.   CAB 65–7, 149–9, 31 May 1940.
3.   FO 371, 24840.
4.   Ivan Maisky, *Memoirs of a Soviet Ambassador* (London, 1967) p. 139.
5.   FO 371, 24845.
6.   CAB 65–6, 108–6, 30 Apr. 1940.
7.   FO 371, 24840, Soviet note 22 May 1940.
8.   Ibid. 29 May 1940.
9.   Dalton Diaries, 19 May 1940; 31 May 1940.
10. FO 371, 24840, 12 June 1940.
11. Ibid., 22 May 1940.
12. Ibid., Cripps telegram 14 June 1940.
13. CAB 65–7, 171–6, 18 June 1940.
14. CAB 65–7, 170–6, 17 June 1940.
15. Sir Llewellyn Woodward, *British Foreign Policy in the Second World War*, vol. 1 (London, 1970) pp. 465–7.
16. FO 371, 24844.
17. Ibid., 17 June 1940. Rothstein interview with Ridsdale 18 June 1940; Sargent to Dalton 22 June 1940.
18. Ibid., Sargent memo. 28 June 1940 with marginal note by Butler.
19. Ibid., memo by Maclean and Collier 19 June 1940.
20. Ibid.
21. Ibid., Sargent to Sir Hughe Knatchbull-Hugessen 11 July 1940.
22. Ibid., Sargent 16 July 1940.
23. Ibid., Maclean 1 Aug. 1940; Butler 2 Aug. 1940; Sargent on Rauschning 22 July 1940.
24. CAB 65–8, 225–2, 13 Aug. 1940.
25. CAB 65–9, 245–5, 9 Sep. 1940; CAB 65–9, 269–8, 10 Oct. 1940.
26. Woodward, *British Foreign Policy*, vol. 1, pp. 479–80. CAB 65–8, 217–2, 1 Aug. 1940 for Cripps' threat to leave.
27. FO 371, 24840.
28. Ibid., Collier memo. 7 Sep. 1940; Maclean 25 Aug. 1940; Sargent to Cripps September 1940.
29. FO 371, 24845, Cadogan 20 Aug. 1940.
30. Cadogan Diary, 17 Aug. 1940.
31. FO 371, 24845, Cripps to Halifax 2 Aug. 1940.

32. Ibid., Butler 12 Sep. 1940.
33. Ibid., Report from Stockholm 7 Sep. 1940.
34. Ibid.
35. FO 371, 24852.
36. FO 371, 24842.
37. Ibid., Dalton to Halifax 9 Oct. 1940.
38. *Daily Worker* 16 Oct. 1940.
39. FO 371, 24845.
40. Ibid., Cripps to FO 19 Nov. 1940.
41. Ibid., Cripps to Halifax 9 Oct. 1940.
42. Woodward, *British Foreign Policy*, vol. 1, pp. 492–4.
43. FO 371, 24845.
44. Ibid., Eden to Cripps 28 Dec. 1940.
45. Harvey Diaries, 15 Jan. 1941.
46. F. H. Hinsley, *British Intelligence in the Second World War*, vol. 1 (London, 1979) p. 199.
47. Ibid., p. 111.
48. Ibid., p. 432.
49. Ibid., p. 438.
50. WO 208, 1758, MI2(b) 27 Jan. 1941.
51. FO 371, 24851, Eden 4 Jan. 1941.
52. FO 371, 29479 Maclean 22 Jan. 1941.
53. WO 208, 1758, Major Tamplin (MI2(b)) 6 Jan. 1941.
54. Hinsley, *British Intelligence*, vol. 1, p. 443.
55. FO 371, 24856, Cripps to FO 1 Feb. 1941.
56. Ibid., Maclean 4 Feb. 1941; Collier 5 Feb. 1941; Sargent 6 Feb. 1941; Cadogan 7 Feb. 1941.
57. Ibid., 22 Feb. 1941.
58. PREM 3, 395–16, 22 Feb. 1941.
59. FO 371, 24856, Eden to PM 24 Feb. 1941.
60. Ibid., Sargent 28 Mar. 1941.
61. Ibid., Cadogan 10 Apr. 1941.
62. Ibid., Eden 15 Apr. 1941.
63. Woodward, *British Foreign Policy*, vol. 1, p. 611.
64. FO 371, 29479, Belgrade to FO 30 Nov. 1941.
65. Ibid., Berne to FO 24 Mar. 1941.
66. Ibid., report by Major Tamplin.
67. Ibid.
68. Martin Gilbert, *Finest Hour: Winston S. Churchill 1939–1941* (London, 1983) p. 1050.
69. FO 371, 29479.
70. Ibid.
71. Gilbert, *Finest Hour*, p. 1051.
72. FO 371, 29479, Mallet to FO 4 Apr. 1941; 15 Apr. 1941.
73. FO 371, 29498. Mallet to FO 8 May 1941.
74. FO 371, 29479, Cripps to FO 23 Apr. 1941.
75. Ibid., 18 Apr. 1941.
76. FO 800, 279.
77. FO 371, 29479.

78. Beaverbrook paper D.415 contains much entertaining material on this incident.
79. FO 371, 29479, P.I.D. 12 May 1941.
80. Ibid., 2 June 1941.
81. *Tass* 13 June 1941.
82. FO 371, 29479, Warner 14 June 1941.
83. FO 371, 29467; CAB 65–18, Folio 163, FO to Moscow 3 June 1941.
84. FO 371, 29483.
85. FO 371, 29482.
86. FO 371, 29484.
87. FO 371, 29482.
88. FO 371, 29483.
89. Hinsley, *British Intelligence*, vol. 1, p. 480.
90. Harvey Diaries, 18 June 1941.
91. CAB 65–8, 61–7, 19 June 1941.

3 RELUCTANT ALLIES

1. Dalton Diary, 22 June 1940.
2. Winston S. Churchill, *The Grand Alliance* (New York, 1962) p. 314.
3. Martin Gilbert, *Finest Hour: Winston S. Churchill 1939–1941* (London, 1983) p. 1122.
4. CAB 65–18, 62–4, 23 June 1941.
5. FO 371, 29466 Moscow Embassy to FO 22 June 1941.
6. H. Ismay, *The Memoirs of General Lord Ismay* (London, 1960) pp. 223 and 225.
7. D. N. Pritt, Manuscript memoirs, p. 525.
8. PREM 3, 395–12, 28 June 1941.
9. Dalton Diary 1 July 1941.
10. Q. J. Reynolds, *Only the Stars are Neutral* (London, 1943) p. 120.
11. Beaverbrook papers, D/425, 8 Oct. 1941.
12. FO 371, 29471, Eden 29 Nov. 1941.
13. FO 371, 32908, Eden 17 June 1942.
14. FO 371, 29489.
15. CAB 65–19, 69–1, 14 July 1941.
16. FO 800–301. Hill's papers are at the Hoover Institution, Stanford University. He also left a volume of somewhat fanciful memoirs. For further details see: Reynolds, *Only the Stars*; Kim Philby, *My Secret War* (London, 1968); and Bradley F. Smith, *The Shadow Warriors* (New York, 1983).
17. This claim is made in F. H, Hinsley, *British Intelligence in the Second World War*, vol. 1 (London, 1979) p. 199.
18. Bradley F. Smith, *Shadow Warriors*, p. 335. I am greatly indebted to this author for much of what follows.
19. FO 371, 36921.
20. WO 204, 1931. My thanks to Bradley Smith for this document.

21. Tolstoy, *Stalin's Secret War*, p. 334.
22. FO 371, 36948, Eden Apr. 1943.
23. FO 371, 47709.
24. FO 371, 43326, 11 May 1944.
25. FO 371, 47620.
26. FO 371, 29491.
27. FO 371, 29587, Peter Hutton to Ridsdale 23 June 1941.
28. Philby, *Secret War*, p. 74.
29. FO 371, 29549. G. M. Young to FO 21 May 1941.
30. Dalton Diary, 25 June 1941.
31. Harold Nicolson, *Diaries and Letters 1939–1945* (London, 1967) 22 June 1941.
32. FO 371, 29466, Duff Cooper to Eden 28 June 1941.
33. FO 371, 29467.
34. FO 371, 29466.
35. CAB 65–18, 62–5.
36. CAB 65–18, 64–6.
37. CAB 65–19, 65–3, Eden to Cripps.
38. Joan Beaumont, *Comrades in Arms: British Aid to Russia 1941–1945* (London, 1980) p. 26.
39. Dalton Diary, 1 July 1941.
40. Ismay, *Memoirs*, p. 225; F. H. Hinsley, *British Intelligence in the Second World War*, vol. 2 (London, 1979) p. 67.
41. FO 371, 29471 for a summary of exchanges on military assistance to Russia.
42. FO 371, 29485; Sir Llewellyn Woodward, *British Foreign Policy in the Second World War*, vol. 2 (London, 1970) pp. 7–9.
43. Gilbert, *Finest Hour*, p. 1133.
44. FO 371, 29467.
45. CAB 65–19, 67–1, 9 July 1941.
46. FO 371, 29486, Leeper 7 July 1941.
47. FO 371, 29485, Cripps to FO 2 July 1941.
48. PREM 3, 395–16, Churchill 10 July 1941.
49. FO 371, 29471.
50. PREM 3, 395–16, Cripps to PM 6 July 1941.
51. Woodward, *British Foreign Policy*, vol. 2, pp. 16–18.
52. CAB 69–19, 72–2, 21 July 1941.
53. FO 371, 29471.
54. Beaumont, *Comrades in Arms*, p. 31.
55. FO 371, 29562.
56. Woodward, *British Foreign Policy*, vol. 2, p. 18.
57. Gilbert, *Finest Hour*, p. 1143.
58. Beaumont, *Comrades in Arms*, p. 34.
59. Ibid., p. 39.
60. CAB 65–19, 84, 19 Aug. 1941; FO 371, 29569, 14 Aug. 1941.
61. FO 371, 29570.
62. FO 371, 29571.
63. FO 371, 29489, Cripps 14 Aug. 1941.
64. CAB 65–19, 87–4.

65. FO 371, 29471.
66. Winston S. Churchill, *The Grand Alliance*, p. 406.
67. Gilbert, *Finest Hour*, pp. 1182–4.
68. Beaumont, *Comrades in Arms*, pp. 47–50.
69. FO 371, 29489, Cripps 7 Sep. 1941.
70. Ibid., message sent 13 Sep. 1941.
71. FO 371, 29471.
72. Gilbert, *Finest Hour*, p. 1200.
73. Ismay, *Memoirs*, pp. 228 and 212.
74. Ibid., p. 228.
75. FO 371, 29469.
76. Reynolds, *Only the Stars*, p. 76.
77. Beaverbrook papers, D/100.
78. Beaumont, *Comrades in Arms*, pp. 68–70 for details.
79. Beaverbrook D/106A.
80. PREM 3, 401–7; text of memo in Woodward, *British Foreign Policy*, vol. 2, pp. 36–9.
81. Ibid., Cripps to Eden 5 Nov. 1941.
82. A. J. P. Taylor, *Beaverbrook* (London, 1972) p. 488.
83. CAB 65–19, 102–8, 13 Oct. 1941.
84. Taylor, *Beaverbrook*, p. 492.
85. H. C. Cassidy, *Moscow Dateline 1941–43* (London, 1943) p. 131.
86. Cadogan Diary, 6 Aug. 1941.
87. Gilbert, *Finest Hour*, p. 1211.
88. FO 371, 29471, Cripps to Churchill 30 Oct. 1941.
89. Ibid., Cripps to FO 13 Nov. 1941.
90. Ibid., Cadogan to Eden 10 Nov. 1941.
91. Harvey Diaries, 3 Aug. 1941.
92. D. N. Pritt, Manuscript memoirs.
93. FO 371, 29614, Bracken to FO 10 July 1941.
94. FO 371, 29741, Churchill draft to Cripps 15 Nov. 1941, rejected by Cabinet 17 Nov. 1941. Gilbert, *Finest Hour*, p. 1236 fails to mention that Cabinet stopped this unfortunate letter.
95. FO 371, 29741.
96. Ibid., Cripps to FO 15 Nov. 1941.
97. FO 371, 29501, Cripps to FO 17 Nov. 1941.

4 FIRST ATTEMPTS AT COOPERATION

1. FO 371, 29487, Cripps to FO 15 July 1941.
2. FO 371, 29488, J.P.C. 17 July 1941.
3. FO 371, 29487, Eden 18 July 1941.
4. Ibid., Lie was later to become Secretary General of the United Nations.
5. Ibid., Collier to Eden 22 July 1941.
6. Ibid., M.E.W. to J.I.C. 29 July 1941.

7. FO 371, 29488.
8. Ibid.
9. FO 371, 29489, Maisky to Eden 15 Aug. 1941.
10. FO 371, 29492.
11. FO 371, 29489, Warner 17 Sep. 1941.
12. FO 371, 32928.
13. PREM 3, 410.
14. FO 371, 29489, Cripps to FO 9 Sep. 1941.
15. PREM 3, 410, PM 20 Oct. 1941.
16. Ibid., 24 Oct. 1941.
17. FO 371, 29493.
18. FO 371, 32928, C.O.S. Committee 14 Jan. 1942; 2 Feb. 1942.
19. Harvey Diaries, 8 Aug. 1941.
20. Hauner, *India in Axis Strategy*, p. 206.
21. F. H. Hinsley, *British Intelligence in the Second World War*, vol. 2 (London, 1979) pp. 81–4.
22. CAB 65–19, 67–1, 9 July 1941; FO 371, 27051.
23. FO 371, 27205.
24. Ibid., Knatchbull-Hugessen to FO 17 Aug. 1941. The Turkish Government claimed that there were 580 Germans in Iran. The British and Soviet Governments claimed that there were 3–5000. The Foreign Office estimated their number at 2000.
25. Ibid., W.O. to C.-in-C. India 23 Aug. 1941.
26. FO 371, 27230 Dalton to L. S. Amery 7 July 1941.
27. Ibid., Eden-Maisky interview 10 July 1941.
28. Ibid., C.-in-C. India 18 July 1941.
29. Ibid.
30. Ibid., Wavell to CIGS 17 July 1941.
31. FO 371, 27231, Committee report 4 Aug. 1941.
32. Ibid., 12 Aug. 1941.
33. FO 371, 27209, Eden to Viceroy of India.
34. FO 371, 27208, Bullard to FO 29 Aug. 1941.
35. Ibid., PM to FO 1 Sep. 1941.
36. PREM 3, 237–2.
37. Ibid., PM to Eden 6 Sep. 1941; PM to Cadogan 3 Sep. 1941.
38. FO 371, 2711, PM to Bullard 3 Sep. 1941.
39. Harvey Diary 25 Aug. 1941.
40. PREM 3, 237–2, C.O.S. memo 31 Aug. 1941; FO 371, 27208, W.O. to C.-in-C. Middle East.
41. FO 371, 27213, Bullard to FO 8 Sep. 1941.
42. Ibid., Cripps to FO 10 Sep. 1941.
43. PREM 3, 237–2, Eden to PM 9 Sep. 1941.
44. FO 371, 27216.
45. FO 371, 27233, memo by Pink.
46. Ibid., 30 Sep. 1941.
47. Ibid., Bullard to FO 5 Oct. 1941.
48. FO 371, 29489, Warner 22 Sep. 1941.
49. Ibid., Cripps to FO 15 Sep. 1941.
50. Ibid., Dew memo 24 Oct. 1941.

51. CAB 65–23, 106–8, 27 Oct. 1941.
52. FO 371, 29491, PM to Stalin 16 Oct. 1941. Eden to Maisky.
53. FO 371, 29471, Cripps to Churchill 26 Oct. 1941.
54. FO 371, 29491, Portal to PM 24 Oct. 1941; Cripps 23 Oct. 1941; Collier to Air Ministry 24 Oct. 1941.
55. FO 371, 29493, FO to Cripps 11 Nov. 1941.
56. WO 208, 1758, J.I.C. report 23 May 1941.
57. WO 208, 1762, 28 June 1941; CAB 79–12, C.O.S. Committee 3 July 1941.
58. WO 208, 1763.
59. CAB 65–19, 65–3, 4 July 1941.
60. FO 371, 29501, Cripps to FO 8 July 1941; FO 371, 29596.
61. FO 371, 29596, C.O.S. Committee 19 Sep. 1941.
62. FO 371, 29598, Berthoud to FO.
63. Ibid., C.-in-C. Middle East 14 Nov. 1941.
64. My thanks are due to Mr Gwynne Elias for his recollections of Mission 131.

5 THE ANGLO–SOVIET TREATY

1. INF 1, 292.
2. Ibid., Report 26 Nov. 1941.
3. Ibid., Report 10 Dec. 1941.
4. Ibid., Reports 22 Oct. 1941, 29 Oct. 1941.
5. Angus Calder, *The People's War: Britain 1939–45* (London, 1969) pp. 263 and 291.
6. INF 1, 292, Report 8 Oct. 1941.
7. Paul Addison, *The Road to 1945* (London, 1975) p. 135.
8. FO 371, 32877.
9. Addison, *The Road to 1945*, p. 137.
10. A. J. P. Taylor, *Beaverbrook* (London, 1972) p. 528.
11. P. F. Jordan, *Russian Glory* (London, 1942) p. 167.
12. FO 371, 29469, Maisky to Eden 17 Oct. 1941.
13. Ibid., Maisky to Eden 21 Oct. 1941.
14. Ibid., Maisky to Eden 27 Oct. 1941.
15. Ibid., Warner, 12 Nov. 1941.
16. FO 371, 29472.
17. CAB 65–21, 122–6, 1 Dec. 1941.
18. FO 371, 29472.
19. FO 371, 29471; CAB 65–24, 111–8.
20. CAB 65–24, Folio 33, Eden to Cripps 17 Nov. 1941.
21. FO 371, 29472.
22. Ibid.
23. CAB 65–24, 118–10, 24 Nov. 1941.
24. FO 371, 29472.
25. CAB 65–24, 120–5, 27 Nov. 1941.

26. CAB 65–24, 124–3, 4 Dec. 1941.
27. FO 371, 29495, Cripps to FO 6 Dec. 1941.
28. FO 371, 32884, Cadogan 11 Dec. 1941.
29. Ibid., Dew 9 Nov. 1941.
30. Details in: Sir Llewellyn Woodward, *British Foreign Policy in the Second World War*, vol. 2 (London, 1970) pp. 221 seq.
31. CAB 64–24, 133–8, 22 Dec. 1941.
32. CAB 65–24, Folio 82, No. 24 HECTIC, Eden to FO 18 Dec. 1941.
33. Cadogan Diary, 17 Dec. 1941.
34. CAB 65–24, 131–2, 19 Dec. 1941.
35. FO 371, 32864, Churchill to Eden 7 Jan. 1942.
36. FO 371, 32875, Eden memo 28 Jan. 1941.
37. FO 371, 32874, Draft memo Jan. 1942.
38. FO 371, 32875, Eden to Halifax 10 Feb. 1942.
39. CAB 65–29, 1–4, 1 Jan. 1942.
40. CAB 65–29, 17–5, 6 Feb. 1942.
41. Taylor, *Beaverbrook*, p. 511.
42. CAB 65–29, 24–2, 25 Feb. 1942.
43. FO 371, 32904, Cadogan memo 31 Dec. 1941.
44. FO 371, 32876.
45. FO 371, 32905, Orme Sargent 5 Feb. 1942.
46. PREM 3, 395–12, Eden to Halifax 10 Feb. 1942.
47. Cadogan Diary, 25 Mar. 1942.
48. FO 371, 32906, Dew 29 Mar. 1942.
49. Ibid., Kuibyshev to FO 1 Mar. 1942.
50. *The Times*, 3 Mar. 1942.
51. FO 371, 32906, Warner 23 Mar. 1942.
52. Woodward, *British Foreign Policy*, vol. 2, p. 239.
53. FO 371, 32863.
54. Ibid.
55. FO 371, 32877.
56. Roy Douglas, *From War to Cold War, 1942–48* (London, 1981) p. 7.
57. CAB 65–30, 52–4, 24 Apr. 1942.
58. CAB 65–30, 56–9, 4 May 1942.
59. CAB 65–30, 66 Annex, 25 May 1942; PREM 3, 399–4 and 5 for the protocol of all the negotiations.
60. FO 371, 36966.
61. PREM 3, 399–6.
62. CAB 65–30, 68–2, 26 May 1942.
63. CAB 65–30, 73, 11 June 1942.
64. CAB 65–31, 85–4, 3 July 1942.

6 CHURCHILL MEETS STALIN

1. Angus Calder, *The People's War: Britain 1939–45* (London, 1969) p. 271.

2. PREM 3, 399–6.
3. FO 371, 32877.
4. FO 800, 300, Clark Kerr to Cripps 26 Apr. 1942.
5. FO 954, 25 part I, Clark Kerr to Eden 27 Apr. 1942.
6. PREM 3, 396–13, Clark Kerr to Warner 18 July 1942.
7. FO 800, 300, Clark Kerr to Warner 12 July 1942.
8. PREM 3, 399–6.
9. PREM 3, 237–11.
10. Ibid., both memoranda are clearly marked as having been handed to Molotov.
11. Cadogan Diary, 10 June 1942.
12. CAB 65–30, 73, 11 June 1942.
13. PREM 3, 237–11, 30 Mission to C.O.S. 29 June 1942.
14. FO 954, 25 part I, FO to Moscow 17 June 1942.
15. Joan Beaumont, *Comrades in Arms: British Aid to Russia 1941–1945* (London, 1980) p. 107.
16. CAB 65–31, 95–2, 24 July 1942.
17. Ivan Maisky, *Memoirs of a Soviet Ambassador* (London, 1967) pp. 311 and 313.
18. PREM 3, 392–2, Air Ministry to HQRAF Middle East 21 July 1942.
19. Ibid., PM to Roosevelt 27 July 1942; Roosevelt to PM 29 July 1942.
20. FO 371, 32911, Clark Kerr to FO 25 July 1942.
21. CAB 65–27, 100. See also: Colin Ross, 'Operation Bracelet: Churchill in Moscow, 1942' in: David Dilks (ed.), *Retreat From Power: Studies in Britain's Foreign Policy in the Twentieth Century*, vol. 2 (London, 1981). The best account is Clark Kerr's diary of the visit in FO 800, 300.
22. Lord Moran, *Winston Churchill: The Struggle for Survival 1940–1965* (London, 1966) entry for 1 Aug. 1942.
23. PREM 3, 76–12.
24. Cadogan Diary, 15 Aug. 1942.
25. Colonel Jacob, *Operation Bracelet*, Manuscript diary. I am most grateful to General Sir Ian Jacob for allowing me to see his diary. Also: PREM 3, 76–12.
26. Arthur Bryant, *The Turn of the Tide* (London, 1957) pp. 461–2, 464.
27. PREM 3, 76–12.
28. FO 800, 300, John Reed to Clark Kerr 19 Aug. 1942.
29. FO 800, 404.
30. Cadogan Diary, 18 Aug. 1942; Dalton Diary 27 Aug. 1942 after talking to Desmond Morton about Churchill's trip to Moscow.
31. Colonel Jacob, *Operation Bracelet*.

7   FRONTS AND FRONTIERS

1. INF 1–319, Report 23 July 1942.
2. Ibid., Report 6 Aug. 1942.

3. Ibid., Report 22 Oct. 1942.
4. Ibid., Report 10 Dec. 1942.
5. Harvey Diaries, 24 Aug. 1942 and 14 Sep. 1942.
6. Ibid., 31 Oct. 1942.
7. Ibid., 14 Nov. 1942.
8. CAB 65–31, 118–2, 25 Aug. 1942.
9. CAB 65–31, Folio 123.
10. Ibid., Folio 127.
11. Ibid., 130.
12. Ibid., 132, Churchill to Roosevelt 22 Sep. 1942.
13. CAB 65–32, 135–1, 7 Oct. 1942, draft telegram to Stalin.
14. PREM 3, 392–3.
15. CAB 65–32, 145–2, 26 Oct. 1942.
16. CAB 65–28, 162, 30 Oct. 1942.
17. CAB 65–28, Folio 104, Churchill to Stalin 5 Nov. 1942.
18. FO 371, 36954, Cadogan 29 Dec. 1942.
19. FO 371, 36972, Eden to Churchill 19 Jan. 1943.
20. Ibid., Cherwell to Churchill, 20 Jan. 1943.
21. Ibid., Alexander to Lyttelton, 8 Feb. 1943.
22. FO 371, 39654, Ismay to Sargent, 22 Feb. 1943.
23. Ibid., Clark Kerr to FO 1 Mar. 1943; Hollis to Sargent 20 Mar. 1943.
24. FO 954, 26 part 2, Warner to Clark Kerr 26 Mar. 1943.
25. FO 371, 36927, Eden to Sinclair 10 Mar. 1943; Churchill to Cadogan 26 Mar. 1943.
26. FO 371, 36928, PM to FO 16 June 1943; Clark Kerr to FO 19 July 1943.
27. Ibid., Cadogan memo 1 Oct. 1943; General Marshall made this suggestion to Field Marshall Dill.
28. FO 371, 37000. Many of the papers are missing in this file. The incident was reported in *The Times* 8 Nov. 1943.
29. Sir Llewellyn Woodward, *British Foreign Policy in the Second World War*, vol. 2 (London, 1970) p. 547.
30. FO 954, 26 part I.
31. Dalton Diary, 5 Jan. 1943.
32. Beaverbrook D/427, 3 Mar. 1942, Beaverbrook to Eden.
33. FO 371, 36928.
34. Beaverbrook D/427, 22 Feb. 1942, Beaverbrook to Eden.
35. FO 371, 36932, Dew minute 11 Feb. 1943.
36. PREM 4, 30–2.
37. FO 800, 301, Warner to Clark Kerr, 16 Mar. 1943.
38. PREM 4, 30–3.
39. Ibid.
40. CAB 65–37, 42 Annex 18 Mar. 1943 and CAB 65–37, 44–2, 22 Mar. 1943.
41. CAB 65–37, 46–2.
42. Joan Beaumont, *Comrades in Arms: British Aid to Russia 1941–1945* (London, 1980) p. 135.
43. Harvey Diaries, 10 Feb. 1943.
44. Ibid., 29 Jan. 1943.

45. PREM 3, 354–8, Cadogan to PM 31 Mar. 1943; PM to Cadogan 3 Apr. 1943.
46. CAB 65–34, 52–2, 12 Apr. 1943.
47. CAB 65–34, 56–5, 19 Apr. 1943.
48. PREM 3, 354–8, Clark Kerr to FO 21 Apr. 1943.
49. Ibid., Stalin to Churchill 21 Apr. 1943.
50. Ibid., Churchill to Stalin 23 Apr. 1943.
51. Harvey Diary, 25 Apr. 1943.
52. Anthony Powell, *The Military Philosophers* (London, 1968) p. 112.
53. PREM 3, 354–8, PM to Maisky 23 Apr. 1943; PM to Stalin 24 Apr. 1943; Stalin to PM 25 Apr. 1943; PM to Roosevelt 27 Apr. 1943.
54. CAB 65–34, 59–1, 27 Apr. 1943.
55. PREM 3, 354–8, Eden to PM 27 Apr. 1943; PM to Eden 28 Apr. 1943.
56. Ibid., PM to Stalin 28 Apr. 1943; Clark Kerr to FO 29 Apr. 1943; Maisky 30 Apr. 1943; Clark Kerr to FO 1 May 1943.
57. CAB 65–34, 62–1, 29 Apr. 1943.
58. PREM 3, 354–8, Eden to Clark Kerr 1 May 1943.
59. CAB 65–34, 66–2, 7 May 1943.
60. PREM 3, 354–8, PM to Eden 10 May 1943.
61. Ibid., Eden to Maisky 12 May 1943.
62. PREM 3, 354–8, FO to Clark Kerr 6 May 1943.
63. FO 371, 36956, Eden to Molotov 9 June 1943.
64. PREM 3, 354–10, Warner to Clark Kerr 28 May 1943.
65. CAB 65–34, 75–2, 23 May 1943, 77–4, 24 May 1943.
66. Harvey Diaries 24 May 1943.
67. FO 371, 37019.
68. FO 371, 37017.
69. FO 371, 36991, 17 Feb. 1943, Report of Ministry of Information and Political Warfare Executive Special Issues Committee.
70. Ibid., Wilson memo 26 Jan. 1943.
71. FO 371, 37054.
72. FO 371, 36983 and 36985.
73. FO 800, 301, Clark Kerr to Warner 5 Sep. 1943.
74. FO 371, 36925.
75. PREM 3, 237–11, PM to Clark Kerr 16 June 1943; Stalin to Churchill 24 June 1943; Clark Kerr to PM 1 July 1943; Churchill to Maisky 3 July 1943.
76. CAB 65–39, Folio 44, Stalin to Churchill 10 Aug. 1943.
77. Harvey Diaries, 30 Aug. 1943.
78. Churchill College, Cambridge, Grigg papers 9/8/3a, Montgomery to Grigg 14 Oct. 1943. Perhaps it should be mentioned that 'Amgot' has no meaning whatsoever in the Turkish language.
79. FO 371, 36991, Wilson memo 25 July 1943.
80. FO 371, 37033.
81. FO 371, 36992 Cripps to Eden 10 Aug. 1943; Bruce Lockhart 9 Aug. 1943; Eden to Churchill 19 Aug. 1943.
82. FO 371, 36990, Churchill to Eden 11 Aug. 1943.
83. Ibid., 28 Sep. 1943.
84. Ibid., Sep. 1943.

85. Ibid., Churchill to Stalin 1 Oct. 1943.
86. Ibid., Eden to Churchill 22 Oct. 1943.
87. Ibid., 23 Dec. 1943.
88. Beaumont, *Comrades in Arms*, p. 161.
89. FO 371, 37045, FO to Washington 17 July 1943.
90. PREM 3, 354–9, Eden to Churchill 19 Aug. 1943.
91. FO 800, 301 Clark Kerr to Warner 10 Aug. 1943.
92. Ibid., Clark Kerr to FO 30 July 1943.
93. Harvey Diaries, 10 Oct. 1943 and 24 Oct. 1943.
94. PREM 3, 355–4, PM to Eden 6 Oct. 1943.
95. Harvey Diaries, 27 Oct. 1943.
96. Woodward, *British Foreign Policy,* vol. 2, pp. 581–94 for a good account of the conference.
97. FO 371, 37030.
98. FO 371, 37031, Clark Kerr to FO 6 Nov. 1943.
99. PREM 3, 136–12, Eden to PM 1 Nov. 1943.
100. Ibid., PM to Eden 1 Nov. 1943.
101. Ibid., Ismay to PM 24 Nov. 1943.
102. King's College, London, Ismay papers 1/5/1a and iv/AVO/3.

8   TEHERAN AND ITS AFTERMATH

1. CAB 88–20, 407, 25 Nov. 1943.
2. FO 371, 36970.
3. Alanbrooke papers. 3/A/10, 1035.
4. Lieutenant-General Sir Giffard Martel, *An Outspoken Soldier: His Views and Memoirs* (London, 1949) p. 221.
5. FO 371, 43288: Liddell Hart papers 11/1944/9.
6. FO 800, 301, Warner to Clark Kerr 1 July 1943.
7. FO 371, 43288, Warner 27 Sep. 1944.
8. FO 371, 43336, Wilson 23 Sep. 1944; meeting with C.O.S. 4 Oct. 1944.
9. Alanbrooke papers, vol. ix, 3/A/ix, 13 Oct. 1943.
10. Collier papers, Liddell Hart Library.
11. PREM 3, 355–6, Eden to PM 17 Nov. 1943; FO 800, 410.
12. PREM 3, 355–6, 23 Nov. 1943, Eden memo 22 Nov. 1943.
13. FO 371, 37031.
14. PREM 3, 76–12, Churchill to C.O.S. 21 Nov. 1943.
15. Lord Moran, *Winston Churchill: The Struggle for Survival 1940–1965* (London, 1966) 28 Nov. 1943.
16. Churchill College, Cambridge, Cadogan papers, 3/13, 30 Nov. 1943.
17. PREM 3, 136–8; 76/12; Moran, *Churchill*, 30 Dec. 1943.
18. CAB 65–36, 169–2, 13 Dec. 1943.
19. PREM 3, 355–6.
20. PREM 3, 355–7.
21. Ibid., PM to Eden 7 Jan. 1944.
22. FO 371, 39386.
23. PREM 3, 399–6, Churchill to Eden 16 Jan. 1944.

24. PREM 3, 355–6, FO to Martin (Cabinet Office) 22 Dec. 1943.
25. PREM 3, 355–7, Moscow to FO 19 Jan. 1944.
26. FO 371, 39386, Eden memo 11 Jan. 1944.
27. Ibid., Sargent 24 Jan. 1944.
28. CAB 65–45, 6–1, Annex 14 Jan. 1944.
29. CAB 65–45, 7–2, Annex 17 Jan. 1944.
30. Cadogan Diary, 17 Jan. 1944.
31. Arthur Bryant, *Triumph in the West* (London, 1959) p. 140.
32. CAB 65–45, 11–1, 25 Jan. 1944.
33. PREM 3, 355–7, Eden to PM 4 Jan. 1944.
34. Ibid., Mikolajczyk to Eden 17 Jan. 1944.
35. FO 371, 39386, Report by Roger Allen 17 Jan. 1944.
36. PREM 3, 355–7, Eden to PM 4 Jan. 1944.
37. CAB 65–45, 16–3, 7 Feb. 1944.
38. PREM 3, 355–8, Churchill to Stalin 28 Jan. 1944.
39. Ibid., Clark Kerr to FO 3 Feb. 1944.
40. CAB 65–45, 15–1, 4 Feb. 1944.
41. PREM 3, 355–8, Eden to PM 5 Feb. 1944.
42. Ibid., 6 Feb. 1944.
43. CAB 65–45, 20–4, 14 Feb. 1944.
44. PREM 3, 355–8, O'Malley 13 Feb. 1944; Cadogan 13 Feb. 1944; Churchill 15 Feb. 1944.
45. CAB 65–45, 21–1, 15 Feb. 1944.
46. PREM 3, 355–9, Clark Kerr to PM 1 Mar. 1944.
47. CAB 65–45, 28–1, 6 Mar. 1944.
48. PREM 3, 355–9, PM to Clark Kerr 10 Mar. 1944.
49. CAB 65–45, 37–1, 21 Mar. 1944; CAB 65–45, 40–1, 27 Mar. 1944.
50. PREM 3, 396–14.
51. PREM 3, 353, Bruce Lockhart 25 Jan. 1944; Moscow to FO 20 Jan. 1944.
52. Ibid., O'Malley to Eden 11 Feb. 1944.
53. Ibid., Eden to PM 25 Feb. 1944; PM to Eden 26 Feb. 1944.
54. FO 371, 39386, Wilson 19 Jan. 1944; FO to Moscow 24 Jan. 1944; Roberts 8 Jan. 1944.
55. FO 371, 39393.
56. FO 371, 43283, J. S. M. Washington to War Cabinet Office 15 Feb. 1944.
57. Ibid., Cavendish-Bentinck, 10 Mar. 1944.
58. Vojtech Mastny, *Russia's Road to the Cold War* (New York, 1979) pp. 133–44.
59. FO 371, 38920 Eden to Resident Minister, Algiers 30 Dec. 1943; memo 17 Jan. 1944.
60. Ibid., Killean to FO 1 Jan. 1944.
61. Ibid., Balfour to FO 12 Jan. 1944.
62. Victor Rothwell, *Britain and the Cold War 1941–1947* (London, 1982) p. 191.
63. FO 371, 38920, Roberts to FO 22 Jan. 1944.
64. See particularly: Nikolai Tolstoy, *Victims of Yalta* (London, 1977) and *Stalin's Secret War* (London, 1981).

65. FO 371, 43382.
66. Ibid., Wilson 28 Apr. 1944.
67. Ibid., MI3(c) 21 Feb. 1944.
68. Ibid., SHAEF memo 25 May 1944.
69. Ibid., Eden 21 July 1944.
70. Ibid., Cadogan 7 July 1944; Wilson 8 July 1944.
71. FO 371, 43307.
72. FO 371, 43382, C.O.S. memo 1 Aug. 1944. The Soviet reply did not come until October.

9 THE BEGINNINGS OF POST-WAR PLANNING

1. FO 371, 43335, 29 Apr. 1944.
2. CAB 81–45, 6 June 1944.
3. FO 371, 43336, 9 Aug. 1944.
4. PREM 3, 355–12, Clark Kerr to FO 11 Aug. 1944.
5. For British attempts to stop Beneš signing a treaty with the Soviet Union see: CAB 65–34, 89–5, 28 June 1943.
6. Dalton to H. N. Brailsford 13 Mar. 1944, Dalton papers IIb, 8/1.
7. CAB 81–45, 9 Nov. 1944.
8. Arthur Bryant, *Triumph in the West* (London, 1959) p. 242.
9. Ibid., p. 289, C.O.S. meeting 2 Oct. 1944.
10. FO 371, 43291.
11. Ibid., Wilson memo 26 May 1944.
12. FO 371, 43351, Sargent 1 June 1944.
13. FO 371, 43636, PM to FO 10 May 1944.
14. PREM 3, 66–7.
15. FO 371, 43636, Eden–Gusev meeting 18 May 1944.
16. Ibid.
17. FO 371, 44331.
18. FO 371, 48928.
19. FO 371, 43636, Wilson memo May 1944.
20. FO 371, 43351, Orme Sargent 1 June 1944.
21. FO 371, 43352.
22. FO 371, 43353.
23. FO 371, 43355, Wilson 9 Nov. 1944.
24. T160, 1373; T236, 290 and 291 for full details.
25. FO 371, 39397.
26. FO 371, 39398, Wilson 30 Mar. 1944.
27. FO 371, 39402, 31 May 1944 and Oliver Harvey's note in FO 371, 39400, 21 May 1944.
28. FO 371, 39402, Eden memo 6 June 1944; PM 11 June 1944; Roberts 22 June 1944.
29. Ibid., Eden 25 June 1944.
30. FO 371, 43304, Eden 31 Mar. 1944.
31. FO 371, 43830.

32. Ibid., Cadogan to Gusev 30 Mar. 1944; Eden 16 Mar. 1944; Wilson 22 Mar. 1944.
33. FO 371, 43834, HQMAAF 11 Dec. 1944.
34. FO 371, 43636, Lord Moyne (Cairo) to FO 21 June 1944.
35. Ibid., Roosevelt to PM 11 June 1944; PM to Roosevelt 11 June 1944; Roosevelt to PM 22 June 1944; PM to Roosevelt 23 June 1944.
36. PREM 3, 66–7, PM to Eden 9 July 1944.
37. FO 371, 43636.
38. CAB 65–43, 103–2, 9 Aug. 1944.
39. CAB 65–47, 103–1, 9 Aug. 1944.
40. FO 371, 43579, Cairo to FO 13 Jan. 1944; SOE Report 13 Mar. 1944; Cairo to FO 16 Aug. 1944.
41. FO 371, 43614, 22 Sep. 1944.
42. FO 371, 43584, McDermott 8 Sep. 1944.
43. FO 371, 43647, Moyne 27 Aug. 1944.
44. CAB 21–1614, FO memo 22 May 1944.
45. Ibid., Duff Cooper to Eden 30 May 1944; Eden to Duff Cooper 25 July 1944.
46. Ibid., Jacob July 1944.
47. CAB 81–45, 11 Aug. 1944.
48. FO 371, 43306, Sargent 18 Aug. 1944.
49. Ibid., Wilson 10 Aug. 1944.
50. Ibid., J. G. Ward (Economic and Reconstruction Department) 15 Aug. 1944.
51. Ibid., Roberts 18 Aug. 1944.
52. CAB 21–1614.
53. CAB 81–45.
54. FO 371, 43306, Wilson 24 Sep. 1944.
55. Dalton Diaries, 9 June 1944.

10 THE POLISH QUESTION

1. PREM 3, 355–12, Stalin to PM 23 July 1944.
2. Ibid., PM to Roosevelt 26 July 1944.
3. Ibid., PM to Stalin 27 July 1944; Stalin to PM 28 July 1944; PM to Roosevelt 29 July 1944.
4. Jan M. Ciechanowski, *The Warsaw Rising of 1944* (Cambridge, 1974) p. 67.
5. FO 371, 39494.
6. PREM 3, 352–12, C.O.S. 3 Aug. 1944; PM to Stalin 4 Aug. 1944.
7. Ibid., C.O.S. to 30 Mission (Moscow) 5 Aug. 1944.
8. Ibid., Stalin to PM 5 Aug. 1944.
9. Ibid., Slessor to C.A.S. 6 Aug. 1944.
10. Ibid., C.A.S. to PM 8 Aug. 1944.
11. CAB 81–41.
12. PREM 3, 352–12, C.A.S. to Slessor, undated.
13. John Ehrman, *Grand Strategy* vol. v (London, 1956) p. 371.

14. PREM 3, 352–12, Eden to PM 8 Aug. 1944.
15. FO 371, 39407, Burgess 6 Aug. 1944.
16. PREM 3, 352–12.
17. FO 371, 39408, Harvey 8 Aug. 1944.
18. FO 371, 39496, Allen memo 10 Sep. 1944.
19. FO 371, 39408, 10 Aug. 1944.
20. PREM 3, 355–12.
21. CAB 88–30. C.O.S. 10 Aug. 1944 and 12 Aug. 1944.
22. PREM 3, 352–12.
23. Ibid.
24. Ibid.
25. Ibid., Slessor to C.A.S. 15 Aug. 1944.
26. Ibid., Clark Kerr to FO 15 Aug. 1944 and 16 Aug. 1944.
27. CAB 65–47, 107–1, 16 Aug. 1944.
28. PREM 3, 352–12, Stalin to Churchill 16 Aug. 1944.
29. Ibid., Eden to Churchill 18 Aug. 1944.
30. Ibid., S. of S. of Air to PM 19 Aug. 1944.
31. Ibid., Churchill to Stalin 20 Aug. 1944; Stalin to Churchill 22 Aug. 1944; Eden to Churchill 22 Aug. 1944.
32. FO 371, 39494.
33. FO 371, 39409, Eden 2 Sep. 1944; Sargent 3 Sep. 1944.
34. FO 371, 39496, Sargent 4 Sep. 1944.
35. PREM 3, 352–12.
36. FO 371, 39496, Clark Kerr to FO 10 Sep. 1944.
37. PREM 3, 352–12.
38. Ibid., Vice Chief of Air Staff 10 Sep. 1944.
39. CAB 65–47, 117–1, 5 Sep. 1944.
40. Ehrman, *Grand Strategy*, p. 376.
41. FO 371, 39410, Roberts 25 Aug. 1944; O'Malley 22 Aug. 1944.
42. FO 371, 39411, Eden 6 Sep. 1944.
43. Ibid., O'Malley 9 Sep. 1944.
44. PREM 3, 355–13, Eden to Sargent 12 Oct. 1944.
45. FO 371, 47577, Cavendish-Bentinck 16 Mar. 1944.
46. FO 371, 39496, Vansittart to Eden 4 Sep. 1944 and 12 Sep. 1944.
47. FO 371, 39420, Roberts memo 6 Dec. 1944; Eleanor Rathbone made a widely-publicised speech in the House of Commons on 15 Dec. 1944.
48. INF 1, 319.
49. FO 371, 39418, Eden memo 2 Dec. 1944; Eden to PM 4 Dec. 1944.
50. FO 371, 43430.
51. FO 800, 414, for a record of this and subsequent meetings.
52. The original of this famous document is in PREM 3, 66–7. For further discussion see: Albert Resis, 'The Churchill–Stalin Secret "Percentage" Agreement on the Balkans, Moscow October 1944,' *American Historical Review*, vol. 83, April 1978.
53. PREM 3, 66–7.
54. PREM 3, 397–3, Churchill to Attlee 18 Oct. 1944.
55. Ibid., Churchill to Eden 23 Oct. 1944.
56. FO 371, 39417, Eden 27 Nov. 1944.
57. CAB 65–48, 157, 27 Nov. 1944.

11   ON THE EVE OF POTSDAM

1. CAB 21–1614, PM to Eden 25 Nov. 1944.
2. Ibid., Moscow to FO 19 Nov. 1944; FO to Moscow 26 Nov. 1944.
3. FO 371, 39418, PM to Eden 25 Nov. 1944.
4. Ibid., Selborne to Eden 8 Dec. 1944.
5. Ibid., Eden to PM 26 Nov. 1944.
6. CAB 65–48, 142–5, 30 Oct. 1944.
7. FO 371, 38921, Roberts 5 Oct. 1944; Churchill 9 Oct. 1944.
8. FO 371, 38927, SOE Report 22 May 1944.
9. Ibid., Hollis to FO 3 Sep. 1944.
10. Ibid., Hollis to FO 27 Oct. 1944; Cadogan to PM 3 Oct. 1944.
11. PREM 3, 355–14, Clark Kerr to FO 25 Nov. 1944; Churchill 26 Nov. 1944.
12. Ibid., Stalin to Churchill 8 Dec. 1944.
13. FO 371, 39421, O'Malley 21 Dec. 1944.
14. Ibid., Harvey 24 Dec. 1944.
15. FO 371, 29420, Warner and Wilson 25 Dec. 1944.
16. FO 371, 47575, Sargent 8 Jan. 1945.
17. FO 371, 47593, O'Malley 11 Jan. 1945.
18. FO 371, 47576, Report by Strang 18 Jan. 1945.
19. Ibid., Cadogan 18 Jan. 1945.
20. CAB 65–51, 7–4, 22 Jan. 1945.
21. CAB 65–51, 10–1, 26 Jan. 1945.
22. FO 371, 47618, Eden 27 Jan. 1945.
23. Ibid., Perkins 28 Jan. 1945.
24. PREM 3, 356–3.
25. FO 371, 47709, Warner to Brigadier Hill 19 Jan. 1945; Warner to WO (MO1(s.p.)) 30 Jan. 1945; WO to FO 5 Feb. 1945; Warner to WO 18 Feb. 1945; Harvey 13 Feb. 1945; Sporborg to Warner 24 Feb. 1945; Wilson 27 Feb. 1945; Sporborg to FO 27 Apr. 1945.
26. Ibid., also: FO 371, 47710.
27. FO 371, 47881.
28. FO 371, 409.
29. Cadogan paper, letters: 7 Feb. 1945; 8 Feb. 1945; 11 Feb. 1945; Diary 11 Feb. 1945.
30. PREM 3, 51–10.
31. PREM 3, 356–3, Sargent 12 Feb. 1945.
32. Cadogan Diary, 20 Feb. 1945.
33. CAB 65–21, 22–1, 19 Feb. 1945.
34. Dalton Diary, 23 Feb. 1945.
35. Nicholson Diaries, 27 Feb. 1945.
36. FO 371, 47578, Pickles 14 Feb. 1945.
37. FO 371, 47580, Cadogan 22 Feb. 1945.
38. FO 371, 47581, Cabinet Conclusions 21 Feb. 1945.
39. PREM 3, 356–9, Clark Kerr to FO 27 Feb. 1945.
40. FO 371, 47580, Moscow to FO 3 Mar. 1945.
41. CAB 65–51, 26–5, 6 Mar. 1945; FO 371, 47481, Sargent 7 Mar. 1945.

42. PREM 3, 356–9.
43. Ibid.
44. FO 371, 37584, Eden to PM 24 Mar. 1945.
45. PREM 3, 356–9, Roosevelt to PM 29 Mar. 1945.
46. FO 371, 47585, PM to Stalin 31 Mar. 1945.
47. Sir Llewellyn Woodward, *British Foreign Policy in the Second World War*, vol. 3 (London, 1970) pp. 520–1.
48. CAB 65–52, 39–1, 3 Apr. 1945.
49. CAB 65–52, 40, 5 Apr. 1945. Bradley F. Smith and Elena Agorossi, *Operation Sunrise: The Secret Surrender* (New York, 1979).
50. CAB 65–52, 44–3, 13 Apr. 1945.
51. CAB 65–52, 50, 24 Apr. 1945.
52. Woodward, *British Foreign Policy*, vol. 3, p. 530.
53. FO 371, 48573, 2 Dec. 1945.
54. Ibid., Pink memo 26 Jan. 1945.
55. CAB 65, 26–5, 6 Mar. 1945.
56. PREM 3, 356–9, PM to Roosevelt 8 Mar. 1945.
57. FO 371, 48552, Le Rougetal 2 Apr. 1945.
58. FO 371, 48123, Houstoun-Boswall 28 Feb. 1945.
59. Ibid., Sargent 6 Mar. 1945.
60. FO 371, 43616.
61. FO 371, 48123, FO to Washington 11 Mar. 1945; FO to Moscow 9 Mar. 1945.
62. FO 371, 48134, Houstoun-Boswall to FO 5 Apr. 1945.
63. FO 371, 48124, Soviet note 6 May 1945.
64. Ibid., FO to PM 8 June 1945.
65. FO 371, 48487.
66. FO 371, 48478, FO to Moscow 5 Jan. 1945.
67. FO 371, 47882, Roberts to Warner, 25 Apr. 1945.
68. Ibid., Sargent 2 May 1945.
69. CAB 79–33, J.I.C. SHAEF (45) 22 (Final) 14 May 1945.
70. CAB 81–46, 27 May. 1945.
71. Ibid., 30 Mar. 1945.
72. CAB 81–45, 17 Mar. 1945, Draft Paper.
73. CAB 81–46, 29 June 1945.
74. PREM 3, 396–12.
75. FO 371, 47076.
76. Arthur Bryant, *Triumph in the West* (London, 1959) p. 469.
77. Ibid., p. 470.
78. FO 371, 47894, 3 Mar. 1945.
79. Ibid., Galsworthy 11 Mar. 1945.
80. Ibid., Sargent to Hollis, 30 Mar. 1945.
81. Ibid., Home Office (Aliens Department) 9 Mar. 1945.
82. FO 371, 47896.
83. Ibid., Wilson 6 Apr. 1945.
84. Ibid., SHAEF MAIN 9 Apr. 1945.
85. FO 371, 39410.
86. FO 371, 47898, Wilson 28 May 1945.
87. FO 371, 47955.

88. FO 371, 47901, Brigadier Firebrace to FO 22 June 1945.
89. FO 371, 47944.
90. FO 371, 47898.
91. FO 371, 47896, 9 May 1945.
92. FO 371, 47899, Firebrace 23 May 1945.
93. FO 371, 47902.
94. Nikolai Tolstoy, *Victims of Yalta* (London, 1977) and *Stalin's Secret War* (London, 1981).

Bibliography

UNPUBLISHED DOCUMENTS

British Library, Department of Manuscripts:
    Oliver Harvey
British Library of Political and Economic Science, London University,
    London School of Political and Economic Science:
    Citrine
    Hugh Dalton
    D. N. Pritt
    Beatrix Webb
Winston S. Churchill Library, Churchill College, Cambridge:
    A. V. Alexander
    Ernest Bevin
    Sir Alexander Cadogan
    Sir Edward Grigg
House of Lords Record Office:
    Beaverbrook
    Lloyd George
Labour Party Archives:
    International Department Correspondence 1932–1946
    Annual Reports
Liddell Hart Centre for Military Archives, University of London, King's
    College:
    Alanbrooke
    Air Vice Marshal Sir A. C. Collier
    Ismay
    Liddell Hart
Public Record Office:
    War Cabinet Papers:
        CAB 65
        CAB 79
        CAB 81
        CAB 84
        CAB 88
        CAB 98
    Foreign Office:
        FO 371
        FO 799
        FO 800

FO 837
FO 898
FO 954
Ministry of Information:
INF 1
Prime Minister's Office:
PREM 1
PREM 3
PREM 4
Ministry of Transport:
T160
T236
T290
T291
War Office:
WO 208

PRINTED WORKS

Addison, Paul, *The Road to 1945* (London, 1977).
Allan, J. S., *No Citation* (London, 1956).
Aplin, John, 'Towards Left Unity', *Left*, March 1942.
Auty, Phyllis and Clogg, Richard, *British Policy Towards Wartime Resistance in Yugoslavia and Greece* (London, 1975).
Avon, Earl of, *The Eden Memoirs: The Reckoning* (London, 1965).
Balfour, Michael, *Propaganda in War, 1939–1945: Organisations, Policies and Publics in Britain and Germany* (London, 1979).
Barker, Elizabeth, *British Policy in South-East Europe in the Second World War* (London, 1976).
——, *Churchill and Eden at War* (London, 1978).
Barman, T., *Diplomatic Correspondent* (London, 1968).
Beaumont, Joan, *Comrades in Arms: British Aid to Russia 1941–1945* (London, 1980).
Beitzell, Robert, *The Uneasy Alliance* (New York, 1972).
Berthoud, Sir Eric, *An Unexpected Life* (Tiptree, 1980).
Bethell, Nicholas, *The Last Secret* (London, 1974).
Bigland, E., *The Key to the Russian Door* (London, 1942).
Bilainkin, G., *Maisky: Ten Years Ambassador* (London, 1944).
Birkenhead, Earl of, *Halifax* (London, 1965).
Birse, A. H. *Memoirs of an Interpreter* (London, 1967).
Bond, B. M., *Liddell Hart: A Study of His Military Thought* (London, 1976).
Brittain, Vera, *Testament of Experience* (London, 1979).
Bruce Lockhart, R. H., *Comes the Reckoning* (New York, 1947).
Burridge, T. D., *British Labour and Hitler's War* (London, 1976).
Butler, R. A., *The Art of Memory* (London, 1982).
Bryant, Arthur, *The Turn of the Tide* (London, 1957).

Bryant, Arthur, *Triumph in the West* (London, 1959).
Calder, Angus, *The People's War: Britain 1939–45* (London, 1969).
Carr, E. H., *Conditions of Peace* (London, 1942).
Carter, H. D., *Russia's Secret Weapon* (London, 1943).
Cassidy, H. C., *Moscow Date-Line, 1941–43* (London, 1943)
Churchill, Winston S., *The Second World War:*
  vol. I, *The Gathering Storm* (London, 1948),
  vol. II, *Their Finest Hour* (London, 1949),
  vol. III, *The Grand Alliance* (London, 1950),
  vol. IV, *The Hinge of Fate* (London, 1950),
  vol. V, *Closing the Ring* (London, 1951),
  vol. VI, *Triumph and Tragedy* (London, 1953).
Ciechanowski, Jan M., *The Warsaw Rising of 1944* (Cambridge, 1974).
Citrine, W. M., *In Russia Now* (London, 1942).
Citrine, W. M., Noel-Baker, P. J., Downie, J., *Finland – Interim Report* (London, 1940).
Coates, W. P., and Zelda, K., *A History of Anglo–Soviet Relations* (London, 1944).
——, *Why Russia Will Win* (London, 1942).
Cole, G. D. H., *Europe, Russia and the Future* (London, 1941).
Cole Margaret (ed.), *Our Soviet Ally* (London, 1943).
Cooke, Colin, *The Life of Richard Stafford Cripps* (London, 1957).
Dalton, Hugh, *The Fateful Years: Memoirs 1931–1945* (London, 1957).
Davidson, Basil, *Special Operations Europe* (London, 1980).
Deane, John R., *The Strange Alliance* (London, 1947).
Deborin, Grigory, *Thirty Years of Victory* (Moscow, 1975).
Dilks, David (ed.), *Retreat from Power: Studies in Britain's Foreign Policy in the Twentieth Century*, vol. II (London, 1981).
——, *The Diaries of Sir Alexander Cadogan 1938–1945* (London, 1971).
Douglas, Roy, *From War to Cold War, 1942–48* (London, 1981).
Ehrman, John, *Grand Strategy, Vol. VI, August 1943–September 1944* (London, 1956).
Elvin, Harold, *A Cockney in Moscow* (London, 1958).
Estorick, Eric, *Stafford Cripps: A Biography* (London, 1949).
Gallacher, Willie, *The Rolling of the Thunder* (London, 1947).
Gilbert, Martin, *Finest Hour: Winston S. Churchill 1939–1941* (London, 1983).
Gladwyn, Lord, *Memoirs* (London, 1972).
Gollancz, Victor, *The Betrayal of the Left* (London, 1941).
——, *Russia and Ourselves* (London, 1941).
Gorodetsky, Gabriel, *Stafford Cripps' Mission to Moscow 1940–42* (Cambridge, 1984).
Gowing, M. M., *Britain and Atomic Energy, 1939–45* (London, 1964).
Greenwood, Arthur, *The Soviet Fighting Forces* (London, 1939).
Haldane, C., *Russian Newsreel* (London, 1942).
Hanak, H., 'Sir Stafford Cripps as British Ambassador in Moscow', *English Historical Review*, vol. XCIIV, Jan. 1979 and vol. XCVII, Apr. 1982.
Harriman, Averell, *American and Russia in a Changing World: A Half Century of Personal Observation* (New York, 1971).

Harrison, Tom, 'Public Opinion About Russia', *Political Quarterly*, vol. 12, No. 4, 1941.

Harvey, John (ed.), *The War Diaries of Oliver Harvey 1941–45* (London, 1978).

Higgings, T., *Winston Churchill and the Second Front, 1940–1943* (London, 1957).

Hinsley, F. H., *British Intelligence in the Second World War*, vol. I (London, 1979) vol. II (London, 1981).

Ismay, H., *The Memoirs of General Lord Ismay* (London, 1960).

Jacob, Alaric, *A Window on Moscow* (London, 1946).

Jordan, P. F., *Russian Glory* (London, 1942).

Kecewicz, Georg V., *Great Britain, the Soviet Union and the Polish Government in Exile 1939–45* (The Hague, 1979).

Knickerboker, H. R., *Is Tomorrow Hitler's?* (London, 1942).

Koch, H. W., 'The Spectre of a Separate Peace in the East: Russo–German Peace Feelers, 1942–44', *Journal of Contemporary History*, vol. x, no. 3, July 1975.

Korbel, Josef, *The Communist Subversion of Czechoslovakia 1938–1948* (Princeton, 1959).

Kot, Stanislaw, *Conversations with the Kremlin and Dispatches from Russia* (London, 1963).

Labour Party, *Stalin's Men – About Turn!* (London, 1940).

——, *Finland: The Criminal Conspiracy of Stalin and Hitler* (London, 1940).

——, *The Communist Party and the War: A Record of Hypocrisy and Treachery to the Workers of Europe* (London, 1943).

Lash, Joseph P., *Roosevelt and Churchill 1939–1941* (New York, 1976).

Leasor, J., *War at the Top* (London, 1959).

Lewin, Ronald, *Churchill as Warlord* (London, 1973).

Lloyd, Lord, *The British Case* (London, 1939).

Loewenheim, Francis L., and Langley, Harold D., *Roosevelt and Churchill: Their Secret Wartime Correspondence* (London, 1975).

Maclean, Fitzroy, *Eastern Approaches* (London, 1949).

Macmillan, Harold, *The Blast of War 1939–1945* (London, 1967).

McNeill, W. H., *American, Britain and Russia* (New York, 1953).

Maisky, Ivan, *Memoirs of a Soviet Ambassador* (London, 1967).

Martel, Lt.-Gen. Sir Gifford, *An Outspoken Soldier* (London, 1949).

Mastny, Vojtech, *Russia's Road to the Cold War: Diplomacy, Warfare and the Politics of Communism 1941–1945* (New York, 1979).

McLaine, Ian, *Ministry of Morale: Home Front Morale and the Ministry of Information in World War II* (London, 1979).

Meehan, E., *The British Left Wing and Foreign Policy* (New Brunswick, 1960).

Miksche, F. O., *Unconditional Surrender: The Roots of World War III* (London, 1952).

Moran, Lord, *Winston Churchill: The Struggle for Survival 1940–1965* (London, 1966).

Morgan, F., *Overture to Overlord* (New York, 1950).

Morray, J. P., *From Yalta to Disarmament: Cold War Debate* (New York, 1961).

Murphy, J. T., *Russia on the March* (London, 1941).

Nicolson, Harold, *Diaries and Letters 1939–1945* (London, 1967).
Page, A., *The Soviet Union* (London, 1943).
Philby, Kim, *My Secret War* (London, 1968).
Polonsky, Anthony, *The Great Powers and the Polish Question 1941–1945* (London, 1976).
Pritt, D. N., *The U.S.S.R. Our Ally* (London, 1941).
——, *Light on Moscow* (London, 1939).
——, *The Mosley Case* (London, 1947).
——, *Must the War Spread?* (London, 1940).
——, *Grigg, Goebbels and Pte. Smith* (London, 1943).
Raczynski, Count Edward, *In Allied London* (London, 1962).
Resis, Albert, 'The Churchill–Stalin Secret "Percentage" Agreement on the Balkans, Moscow October 1944', *American Historical Review*, vol. 83, Apr. 1978.
Reynolds, Q. J., *Only the Stars are Neutral* (London, 1943).
Roskill, Stephen, *Hankey, Man of Secrets*, vol. III 1931–63 (London, 1974).
Ross, Graham, 'Foreign Office Attitudes to the Soviet Union 1941–1945,' *Journal of Contemporary History*, vol. 16, July 1981.
Rothwell, Victor, *Britain and the Cold War 1941–1947* (London, 1982).
Sloan, P. A., *Russia in Peace and War* (London, 1941).
——, *Russia Resists* (London, 1941).
Smith, Arthur L., *Churchill's German Army: Wartime Strategy and Cold War Politics, 1943–1947* (London, 1977).
Smith, Bradley F., *The Shadow Warriors: O.S.S. and the Origins of the C.I.A.* (New York, 1983).
Smith, Bradley F. and Elena Agarossi, *Operation Sunrise: The Secret Surrender* (New York, 1979).
Stoler, Mark, *The Politics of the Second Front* (Westport Connecticut, 1977).
Strang, Lord, *Home and Abroad* (London, 1956).
——, 'Prelude to Potsdam: Reflections on War and Foreign Policy', *International Affairs*, vol. 46, July 1970.
Taylor, A. J. P., *English History 1914–1945* (Oxford, 1965).
——, *Beaverbrook* (London, 1972).
Thompson, Kenneth W., *Cold War Theories*, vol. I 1943–1953 (Baton Rouge, 1982).
Trukhanovsky, V., *British Foreign Policy During World War II, 1939–1945* (Moscow, 1970).
Tolstoy, Nikolai, *Victims of Yalta* (London, 1977).
——, *Stalin's Secret War* (London, 1981).
Wasserstein, Bernard, *British and the Jews of Europe 1939–1945* (Oxford 1979).
Weil, Ursula and Otto, *Churchill und der britische Imperialismus* (Berlin, 1967).
Werth, A., *The Year of Stalingrad* (New York, 1947).
Wheeler-Bennett, Sir John, *Action This Day: Work with Churchill* (London, 1968).
White, M. B., *Russia at War* (London, 1942).
Winterton, P., *Report on Russia* (London, 1945).
Woodward, Sir Llewellyn, *British Foreign Policy in the Second World War*, 5 vols (London, 1970–6).

Index

Index